ENGAGING

AUGUSTINE

ON ROMANS

Romans Through History and Cultures

Receptions and Critical Interpretations

CRISTINA GRENHOLM AND DANIEL PATTE, SERIES EDITORS

The series, *Romans Through History and Cultures,* includes a wealth of information regarding the receptions of Romans throughout the history of the church and today, in the "first" and the "two-thirds" world. It explores the past and present impact of Romans upon theology, and upon cultural, political, social, and ecclesial life, and gender relations.

In each volume, the authors contribute to an integrated practice, "Scriptural Criticism," which takes into account: with contemporary biblical scholars, that different readings can be grounded in the same text by different critical methods; with church historians and practical theologians, that the believers' readings interrelate biblical text and concrete life; and with theologians, that believers read Romans as Scripture.

The cover art skillfully represents that any interpretation of a scriptural text is framed in three ways: a) by an *analytical frame* that reflects each reader's autonomous choice of a textual dimension as most significant--see the individual studying the text; b) by a *contextual/pragmatic frame* shaped by a certain relational network of life in society and community--see the people joining hands; and, c) by a *hermeneutical frame* inspired by a certain religious perception of life--see the bread and chalice and the face-to-face encounter.

By elucidating the threefold choices reflected in various interpretations of Romans through the centuries and present-day cultures, the volumes in the series--which emerge from a three-year Society of Biblical Literature Consultation and an on-going SBL Seminar--raise a fundamental critical question: Why did I/we choose this interpretation rather than another one?

ROMANS THROUGH HISTORY AND CULTURES SERIES

ENGAGING
AUGUSTINE
ON ROMANS

Self, Context, and Theology in Interpretation

Edited by

Daniel Patte and
Eugene TeSelle

Trinity Press International
Harrisburg Pennsylvania

To **Krister Stendahl**

Teacher, Scholar, Bishop, Friend

Cover art by Elizabeth McNaron Patte

Trinity Press International, P.O. Box 1321, Harrisburg, PA 17105
Trinity Press International is a division of The Morehouse Group.

Cover design: Corey Kent

Library of Congress Cataloging-in-Publication Data
Engaging Augustine on Romans : self, context, and theology in interpretation / edited by Daniel Patte and Eugene TeSelle.
        p. cm. – (Romans through history and cultures series)
    Includes bibliographical references and index.
    ISBN 1-56338-407-8 (alk. paper)
        1. Bible. N.T. Romans—Criticism, interpretation, etc.—History—Early church, ca. 30-600. 2. Augustine, Saint, Bishop of Hippo. I. Patte, Daniel. II. TeSelle, Eugene, 1931 – III. Series.

BS2665.52 E54 2003
227'.106'092—dc21   2002074041

Printed in the United States of America

02 03 04 05 06 07 10 9 8 7 6 5 4 3 2 1

Contents

Abbreviations

Marginalia (see Introduction, pp. 5-6)

A **Analytical frames:** textual features viewed as most significant in the
interpretation, and/or analytical models that focus the attention on these.

H **Hermeneutical frames:** theological concepts emphasized in the interpretation
of the text; the interpreter's (Augustine's, a modern scholar's) religious
perception of life as interpreted with the help of the text.

C **Contextual frames:** biographical factors, social location, relations of power and
authority of the contexts of both the text and the interpreter which influenced
the interpretation of the text and/or were interpreted with the help of the text.

Research Tools

AM   *Augustinus Magister*

Aug-Lex   *Augustinus-Lexikon,* hrsg. von Cornelius Mayer, Erich Feldmann, Karl
Heinz Chelius. Basel: Schwabe, 1986- .

RAC   *Reallexikon für Antike und Christentum. Sachwörterbuch zur
Auseinandersetzung des Christentums mit der antiken Welt,* ed. Theodor
Klauser. Stuttgart: Hiersemann, 1950- .

Editions and Translations

ACW   *Ancient Christian Writers: The Works of The Fathers in Translation.*
Washington, New York, 1946- .

BA   *Bibliothèque Augustinienne. Oeuvres de Saint Augustin.* Paris, 1947- .

BAC   *Biblioteca de Autores Cristianos. Obras de san Agustín.* Madrid, 1951- .

CC   *Corpus Christianorum.* Series Latina. Turnholt: Brepols, 1953- .

CSEL   *Corpus Scriptorum Ecclesiasticorum Latinorum.* Vienna, 1865- .

FOC   *The Fathers of the Church: A New Translation.* New York, Washington,
1947- .

NBA   *Nuova Biblioteca Agostiniana. Opere di Sant'Agostino.* Rome, 1976- .

PG   *Patrologiae Cursus Completus. Series Graeca*, ed. J. P. Migne. Paris: Migne, 1857-1866.

PL   *Patrologiae Cursus Completus, Series Latina*, ed. J. P. Migne. Paris: Migne, 1844-1864.

PLS   *Supplementum to the Patrologiae Cursus Completus, Series Latina*, ed. A. Hamman. Paris: Garnier Frères, 1958-63.

SC   *Sources Chrétiennes*. Paris: Éditions du Cerf, 1941- .

Augustine's Works

C.Acad.	*Contra Academicos (CSEL 63, CC 29)*	*Against the Academics*
De ag.chr.	*De agone christiano (CSEL 41)*	*The Christian Struggle*
De bapt.	*De baptismo (CSEL 51)*	*On Baptism*
De beat.vit.	*De beata uita (CSEL 63, CC 29)*	*Life of Happiness*
De bon.coniug.	*De bono coniugali (CSEL 41)*	*The Good of Marriage*
De bon.vid.	*De bono uiduitatis (CSEL 41)*	*The Good of Widowhood*
De cat.rud.	*De catechizandis rudibus (CC 46)*	*Instructing the Unlearned*
De civ.Dei	*De ciuitate Dei (CC 47,48)*	*The City of God*
Conf.	*Confessiones (CC 27)*	*Confessions*
Conl.Max.	*Conlatio cum Maximino Arrianorum episcopo (PL 42)*	*Debate with Maximinus the Arian*
De cons.ev.	*De consensu euangelistarum (CSEL 43)*	*The Agreement of the Gospel Writers*
De cont.	*De continentia (CSEL 41)*	*On Continence*
De corr.et gr.	*De correptione et gratia (PL 44)*	*Rebuke and Grace*
C. Cresc.	*Ad Cresconium grammaticum partis Donati (CSEL 52)*	*Against Cresconius*
De div.qu.	*De diuersis quaestionibus octoginta tribus (CC 44A)*	*Responses to Various Questions*
C.du.ep.Pel.	*Contra duas epistulas Pelagianorum (CSEL 60)*	*Against Two Letters of the Pelagians*
De doct.chr.	*De doctrina christiana (CSEL 80, CC 32)*	*On Christian Instruction*
Dulcit.qu.	*De octo Dulcitii quaestionibus (CC 44A)*	*Responses to Eight Questions from Dulcitius*
En.Ps.	*Enarrationes in Psalmos (CC 38, 39, 40)*	*Expositions of the Psalms*
Enchir.	*Enchiridion de fide spe et caritate (CC 46)*	*Handbook on Faith, Hope, and Love*
Ep.	*Epistulae (CSEL 34, 44, 57, 58,88)*	*Letters*

C.ep.Man.	Contra epistulam Manichaei quam uocant fundamenti (CSEL 25.1)	Against the Fundamental Epistle of Mani
C.ep.Parm.	Contra epistulam Parmeniani (CSEL 51)	Against the Letter of Parmenianus
De don.pers.	De dono perseuerantiae (PL 45)	The Gift of Perseverance
Ep.Rom.inch.exp.	Epistulae ad Romanos inchoata expositio (CSEL 84)	Unfinished Exposition of the Epistle to the Romans
Exp.ep.Gal.	Expositio epistulae ad Galatas (CSEL 84)	Exposition of the Epistle to the Galatians
Exp.prop.Rom.	Expositio quarundam propositionum ex epistula apostoli ad Romanos (CSEL 84)	Propositions from the Epistle to the Romans
C.Faust.	Contra Faustum Manicheum (CSEL 25.1)	Against Faustus the Manichaean
C.Fel.	Contra Felicem Manichaeum (CSEL 25.2)	Against Felix the Manichaean
De fid.et op.	De fide et operibus (CSLE 41)	Faith and Works
De fid.et symb.	De fide et symbolo (CSEL 41)	Faith and the Creed
De fid.invis.	De fide rerum inuisibilium (CC 46)	Faith in Things Unseen
C.Fort.	Acta contra Fortunatum Manichaeum (CSEL 25.1)	Against Fortunatus the Manichaean
C.Gaud.	Contra Gaudentium Donatistarum episcopum (CSEL 53)	Against Gaudentius
De gest.Pel.	De gestis Pelagii (CSEL 42)	The Proceedings of Pelagius
De Gen.ad litt.	De Genesi ad litteram (CSEL 28.1)	Literal Commentary on Genesis
De Gen.imp.	De Genesi ad litteram imperfectus (CSEL 28.1)	Unfinished Literal Commentary on Genesis
De Gen.adv.Man.	De Genesi aduersus Manicheos (PL 34)	On Genesis Against the Manichaeans
De gr.et lib.arb.	De gratia it libero arbitrio (PL 44)	Grace and Free Will
De gr.et pecc.	De gratia Christi et de peccato originali (CSEL 42)	The Grace of Christ and Original Sin
De imm.an.	De immortalitate animae (CSEL 89)	The Immortality of the Soul
In Io.ep.	In epistulam Iohannis ad Parthos (PL 35)	The First Epistle of John
In Io.ev.	In Iohannis euangelium tractatus CXXIV (CC 36)	Expositions of the Gospel of John
Adv.Iud.	Aduersus Iudaeos (PL 42)	Against the Jews
C.Iul.	Contra Iulianum (PL 44)	Against Julian
C.Iul.imp.	Contra Iulianum opus imperfectum (PL 45, CSEL 85.1)	Unfinished Work against Julian
De lib.arb.	De libero arbitrio (CSEL 74, CC 29)	Freedom of Choice
C.litt.Petil.	Contra litteras Petiliani (CSEL 52)	Against the Writings of Petilian

De mag.	De magistro (CSEL 77, CC 29)	The Teacher
C.Max.	Contra Maximinium Arrianum (PL 42)	Against Maximinus the Arian
De mend.	De mendacio (CSEL 41)	On Lying
C.mend.	Contra mendacium (CSEL 41)	Against Lying
De mor.	De moribus ecclesiae catholicae et de moribus Manicheorum (PL 32)	The Morals of the Catholic Church and the Manichaeans
De mus.	De musica (PL 32)	On Music
De nat.bon.	De natura boni (CSEL 25.2)	The Nature of the Good
De nat.et gr.	De natura et gratia (CSEL 60)	Nature and Grace
De nupt.et conc.	De nuptiis et concupiscentia ad Valerium (CSEL 42)	Marriage and Concupiscence
De op.mon.	De opere monachorum (CSEL 41)	The Work of Monks
De ord.	De ordine (CSEL 63, CC 29)	On Order
De pat.	De patientia (CSEL 41)	On Patience
De pecc.mer.	De peccatorum meritis et remissione et de baptismo paruulorum (CSEL 60)	The Merits and Remission of Sins
De perf.iust.	De perfectione iustitiae hominis (CSEL 42)	Human Perfection in Righteousness
De praed.sanct.	De praedestinatione sanctorum liber ad Prosperum et Hilarium (PL 45)	The Predestination of Saints
De quan.an.	De animae quantitate (CSEL 89)	The Greatness of the Soul
Qu.evang.	Quaestiones euangeliorum (CC 44B)	Questions on the Gospels
Qu.Hept.	Quaestionum in Heptateuchum libri VII (CC 33)	Questions on the Heptateuch
Qu.vet.	De octo quaestionibus ex ueteri testamenti (CC 33)	Replies to Eight Questions on the Old Testament
Retr.	Retractationes (CSEL 36, CC 57)	Reconsiderations
C.Sec.	Contra Secundinum Manicheum (CSEL 25.1)	Against Secundinus the Manichaean
Serm.	Sermones (PL 38,39; CC 41; PLS 2; SC 116)	Sermons
Serm Dolbeau	Vingt-six sermons au peuple d'Afrique, ed. Francois Dolbeau (Paris: Institut d'Etudes Augustiniennes, 1996)	
C.serm.Ar.	Contra sermoneum Arrianorum (PL 42)	Against the Sermon of the Arians
De serm.dom.mon.	De sermone domini in monte (CC 35)	On the Lord's Sermon on the Mount
Ad Simpl.	Ad Simplicianum (CC 44)	Replies to Simplicianus
Solil.	Soliloquiae (CSEL 89)	Soliloquies
De spir.et litt.	De spiritu et littera ad Marcellinum (CSEL 60)	The Spirit and the Letter

De Trin.	*De trinitate (CC 50, 50A)*	*The Trinity*
De util.cred.	*De utilitate credendi (CSEL 25.1)*	*The Usefulness of Belief*
De ver.rel.	*De uera religione (CSEL 77.2, CC 32)*	*True Religion*

Chronology of Major Events and Writings

(adapted from the chronology in the article by Fredriksen, n. 2)

354	Birth of Augustine in Thagaste
386	Conversion in Milan
389	*De Genesi contra Manichaeos* (*On Genesis Against the Manichees*)
991	Ordination as presbyter in Hippo
392	Debate with Fortunatus in Hippo
393	*De Genesi ad litteram imperfectus liber* (*Incomplete Commentary on Genesis*)
394–95	Commentaries on Romans and Galatians *Ep.* 28 to Jerome on Galatians 2
395	Consecrated co-adjutor bishop in Hippo
396	Death of Valerius; Augustine becomes bishop of Hippo *Ad Simplicianum* (*Responses to Simplicianus*), "triumph of grace over freedom of choice" *De doctrina christiana* (*On Christian Instruction*)
397	*Ep.* 40 to Jerome on Galatians *Confessions*
397–98	*Contra Faustum* (*Against Faustus the Manichaean*)
401–14	*De Genesi ad litteram* (*On Genesis According to the Letter*)
404	Receives *Ep.* 75 from Jerome
405	*Ep.* 82 to Jerome on Torah observance
412	Beginning of Pelagian controversy
413–27	*De civitate Dei*

–INTRODUCTION–

Engaging Scripture

Patristic Interpretation of the Bible

Eugene TeSelle

In the "Overture" to the first volume, Grenholm and Patte develop what they call "scriptural criticism," an "integrated tri-polar" approach to the interpretation of Scripture. On the basis of a consideration of the actual practice of interpretation, they find

> three "poles" (what is interpreted): the scriptural text, the believer's life context, and the believer's religious perceptions of life.

They root these in

> three modes of existence on the part of the reader or believer: autonomy, relationality, and heteronomy,

and they defend, furthermore, the legitimacy of

> three basic "modes of interpretation" or methodologies: analytical, contextual-pragmatic, and hermeneutical-theological,

which, in each scriptural interpretation, is reflected by

> three interpretive frames: analytical, contextual, and hermeneutical.

This tri-polar approach to the human situation and to the process of interpretation finds support in a number of contemporary discussions. Edward A. Farley's widely influential approach to theological education as *paideia* finds in it three irreducible aspects:

> a disciplining of the interpretation of the events and texts of traditions, of the interpretation of the vision or content under the

posture of truth and reality, and of the interpretation of these things under the posture of praxis or action (Farley 1988, 138).

And those who have reviewed the "academic study of religion" in graduate programs tend to find them grouping into three clusters of disciplines:

Historical Studies of "Texts and Traditions" (in the West, Biblical Studies followed by History of Judaism or History of Christianity); Critical Studies of Religion (anthropology, psychology and sociology of religion, philosophy of religion); and theological Studies (theology, ethics, practical theology).

The test of this tri-polar approach, of course, will come in its actual practice, which takes two quite different modalities.

On the one hand, these methods are distinct, and it is usually assumed that each of them can go its own way. In the scholarly world we can easily identify the "professional guilds" involved in each of these clusters of disciplines. The differentiation between biblical exegesis and doctrinal theology — what Cristina Grenholm calls "Gabler's gap" and Krister Stendahl has termed the difference between "what the Bible *meant*" and "what the Bible *means*" (Stendahl 1962, I:419-22) — has been very useful for more than two hundred years, and it is a major reason for the progress made in the study of classic texts. Theologians as well have acknowledged the distinction. It is clear that they do not simply derive their assertions from Scripture, whether by prooftexting or deduction or some more complex process, and it would be far-fetched to defend the statements made by theologians as "exegesis" or even as "hermeneutics." Karl Barth said that the task of dogmatics is not to ask "what the apostles and prophets have said, but *what we ourselves must say* 'on the basis of the apostles and prophets' [cf. Eph 2:20]" (Barth 1936- , I/1, 16).

At the same time these disciplines cannot be closed against each other, for they define each other and interact with each other in varied ways. When textual and historical studies claim to exercise "autonomy" in the study of classic texts without interference from theology or from religious institutions, they discover that they have been influenced by them nonetheless; "Gabler's gap," in other words, is closed in many ways, surreptitiously or overtly. Those who claim to avoid doctrinal or theological presuppositions turn out in fact to bring many presuppositions — from their own ecclesial tradition, or from their critical rebound against it, or from an anti-theological bias which operates with quite different presuppositions, but presuppositions nonetheless.

The study of a religious text must take into account the meaning of the text, and this involves both philology and a close analysis of the "discourse" of the text. Yet one must also take it into account that, in the historical context, readers (including the first reader, the author) interpreted the text in terms of their own lives, and conversely interpreted their lives in terms of the text. Both the text and the readers' context must be studied with the aid of anthropology, sociology, psychology, political science, and other disciplines. The readers also interpreted the text in relation to their religious experience, and their religious experience in terms of the text. Theological convictions were, and are, an important factor in dealing with a text. And so on.

Context can have multiple meanings. (1) We may mean the historical context in which the text was produced (e.g., first-century Galilee or Syria), and the perhaps quite different context in which it was read, even in its own time. (2) We may mean the context in the present from which questions are asked; and this may range from quite specific vocational concerns (when the context is ministerial education, inevitably the Bible will be approached as "the church's book") to a more diffuse interest in "spirituality," raising the reader's own questions, and even to the deepest preoccupations of the culture, what Tillich calls the "question side" of the correlation between cultural questions and religious answers (Tillich 1951, 59-66). (3) Context may also mean the practical or ethical situation in which the Bible is approached, seeking answers to basic questions. Here one is doing a kind of "theological" interpretation, and it is not simply the "application" of an already complete theology to a new set of issues, because the practical issues themselves raise new questions for the Bible and for one's theology (think, for example, of Dietrich Bonhoeffer reading the Bible in 1938 — or in 1944).

Context can be a far more contested issue than this, of course. Feminist and liberationist and post-colonial thinkers have been able not only to identify "blind spots" in earlier interpretations which result from the social location of scholars (who are usually male, European, and dependent upon established institutions), but to illuminate new aspects of the text and its context by making of their own experiences and perspectives. Indeed, one of the "growth industries" within biblical studies itself in recent decades has been the analysis of social institutions in all their many aspects, including issues of power, class, race, gender, sexual orientation, and disability. This approach brings "text" and "context" together to a new degree, so closely that some scholars are convinced that the Bible is nothing but a reflection of the social relationships of the various times when it was written — that the Bible is, in a word, "ideology" justifying the power relationships of the times, or, if not that, a form of "social criticism" which may be expressed, of course, in the mode of "utopia," correcting or compensating for or transcending the existing relationships.[1]

By the time we reach this point we have discovered the inevitability of the tri-polar approach to interpretation, with "text" and "context" being supplemented by "theology" or perhaps by some form of "anti-theology," a programmatic opposition to what theology assumes and asserts; indeed, when an interpreter moves between text and context (either past or present), some kind of theology or anti-theology is likely to set the rules of inference and give some kind of backing for those rules. When text is "applied" to some contemporary context (e.g., to interpret the meaning of the context, or to ask about ethical implications in this particular setting), the principle of mediation is at least implicitly theological. And when text is "reduced" to context, regarded as nothing more than the expression of power relationships or cultural assumptions of the time, it is done on the basis of the "critical principle" that no text is to be taken at face value.

Theologians in the modern world, after the rise of the social sciences and many forms of philosophical "critique of religion" (e.g., by Feuerbach and Marx, Nietzsche and Freud), have set themselves the task of showing how the Bible, with its all-too-human origins and modes of expression, can still function as the Word of God. Karl Barth recognized the problem and confronted it with his usual audacity. When Rudolf Bultmann, in a review of Barth's *Romans*, pointed out that "other spirits" as well as the Spirit of Christ are to be heard in the Bible, Barth "one-upped" him, suggesting that "there are in the Epistle no words at all which are not words of those 'other spirits' which he calls Jewish or Popular Christian or Hellenistic or whatever else they may be" — and yet asserting that the Spirit of Christ can speak through them all (Barth 1933, 16). Feminists and liberationists have taken a similar approach; Schaberg, for example, writes:

> Feminist hermeneutics, then, is profoundly paradoxical. It sees the Bible as both ally and adversary in the struggle for human rights, equality, and dignity. The biblical God, both helper and enemy, friend and tormentor, cannot simply be identified with God (Schaberg 1990, 8).

And yet the biblical text is not simply passive to contextual or theological interpretation. We often find, as Grenholm and Patte have said, that it "reads and interprets" the other two modes of approach (Grenholm and Patte 2000, 15). Rilke's poem, "Archaic Torso of Apollo," evokes the phenomenon in a striking way:

> ... there is not the least
> Of parts but sees you. You must change your life.[2]

The ancient world would not have been surprised at this poem. A major function of philosophical texts was not to express the author's own experiences or feelings (Romanticism had not yet been invented) but to engage and form and transform the reader, in the manner of what a later era has called "spiritual exercises" (Hadot 1995, 82ff., 102ff.).

In some cases the text, although written in former times, seems to speak directly to the reader in the present: "I will be your God and you will be my people" (Jer. 7:23, 31.33); "You shall love the Lord your God" (Dt. 6:4), "You shall love your neighbor as yourself" (Lev. 19:18), "You shall love the stranger as yourself" (Lev. 19:34); "Hear the word of the Lord" (passim); "Inasmuch as you did it to one of the least of these, you did it to me" (Mt. 25:40). But even where there is not direct address which the reader takes to heart, the text may open up what Karl Barth called "the strange new world in the Bible," framing life's questions in a different but appealing way and offering challenging new "examples" or "case studies."

Marginalia

In order to facilitate the practice of scriptural criticism by biblical critics, church historians, Augustinian scholars, theologians, including pastors, priests, seminarians, as we did in the first volume the editors signal the presence of analytical, hermeneutical, and contextual frames–be they those of the interpretation of Romans by Augustine or those of his interpreters.

"A" : **Analytical Frames** involve *critical categories* which can be either defined in terms of textual features and characteristics (the rhetoric of the text, its logic, etc.) viewed as particularly significant or in terms of the analytical model (e.g., canons of consistency). Wherever pertinent, we underscore here Augustine's readings of specific passages of Romans, as noted by the authors of the essays. Our hope is to facilitate in this way the work of biblical critics who want to identify how Augustine interpreted specific passages of Romans.

"H" : **Hermeneutical Frames** involve *hermeneutical and theological categories* defined in terms of the religious perception of life in Augustine, or the author of the essay, or again the text. Wherever pertinent, for the sake of biblical critics, we underscore here how certain hermeneutical or theological categories are related to Augustine's readings of specific passages of Romans.

"C" : **Contextual Frames** involve *pragmatic bridge categories*, which are context-specific and defined in terms of relational issues. As noted above, the contextual frames might refer to the context of the first readers of the text (Paul and the Romans), of Augustine as interpreter, or of present-day interpreters of Augustine. The web of relationships in a given context includes all the relations governed by structures of power and authority, and thus by structures of inclusion and exclusion. Here also, wherever pertinent, for the sake of biblical critics we underscore how certain contexts are related to Augustine's readings of specific passages of Romans.

"I" : Interplay of Frames involves situations in which two or three frames – Analytical, Hermeneutical, and Contextual frames – are at play simultaneously.

Part I : The Bible as a Problem in the Early Church

I We have begun from the standpoint of contemporary analyses of the process of interpretation, on the tentative assumption that these are the cumulative insights of experienced and self-critical scholars. Taking this "tri-polar" approach to biblical interpretation as a hypothetical model, we may also ask to what extent it was shared by Augustine and his cultural world, the world of Greco-Roman culture and the "fathers and doctors" (including mothers, of course) of the early church.

A As Thomas F. Martin points out in his essay in this volume, Augustine — who began his professional career as a grammarian before becoming a successful teacher of rhetoric — knew the importance of investigating the text as text. Well before the modern study of "the Bible as literature" he engaged in it. Furthermore, he knew the importance of what we call today semantics and semiotics, the theory of signs, and in fact helped to develop that theory for the middle ages and modern times. The marks read by the eye, the sounds heard by the ear, the conventional associations of words are, to be sure, important vehicles of communication; but for Augustine "understanding" meant something more, an intelligibility and coherence which was to be sought "beyond" these signs.

H The problem of interpretation has always been with the Christian church — and before it the Hellenistic synagogue. Educated Greeks were offended by the barbaric style of the Septuagint, and the Old Latin (the version which Augustine used) was even worse, the result of not one but two stages of literal, unidiomatic translation. Augustine was so offended at the style of this translation that he went into a nine-year detour among the Manichaeans, who rejected the Old Testament as the work of a different deity than the God of Jesus Christ. Even without the vicissitudes of translation, there were narratives which depicted God as walking in the garden, acting with a strong right arm, or responding with anger and then repentance. Clearly these needed to be "interpreted." So did passages like the ending of Psalm 137 (136 in the Greek and Latin numbering), "Blessed are those who take your little ones and dash them against a stone"; Augustine thought it meant that vices should be identified and exterminated while they are still small, lest they grow to adult power (*En.Ps.*

I The interaction of the three poles, not only today but in the ancient world.
A The importance of textual study.
H The need for interpretation of the Bible.

136,21). Jonah seemed to be a false prophet, for his statement "In forty days Nineveh will be destroyed" (Jon. 3:4) seemed to be falsified by the city's repentance. No, Augustine says, the wicked Nineveh was destroyed through repentance, and a good Nineveh was thereby constructed (*De civ.Dei* XXI, 18 and 24).

We shall discuss the patristic methods of interpretation — especially allegory and typology — at a later point, noting in particular the way they involve an interaction between the "textual" and the "theological" dimensions. But Augustine and other ancient writers were not unaware of "context."

C For one thing, they were aware of the individuality of the biblical authors, for they did not usually have the Bible in one volume (one-volume copies of the Bible began to be produced during the fourth century, but these great codices were limited in supply, used for liturgical or scholarly purposes in a few major centers; and in any case one had to have an agreed-upon canon, which was only then reaching definiteness). They thought in terms of "David" or "Paul" since they handled them in separate codices, and they were not surprised to find differences among them.

They also took an interest in the circumstances under which biblical writings were produced. This was especially true of the letters of Paul; from the second century on, there were various "prologues" to the Pauline corpus which attempted to set the letters in chronological order and understand their context (Dahl 1978, 2000). Both Galatians and Romans, furthermore, give much attention to the relationship between Jews and Gentiles, not only "theologically" but in relation to specific controversies involving these groups in the local churches; they directly *invite* contextual interpretation. Peter Gorday's essay in particular will deal with fourth-century attempts to understand the relation between Jews and Gentiles in the first-century church.

C The early church, furthermore, was intensely aware of its differences from the surrounding culture. There were constant questions concerning idolatry, immorality, and what to do with those who had fallen into apostasy. Early Christians were not surprised, then, to find the Bible reversing the values that were familiar in the surrounding culture.

And yet the church was also trying to gain recognition from those with power and authority in the society. It had the reputation of being a group of rebels or subversives, and it tried to bridge the gap by doing away with misunderstandings, at times by trying to seem as much like the surrounding society as possible. Already within the New Testament Christians are told to honor those who have political authority and not to try changing

---

C The ancients' awareness of historical context.

C The early church's relation to Graeco-Roman culture — negatively, but also positively.

social customs (including slavery and the subordinate role of women) too drastically. By the time of Augustine, when rulers were Christians and were beginning to enforce Christian orthodoxy, there were further reasons not to emphasize differences from dominant groups in the society and the state; conflict came to be centered upon *religious* differences from pagans, from Jews, and from other Christians. Augustine had to defend Christianity against accusations that its language about nonviolence was incompatible with public order and the safety of the empire; in response he pointed to those passages in the New Testament in which soldiers are told not to leave their service but to carry it out with integrity, and he became one of the first theorists of justifiable war. During the fourth century, furthermore, the monastic movement was catching on; both men and women were forsaking marriage and the family, as Augustine himself did. Under the circumstances it could seem that Christianity was hostile to these traditional institutions — especially since the monastic movement often made negative statements about sex, marriage, and reproduction. While Augustine was aware of the "preferential option for celibacy" in Jesus (Mt. 19:12, Lk. 20:35-36) and Paul (I Cor. 7:7-8, 32-35, 38) and the Revelation to John (Rev. 14:4), he also defended the role of marriage; and in order to ease his task he paid almost no attention to those passages in which Jesus redefined the family, asking who were his mother and siblings (Mt. 12:48-50; Mk. 3:33-35; Lk. 8:19-21), setting parents and siblings in a position of lesser importance than his message (Mt. 10:34-39; Lk. 14:25-26), and promising an alternative family in which the role of father is omitted (Mt. 10:34-39; Lk. 14:25-26). From a distance of fifteen centuries it is easy to see the influence of "contextual" factors like these and to condemn Augustine for his too easy acceptance of war, slavery, and traditional marriage — or for his negative attitudes toward sexual desire.

H Without denying these contextual influences, it is more fruitful to look at the "theological" reasoning that not only justified these positions but in the process qualified and limited them in important ways, avoiding, for example, a wholehearted endorsement of war even while Augustine saw a place for it in the life of governments, and avoiding an overly negative assessment of sexuality as the result of an alien force even while he seems preoccupied with the dangers of desire.

Patristic Biblical Interpretation

C H Let us focus attention on the methods of biblical interpretation that were most often practiced in the patristic period, especially by Augustine.

H   Augustine tries to surmount his context with the aid of theological reasoning.
C H   Principles of interpretation during the patristic period.

We can tease out a number of distinct issues, which will be dealt with in succession.

Allegorization and the Issue of Genre

I We have already noted that Jews and then Christians in the ancient world had difficulties with the Bible. The Greeks had already felt similar difficulties over the epics of Homer, their religious and cultural classics. Some of them differentiated between passages which describe what is *impossible* (what could not have happened as narrated, or what is unworthy of the divine), which they called "myth"; what is *possible but not actual* (what could have happened but did not), which they called "fiction"; and, finally, what is *both possible and actual,* which they called "history" (Pépin 1955 and 1966; Grant 1952 and 1957; Torjesen 1986). Origen adapted this interpretive scheme to the Bible and used the biblical terms "enigma" and "parable" for the first two. His theory was that Scripture is intentionally strewn with "stumbling blocks" as clues that there is a "higher" — or simply "other" and "different" — meaning than the literal one. Origen went on to suggest that not all passages in Scripture have a literal or historical meaning, but that all of them, not only those with stumbling blocks, have this higher meaning (*De princ.* IV,ii,8-9;iii,1-6).

A It should be obvious to any reader of the Bible that it is concerned to speak of something more than empirical facts. The point has often been made in recent centuries, for example, that the Bible is not a scientific textbook and the first chapter of Genesis should not be correlated with various events spoken of in contemporary scientific cosmology, or that the book of Jonah may not be intended to be a "historical statement" at all. Any passage must be understood in light of its genre — both the context in which it is said and heard, and the manner in which it is said — and this is more determinative of its meaning than the "literal" meaning of the terms. We must be cautious, then, not to make a "genre mistake," construing a passage in a way that is inappropriate to what it is saying and how it is saying it. The canonical books of Kings, for example, refer us to other histories for a fuller account of events (I Ki. 11:41, 14:19 and 29), implying that they have earlier and fuller "historical sources" and that their own narrative picks out only the most "significant" events and interprets them in terms of divine promise, chastisement, and restoration. Augustine was aware of these other books (*De civ.Dei* XVIII,38), and concluded that they were produced by human beings using "*historica diligentia,*" while the canonical histories were authored by God, speaking

---

I The text itself seems to invite "interpretation."
A How not to misread the Bible: the importance of genre.

through human "prophets," to give the divine interpretation of an already well-known story.

Attention to genre is a modern version of the point made by Origen that not all passages in Scripture have a "literal" meaning, though all have an "allegorical" meaning. Augustine anticipated our own approach to the question: a totally fictitious narrative, he said, can be told for the sake of truth (*C.mend.* xiii,28; *Qu. evang.* II,v,1 and li,1). He could have affirmed the declaration of Thomas Aquinas that in the case of parables, which clearly do not refer to historical events, the "parabolic meaning" *is* the literal meaning (*S.T.* I, q. 1, a. 10, ad 3). These are, in the language of the current series, *analytical* issues, and the ancients were already aware of them.

C H When Origen and his followers suggested that Scripture has certain "stumbling block" passages which are an invitation to allegorization, their solution was often to interpret some components of the text metaphorically, that is, with meanings "transferred" from the accustomed use of the words to new and different use. To take only the simplest examples, Origen often interpreted "heaven" to be the "heaven of heavens" above the visible heaven, the realm of minds or spirits; he interpreted the "land of promise" to be that same realm, the "pure land" (*De princ.* II,iii,6; II,ix,2-3; III,vi,7-9). A passage may be treated as a juxtaposition of distinct and otherwise incompatible metaphors, somewhat like the "metaphysical poetry" of John Donne and his generation. In fact, this kind of poetic achievement probably rests upon the interpretive theory that was inherited from Origen and Augustine and further developed by the middle ages; the method of dealing with the Bible and other classic texts then gave rise to a distinctive method of literary practice, certainly from Dante on.[3] However this may be, Augustine interpreted many details in the Bible as metaphor. For him the light of the first day, before the sun and stars were created, began with God's call to the angels to turn to God ("Let there be light") and was completed with their turning and becoming light; the six days were their "ordered knowledge" of created things, first in themselves ("evening knowledge"), then as this knowledge was referred to the glory of God ("morning knowledge"); and, since the six days are really one day, they also know all these things with "noonday knowledge" in the divine ideas (TeSelle 1970, 131-46). The Psalms are interpreted to be the utterance of "the whole Christ, head and body" — sometimes crying out in anguish or struggle, sometimes rejoicing in the glory of God, sometimes expressing gratitude for divine grace. Examples like these indicate that allegorization was not some kind of complex system of "coding and de-coding" but a metaphorical reading of Scripture which found greater coherence and intelligibility

---

C H   The nature and role of metaphor.

in it than a flat-footed "literal" reading could ever discover. In the language of the current series, we are not dealing solely with analytical matters, for the interpreter in his/her own situation is moving between text and life and meaning; the poles, then are *contextual* and *hermeneutical.*

H Since there has been much theoretical discussion of the nature of metaphor in our own day, we might note that Augustine's own theory of metaphor (the use of what he called *signa translata*, tranferred signs) is that a word refers "properly" to a specific thing, and then that thing is used to signify something else (*De doct.chr.* II,x,15; cf. III,xxxvii,56). By this he does not mean a *particular* thing, of course, but rather a *kind* of things, whose typical characteristics are connoted by the conventional meaning of the term. When we combine words in new ways to form sentences and whole narratives (shifting, as modern semiotics would put it, from meaning to reference, or from *langue* to *parole*), the characteristics which belong to the conventional usage of a word are employed in different or even contradictory ways between one sentence and another, as Augustine notes. This may be true even of a word's conventional or "literal" use, but it is more dramatic when a word is used metaphorically. Augustine points out that the Bible uses words like "lion," "leaven," and "serpent" with both positive and negative connotations, picking up one or another characteristic of these kinds of things in order to make its point (*De doct.chr.* III,xxv, 35-36).[+]

We have been emphasizing that allegorization can often take the form of metaphorical interpretation, which, while it can be especially original and stimulating when there are unaccustomed combinations of words, is a regular practice even in "ordinary language." But this is not all that is involved in allegorical interpretation, and we must raise other kinds of questions about it.

Allegorization as Theological Interpretation

C The practice of allegorization is often viewed in our sophisticated modern world as a failure to engage in cultural de-centering, because it imposes the reader's own world upon the text rather than asking about the world of the text. I It is well known, of course, that allegorization could involve some far-fetched readings of the Bible, which often amounted to "reading in" a Platonist theory of the differences between body and soul and the sensible and intelligible realms. Allegorization, we might say, illustrates in a striking way the difference between text and theology,

---

H Augustine's theory of metaphor.
C The practice of allegorization is culturally rooted.
I Allegorization is one way (not the only way) of moving between text and theology.

between "what the Bible *meant* "(at least in its literal meaning, to those who were unable to move beyond it) and "what the Bible *means* "(at least to properly spiritual interpreters, operating with the certitudes of their own time).

H The procedure followed by the allegorizers is not the only way of dealing with problematical texts; it had its critics in antiquity as well as the modern world. It makes several quite specific assumptions: it not only (1) has difficulties with the literal text, but it (2) operates with an alternative view of the nature of things, often derived from the surrounding culture with its non-biblical experiences and thought, and this view (3) is held with such certitude that there is a conviction that it must offer decisive clues to the meaning of the biblical text itself, indeed, to the intention of its divine author.[5]

H Perhaps the interpreter's world view overpowers that of the Bible. Perhaps there is what Gadamer (1989, 302-7, 374-75, 576-77) calls a "fusion of horizons," a mutual transformation of both outlooks. Or perhaps the biblical perspective remains the determinative one. Origen, to be sure, reinterpreted the literal sense of the Bible with his theory that created souls live through a long succession of worlds, both before and after this one, on their return to the presence of God. But the case can be made that he interpreted this long journey in a manner that is shaped more by the Bible than by Plato, seeing the entire history of creation as a drama played out between human freedom and divine grace. Schleiermacher once said that, "after all that I have passed through, I have become a Herrnhuter [Moravian] again, only of a higher order" (Gerrish 1984, 26-27). On this reading of Origen one could say that he was "a biblical theologian of a higher order," examining what intelligent and free spirits would do in all possible worlds, under all conceivable circumstances. He himself thought in terms of a temporal succession of worlds; others, less adventuresome, in terms of an overworld of angels and demons, principalities and powers; our own age is more likely to think in terms of a spatial plurality of planets revolving around many stars in many galaxies.

A   However we judge these matters, it must be noted that allegorization is not incompatible with careful historical study. In fact Porphyry, Origen's younger contemporary and the originator of historical criticism of the Bible (suggesting, for example, that the book of Daniel was written during the time of Antiochus IV and the Maccabees), was also a practitioner of allegorical interpretation of the Greek classics and of more recent oracles. Origen himself was a careful textual scholar and paid close

---

H   What allegorization assumes.
H   Does allegorization overpower the text?
A   Close textual and historical analysis is not irrelevant to allegorization.

attention to the chronological sequence of the events that are narrated in the Bible. If one is to determine what in a text is impossible, or possible but not actual, then rigorous historical discipline is needed. Careful delineation of the "literal" or "historical" meaning may be presupposed by the allegorical interpreter as furnishing indications that there are other, more spiritual meanings.

This is not to say that historical readings are necessarily determinative, exercising a kind of veto power over theological readings. To differentiate between the actual, the possible, and the impossible is to recognize the *distinctions* among them, but this is not to ignore the *continuities* between them as long as they remain distinct in the interpreter's own mind; close analysis of the "historical" meaning can yield clues to other meanings that are not so narrowly historical. We have already seen that Origen felt that *all* passages of Scripture had a spiritual meaning, even those that had a literal or historical meaning. The various aspects may interpenetrate in the same text (may be "interwoven," to use a favorite metaphor of both Origen and Augustine) just as well as they may be expressed in different texts.

A It is of more than passing interest that the same differentiation between "myth," "fiction" or "legend," and "history" was utilized by D.F. Strauss in the nineteenth century and by Rudolf Bultmann in the twentieth (Strauss 1972, 75-93; Bultmann 1958 and 1963). **H** Their understanding of the non-literal meanings was no longer that of Origen and Porphyry, an overworld of minds and souls. In Strauss's case it was the hidden unity of the divine and the human which had been uncovered by Hegel; in Bultmann's case it was the existential posture of human life aware of its own mortality. The similarity between them and Origen is that careful attention to text and history not only is compatible with the search for less evident meanings; it is in a sense the precondition for such a search, reminding the reader that the meaning of the text is not primarily, and certainly is not exclusively, the literal or historical one.

H In all such approaches a metaphysical conviction is at work: that historical facts as such are not the point of the Christian message, which has a coherence and intelligibility far surpassing any set of facts; or, if this message is somehow "expressed" in historical facts (a process that is understood in one way by Platonism and in quite a different way by Hegelianism), it is important to move beyond the means of expression to the truth being expressed.

The "theological" principle of interpretation need not be Platonist or Hegelian or existentialist, of course. For Karl Barth the aspect of

---

A Similarities with modern historical criticism . . .
H . . . yet in a different hermeneutical framework.
H The role of theological or metaphysical convictions in this kind of interpretation.

Scripture that goes beyond literal or empirical meanings is the Word of God, always coming afresh as the "event" of direct address to the person, who is thereby called and enabled to respond. Barth has become the patron saint of a wide range of "biblical theology" and "narrative theology" movements (Fowl 1998). Hans Frei championed what he called the Bible's "literal" or "narrative" meaning as against its "factual" meaning as determined by historical criticism (Frei 1974 and 1986). For the "canonical criticism" movement associated with Brevard Childs, the narrative is that of the entire Christian canon understood as a unit, so that "intratextual" cross-references are not only inevitable but completely legitimate.

H In recent decades there has been almost as much discontent with Hegelian or existentialist, Barthian or canonical readings as with Platonizing ones; all of them are accused of being too "totalizing" in their claims. And yet the alternatives being put forward today are not all that drastically different. Narrative interpretation, as we have already mentioned, tells us not to be overly concerned with the "factual" or "historical" or "positivistic" meaning of a text, since what is important is the narrative framework that defines and gives context to the individual episodes. There are others who develop theories of the "performatory" character of all language: language is "discourse," a mode of action; we act by speaking, we can make something to be so by saying so. For Barthians, of course, this is a description of how the Word of God speaks to the human subject, calling for, and calling forth, a positive response. The "hermeneutic of suspicion" and "deconstruction," however, find more sinister overtones in these performatory functions of the text, for it may amount to nothing more than "constructing" a world out of nothing, with no better grounding than the wishes of the speaker or writer, and with no better purpose than to enhance power or position. To discover this background we are urged to look for the "disruptions" in the text — a new version of Origen's "stumbling blocks," but with the damning conclusion that the overworld of meanings is nothing more than a means of exerting power over readers or hearers, making the actual seem inevitable, power seem legitimate, and compliance seem the only reasonable choice. We have not traveled far from the spirit of allegory; the difference is that contemporary "post-modern" approaches are at best relativistic or "historicist" in the conclusions they draw, finding rather little where ancient allegory saw an intelligible world inhabited by souls and spirits, and at worst are downright negative, developing an "anti-theology" which accounts for all the meanings with an alternative explanation, one which is "contextual" in one of the senses discussed above, in effect reducing the text to a function of its context.

H Is theology reducible to social context?

I Most historians and theologians are likely to take a somewhat different approach. They begin by looking at the individual authors or traditions in their own right, and even at the historical "strata" of traditions — asking, for example, about the teachings of the historical Jesus; then about the theology of the "Q community" at various stages as it dealt with new issues; then about the theology of "Luke" as he reworked the Q tradition and joined it with other traditions; then about the Fourth Gospel as a total reinterpretation of the gospel tradition which, even though it has little independent value for finding the "historical Jesus," shows how Jesus' significance was interpreted by at least one tradition in the early church. Then it is appropriate to continue with the "reception" of these various biblical writings in the life of the church, taking note, for example, of the pervasive influence of the Gospel according to Matthew through the centuries, partly because of the assumption that it was the first one written, but largely because it was written and read as a kind of "church order," relevant to the governance of the church and to the Christian life more generally (one thinks, for example, of the use of the instructions to the missionaries in Matthew 10 in the history of ascetic and monastic movements, climaxing with the mendicant orders of the middle ages). This is a more descriptive, pluralistic, and historical or process-oriented approach, letting the "theologies" of the biblical writings speak in their different voices and in the process asking how earlier writers influenced later ones and in turn were unified, revised, or "corrected" by them.

As critical historical investigation does its work, peeling away layer after layer of reinterpretation, we may find the "original" events diminished almost to nothing, or looking quite different from what had been imagined, or susceptible of being construed in conflicting ways (we need only think of the various depictions of the "historical Jesus" in contemporary scholarship). Under such circumstances several quite different responses are possible. Some, whose interest is primarily *historical*, totally reject the later theological elaborations upon the original events as unfounded and illegitimate. Some, whose interest is *contextual*, see these writings as expressions or instruments of the life of the church and Greco-Roman society. And still others, whose interest is *theological*, see the process of elaboration and growth as a legitimating warrant for theology — a kind of theology, however, that no longer grounds itself upon historical events alone, though it takes them into consideration, but engages in broader reflection upon the human situation, the nature of the world, and questions of ultimacy without feeling totally bound to particular facts and events. Two prooftexts for ancient Platonists and modern Hegelians are Jesus' statement (Jn. 20:17), "Do not touch me!" and

---

I   Seeking a genuinely tri-polar approach to biblical texts.

Paul's analogous statement that he is no longer concerned to know Christ "after the flesh" (II Cor. 5:16). In other words, one is not to hold onto the historical particulars but let the wider relevance of the Christian message come into its own.

H It is, however, precisely because allegorization and its modern substitutes emphasize broad theological principles that there are many who fear its abstractness and the universality of its claims. They are likely to want more rooting in historical events, understood not merely as illustrations or reminders of general truths but as actualizations of human potentialities and of divine grace. This is the reason for the growth of theories of typology as contrasted with allegorization.

From Allegory to Typology

H The difference between the letter and the spirit, between *historia* and *figura*, need not be seen in terms of a stark duality. The historical events narrated by the literal meaning of the text were often understood to have additional significance. Already in ancient Israel there was the growth of what has come to be called "typology," the interpretation of earlier events as an anticipation or foreshadowing of later events. Contemporaneous struggles could be seen as a kind of repetition of God's overcoming of chaos in creation (Isa. 51:9-11), the return to Jerusalem from Babylon as a new Exodus (Isa. 43:15-19). In the New Testament this tendency increases. Adam can be seen as a foreshadowing of Christ (Rom. 5:12-14; I Cor. 15:21-22, 45-50), as can certain events during the Exodus (I Cor. 10:4); Christ's death and resurrection as a new Exodus (Lk. 9:31), and Christ as the "end" — fulfillment, perhaps also termination—of the law (Rom. 10:4) or as the new Moses who fulfills the law (Mt. 5:17) or as the High Priest who in offering himself brings the sacrifices to an end (Heb. 10); and Noah's ark as a foreshadowing of salvation through the waters of baptism (I Pet. 3:20-21).

H Allegorization, to be sure, was the predominant method of interpretation during the patristic period; but the theory of typology was growing quietly in the midst of this culture of allegorization. (Allegorization is usually linked with the tradition of Alexandria, typology with that of Antioch.) The difference between the two is that allegorization tends to seek "spiritual" or "intelligible" meanings as contrasted with sensory ones, while typology is confident that some events, *precisely as events*, can also be signs of future events. The former, as Cameron puts it, sees a disjunctive

---

H How to return from theory to events.
H Typology as a different approach to events and their meaning. Rom. 5:12-14; 10:4.
H The difference between allegorization and typology.

relation between sign and referent, the latter a conjunctive relation.[6] We ourselves often speak about "significant" events, as though they carry some kind of meaning beyond what they are in themselves. In typology the connection is mediated by the "sign" character of the earlier events, in other words, by something "intelligible" about them when they are viewed within a broader continuity through time. Events seem to signify something larger than themselves, or establish a trajectory that seems to require a fulfillment beyond what is contained within the events themselves.

H   Augustine, disappointed at the barbarous language of the Old Testament, had followed the Manichaeans in their rejection of this entire part of the Bible. He changed his evaluation of it, as Fredriksen points out in her essay in this volume, when he learned from Ambrose how to allegorize; then he gradually learned the nascent theory of typology and helped to bring it to fuller formulation, handing it on to later Western thought. (He tends to use the term *figura* for narratives of events that signify other events, and *allegoria* for texts that only have intelligible meanings [Dawson 1999].) He was aware, for example, that the rituals of ancient Israel were different from the Christian sacraments; yet he affirmed that they were signs of the same faith and the same grace, differing only in that ancient Israel believed in Christ as still to come, while the church believed in Christ as having already come (*De cat.rud.* xvii,28).[7] Israel's rituals are viewed as subordinate, of course, and as having been superseded by the Christian sacraments, for the reason that the meaning which is "latent" in Israel becomes "patent" in the gospel of the church (*Q.Hept.* II,73).[8] At the same time Augustine helped Christians to take a more positive attitude toward their Jewish neighbors, an attitude that bore fruit in the medieval church's official opposition to violence and forced coercion (quite compatible, in practice, with various forms of discrimination and pressure against Jews), and in the "philo-Semitism" of some Europeans during Reformation and modern times. The point is that there are varied "theological" understandings of the relationship between Jews and Christians, and our decisions among them will make a difference both in our interpretation of passages in the Bible and in our actual behavior in the world.

H   Typological readings of the Bible have been familiar since the middle ages, when the famous fourfold meaning or "*quadriga*" was gradually developed out of John Cassian's discussion of the historical meaning and three spiritual meanings based on Origen (the rather erratic course of this development, which did not reach finality until the thirteenth century, is traced by de Lubac 1948 [1984] and 1959, I:187-

---

H   Augustine's theory of typology.
H   Medieval and modern uses of typology.

219). The "literal" meaning is usually an event or reality in ancient Israel (the Exodus, or Jerusalem); the "allegorical," or really the typological meaning, foreshadowed by the first, is an event or reality in the New Testament (Christ's new "exodus" in Jerusalem [Lk. 9:31], or the church as Jerusalem, God's new dwelling place); the "moral" meaning finds an inward and personal significance of these outward events or realities (exodus from sin to salvation, or the soul as God's dwelling place); and the "anagogical" meaning is the eschatological promise toward which all of these point (eternal life in the heavenly Jerusalem). It is one way of finding unity in the entire Bible. In a less elaborate mode, some nineteenth- and twentieth-century biblical interpreters and theologians have used the typological approach, usually in the form of "biblical theology" or "theological interpretation," with the expectation of finding continuity and consistency throughout the Bible. The Barthian tradition and "narrative criticism" are perhaps the most important contemporary movements which owe much to the tradition of typological interpretation.

C How did Augustine come to shift his emphasis from allegory to typology, without ever abandoning the first? Fredriksen's essay traces Augustine's increasing interest in the interpretation of the Bible *ad litteram*, focusing attention on several quite specific "contextual" factors: his reading of Galatians and his controversy with Jerome over the nature of the dispute between Peter and Paul in Antioch; his reading of the Donatist Tyconius, who showed him how the biblical message could be "de-eschatologized" and re-read in terms of tensions within the historical life of the community of faith; and the need to defend the Old Testament against the Manichaeans by showing that it is a "Christian" set of books.

The Hermeneutical Role of the *Regula Fidei*

H When Augustine reflected on what he was seeking while interpreting the Bible, he often mentioned, as Martin reminds us, the *regula fidei*, the "rule of faith" — concretely, the creed which was learned at baptism. The importance of the rule of faith is that it deals with two indispensable topics: the eternal Trinity, and the Trinity's promises and actions in human history (*De uer.rel.* 1,99; *De lib.arb.* III,xxi,60; *De ag.chr.* 19). (The "holy church," mentioned in the third article of the creed, was understood not as an object of faith but as the object of God's actions and that "through which" and "from within which" one believed in the Trinity [*Serm.* 215,9].) The *regula fidei* could find some surprising applications; when the Pelagians suggest that some human beings might not be

---

C Augustine's move from allegorization toward typology.
H The "rule of faith" as the doctrinal norm.

corrupted by the first Adam and therefore might not need healing by the second Adam, Augustine declares this to be contrary to the *regula fidei* (*De gr.Chr.et pecc.orig.* II,xxix,34).

H To mention the *regula fidei* is not to resolve all problems, however; it is, in fact, to introduce new ones. As J. Patout Burns commented in discussion, Augustine used the creed in two forms, basically similar but with a number of differences in wording — that of Milan and that of North Africa. If, furthermore, the purpose of the *regula fidei* is to ensure unanimity of belief, Augustine's theology fails on this score. His insistence on predestination and grace was not well received by many in the church, and when Vincent of Lérins said that the orthodox faith is that which is believed "always, everywhere, and by all" (*Commonitorium* ii,5), he said it in order to exclude Augustine's doctrine as an innovation *not* supported by the tradition of the church at large. And finally, Burns pointed out, Augustine adhered to the harsh North African doctrine, expressed in a classic way by Cyprian, that "outside the church there is no salvation." This denial of salvation, not only to non-Christians, but to all Christians not in communion with the Catholic Church, was not affirmed by the church of Rome in Cyprian's day, and it has been explicitly rejected by the Roman Catholic Church in more recent times.

H We must also remind ourselves that Augustine did not passively repeat the words of the creed as though they contained the whole truth. The local baptismal creeds, to begin with, had to be interpreted by the decisions of councils, especially that of the Council of Nicaea in 325 which established the full divinity of the second person of the Trinity as a doctrinal benchmark. And even this council, in declaring that the Father and the Son were "of the same substance," failed to state clearly how they were distinct from each other; this question was debated throughout the fourth century, being eventually resolved when Gregory Nazianzen and Gregory of Nyssa singled out the notion of "relation" as the point of the Bible's language about "Father" and "Son." Augustine also found it necessary to go beyond the words of the Nicene Creed when it came to the interpretation of statements by and about Jesus in the gospels; probably following Athanasius and Hilary of Poitiers, he formulated what he called the *canonica regula*: that those passages which speak of his weakness refer to his humanity, while those which speak of his power and knowledge refer to his divinity (*De Trin.* II,i,4).

H Augustine's work *On the Trinity*, which stretches to fifteen books and took twenty years in the writing, is an attempt to go beyond the mere words of Scripture, and beyond the *regula fidei*, to a more comprehensive

---

H Historical complexities in the nature and use of the rule of faith.
H Changing interpretations of the rule of faith.
H Understanding must go beyond the literal meanings of scripture and doctrine.

and explicit "understanding" of what is believed. Even when he was dealing with the essentials of the faith, then, Augustine emphasized that faith must seek understanding. In the process he had to counter many misunderstandings. God is not gendered; the only point in speaking of God as "Father" and "Son" is relationality; the virgin birth does not mean that the Holy Spirit is in any sense the "father" of Jesus; and the procession of the Spirit from the Father through the Son does not mean that the Spirit is the "grandson" of the Father. This is a rather thorough demythologizing, or at least de-literalizing, of the language of Scripture and the creeds (TeSelle 1999, 436).

H There are passages in Augustine's work on the Trinity that attempt to formulate the doctrine in a more precise way. Some of them have even found their way into the so-called Athanasian Creed, named more precisely the *Symbolum Quicunque* from its opening words ("Whoever desires to be saved must above all hold the Catholic faith"). It does not come from Athanasius; it was formulated around 525 in southern Gaul, perhaps by Caesarius of Arles or those associated with him. In any case it came to be a standard of orthodoxy, a far more definitive formulation of the *regula fidei* than either the old baptismal creeds or the Nicene Creed. Some of its language clearly comes from Augustine, as when it says,

> Thus the Father is God, the Son God, the Holy Spirit God; and yet there are not three Gods, but there is one God. Thus the Father is Lord, the Son Lord, the Holy Spirit Lord; and yet there are not three Lords, but there is one Lord (Kelly 1964, 27-29, 83-84, notes the parallels with *De Trin.* V,viii,9 and VIII,i,1).

These driving affirmations have an air of dogmatic certainty and exactitude about them, and through the centuries they have evoked the thrill of discovery in some but have caused others to turn away with disgust. When Augustine uttered them he thought that he was gaining a degree of understanding that went beyond mere belief on the basis of authority.

C Augustine did not suppose, however, that he was thereby formulating statements that could be a substitute for growth in faith and understanding. He still called for an ongoing process of personal initiation. In the later books of *On the Trinity*, therefore, he keeps relativizing and de-stabilizing his own discoveries. While he affirms that faith is the beginning of certitude, he also reminds himself that knowledge cannot be complete until God is seen face to face after this life. Therefore it is better to keep on seeking than to presume that one has found; better yet, God is

---

H   Augustine's own contribution to the rule of faith.
C   Recontextualizing dogma as personal quest.

to be sought even after being found, and when God is found more sweetly, God must continue to be sought all the more eagerly (*De Trin*.IX,i,1; XV,ii,2).

It was very much in Augustine's spirit, therefore, that F.D. Maurice reinterpreted the bold first line of the *Quicunque* to mean quite simply "that eternal life is the knowledge of God, and that eternal death is Atheism, the being without him" (Maurice 1957, 328; cf. the entire discussion, 326-31). **C** Such a perspective may actually be more faithful to the original meaning of the *regula fidei*, for the creed was first used in baptism and soon found additional use as a convenient summary of the "apostolic proclamation," the good news that goes to all the nations (Irenaeus, *Adv.haer*. I,10,1; III,4,2; III,16,6; Tertullian, *De praescr.adv.haer*. 13 and 21). It functioned as a kind of "common denominator" among the many apostolic churches in an era when there was diversity and conflict over many points. In the next generation, Origen understood the creed in the same way, as a summary of the "essentials" of the apostolic proclamation which left many items open, inviting further, more diligent inquiry (Origen, *De princ*. I, praef).[9]

H There is, to be sure, a "hard-line" Augustine who takes seriously the rule of faith and the rule of life. But it is precisely because these are read as being addressed to the reader that a space is opened up for a personal process of initiation — an initiation in understanding (*intellegere*), as we have just seen, but also in love (*caritas*); and both kinds of growth, Martin will emphasize, must be *ad salutem*, for the salvation and fulfillment of the person involved.

Thus Augustine explicitly made a place for freedom of interpretation and judgment (*C.Faust*. XI,5; *Ep*. 147,4; *De civ.Dei* XXI,6). He defended the validity of multiple interpretations of Scripture (*De doct.chr*. III,xxvii,38; *Conf*. XII,xiv,17; xxv,34; xxx,42). **H** He even made the rather audacious statement that Scripture *must* be interpreted figuratively *wherever* it does not concern faith or love (*De doct.chr*. III,x,14-15). Calling upon Augustine as precedent, Elisabeth Schüssler Fiorenza (1984, 14) has used this same principle to assert that revelation is to be found in and through the Bible only in "matters pertaining to the salvation, freedom, and the liberation of all, especially women." The inference she draws is that "the canon and norm for evaluating biblical traditions and their subsequent interpretations cannot be derived from the Bible or the biblical process of learning within ideologies, but can only be formulated within the struggle for the liberation of women and all oppressed people" (60).

C Recontextualizing the creed in the life of the church.

H Dogma opens the way to a personal process of initiation, and hermeneutical theory must return to human life.

H Augustine's audacious hermeneutical principle.

Schüssler Fiorenza goes well beyond what Augustine said and meant. Yet she is continuing a line of reflection which he started.

C Augustine may not have been as far from a "liberationist" perspective as we often think. In listing the Decalogue or Ten Commandments, Augustine followed the text of Deuteronomy 5 rather than Exodus 20. Here the prohibition on desiring the neighbor's wife comes first; then there is a prohibition on coveting the neighbor's property. (To keep a total of ten, the prohibition on other deities was understood to include the making of images.) This numbering is reflected in some early Christian writers, in the medieval Masoretes and Moses Maimonides, and most influentially in Augustine (Reicke 1973, 9-12; Schindler 1996, 246-55).[10] Augustine's enumeration of the commandments was followed by the medieval Catholic Church and by Luther; their catechisms still divide the commandments in this way, with three in the "first table" dealing with one's relationship with God, and seven in the "second table" dealing with one's relationship with other human beings.

The text of the Decalogue in Exodus 20, by contrast, includes the neighbor's wife, as well as male and female slaves, in the middle of a list of the neighbor's property. This is the enumeration used by Calvin and the churches influenced by him (the separate enumeration of the commandment against images helped to reinforce the iconoclasm of the Calvinistic churches). Today when state legislatures are thinking about permitting or requiring the Ten Commandments to be posted in public schools, they probably assume that the Calvinist version is the correct one. What they seek would in fact amount to an "establishment" of one religious tradition and prejudice against another tradition whose religious instruction still lists the commandments in a different way. An even more interesting issue is that Deuteronomy's enumeration, reflected in the Catholic and Lutheran traditions, seems closer to a "feminist" version of the Decalogue. Augustine is not often viewed by feminists as one of their champions. Yet he did consider women to be the spiritual equals (though not the bodily equals) of men, and in this specific case he clearly resisted including them within a longer list of the husband's property. It may well be, then, that not only Catholics and Lutherans but others will want to insist on keeping these commandments distinct.

H But let us look further at his invitation to interpret Scripture in light of the twin law of love, asking how and to what extent Augustine sketches the possibilities for a "reader-oriented" interpretation of Scripture.

C Embryo of liberationism in Augustine.

H Augustine's "reader-oriented" hermeneutic.

Augustine's Charter for a "Reader-Oriented" Interpretation

H The audacious statement that Scripture must be interpreted figuratively wherever it does not concern faith or love appears in Augustine's work *On Christian Instruction* (concerning this work see esp. Arnold and Bright 1995; Pollmann 1996; English 1995). It was written just before the *Confessions*, at a crucial turning point in his life and thought. He had just become a bishop; he was in the midst of a drastic change in his views on grace and conversion; and (most to the point in this connection) his aspirations had become more humble, no longer expecting an unblinking contemplation of God but deferring that hope to the situation following death. This work is perhaps the first fully developed theory of signs in antiquity, certainly among Christian writers (Pollmann 1996, 174-76), and it draws together motifs from Stoicism, neo-Platonism, and especially the Aristotelian theory of rhetoric (Pollmann 1996, 160-67, 195). It is well known that Augustine held the neo-Platonic theory that sensible things and words are signs or reminders of pure intelligibles; his early work *On the Teacher*, written in 389, is an especially blatant expression of that theory. In *On Christian Instruction*, written seven years later, Augustine's thought becomes far more complex than this, in at least three important respects.

H 1. In this work Augustine shifts his emphasis from the intellect to the affections. The reason is that human beings, who should have enjoyed the direct intuition of the divine light, have fallen away from it and are no longer able to endure the divine presence. Now they are "sojourners" in the sensory world, and their return to the divine light is a journey of the affections; hence the focus on love of God for God's own sake, the desire for a more complete communion with God, and the eventual enjoyment of God which alone brings true fulfillment to human life.[11] Christ in his divinity has always been the goal; but through the incarnation he has also become, in his humanity, the indispensable way toward the goal (*De doct.chr.* I,xi,11; xxxiv,38). Everything is set in motion because of the situation of fallen humanity; God is that *to which* all else is set in relation, *to which* all else ought ultimately to be "referred" (and both affections and signs can be "referred," set in relation to something else; that is the character of what modern philosophers call, on the basis of a line of inquiry stimulated by Augustine, "intentionality"). This is why Augustine says in Book I that God alone is to be "enjoyed" while all else is to be "used," then puzzles over the question whether human beings are to be used or enjoyed, and finally concludes that they are to be loved "in God."

H Augustine had assumed the possibility of an unblinking contemplation of God, but now he concludes that it is impossible.

H Humanity as distanced from God.

H 2. The journey is directed by signs. The function of signs is to refer to realities other than themselves, just as acts of will ought to refer created things to God. But signs can be dangerous, Augustine says, especially in religious matters. While religious signs ought to point to God and participate in God's gracious activity, they may be taken too literally (and Augustine cannot refrain from mentioning the Jews here); or they may erroneously point to the physical elements, as in the religions of the Gentiles (*De doct.chr.* III,vii,11-ix,13); or they may become the vehicle for deception by the demons (II, xxiii,35-xxiv,37). Hence the importance of finding the right signs — and interpreting them rightly. The created world itself ought to have been an adequate expression of God, and Augustine compares those who love created things rather than the creator to people who, in hearing a speaker, listen to the voice and syllables rather than the message of which they are signs (*De lib.arb.* II,xv,43; cf. *De doct.chr.* II,xxi,32). But this, of course, is precisely what has happened. Scripture is a more carefully articulated set of signs designed to lead the human race toward God and the enjoyment of God.

H 3. The work is therefore framed by the question how to interpret the Scriptures. And the nature of that task is not self-evident. In a polemical introduction to the work, Augustine attacks unnamed opponents who claim divine assistance (perhaps charismatics; perhaps Platonists as well, with their theory of inward illumination) and are contemptuous of human reflection on the problems of interpretation. Augustine defends a more "critical" approach. The one he develops is not primarily cognitive, does not approach interpretation as a scholarly endeavor in either theology or history; it is practical, undertaken for the sake of human beings and their movement toward the enjoyment of God. Attention is focused on the contemporaneous relevance of the Bible in the ongoing present. The work is conceived accordingly on the rhetorical model, beginning with *inventio*, the discovery of what ought to be taught, and concluding with composition and delivery in light of the three purposes of rhetoric: to instruct, to persuade, and to delight. **H** As Martin points out in his essay in this volume, Augustine drastically decentered the rhetorical practice of *inventio*, subordinating it to the biblical text, with the task of understanding "those things which ought to be understood." While Augustine stopped writing near the end of Book Three and did not complete the entire work until three decades later, in 427, the fourth book — which deals with the other aspect of rhetoric, the process of delivery — is probably close to what he originally intended; **C** if anything his original purposes were reinforced, for in the meantime the controversy with the

---

H The need for method.

H The crucial role of the biblical text in Augustine's hermeneutical theory.

C Early Augustine's interpretation of Rom. 5:5; 1:18-23; and 2:14-16 and during later controversies.

Pelagians had strengthened his convictions about the role of the affections, which, he is now persuaded, are influenced not only by rhetoric but by divine grace acting immediately upon the human heart. For many years he had interpreted Romans 5:5 to mean that love for God is poured into the heart by the Holy Spirit; he had begun to suggest that the experience of love within oneself is an experience of the Holy Spirit, who is Love from Love (*In ep.Io.* viii,12-14; ix,10; *De Trin.* VIII,viii,12); now he declares even more strongly that only God can arouse delight in the good within a heart that has become accustomed to desiring lesser things (Burns 1980).

Gathercole's essay on Augustine's interpretation of "natural law" is also pertinent to this late development in Augustine's thinking. The early Augustine assumed (on the basis of Rom. 1:18-23 and 2:14-16) that human beings are able to know the law and do what it demands. As he took the effects of sin more seriously, he emphasized the role of distorted impulses and erroneous judgments in human life. His later view, therefore, was that natural law and natural capabilities, while they are never lost, can come into exercise only when human nature is restored with the assistance of grace; natural law is fulfilled, then, only by the elect, and only partially even by them.

I In *On Christian Instruction* Augustine clearly tilts the interpretation of Scripture not toward exegesis of the text, not toward historical study of its background and its meaning in its time, but toward "doctrine" in the sense of the activity of teaching or proclaiming. He is writing here for the preacher, not for the contemplative reader who seems to be assumed in many passages of *On the Trinity.* His emphasis, as we have said, is not so much cognitive as affective, not so much theoretical as practical, focused not on the past but on the present and future. His concern, to put it in Stendahl's language, is not with "what the Bible *meant*" but with "what the Bible *means*" — and not even that, for his concern is finally not with what the Bible means and says but with "*what we ourselves say on the basis of the Bible*" (cf. Barth 1936- , I/1, 16). It is a combination of "interpretation" and "application" and "proclamation."

H How does he justify this reader-oriented approach? We can identify a number of theological reasons for it.

1. In his theology we find both an intensification of concern with human subjectivity and an interest in the universal mission of the church to all peoples. His "turn to the subject" brought a new degree of attention to consciousness and the affections, indeed, an attempt to describe both cognition and volition with the greatest generality, accounting for all acts of knowing and willing and attempting to discover their conditions of possibility. Because of this he also gained a new degree of confidence in

---

I A tripolar approach to reading the Bible.
H Theological justifications of this approach.

the universality of the Christian message as not limited to any language or people, any culture or political realm.

2. He had what we might call a "philosophy of religion," inherited from a broadly Aristotelian understanding of human life as a quest for happiness or fulfillment. We all seek happiness; but it is not self-evident in what happiness will consist. On the basis of Cicero's *Hortensius* he described happiness as that situation in which what is *best* is both *loved* and *possessed* (*De mor.*I,iii,4; *Ep.* 130,10; *De Trin.* XIII,v,8 [where Cicero is explicitly quoted]). His own conviction was that true happiness or fulfillment is to be found only in the contemplation of God, an end which is *worth having,* can be *attained,* and with full *security.*

3. Augustine's understanding of grace increasingly reinforced these tendencies. He had begun with a fairly conventional belief in the interaction between free choice and the operation of grace, on the principle that grace will be received most gratefully after human beings are brought to an awareness of their need for it. **H** But in 396 he became convinced, on the basis of Romans 9:14, that grace comes as a result of divine predestination; "I defended the free choice of the will," he later said, "but the grace of God prevailed" (*Retr.* II,1, referring to *Ad Simpl.* I, q. 2,10-22). After a silence of fifteen years he returned to the theme during the Pelagian controversy, and twenty years after first being persuaded about predestination he came to an intensified version of it — that no one can delight in the law of God except when God directly arouses the affections.

This change occurred in 417, and some see Augustine's thought becoming grim and cold. The essays by Martin and TeSelle, however, call attention to the ways he continued to defend human freedom and the role of the affections, with the added insistence that they are guided and nurtured by divine grace, which offers a stability which human freedom cannot give to itself. **C** Augustine did not cease to use the principle of love in interpreting the Bible; if anything he intensified it, declaring, as Martin points out, that an interpretation will be "outrageous" and "inopportune" and "inappropriate" if it is not applied in a salutary way to human weakness (*De don.pers.* xxii,61). It is worth noting that in precisely this passage he is urging the preacher to shift from theoretical statements to practical ones, using direct address in "second person" so that the language of predestination will be employed in a hopeful way.

H Augustine's theology is intensely "personalist" in its understanding of both human life and God, and many in the modern world have found such an approach appealing. He, along with Ambrose, is at the source of a tradition of personal piety in Western spirituality which emphasizes that

---

H Augustine's interpretation of Romans changes with a new belief in predestination. Rom. 9:14.

C Preaching ought to use direct address.

H The hermeneutics of love.

love for God goes beyond the "servile fear" of a slave toward a master, beyond the "mercenary" attitude that seeks a reward, but is characterized by mutual affection between God and human beings. A classic expression is a sonnet published in Spanish in Madrid in 1638. (It is often assumed to have been written by Francis Xavier or Teresa of Ávila, merely on the strength of their reputations. After a manuscript copy, written only ten years later by an Augustinian in Michoacán, Mexico, was found early in the twentieth century, some claimed it for the New World; but this attractive thesis has not received much support [Huff 1948, 29].) The most famous English paraphrase goes this way:

My God, I love thee, not because
I hope for heaven thereby;
Nor yet since they who love thee not
Must burn eternally.
. . . . .
Not with the hope of gaining aught,
Not seeking a reward;
But as thyself hast lovèd me,
O ever-loving Lord (Caswall 1873, 152).
. . . . .

H At the same time, it is only fair to note that there are critics who find all of this "too good to be true." If he posits a "mothering God" who is in charge of all that happens, at least for the elect (O'Connell 1983), then this might be nothing more than the final expression of his fixation on his mother. Connolly, who stands in the tradition of Nietzsche, accuses Augustine of seeking "revenge" against the realities of the human condition (Connolly 1991, 138, 139), and addresses him boldly:

You speak, Augustine, to an ear located in the interior of the self, an ear that muffles the sounds of death so that it can receive any murmur on behalf of an afterlife, an ear that drowns out sounds that equate death with oblivion, an ear that listens to secret appeals for revenge against a world that is cold and indifferent to the desire to escape oblivion, an ear that would rather hear the voice of the other through a code of heresy, damnation, apostasy, sacrilege, and sinfulness than sacrifice the possibility of eternity (138-39).

Whatever our final judgment about these issues, it is clear that Augustine does adopt a reader-oriented approach to interpretation that, even while it affirms the Bible *ad litteram,* is not afraid to go "beyond" the letter of the

---

H Or was Augustine too confident about God and the good?

Bible in a number of important ways. Let us now try to gain a comprehensive picture of the procedures that he follows.

Leveraging the Language of the Bible

H Augustine, precisely in affirming the Bible *ad litteram*, goes "beyond"
its literal sense. In some cases this is done by reading it allegorically
(which often means metaphorically); but of course the metaphorical or
parabolic sense of the Bible may in fact be its "literal" sense, as Augustine
himself points out. In other cases it is done by reading the Bible
typologically; the typological sense is even more clearly "literal," for the
biblical narrative refers to events which are in turn understood to be
"signs" of later events. In both cases the point is that the biblical text may
have dimensions of meaning that are not at first apparent but come to
light after a more careful reading, asking whether it narrates something
impossible or improbable or unworthy of God, or inquiring into the
connections among events that, while widely scattered in time, may reflect
a coherent divine purpose.

A There are other ways Augustine goes "beyond" the text of the Bible,
and here again the time dimension becomes an important factor. He
knows, for example, that the Septuagint, the Greek translation of the
Hebrew Bible, is at variance with the Hebrew text at some crucial points.
And yet he argues for use of the Septuagint on providential grounds: the
Jews had failed to transmit the Bible to the nations, and the task was then
assumed by the legendary seventy translators at the time of the Hellenistic ruler Ptolemy, making some adaptations to Greek culture (*De doct.chr.*
II,xv,22).

A Or again, various acts that we consider immoral are narrated of the
patriarchs and the prophets (polygamy, concubinage, the Israelites' taking
their Egyptian neighbors' jewelry, Hosea's marrying a prostitute). Such
acts, Augustine says, are to be left in the past by interpreting them as
figures; in other words, the meaning of the events is to be retained in
understanding, but the deeds themselves are not to be transferred to our
own morals in the present (*De doct.chr.* III,xii,18-xxiii,33). (The same
thing was done by slaves and abolitionists in nineteenth-century America,
viewing Paul's exhortations about slavery as too dead a letter to be the
living word of God.)

This is not all. The Bible speaks of God "hardening the hearts" of
Gentiles and even the people of Israel (Ex. 4:21; Is. 6:9-10; Mk. 4:23 parr).
Some of Jesus' parables have offensive features; we immediately think of
the unjust steward (Lk. 16:1-9), the man who finds a treasure and secretly

---

H A summary of Augustine's hermeneutical rules.
A Are the differences between the Hebrew and the Greek texts of the Bible justifiable?
A Problems with the Bible which demand interpretation.

buys the field (Mt. 13:44), or taking the reign of God by violence (Mt. 11:12-13 = Lk. 16:16). **H** The gospel according to Mark repeatedly reproaches the disciples for their failure to understand what Jesus says and does — a healthy reminder, we might say, that it is not only we who question the text of the Bible, for the Bible also questions us.

A Even more drastic issues can arise. Augustine was confident that Jesus' actions conveyed a message, that they were significant, even eloquent; deeds can speak, and if we understand them they become words (*Serm.* 95,3). But they are not always so clear and unambiguous. On one occasion Jesus said that he was not going up to Jerusalem for the Feast of Tabernacles, but then he went up "secretly," or at best "privately" (Jn. 7:2-10); Augustine, aware of the charge that Jesus lied on at least this occasion, felt compelled to interpret this sequence of events pedagogically (*Serm.* 133). Again, when Jesus walked over to the fig tree to see whether it had any fruit (Mt. 21:19), he could not have been ignorant. **H** His action, while a "fiction," did not amount to deception; it was a figurative act, "inviting understanding rather than causing error" (*Serm.* 89,4). Any misinterpretation on the part of the onlookers must be the result of wrong judgment on their part, not of deception on Christ's part.

H What, then, are we to make of the disagreement between Peter and Paul in Antioch, recounted in Galatians 2:11-14? Gorday's essay traces a conflict in interpretation between Jerome, who thought that the disagreement must have been simulated to convey a message to believers in Antioch, since apostles could not really differ over an issue so fundamental as the observance of the Jewish law, and Augustine, who in this case saw no pedagogical function in the altercation between Peter and Paul and viewed Jerome's interpretation as a totally inappropriate encouragement of lying. It is not always easy to differentiate between pedagogy and deception!

Gorday notes that both Origen and Chrysostom offered more subtle explanations of the dispute, suggesting that Peter, because of his anxiety to maintain his relationship with Jewish Christians, did indeed commit an offense against the gospel, and that this error was then corrected by Paul, to the edification of all. **H** On this reading, the conflict was genuine but had pedagogical results through a kind of "indirect communication." The issue, of course, is whether it was intentional on their part, or providential (as Origen and Chrysostom suggested), or becomes instructive only in hindsight.

H The text may question the reader.
A Other problems with the Bible.
H Are we to differentiate between fiction and deception?
H A dispute about the nature of the apostles' authority.
H If the episode is instructive, how and why did it become so?

H In these and other ways the Bible invites, in fact demands, the exercise of good judgment, which begins with a hard-headed assessment of the tensions within the text, or of what actually happened, or of what is worthy of God, or of what can be considered right or good in our own day. The text itself may raise questions which make us seek new and different meanings. Augustine preached two sermons on the Canaanite woman (Mt. 15:21-28) about the same time as his sermons on Romans 7 (*Serm.* 154A = Morin 4; *Serm.* 77A = Guelferbytanus 33).[12] He notes that Jesus, in saying that it is not right to take the children's food and give it to the dogs (the Gentiles, to whom she belonged), blocked her, created an *aporia*[13]; she quite properly responded with a new thought, that even the dogs get the crumbs that fall from the table, and he praised her for it, since she was seeking a share in a salvation that she knew was not hers by right.

The process of interpretation as Augustine traces it, then, very often involves a "rebound" against the obvious meaning of a passage and a "leveraging" of further meanings. How does this happen? Let us consider the process — and the justification offered by Augustine — in the light of the three perspectives that were identified earlier.

A 1. It may happen *textually* — perhaps through the very genre that is used, perhaps by posing problems through "hard sayings" or by the nature of the narrative itself, perhaps by arousing expectations that set a new trajectory toward the future, in the fashion of typology. At least that is how Augustine interpreted the "transition" of Exodus and Passover, as a sign or figure of the *intentio* of Philippians 3:13 which strives toward new life and the city of God (*De civ.Dei* XVII,7).

H 2. It may happen *intertextually*, as the interpreter becomes aware that a particular passage seems incongruent with other important passages in the Bible. There are many examples of this in Augustine's sermons and commentaries and theological writings, for he was constantly moving back and forth through the Bible; La Bonnardière has developed a method of dating Augustine's works by plotting his biblical citations and the associations among them, their *orchestration scripturaire* (La Bonnardière 1960- and 1965). One dramatic instance of intertextual stimulation can be seen in his first attempt at a commentary on Romans, written about 394, which never gets beyond the opening verses. First he is concerned that Paul only mentions "God our Father and the Lord Jesus Christ" (Rom. 1:7) without naming the Holy Spirit, then he decides that this is done in speaking of "grace and peace," since grace and peace are God's gift, indeed, the Spirit *is* God's Gift (*Exp.inch.Rom.* 11-13). This reminds him of the statement in the gospels that the only unforgivable sin is the sin against the Holy Spirit (Mt. 12:31-32 was his primary point of

---

H The necessity of inquiry, interpretation, and judgment.

A Augustine's emphasis on the analytical frame and textual evidence.

H Augustine's use of intertextuality and the *regula fidei* as parts of his hermeneutical frame. Rom. 1:7.

reference), and he quickly comes to the insight that this must be despair over the grace of God, impenitence, spurning the means of grace offered through the one church which alone has the Spirit.[14] There may be many unexpected resonances among biblical passages, especially for an interpreter aware of his doctrinal responsibilities and guided by the *regula fidei*!

C 3. It may happen *contextually*, through the character of the problems that are raised for human life — in biblical times, or in our own day, or for human life considered more generally. At times there is an affirmation of cultural perspectives, as when the "wisdom literature" borrows themes and language from Mesopotamia and from Egypt. Augustine, following Irenaeus and others, defends this as being like the Israelites' "spoiling the Egyptians," taking what belongs to God and putting it to a more appropriate use (*De doct.chr.* III,xl,60-61). More often there is a challenging of these perspectives. Either way the cultural setting may amount to the "question side" of a correlation which is then "answered" with the assertions of faith.

H 4. It may happen *theologically*, making affirmations about God or the human self or the world that seem inconsistent when we move from one passage to another; then they require us to engage *die Sache selbst*, by which we mean not a presumed reality but the issue under discussion — evil or providence, justification or human happiness, the character of God. Once the text raises certain points, there is no going back; just as in a court of law or a parliamentary debate one may raise a topic and then find that the discussion has taken a very different direction than one had anticipated, similarly the Bible raises a number of difficult topics, approaches them with a variety of perspectives, and requires the reader to come to his or her own judgments. Once the topic has been raised — by the text, by readers, by a tradition of use or debate — a trajectory has been established, and one must continue the inquiry.

In all of these ways the Bible seems to be self-transcending, going beyond the plain letter of its text and inviting new judgments.

H Augustine knew that signs are not always clear and transparent, and he devoted much of Book III of *On Christian Doctrine* to "ambiguous" signs. Derrida in our own day has emphasized how a language is constituted by a multiplicity of signs which relate to each other in a shifting network of meanings, constantly destabilizing each other and "deferring" meaning further. Augustine would not be surprised; he commented that, when we try to explain words with the help of other words, it is like rubbing fingers together and then trying to differentiate which does the rubbing and which the feeling (*De mag.* 14). Derrida's world view is, we might say, Platonism without either the Demiurge or

---

C Augustine's contextual frame
H The instability of language.

the realm of ideas to give stability. Augustine was aware, as a Platonist, of the plurality and instability of finite beings, sensory experience, and the language which tries to narrate them, always uncertain and hastening on. At the same time he refused to despair of the possibility of gaining coherent, though limited, knowledge of the finite world, human being, and God, engaging in neither a wholesale demolition nor a wholesale defense of language and its capabilities.

H Precisely because of his confidence in human thought, Augustine was prepared to make judgments about *die Sache selbst*, the issue itself. He praised Porphyry for coming to a different judgment than Plato: here was a Platonist criticizing Plato, and this, he concluded, was very much in the spirit of Plato (*De civ.Dei* X,30). He also devoted much attention to the mistakes of judgment we can make, wrongly interpreting our experiences; one major hazard that he identified is the use of sensible things as the model for thinking about ourselves and about God (*Conf.* III,vi,10; *De Trin.* XI,v,9). Thomas Aquinas thought that he saw a different error of judgment in Augustine; he was so imbued with the doctrine of the Platonists, Aquinas says, that he misinterpreted the fact that intelligibles are in our minds in an "immaterial" way and assumed that it proved that those same intelligibles exist independently in an immaterial way (*S.T.* I, q. 84, a. 5). In more recent times we have seen other, more radical "critiques of knowledge" which trace the ways we misconstrue and misinterpret what is given in experience — sometimes on the basis of self-interest or desire or imagination, sometimes on the basis of social and linguistic conventions, sometimes on the basis of ideologies which entice us to interpret our experience in accordance with the interests of dominant social classes. But this is very much in the spirit of Augustine, as we have just seen, for he was interested more in the truth than in what people have said or supposed, more in God than in what has been thought about God, even when it is expressed in the words of Scripture. The process of interpretation is unpredictable and unconstrained.

Are There Contemporary Parallels?

C H Augustine's perspective in *On Christian Doctrine* looks very much like what is called today "liberal" or "liberationist" or "revisionist" theology. The similarity is not merely in the flexible attitude taken toward the letter of the Bible, but in the "material principle" that is emphasized, namely the twin commandment of love for God and neighbor (Augustine will often add the stranger and the enemy, too). The love commandment had not been used very much prior to Augustine as a

---

H   The necessity, and the possibility, of critical thinking.
C H   Similarities of structure between Augustine and modern liberal theology.

summary of the Christian life. Now he was drawn toward it because of its comprehensive applicability to all possible situations and its reliability as a guide to all acts of willing.[15]

This rather free-wheeling approach to the biblical text is not the only one that we find in Augustine's writings, either before or after *On Christian Doctrine*, though it is not inconsistent with them. Perhaps in this work he was caught by the momentum of his own reflections and drew implications that were somewhat misleading. However that may be, Augustine did not allow this hermeneutical principle to lead him into undisciplined subjectivity. **H** When he broke off writing *On Christian Doctrine* he started the *Confessions*, a work which is intensely personal, to be sure, but one in which he seeks structure in his life by setting his quest in the context of prayer, and getting orientation from the passages of Scripture that pepper its pages, and in the final books placing his own story within the story of the whole cosmos. If he was interested in the human subject, he knew that the human subject is *situated* and must be seen in relation to other persons, to culture, to the cosmos, and to God.

Nonetheless he did say these things in *On Christian Doctrine*, and he offers an interesting justification for contemporary tendencies that are similar in emphasizing the central and most comprehensive features of the biblical message and using these to judge all its other features. **C** We should not find this surprising, for it took the early church a number of centuries to draw together a canon of apostolic writings and come to some kind of agreement about the basic doctrines of Christianity. Augustine himself, who brought a new degree of coherence to Christians' thinking about the biblical story and the Trinity, and especially about grace and free will, was praised by Jerome (in his *Ep.* 141) as the "second founder of the ancient faith"; earlier Jerome had used similar language about Origen, calling him "a teacher second only to the great apostle" (preface to Jerome's translation of Origen's homilies on Ezekiel). Christians in that era were aware of how *little* they knew about the way their faith and ethics held together. Perhaps the same attitude would be salutary even in our own day, when there is a vast accumulation of doctrinal statements and systematic theologies. At least that what liberals and revisionists encourage us to keep on doing.[16]

H The complexities of using the Bible in our own day are highlighted by the title of a book on biblical interpretation, *Slavery, Sabbath, War, and Women* (Swartley 1983). In at least these four areas — certainly not minor points! — we do *not* follow the letter of Scripture and are glad to call upon principles such as "interpretation," "the fundamental message of the Bible," and "Christian freedom." In our time most of us use gender-inclusive

---

H The personal is corrected by the textual and the theological.
C The indefiniteness of the early church's canon and doctrine.
H C The impossibility of biblical literalism.

language about human beings and God. But some do not, on the grounds that the Bible refers to God with the masculine pronoun. And yet these same persons usually assume that the New Testament talks about people "sitting" to eat, when it actually says that they were reclining, whether at table or in the feeding of the multitudes in the fields. It is difficult to be a consistent biblical literalist!

C Beyond these four areas there is the even more contested question of same-sex relationships, which seem to be condemned unconditionally in various passages of Scripture (six to twelve, by various counts). But here as well there seems to be a place for interpretation and Christian freedom rather than the simple repetition of biblical passages, for we must not only understand them in their own cultural setting but then take responsibility for setting policies that will be appropriate to our own science and culture but also in accord with the basic spirit of Scripture.

What are we to make of the narratives of Sodom (Gen. 19) and the Levite's concubine (Judg. 19)? They deal with the gang rape of travelers, an act of personal violence which was also an act of contempt toward the host, who was obligated to offer hospitality and protection. In both stories it is clear that it was permissible to give women over to the sexual aggression of males — either the host's own daughters, as Lot did, or both one's own daughter and the traveler's concubine, as the Levite's host suggested. Females were, on a relative scale, more expendable. The attitude, then as now, was, "Well, at least there are no unnatural acts going on here" and "Men are just like that."

C It is important, then, to see the *reasons* for the widespread condemnation of homosexual acts in the Biblical tradition. One, as we have just seen, is a concern about *violence* and *lack of consent*, a dramatic instance of humiliation and violation. If one side of the relationship is aggression, the other side is *passivity*, a role regarded as inappropriate for males; hence the prohibitions on a man lying with a man "as with a woman" (Lev. 18:22 and 20:13). This may be the reason for a New Testament passage like I Cor. 6:9-10, where the two words that are used may apply respectively to the passive and the active partners.[17] More broadly, certain kinds of same-sex relations, on the part of both women and men, were taken to be *disruptions of natural order*, symptomatic of the *wider* disruptions of natural order that follow from human sin (Rom. 1:26-27). Paul speaks of them as being "against nature" or contrary to the "natural use of women." But in what sense? Because they do not lead to procreation? Or because the natural order was assumed to include the primacy of males and their monopoly on the "use of women" (Rom. 1:27)? Or perhaps because persons who were naturally heterosexual were engaging in homosexual acts?[18]

C How shall we approach current issues?
C Interpreting the Bible in its own context. Rom. 1:26-27.

Thus we have issues of *religious taboo* as well as those of *violation of "natural order," lack of procreation, humiliation of others, lack of consent,* the widespread presence of *sacred prostitution.* and, we should also add, *sexual activity for hire.* All these concerns, it must be said, are far more definite in Roman law than in the biblical writings themselves. **I** Once we see the reasons for traditional attitudes toward homosexual acts, we are obliged to ask the further question whether these biblical prohibitions apply to *all* same-sex relationships, or only to those which involve violent assault, humiliation of the victim, a mercenary relationship, or sexual perversity which is *against* one's own natural inclinations, and thus do *not* apply to consenting relationships between mature adults. The issues of interpretation continue in our own day, and they are not susceptible of facile solutions.

The Selection and Transmission of Augustine's Interpretation

The chief question with which this volume is concerned is the influence of Augustine upon the reading of Romans in the West. It is important, then, to ask how it happened, to look into its "transmission history."

A C The Augustinian interpretation of Paul's epistles was transmitted to the middle ages, not primarily through Augustine's own writings (though these were copied and read), but through excerpts. Let us note what this involved. Augustine himself engaged in the exposition of biblical passages in something less than a "systematic" way, sometimes in sermons and sometimes in written commentaries. In the transition from the ancient world to the early middle ages, much of the intellectual activity amounted to a "salvage operation," selecting the most usable comments or those that dealt with important or difficult biblical passages. These were strung together in the order of the text — first the Bible as a whole, then the various *corpora*, especially the H exaemeron (the six days of creation), the Psalms, the gospels, and Paul. These excerpts then developed into "glosses" in the eleventh and twelfth centuries, which in turn gave rise to the full-fledged "commentaries" of the thirteenth century.

The first collection, moving through the entire Bible, was made by Eugippus, an abbot near Naples, using a collection of Augustine's writings held by the virgin or nun Proba. This was expanded by Bede in England, adding other passages (Hurst 1999, 8-9). Bede in turn was one of the sources for Florus of Lyons, whose compilations — now divided into the various *corpora* within the Bible — were influenced by the ninth-century disputes over grace and predestination, which, of course, had been originally started by Augustine (for these and other writers, see McNally

---

I Moving from context to hermeneutics.
A C Augustine's influence on later interpreters; the nature of excerpts.

1959, 109-10). During the eleventh century the "glosses" evolved, flowering during the "eleventh-century Renaissance" for the reason that they were widely used in instruction, gaining a kind of conventional authority and being constantly expanded and improved. Major contributions were made by Anselm of Laon, Gilbert de la Porrée, and Peter Lombard; the latter also incorporated some sections of his own *magna glossatura* into his doctrinal work, the *Four Books of Sentences* (Smalley 1983, 64-66; Domanyi 1979, 34-37; Colish 1994, 192-225; Matter 1997, 83-111; Bougerol 1997 113-164). Augustine and others had already raised philological or doctrinal issues; as discussion of such issues became more complex, the scholastic method gradually evolved, and this meant identifying problems or inconsistencies, enunciating *quaestiones*, and resolving them through a process of argumentation. The glosses were also utilized in the more specialized biblical commentaries of Herbert of Bosham, Stephen Langton, and Hugo of St. Cher. By the time of Thomas Aquinas's commentary on Romans there was an impressive heritage of philological, hermeneutical, and theological insights that could be brought to bear in explicating Paul.

C Then something new happened. The Renaissance and Reformation looked past these medieval collections and commentaries to the text itself, quoting the advice of Cyprian (*Ep.* 74,11), which had also been quoted by Augustine (*De bapt.* V,xxvi,37), to "return to the sources and from there construct a channel to our own times." An attempt was made to read Paul's text in a fresh way, though it was impossible, of course, to ignore either the concerns of their own time or the tradition of interpretation they had received from the middle ages.

C Looking back over the process one cannot help raising several questions. By what principles did the earlier compilers choose the passages which they excerpted (e.g., usefulness in interpreting difficult passages, ease of reading, agreement with their own doctrine)? By what principles did the later compilers supplement or correct them with other passages? How did the selection of passages shape the interpretation of Romans? Conversely, how did the dominant interpretation shape the selection of passages and the framing of issues? What issues were obscured or totally omitted in this process of selection? And when there was a change of method and genre at the time of the Reformation, how much of a corrective did it offer, and what new problems did it introduce? These are questions which we cannot address here, but they will be the subject of future volumes in this series.

C A new attempt to "return to the sources."

C Was there distortion in the process of selection and transmission of Augustine's writings?

Part II : Contemporary Issues Concerning
Paul's Interpretation of Romans

C It should be no surprise to learn that Augustine is often held responsible for an influential but disastrous misinterpretation of Romans 7 (see esp. Stendahl 1960). **C** It is clear from Augustine's writings that he distrusted desire in general, and sexual desire in particular. This came out most strongly in the controversy, late in his life, with Julian of Eclanum. Julian was married (in fact the epithalamium had been written by the bishop Paulinus of Nola); while he lived in chastity after he became a cleric, in accordance with the by then established custom of the church, he took a positive view of sexual pleasure, regarding it as good in itself and wrong only in excess. Augustine, perhaps out of remorse over his earlier life, saw sexual ecstasy as the chief instance of the soul's division against itself, a dramatic demonstration of how it can come to be captured by its irrational impulses (Lancel 1999, 587-88, 595). In the sermons newly discovered by Dolbeau, Augustine recalls that during his younger days in Carthage there was no separation of the sexes in the basilica (*Serm. Dolb.* 2,5). We have known that he started a sexual relationship (probably with his concubine) in church (*Conf.* III,iii,5); in this newly discovered passage he indicates that it began with more than glances across a crowded nave and in fact involved what we today would call "inappropriate touching." There was much that he later regretted; in the view of many he regretted it too much. He joined the Manichaeans, who were convinced that the glow of sexual delight is a trick of the powers of evil to keep the fragments of light imprisoned, generation after generation, in their world; after the birth of one son he and his concubine successfully avoided conception. His conversion to Catholic Christianity took the specific form of a commitment to celibacy. For several decades he held a vague belief in the soul's preexistence and wandering away into an earthly body; after he gave up this view, he was convinced that Adam and Eve in the earthly Eden would not have experienced irrational desire, since their sexual activity would have been under the control of reason and will (*De civ. Dei* XIV,24). While Augustine is not the only cause for feelings of shame and guilt about sexual desire, he is certainly the most authoritative source for them in Western culture, both Catholic and Protestant.

   C Stendahl recalled that he had been prepared for confirmation by the father of Ingmar Bergman, and to those who know the grim atmosphere of his films this seems to be self-sufficient justification for Stendahl's

---

C   Was Augustine the source of an important misinterpretation of Romans? Romans 7.
C   The personal factor in Augustine's thought.
C   Stendahl's self-professed context.

questioning of "the introspective conscience of the West." The autobiographical element is not absent from Stendahl's own work, then. Stendahl
has also noted that in the United States he lived in the first society since
ancient Alexandria to include Jews as full participants in academic and
civic life. To point this out is neither to praise his work nor to damn it,
but to note that the hermeneutical context is always pertinent. In his
presentation to the Romans seminar he said, "When forty-some years ago
I began to speak of Paul as an extrovert with a robust conscience, in sharp
contrast to the sensitivities of Augustine and Luther as they read and
expounded the apostle, my focus was of course justification by faith as it
was taught in my native land."

H   Augustine's interpretation of Romans 7 may confirm all that
Stendahl said of it in 1960 — that a commonplace observation (the
difference between what we ought to do and what we actually do) is taken
out of proportion, as though it probes the deepest mysteries of the human
heart and of divine wisdom. Rudolf Bultmann, too, said much the same
thing about the many parallels in ancient literature, dismissing them as
irrelevant to Paul's argument (Bultmann 1952-55, I: 248) — though with
different import, since Bultmann wants to reinforce the Lutheran doctrine
of justification by faith and its opposition to any form of salvation by
human effort, while Stendahl wants to shift the focus to the historical
interaction between Jews and Gentiles.

I   The essay by TeSelle explores the Augustinian trajectory of
interpretation of Romans 7, not only in Augustine but through the middle
ages and the Reformation, then into modern philosophy and theology.
During the meeting of the Romans Consultation in 1998 he acknowledged
that there are some who would consider this simply going farther and
farther down a dead end — exegetically and systematically. But at
precisely this point Stendahl broke in and suggested that it might have
been "a live end"; he was suggesting, in other words, that interpretation
is an ongoing process, not limited to the original situation or to the
original text or to "what the text meant."

H   After noting all of these issues, we must also remind ourselves that
the differences between the Augustinian interpretation and other
interpretations should not be stated too starkly.

First, we do not have an either/or. Augustine was also aware of the
historical relationship with Israel. He took Romans 9-11 seriously, and in
his correspondence with Jerome (examined in this volume by Gorday) he
championed the first-generation Jewish Christians who continued to
observe the law, since these practices were *adiaphora* — but only for the
first generation (when Jerome asked whether a bishop might permit

---

H   Has Romans 7 been misinterpreted?
I   How do text, context, and theology relate? Romans 7.
H   Perhaps Augustine's interpretation is not drastically different from the alternatives.
Romans 7 and 9–11.

observance of the law in his own time, Augustine felt obliged to say No). Augustine's "psychological" interpretation, furthermore, was framed by the historical sequence in which the human race develops — before the law, under the law, under grace, in peace. And in preaching on Romans 7 he also took note of the gospel story of the Canaanite woman, a Gentile who refused to be excluded from the benefits given to Israel. The two approaches are certainly within conversing distance of each other.

C The psychological interpretation, furthermore, does have historical justification. Theissen (1987) has explored the many parallels in Greek literature and philosophy, and Paul may in fact be assuming that background as he writes (Stowers 1995). Räisänen (1983, 232-36) thinks it reflects Paul's problems with a law that was to be obeyed simply because it had been commanded, without clear motivation either in God or among human beings. **C** Lüdemann has suggested that Romans 7 reflects the inward conflict between Saul the persecutor, who thought that the law clearly ruled out loyalty to one who had been crucified, and his unconscious attraction toward Jesus and the Christian message (Lüdemann 1996, 69-74). **C** Nanos interprets Romans 7 in the context of Romans 9-11 and Galatians 2 as the manifestation of Paul's internal wrestling with Jewish feelings of superiority over Gentiles, not only before but after conversion to Christianity (Nanos 1996, 358-65).

H But let us consider Stendahl's claim that Romans 7 merely alludes to common human problems with *obiter dicta*, banal commonplaces that are not central to the epistle as a whole. On this thesis, the "psychological interpretation" inappropriately utilizes Romans 7 as a Rorschach blot upon which to project concerns alien to the text.

Desire has been a problem throughout the history of the West, not excluding the twentieth century. The century dawned in the midst a *fin de siècle* fascination with *décadence*, and it has seen a succession of "sexual revolutions." And yet there are also counter-trends. Early in the century, Max Weber showed us how the "work ethic" develops rational, methodical mastery of our impulses; the consequence is a very effective control over the world and its resources as well. The orthodox Marxists of the Old Left, quite unlike the "counter.culture" and the New Left, affirmed many features of the work ethic, hoping only to liberate it from its alienating and undemocratic features under capitalism. In our own day we find a certain type of political thinker praising the "producer ethic" of those who "work hard and play by the rules" and condemning Marxism, the welfare state, and Keynesian economics alike as "a moral rehabilitation of desire"

C Similarities between Romans 7 and Greek thought.

C Does Romans 7 express Paul's unconscious conflicts over Jesus and the first Christians?

C . . . or perhaps over Jews' superiority over Gentiles? Romans 7 and 9–11.

H Are the questions (and answers) of later centuries being projected into the text? Romans 7.

(Lasch 1991, 173-76, 52). For this school of thought, attempts at liberation simply abandon us to our own desires and give us no other purposes than those we already have. The 1998 meeting of the Consultation on Romans was held at Disney World, in a room presided over by pictures of Marilyn Monroe, during the sixth regnal year of Bill Clinton while he was under accusation because of his relationship with Monica Lewinsky. The issue of desire is neither antiquated nor irrelevant. And we have been considering here only the most obvious aspects of desire, saying nothing about desire in its "spiritual" dimensions of ambition, pride, and self-centeredness.

H   Might it be, then, that a passage like Romans 7 invites further inquiry into the dynamics of the human heart, inquiry more explicit than what is contained in the text itself? On that hypothesis, the history of interpretation in the West after Augustine, even if it should be incidental to Paul's concerns, was not only inevitable but was well worth doing. In the history of doctrine and of literary interpretation more generally, once certain questions are raised it is necessary to pursue them, because they are attempts to probe the mysteries of the human condition.

Looking Once Again at Romans 7

A   To whom, and in what situation, does Romans 7 apply? To the the Jew who finds that the law cannot overcome the power of sin? or to the Gentile who, bereft of the Jewish law, remains captured by the Greek culture of desire? or to both of them because of the general human condition of weakness, perhaps also the temptations of both to make too much of their own status? And at what point does it apply? Prior to becoming a Christian, so that Romans 7 indicates the problem which the grace of Christ solves? Or might it apply even to the Christian, suggesting that this person, far from being free of temptation, experiences conflict with even greater intensity?

A   Paul himself bears considerable responsibility for the conflicting interpretations of Romans 7, for his language points the reader first in one direction and then in another, and it is difficult to find total consistency, either grammatical or systematic. I   The relation of the text to the interpreter can be characterized in various ways. Thinking of the text *passively*, it can be viewed as a Rorschach blot or a "Rashomon" incident in which different inclinations and preconceptions can find what they are looking for. Thinking of the text more *expressively*, it looks like the playing out of a struggle among conflicting feelings and thoughts. Paul's

---

H   Or are these later interpretations both inevitable and legitimate? Romans 7.
A   To whom does Romans 7 apply?
A   Uncertainties of the text.
I   How is the text related to the interpreter?

language is full of what grammarians call anacoluthon (lack of consistent sequence) and ellipsis (leaving out terms that are grammatically necessary); he seems to be thinking and correcting himself as he writes or dictates. To put it more *existentially*, the text interrogates the reader, asking how one understands oneself, what struggles one undergoes, how one tries to resolve them. To put it *theologically*, the text invites concern with the issue — or cluster of issues — dealt with in this chapter.

A At first glance, Paul seems to frame the chapter with an antithesis between freedom for sin and freedom for God (Rom. 6:20-23), the law of sin and death and the law of the Spirit of life (Rom. 8:2). Viewed this way, chapter 7 might be seen as stating the problem and chapter 8 the answer. One simple reading of the chapter, then, is to see a "diachronic" sequence from the one chapter to the other. Today, when scholars are aware of the eschatological framework of early Christianity, the contrast is often seen as that between the "old age" which is passing away and the "new age" which is dawning, between the "old humanity" in Adam and the "new humanity" in Christ.

H But matters are not quite that simple. Within chapter 7 itself there is a kind of "synchronic" opposition between the "I" who is speaking, who affirms the law at least with "the mind," and "the flesh," or "sin dwelling in the flesh," which is almost split from the self or the mind. Even if we do not follow Jerome and Augustine in seeing this as a conflict within the Christian, we must take into account the language of present conflict; if it belongs to the transition from flesh to spirit, from the old age to the new, the transition is conflict-filled. This creates a further difficulty, for the language of conflict between flesh and spirit seems to suggest a metaphysical dualism, and fourth-century commentators knew that this was the heresy of the Manichaeans — the doctrine that human life is influenced by two independent factors, two "substances," one good and one evil.

In the patristic period these dualistic implications were softened in two ways. One was to apply the theory of habit, or more precisely custom, and any educated commentator would be acquainted with the dictum that custom becomes "second nature." Pelagius, like the early Augustine, interpreted the statement "it is no longer I who do it" (Rom. 7:17 and 20) to suggest that sin begins willingly, but then custom, *consuetudo*, takes over, and the addiction to sinning becomes almost autonomous, a necessity that is no longer one's own, yet different from nature (*In Rom.* 7:17). The other was to attempt to enunciate carefully the nascent doctrine of original sin; and since original sin was believed to be transmitted through physical generation, it tended to be linked (if only symbolically) with the body more than with the mind.

A Trying to construe the text. Rom. 6:20-23 and 8:2 as framing Romans 7.
H How is the language of conflict in Romans 7 to be interpreted? Rom. 7:17 and 20.

H There are even more difficulties, however. The text twice suggests that the law itself is part of the problem, then quickly denies that the law is "sin" (Rom. 7:7) or the cause of death (Rom. 7:13). What, then, is the issue? Sin was dormant until the law entered the picture, but then sin "revived" and the commandment led to death (Rom. 7:7-10; cf. 5:13). In what sense? For Pelagius it means that after hearing the commandment we cannot be ignorant of our sin; when sin is committed knowingly, as "transgression" of an explicit prohibition, condemnation is beyond question, and the law, weakened by the flesh, cannot set one free from the law of sin and death (*In Rom.* 7:9-13). Origen is more complex, focusing on the psychological struggle of one who forms good purposes but cannot carry them into effect without long practice and effort. The contrast between "willing" and "completing" is explicit in Rom. 7:19, and Origen, who was well acquainted with the Stoics' theory of psychological conflict, sees that the conflict is intensified in the person who is aware of what the law demands and wishes to carry it out but cannot. In other words, Origen too has a "psychological" interpretation of Romans 7, the "beginning of conversion," when it has not yet taken full effect, while Romans 8 deals with the person who is "in Christ," freed by the Spirit (Bammel 1997, 515-20).

In other ways, too, the law might intensify sin; most of these were already suggested by the early commentators. Perhaps it intensifies sin by suppressing it, damming it up so that it eventually breaks forth with even greater force. Perhaps its explicit prohibitions intensify the internal struggle with sin (as Origen emphasized). Perhaps the law even tempts one to sin by suggesting forbidden possibilities for the first time. Perhaps condemnation by the law causes despair about salvation. Perhaps the law, precisely because of the totality of its demands, encourages self-deception and hypocrisy.

H There are some sentences which suggest that the problem is neither "the flesh" nor "the law" but *sin itself*, able to use the law deceptively; this is how sin becomes sinful beyond measure. There are several ways this might happen.

Origen, followed especially by Ambrosiaster, suggested that "sin" actually means the devil, Satan. Although a generic term like "sin" or "apostasy" can be used to designate the power of sin that is at work in all particular agents, the devil can be identified as the first and chief agent, responsible for the sins of others and continuing to lead them into temptation.

H   How does the law intensify sin? Rom. 7:7-10; 7:13; 7:19; 5:13.

H   Perhaps not the law but sin is the problem. Rom. 3:20 and 28; 4:5; 10:5-6; 6:20-22; 8:5; 8:6-7.

In the Lutheran and Bultmannian tradition of interpretation, by contrast, the sin in question is legalism or self-justification, an attempt to secure one's own status through the law (for Luther, of course, the attempt at self-justification may be Satan's final, most clever temptation, a sure way of keeping sinful humanity in his own camp). It is undeniable that for Paul one's standing before God cannot be made secure through obedience to the law (Rom. 3:20 and 28, 4:5, 10:5-6; cf. Gal. 2:16 and 3:11). But the rhetoric is escalated even further if the problem is not simply the weakness of the law but the deceptive way sin exploits the law and the noblest aspirations of the human mind and will; in this way, then, sin reveals how sinful it can become. Desire, ἐπιθυμία, means not merely the passions of the flesh but any mode of self-assertion against God, including the most zealous attempts to prove one's righteousness. The text supports this emphasis upon erroneous valuations and decisions on the part of the human subject, who is either free for sin or free for righteousness (Rom. 6:20-22), sets the mind on the flesh or on the Spirit (Rom. 8:5), or follows the "prudence" of either the flesh or the Spirit (Rom. 8:6-7).

A All the different lines of interpretation converge in Romans 7:21, a major crux for interpreters, a verse which has no variant readings in the textual tradition and yet remains difficult to construe. Each of the grammatical solutions that have been proposed, first by "native speakers" of Greek during the patristic period and in more recent times by sophisticated philologists, has some degree of difficulty about it. (One possibility, of course, is that Paul shifted his thought once or even twice while dictating the passage.) The verse is translated in the King James Version with remarkable ambiguity: "I find then a law, that, when I would do good, evil is present with me," or by Dunn with even more literal ambiguity, "I find then the law, for me who wishes to do the good, that for me the evil lies ready to hand" (Dunn 1988, 392). If we press beyond ambiguity, how are we to construe the verse?

A 1. The law mentioned could be the "different kind of law," the "law of sin," mentioned a few verses later (Rom. 7:23 and 25), the "law of sin and death" (Rom. 8:2); indeed, by the middle ages there was a textual tradition which inserted "*aliam* legem," "*another* law," in this verse. Calvin thought that the law referred to was the tyrannical law which resists the law of God (Calvin 1960, 153). This is the preference of Cranfield in the recent commentary on Romans in the International Critical Commentary series (Cranfield 1975, 362).

2. The Revised Standard Version translates the verse, "So I find it to be a law that when I want to do right, evil lies close at hand." This makes the law in question something like what we now call a scientific law, a

---

A A grammatical puzzle: Rom. 7:21.
A Alternative ways of construing Rom. 7:21, in terms of Rom. 7:23, 25; 8:2

generalized statement that always turns out to be confirmed in experience, perhaps a kind of objective necessity, perhaps even the providential will of God. This was the preference of Sanday and Headlam in the older ICC commentary (1895, 182). Räisänen (1991, 63-64, 69-94) shows that this meaning of the term was current in Paul's era and argues that Paul exploits several different nuances of law in Romans 7:21-25.

3. The classic suggestion of Vaughan is rather different, requiring an idiomatic interpretation of the opening words: "I find then with regard to the law. . . " He thinks that the continuity in Paul's thought was broken twice during the writing of the sentence: that he started to say "I find then the Law powerless to effectuate in me that well-doing which my will approves," then for the sake of clarity repeated "for me" (1885, 143). This is the reading preferred recently by Meyer: "So, then, as far as the (Mosaic) law is concerned, the outcome . . . is that for me, the very one who wishes to do the good, evil is what I find at hand" (1990, 79). For him the point of the entire passage is that the law, which is good, can be corrupted by the power of sin to accomplish exactly the opposite of what it intends.

4. And thus from a "Lutheran" perspective the point of the sentence may be the limitations of the law — not merely its inability to overcome sin but its susceptibility to being misused and exploited by sin. Karl Barth adventurously paraphrases, "I find then the reality of the law exposed..." (1933, 266).

A   The patristic commentators, in contrast to all these modern interpreters, construe the sentence positively in the light of what comes immediately after it, "I delight in the law of God" (Rom. 7:22). In fact Origen (or his translator Rufinus) understood verses 21-22 to be inverted in their order, and he untangled the thought as follows:

> Therefore because evil lies near to me when I will to do good, I find the law of God and delight in it after the inward person (Bammel 1997, 513).[19]

Ambrosiaster, the unknown writer in the West, sees it similarly: the law of Moses strengthens the will against sin, which dwells in the flesh and inclines one to do other than what one wills; because Ambrosiaster thinks that sin affects the flesh but not the mind, he intensifies the conflict between these two aspects of human life (*Ad Rom.* 7:21). Pelagius is in the same tradition: "When I will, I find that I have a law to do good against the evil that lies near" (*In Rom.* 7:21).

A   Ancient construals of the same verse. Rom. 7:21-22.

I Augustine is not unique, therefore, when he understands it to mean "I find, then, that the law, when I will to act, is a good thing, because evil lies near to me."[20] And yet there are serious grammatical difficulties with Augustine's particular interpretation.[21] The Greek cannot mean that the law is "a good thing"; in the Greek, "good" clearly is the object of the doing, completing the phrase "the one who wishes to do the good." In addition, Augustine probably misconstrues the Greek ὅτι; when the Latin translated it *quoniam*, Latin-speakers often understood it to mean "because," while the Greeks understood ὅτι in this grammatical position, introducing a noun clause, to mean "that." There were serious linguistic discontinuities, in other words, between Greek and Latin speakers, and Augustine seems to have pressed them beyond all legitimate grammatical bounds. And yet as Augustine read the chapter and tried to understand it in a connected way his interpretation converged with that of most of the Greeks.

Relating the Cosmic and the Personal Dimensions of Paul

The issue highlighted by Stendahl is not the only instance in which Augustine is alleged to have re- or mis-interpreted Romans. **C** Riches draws attention to the question raised by Schweitzer early in the twentieth century, and emphasized more recently by E.P. Sanders, whether the Augustinian (and, more proximately, the Lutheran) tradition had obscured the place of apocalyptic eschatology in Paul. This would mean that Augustine glossed over those aspects of Paul which assumed some kind of cosmic dualism (the influence of angelic and demonic powers, the antithesis of the "old age" and the "new age," and the imminent transformation of the world with the return of Christ) and replaced it with a "juridical" concern for justification, to use Lutheran language, or with a more "introspective" approach to the human situation, to use Stendahl's language. (TeSelle's essay in this volume calls attention to a striking example of exactly this kind of "glossing over" when Augustine interprets the "creation groaning in travail" of Romans 8 to apply not to the entire cosmos but to the whole human being, body and soul, already being transformed by grace but not yet enjoying the full peace of resurrection and eternal life.)

C In defense of Augustine, Riches argues that his "introspective" interests did not constitute a drastically new departure, because there had been others in the ancient world who spoke openly of their religious

---

I Augustine was wrong grammatically, but he may have been right hermeneutically.

C Was Paul more influenced by apocalyptic than the Augustinian and Lutheran tradition recognizes? Romans 8.

C An "introspective" concern for personal religious quests was a part of ancient culture.

quests, describing their uncertainty or lack of orientation which was then followed by a new degree of conviction and dedication which is often termed "conversion" by modern scholars. **C** The quest was not purely individual, however. The Greco-Roman world was aware of a multiplicity of religious options, advocated by philosophical schools and religious communities to which one could voluntarily adhere as well as by ethnic traditions which were not voluntary to the same degree. Conversion usually meant a change from one community to another, and in this sense Riches acknowledges Stendahl's interest in the relationship between Jews and Gentiles. This, he argues, does not negate "introspective" or "autobiographical" concerns, for the shift from one community to another was often described in terms of a personal religious quest. Paul himself makes much of his change from one Jewish group, the Pharisees, to another Jewish group, the nascent Christian movement, which found a place for not only Jews but Gentiles in its message and its life. Thus it would be misleading to suggest that an interest in more personal issues comes from a new and different framework imposed by Augustine, or that it is necessarily to be set in opposition to a concern for ethnic groups and religious communities.

C H Riches refocuses the argument by suggesting that Augustine *did* reinterpret Paul in *another* crucial respect: because of his own conversion from Manichaeism (which thought of good and evil as independent cosmic principles) to neo-Platonism (which thought of evil as a privation of good), he rejected any "dualist" explanation of the origin of evil. In its place he made free choice the source of human evil and emphasized the more "introspective" aspect of the struggle between good and evil as it is evoked by Paul. This in turn meant that he found himself compelled (by the authority of Scripture itself, he was convinced) to give an increasingly larger role to divine grace in the attempt to overcome evil within oneself.

A Riches is aware that Augustine did not promote a totally introspective or subjective or existentialist interpretation of the Christian life. Even in the case of the *Confessions*, which many think of as the spiritual autobiography *par excellence*, the closing books return to cosmic themes — the creation of the material and spiritual realms, the fall of some angelic powers and the faithfulness of others as God's agents in the world, and the eventual transformation of the entire cosmos, material and spiritual.

It may be, however, that Riches makes too much of a differentiation between the cosmic and the moral or introspective, such that it is easy to infer that we must think in terms of either the one or the other. In

---

C This quest, while intensely personal, also involved adhering to a community or changing from one community to another.

C H Augustine's reaction against Manichaeism may have led him to reject apocalyptic and emphasize freedom in considering evil.

A Augustine's thought still retains many cosmological dimensions.

Augustine's picture of the world an essential role was played by both angels as ministers of good and demons as tempters and deceivers. He saw punishment and reward at work in natural and historical events, enough to confirm faith in God's providence but not enough to diminish hope for a future world. Paul's "two ages" were reflected in his sense of inward struggle, confidence in the present work of grace, and hope for the final restoration of both body and soul. His was not a totally "existentialized" interpretation of Christianity.

Gorday in his essay reminds us that Käsemann takes a rather similar approach to Paul — an approach that Gorday calls universal/theological as against Stendahl's, which emphasizes situational/personal factors. Käsemann can agree with Stendahl on two counts: first, that Paul was not primarily concerned to proclaim a universalizing anthropology, and second, that there has been, since Augustine, an excessive psychologizing of Paul. He differs from Stendahl, however, in judging Paul's overarching concern to be not the Gentile mission, with the accompanying question how it related to the heritage of Israel, but the imminent return of Christ, understood in terms of the apocalyptic contrast between the "old age" and the "new age." Therefore Käsemann reinterprets justification along "cosmic" lines and his entire commentary on Romans looks for universal features of the human situation hiding behind particular issues (such as the relationship between Jews and Gentiles) and the specific beliefs of the time (especially the apocalyptic eschatology which influenced Paul and many others).

H Riches, by highlighting the issue of dualistic versus moral conceptions of evil, has done the service of reminding us that Augustine rethought this as well as most other aspects of Christian doctrine, warning against formulations that seem to suggest that evil is an independent power and trying to extend the rather different conceptuality of *moral agency* — human, angelic, and divine — wherever it may be applicable. In the process Augustine found a middle way between cosmic dualism, which is too facile in finding ultimate good and evil ready at hand in the world of everyday experience, and the kind of naturalism, ancient or modern, that limits its field of awareness to what is observable and measurable. He was aware, as Kant would be later, that the moral transcends what is objectively observable and must be traced with different methods. *The City of God* has often been praised for its recognition that the formative influences on human life are not empirically identifiable but are to be found in the two "mystical cities" based on contrary loves. A totally "immanent" understanding of human subjectivity and human society, he would argue, soon betrays its inadequacies. Even to will the good is to go

---

H Perhaps Augustine reshapes the more cosmic aspects of Christianity with his more neo-Platonist theory of moral evil.

beyond what is given to us in sensory experience. But the mystery of evil
lies couching at the door, too, in possibilities of which we cannot help
being aware and which we may well choose through selfish desire or lack
of attention to the good, perhaps "pulled" as well by temptation from
demonic powers, from ideology, or from political coercion. Once we begin
thinking along these lines, furthermore, we cannot help inquiring as well
about the role of divine freedom, which sometimes manifests itself as
grace, as assistance in the human struggle, but at other times contradicts
what we wish or anticipate and requires us to think of the divine as
mystery as well as mercy.

How Are We to Construe Romans as a Whole?

I The essay by Gorday sets Paul in the context highlighted by the
"Scandinavian school," namely the relationship between Jewish and
Gentile Christians and, more broadly, between Paul's Gentile mission and
the Jewish heritage of Christianity. It examines this set of issues in the
mirror of the "incident at Antioch" (Gal. 2:11-21), which provoked quite
different interpretations by Jerome and Augustine. Gorday then asks
whether Romans is to be interpreted in this same context. Put most
simply, the question is whether the "meaning" of Romans is "theologi-
cal/universal," a generally applicable Christian interpretation of the
human situation, or "situational/personal," Paul's own biography and
specifically the tensions between Jewish and Gentile Christians which are
reflected several times in the extant epistles. But of course matters are not
this simple. Issues are raised in all three of the dimensions that are the
theme of this series. Some are *textual/analytical* (not only the wording of
particular passages but their place in the whole epistle and the influence
of contemporary genres such as the Stoic diatribe). Some are *biographi-
cal/contextual* (specifically, what provoked this particular letter and Paul's
mode of dealing with it). And some are *theological/hermeneutical* (what
broader theological assertions are made or implied or provoked). We
cannot begin with one of them and then move self-confidently to the
others, for there is constant interaction. Our textual judgments are likely
to be influenced by our construal of the historical situation in which Paul
wrote and by our own convictions, both sociological and theological, about
human life.

Gorday's essay thus draws together and gives specificity to the triple
schema that has been followed, at least heuristically, in this series. In
addition, it connects rather dramatically with a theme that emerged in the

---

I Interpreting Romans — textually, biographically, theologically.

first volume of this Romans Through History and Culture series. **C** In that volume, several essays made a definite advance on the question of Paul's Jewishness and his relation to Judaism and Jewish Christianity in his time. This is an issue that comes to fullest expression in Romans 9-11, precisely the section that has been the focus of attention for the "Scandinavian school" but was also, perhaps ironically, the source of several of Augustine's decisive prooftexts for predestination and grace. It is usually said that Augustine misunderstood and misinterpreted these passages. **H** We shall want to examine that question in a "hermeneutical" way, with full awareness of the many other difficulties in interpreting this section of Romans. In the process, I suggest, we may discover new relationships between textual, contextual, and hermeneutical issues.

A In that first volume, Campbell (2000, 190-91) points out that recent scholarship has raised new questions about Romans 9-11. There have been some who question whether the section even comes from Paul. Others find that chapters 9-10 follow "reasonably well" from chapters 1-8; but the consequence is that their discrepancies with chapter 11 are intensified, isolating chapter 11 and suggesting either that the text lacks integrity or that Paul changed his mind during the process of writing these chapters.

The issue is this: the general tenor of chapters 9-10 seems to be that the majority of Jews have failed to respond to the gospel of the Messiah and that God is free to call the Gentiles in their place. Then Paul suddenly asserts that God has not rejected Israel as "God's own people" (Rom. 11:1); indeed, they remain the olive tree into which the Gentiles have been grafted "against nature" (Rom. 11:24), and their conversion is intended, in God's providence, to arouse jealousy on the part of the Jews so that they will eventually accept the same gospel. All of this manifests, of course, the complex dialectic of being saved by faith in God's mercy, so that both Jews and Gentiles must guard against boasting of their status before God and each other.

A Campbell (194-98) argues that Romans 11 does *not* indicate a sudden change in Paul's thinking. He finds a number of "forward-looking" passages which prepare the way for it throughout Romans. There is not only the repeated formula that the gospel goes "to the Jew first, then to the Greek" (Rom. 1:16, 2:10). There is also the assertion that Abraham is "the father of us all" (Rom. 4:16), i.e., of both Jewish and Gentile believers. And there is the statement that the vessels of mercy are "not from the Jews only but also from the Gentiles" (Rom. 9:24). All of this means, then,

---

C Taking Paul's context seriously. Romans 9–11.
H Interpreting Augustine from a hermeneutical point of view.
A Does chapter 11 fit into Romans?
A Or perhaps chapter 11 *does* fit.... with Rom. 1:16; 2:10; 4:16; 9:24

that Paul from the first is reasoning not *exclusively*, in terms of *either* Jews or Gentiles, but *inclusively*, including *both* Jews and Gentiles (194); that there has been "an extension of Israel's privileges to Gentiles" and not "a transfer of them away from Israel," an affirmation rather than an annulment of Israel's status as the covenant people (197). The continued stress upon God's election is to be interpreted, then, to mean not primarily that God can reject some — Esau, the Gentiles, unbelieving Jews — but that God has the "right to be patient with Israel" (199), that God "is not obligated to discard Israel" (202) but is free to be compassionate to both Jews and Gentiles in fulfilling the purpose of bringing all to salvation.

   H   Given this emphasis upon divine freedom and mercy, it is not surprising that Augustine came to be persuaded about predestination and grace when he read Paul's statement that God elected Jacob rather than Esau "when they were not yet born and had done nothing either good or bad, so that God's purpose of election might continue, not because of works but because of God's call" (Rom. 9:10); or that he used the statement that "God's gifts and call are irrevocable" (Rom. 11:29) to buttress these convictions against the Pelagians and champion the gift of perseverance (Sievers 2000, 142); or that he used as the clinching argument Paul's doxological exclamation, "O the depths of the riches and wisdom and knowledge of God!" (Rom. 11:33), emphasizing the mystery of divine freedom beyond all that can be explained or explored by human reasoning. It is true that Augustine applied these statements to individual predestination, while Paul was talking primarily about the call addressed to Israel and to the nations, considering the responses of individuals only within this more corporate context. But Augustine himself was not unaware of the broader history of the human race and the distinction between Jews and Gentiles. In any case, the emphasis on the freedom and priority of divine grace, misapplied or not, remains.

   A   A crucial hermeneutical question, whether we are thinking individually or collectively, is whether Paul understands election to be a matter of *either/or*, with the exclusion of some, or of *earlier/later*, with some being called prior to others and for their benefit. The latter understanding of election, which has become pervasive in German theology, was first put forward by Schleiermacher as a modified version of Calvin's supralapsarian predestinarianism, making use of Paul's affirmations (Rom. 3:9, 5:18, 11:32) that God first condemns all, then wills the salvation of all (Schleiermacher 1928, 536-60; Romans 10-11 is mentioned twice, 538 and 554).

   H   Paul's statements about God's freedom and mercy are what persuaded Augustine about predestination. Rom. 9:10; 11:29, 33.

   A   According to Paul, is election exclusive, *either/or*, or inclusive on a time line, *earlier/later* (Schleiermacher on Romans 10-11)?

C   The specific context within which Paul is saying this, Campbell argues, is that the Gentile Christians in Rome (to whom the letter was written) had already formed "a specific view of Paul" (191), namely a "one-sided, Gentile-sided, image of Paul" (205). In them, Campbell suggests, Paul might have encountered for the first time "a supersessionist form of Christianity," and one "that his own mission, at least as it was reported, had helped to produce" (206). A corrective was clearly needed. Hence Paul's insistence on the formula "to the Jew first, then to the Greek" (Rom. 1:16, 2:10) and his assertions that the Jews continue to have "the oracles of God" (Rom. 3:2), the covenants and the promises and much else (Rom. 9:4-5).

C   The essay by Mark Nanos reinforces these points, emphasizing even more strongly that Paul did not abandon Judaism but thought of himself as a Jewish reformer, though in quite a different way, of course, than other Jewish reformers of the time. Christianity for him was not a "Gentile movement," as many tend to assume (Nanos 2000, 215); it was part of his Jewish identity. The controversies reflected in Galatians and other letters concern, then, "the proper means for including Gentiles as full children of Abraham since the coming of Christ" (219). The difference between Jews and Gentiles continues, but in a way that includes both of them in the purposes of the one God, with the consequence that the "pro-Gentile" passages are compatible with and even presuppose the "pro-Jewish" ones (223).

Thus far we seem to have confirmation of the "Scandinavian school" emphasis upon the corporate calling of Israel and the nations, not the election and predestination of individuals as in Augustine. And yet the relationship between Jews and Gentiles may not be as simple as this. Paul develops a complex dialectic, not only in Romans 9-11 but through the earlier chapters as well. A   Its complexity is highlighted by Brawley (2000, 86) when he suggests that Paul, precisely in making Abraham "the father of us all" (Rom. 4:16), emphasizes that he was this *because of his faith*, while he was, in effect, *still a Gentile* (cf. Rom. 4:10), and thus that Abraham "is not first of all ancestor of Israelites but of Gentiles who believe," and the purpose of his circumcision is "that he might also be the ancestor of Israelites who believe." "In this case," he concludes, "Israel is added to the Gentiles rather than the inverse" (86). H   This seems to

---

C   In writing Romans, Paul was addressing a Gentile church. Campbell on Rom. 1:16; 2:10; 3:2; 9:4-5.

C   Paul's Gentile mission was rooted in Judaism. Nanos and Scandinavian School on Romans 9-11.

A   What does it mean to say that Abraham is "the father of us all"? Brawley on Rom. 4:10, 16.

H   Some aspects of Paul may call for a "theological/universal" approach.

confirm a more existential Paul, who may perhaps be interpreted in what Gorday calls a "theological/universal" way.

At this point we must also recall the points made in one way by Käsemann and in another way by Riches, that Paul was deeply influenced by apocalyptic thought with its contrast between the "old age" which still continues and the coming "new age" which is already at work through Christ and the Spirit. Whether Paul was fully aware of its "theological/universal" implications or not (and Käsemann is willing to concede that he may not have been), these implications were there, he argues, and thus it is legitimate to draw them out in our interpretation of Paul.

On the basis of these reflections let me venture a rash, and certainly speculative, theological account of a two-way movement in Romans which, not accidentally, has relevance to some major Augustinian themes. Using Gorday's terminology, the first movement will be from "theological/universal" to "situational/ personal" themes; the second will be just the reverse.

H One movement is from individual or existential issues — or perhaps more accurately, following the lead of Käsemann and Riches, from apocalyptic concerns which by the nature of the case involve all human beings — toward the more specific details of human life. Augustine saw in Paul an interpretation of universal human history which goes through four stages of spiritual development: "before the law, under the law, under grace, and in peace." The Gentiles represent the first stage; Israel, with its law, the second; Christian believers, who are offered grace through faith, the third; and the eschaton toward which they are striving the fourth. There is much in Romans that suggests precisely this movement outward from the center of the self, or, to put it in an alternative way, from the universal human situation to more specific historical contexts. Some recent scholars find a somewhat similar process of unfolding. Käsemann (1980, 196-97) gives a number of reasons for understanding the "I" of Romans 7 to be Adam, who anticipates the destiny of all subsequent human beings, and then goes on to suggest that verses 7-13 deal with the past, while verses 14-25 are in the present tense, evoking the struggles of post-Adamic humanity.

A What is the evidence for this emphasis in the interpretation of Romans? Paul speaks of understanding the invisible God through the things that are made, with the result, however, that human beings are "without excuse" (Rom. 1:18-20); of the law written on the human heart, which means that those who sin without the law perish without the law (2:12-15); of the spread of sin to all "insofar as all sinned" (5:12); of the

---

H An existential or "theological/universal" reading of Romans. Käsemann on Romans 7.

A Textual warrants in Romans. TeSelle on Rom. 1:18-20; 2:12-15; 5:12; 8:2; 7:13; 4:1-12; 6:8.

"law of sin and death" (8:2) which is able to pervert even the law to its purpose, showing that it is sinful beyond measure (7:13); of the justification of Abraham through faith, prior to any works of the law (4:1-12); and of the fulfillment of this promise in Christ, dying to sin and rising to new life (6:8). The "introspective" or "universalizing" interpretation of Paul is not inappropriate.

A   H   And yet there is also the opposite movement, from specific historical relationships to the inward self or to issues that affect all human beings. It happens first, perhaps, in the spread of sin from others (Rom. 5:12), then in the demonstration of the inability of the law to remedy the situation (Rom. 7). But just as in Adam all die, so in Christ all are made alive (Rom. 5:18-19; cf. I Cor. 15:22); where sin abounds, grace abounds all the more (Rom. 5:20), with hope for the restoration of "the whole creation" (8:18-25). It is in this more situational or interpersonal context that Paul raises the question of Israel and the nations and concludes with his suggestion that they exist for each other — the Jews as the source of salvation for the Gentiles, the Gentiles as the ones who will make the Jews jealous for the same salvation, but all of them exhorted to respond to their salvation with fear and trembling. One is saved not as an isolated individual but only within the corporate life of Israel and the church, and it is only after discussing this complex historical dialectic that Paul engages in ethical exhortation (Rom. 12-15) and describes Christians as "one body in Christ" (Rom. 12:5). Augustine, whatever his distorting influence, was aware of these aspects of Paul. He took a pervasive interest in the corporate history of salvation from Abel on, and he insisted against the Donatists that salvation is impossible outside "the unity of the Spirit in the bond of peace" (Eph. 4:3), namely within the one universal church, despite — or because of — its diversity and its internal tensions.

H   This brings us to a point that is especially emphasized by Gorday as he considers the conflicting interpretations advanced by Jerome and Augustine concerning the "incident at Antioch" and, more generally, the relation between Jews and Gentiles, law and gospel. On either view, he suggests, it is possible to move from the more specific "situational" or "personal" dimensions of the text toward more theological and thus more universally applicable interpretations.

The approach taken by Jerome, following the Greek tradition, begins with an analysis, often in great detail, of personal and situational factors. This could mean that we are invited to give a purely "contextual" account of the issues raised in the text, understanding them sociologically or culturally and leaving matters there; the consequence then could be that

---

A   H   A more "historical" or "situational/personal" reading. TeSelle on Rom. 5:12; Romans 7; Rom. 5:18-19; 5:20; 8:18-25; Romans 12—15; Rom. 12:5.

H   How can we move from more "situational/personal" to more "theological/universal" considerations?

Paul remains isolated in the past, stuck in a situation that is alien to us because of radically different assumptions. But Gorday argues that this approach, represented by the Greek tradition and Jerome in antiquity and by the Scandinavian school in our own time, is quite capable of drawing broader implications — about the vulnerabilities of the apostle, for example, or, in the spirit of Romans 11, about the temptation of both Jews and Gentiles to boast about their status and the inappropriateness of that response in light of the character of God's grace.

The contrasting approach taken by Augustine and anticipated by earlier Latin writers, while it seems to leap much more quickly to theological generalizations, was not unaware of historical particularities; if anything it was stronger in its acknowledgment of the legitimacy of continued observance of the Jewish law, at least during the first Christian generation. The reason Augustine was able to do this, as both Fredriksen and Gorday emphasize, is that he made much of the "sign" character of the Jewish ceremonies, not only before but after Christ. They were, in effect, taken out of the realm of sheer particularity and were given from the first a "universalizable" role of signifying the same grace that is manifested in Christ. Augustine even saw continuing value in what the Jews of his own time were doing, on the principle that by carrying these "signs" throughout the world they offered independent confirmation of the Christian message. Gorday's point, if we may phrase it in terms of the tri-polar approach taken in this series, is that what was done by the Greeks and Jerome cannot be stereotyped as purely "contextual," though it starts there, any more than what was done by the Latins and Augustine can be stereotyped as purely "hermeneutical," though that tends to be its emphasis from first to last.

H Perhaps Augustine misunderstood Paul and shifted the interpretation of Romans in too "introspective" and therefore too "universalizing" a direction. Even if this should be true, we must also take note of the fact that his theological perspective was fundamentally transformed — not once but several times — by his encounter with Paul. It was precisely the "introspective" Augustine, ironically, who, asking how the individual can move from sin to faith, learned from the Paul of Romans 9-11; perhaps there is some analogy or congruence between the more introspective and the more social aspects of the Christian life! The first major crisis in his theology was brought about by his reading Rom. 9:10, where Paul speaks of God's choosing Jacob rather than Esau before they were alive, before they could have done anything in the body, before they could even have responded inwardly with faith (*De div. quaest. ad Simpl.*, I, q. 2, written in 396 or 397, just prior to the *Confessions*). His answer was that those who

---

H Whether Augustine misunderstood Romans or not, his emphasis on predestination and grace was based upon passages in Romans 9-11. Rom. 9:10; 11:29; 11:33.

have been elected by God are called in a way "congruous" with their condition, that is, in a way that God knows will receive a positive response. A second major crisis came later, at the height of the Pelagian controversy, when Augustine began quoting the statement that "God's gifts and call are irrevocable" (Rom. 11:29); he spoke of God's giving an "invincible delight" in the good, and this, he said, is the only basis for perseverance in faith. In both cases, furthermore, he backed up his assertions with Paul's exclamation, "O the depth of the riches and wisdom and knowledge of God" (Rom. 11:33), relying, in other words, upon the mystery of God's freedom and mercy in place of human explanation or human effort. Unity and coherence come not from the cosmos or from history, not from personal continuity or human purposiveness, but from the freedom of God, which is often manifested most reliably and most efficaciously in the *discontinuities* of human life.

These suggestions, rash though they may be, are intended to be introductory to the essays in this volume. Let us see how their various readings illuminate the text, the various contexts, and the hermeneutical issues involved in the reception of Romans through the centuries and in our own time.

Notes

1. The terms are being used in the sense made classic by Mannheim 1936. For Mannheim "ideology" is a belief system whose function is to explain and justify the existing order of society, "utopia" the envisagement of a better order, with at least implicit criticism of the existing order. Similar notions are to be found in the large body of literature associated with liberation theology.

2. Rilke 1987, 3. Reprinted with the permission of Farrar, Straus and Giroux, publisher.

3. This thesis is especially associated with Professor D.W. Robertson, Jr., of Princeton University; medievalists often speak of "Robertsonians" or "the Princeton school." Distinguishing features of this tradition are a) interest in the way literary theory influenced literary practice during the middle ages, b) attention to difficulties and disruptions in the text as signals that some further meaning is to be sought, and c) awareness that the text often conveys the useful through the enjoyable, the *utile* through the *dulce*. It should not be surprising, then, that Robertson translated and wrote an introduction to Augustine's *On Christian Doctrine*. Later poetic practice is analyzed (without reference to the medieval background, however) in Lewalski 1979.

4. This point might have been suggested to him by Tyconius, who in his Rule VII notes that metaphors like "morning star" and "mountain" are applied in Scripture to both Satan and God (*Liber regularum* 70-85).

5. Stephen's speech in Acts 7 is a remarkable example of this kind of importation of new meanings, for when Stephen (who has a Greek name, is called one of the "Hellenists," and was doubtless educated in the Diaspora) reads about God's instructions for making the tent of witness "according to the pattern (τύπος) he had seen on the mountain" (Act 7:44, citing Ex 25:40) he is struck by the parallel with Plato's *Timaeus*, which tells how the Demiurge or Artisan formed the world in accordance with the pattern (παράδειγμα), the intelligible realm. This understanding of the passage in Exodus was already anticipated by Philo of Alexandria (*Quaestiones in Exodum* II,52; II,82; II,90).

6. For a thorough and critical survey of various theories of typology, see Young 1994; for a discussion of allegory and typology in Augustine, Cameron 1999.

7. As Martin points out in his essay in this volume, Augustine saw the church of the elect, the body of Christ, as the unifying theme of the biblical story, from Abel onward, so that the whole of Scripture confesses Christ and the church (see esp. *En.Ps.* 79,2).

8. There are similar contrasts between *velatio* and *revelatio* (*Serm.* 300,3), *occultatio* and *revelatio* (*En.Ps.* 45,1), *occultatio* and *manifestatio* (*De cat.rud.* iv,8).

9. Among the questions which the creed leaves open, according to Origen, are whether God created other worlds before this one, and whether there will be further worlds after it. While this may be an extreme and unusual example, a question which would not have occurred to very many Christians in his day or in ours, it is still a dramatic illustration of the way the creed, even in drawing definite lines, leaves much undefined.

10. In *C.Faust.* XV,7 Augustine lists all the commandments in this way. He justifies the differentiation between the ninth and tenth in his *Quaest.Exod.* 71. The point that the prohibition of desire leads toward the positive command of love, already made by Paul (Rom 13:9), is emphasized in *De spir.et litt.* xxxvi,64–66.

11. *De doct.chr.* I,iv,4 spells out the theme of sojourning, *peregrinatio*, for the first time in Augustine's writings, on the basis of Paul's language of "sojourning away from the Lord" (II Cor 5:6); he also uses Paul's image of "reaching forward" to a future that is different in character from the present (Phil. 3:13).

12. For Augustine's use of this pericope see La Bonnardière 1986, 117–43.

13. Augustine's word is *"aporiabatur"* (*Serm.* 154A,3), a Greek term for blockage, setting in narrow straits, impasse, often used in rhetoric for creating confusion or posing a dilemma.

14. *Exp.inch.Rom.* 14–23, following his earlier reflections in *De serm.Dom.* I,xxii,75. He comes back to the same point in *Serm.* 71 from the year 417, devoted completely to this theme.

15. *Caritas* is always to be willed, Augustine says, and *cupiditas* is always to be avoided (*De doct.chr.* III,x,15). Love is what directs the affections toward God and sets everything in perspective. He even utters the maxim, "Love and do as you will" (*In ep.Io.* vii,8; x,7), though in Augustine's hands it is not an early version of situation ethics but a statement of confidence that in the coercion of the Donatists love cannot go wrong, even when the means seem harsh. We can understand the need for "tough love" when it is appropriate; but we also know that, lacking guidelines and accountability, it can lead to child abuse, the "battered wife syndrome," manipulative social policies, and totalitarian government.

16. A distinguished recent example of a theologian who insisted on revisiting patristic debates and holding open the possibility of arriving at different conclusions is Maurice Wiles (see esp. Wiles 1967, 1974, and 1976).

17. This is not beyond dispute, however. The first term, μαλακοί or "soft," was applied in Greek writings to all kinds of weak-willed persons, and in the exegetical tradition it was generally interpreted to apply to masturbation, not to same-sex relations. The second term, ἀρσενοκοῖται or "those who lie with men," is probably derived from the Septuagint's translations of Leviticus 18:22 and 20:13 and depends upon the meaning of those passages at various stages of transmission, translation, and reception.

18. Rom. 1:26-27 speaks of women who "change" the "natural use" into what is against nature, and men who "leave" the "natural use of the woman" in an unseemly way. The sign of disorder may be, then, acting against heterosexual inclinations, rather than having homosexual inclinations. If the Bible is to be used legalistically, then close, legalistic analysis of all the texts is required.

19. In the context, Origen clearly thinks of the law both as that which comes from the life-giving Spirit (508) and as the natural law (510). For textual issues concerning the translation, see Bammel 1985, 358. It is uncertain whether this interpretation, found in Rufinus's Latin translation, actually goes back to Origen, for it assumes that ὅτι means "because," not "that"—easier for the Latin *quia* than for the Greek ὅτι in this position. The *Biblia Patristica* lists no other treatment of Rom 7:21 in Origen's works,

and thus it is impossible to cross-check his understanding of the verse. If the interpretation is Origen's own, then he somehow stressed a connection between "finding the law" (vs. 21) and "delighting in the law" (vs. 22).

20. His construal of it is evident from his expositions of the passage, first in his reply to Simplicianus in 397: "I find the law to be a good thing to me when I will to do what the law commands, because evil keeps me from doing it easily" (*De div.quaest.ad Simpl.*, I, q. 1,12); far more starkly, in one of his anti-Pelagian writings he paraphrases it: "It [the law] is a good thing to the one who wills to act, but evil lies near because of desire, to which one who says 'It is not longer I who do it' does not consent" (*C.du.ep.Pel.* I,x,19). In an anti-Manichaean vein he emphasizes "lies near *to me*," because "it is not that the flesh is not mine, or from another substance or another principle, or that the soul is from God and the flesh is from the race of darkness" (*Serm.* 154,15).

21. Letter from Paul W. Meyer, March 2, 1999, in response to the apparent similarities between his interpretation of the verse and Augustine's.

Bibliography

Arnold, Duane W.H., and Pamela Bright (eds.). 1995. *De doctrina christiana: A Classic of Western Culture.* Christianity and Judaism in Antiquity 9. Notre Dame: University of Notre Dame Press.

Balch, David L. (ed.). 2000. *Homosexuality, Science, and the "Plain Sense" of Scripture.* Grand Rapids: Eerdmans.

Bammel, Carolyn P. Hammond. 1985. *Der Römerbrief des Rufin und seine Origenes-Übersetzung.* Freiburg: Verlag Hereer.

———. 1997 (ed.) *Der Römerbriefkommentar des Origines. Kritische Ausgabe der Übersetzung Rufins.* Freiburg: Verlag Herder.

Barth, Karl. 1933. *The Epistle to the Romans.* Translated from the Sixth Edition by Edwyn C. Hoskyns. Oxford: Oxford University Press.

———. 1936- . *Church Dogmatics.* Edinburgh: T.& T. Clark.

Baur, F.C. 1972. The Life of Jesus, Critically Examined. Edited and with an Introduction by Peter C. Hodgson. Translated from the 4th German Edition by George Eliot. Philadelphia: Fortress Press.

Bougerol, Jacques-Guy. 1997. "The Church Fathers and the *Sentences* of Peter Lombard." Pp. 114-64 in *The Reception of the Church Fathers in the West: From the Carolingians to the Maurists.* Edited by Irena Backus. Leiden: E.J. Brill.

Brawley, Robert L. 2000. "Multivocality in Romans 4." Pp. 74-95 in *Reading Israel In Romans: Legitimacy and Plausibility of Divergent Interpretations,* ed. Cristina Grenholm and Daniel Patte. Harrisburg: Trinity Press International.

Bultmann, Rudolf. 1952-55. *Theology of the New Testament.* Translated by Kendrick Grobel. London: SCM Press.

———. 1958. *Jesus Christ and Mythology.* New York: Scribner.

———. 1963. *The History of the Synoptic Tradition.* Translated by John Marsh. New York: Harper & Row.

Burns, J. Patout. 1980. *The Development of Augustine's Doctrine of Operative Grace.* Paris: Études Augustiniennes.

Calvin, John. 1960. *The Epistles of Paul to the Romans and to the Thessalonians.* Translated by Ross Mackenzie. Edinburgh: Oliver and Boyd.

Cameron, Michael. 1999. "The Christological Substructure of Augustine's Figurative Exegesis." Pp. 74-103 in *Augustine and the Bible,* edited and translated by Pamela Bright. Notre Dame: University of Notre Dame Press.

Campbell, William S. 2000. "Divergent Images of Paul and His Mission." Pp. 187-211 in *Reading Israel In Romans: Legitimacy and Plausibility of Divergent Interpretations,* ed. Cristina Grenholm and Daniel Patte. Harrisburg: Trinity Press International.

Caswall, Edward. 1873. *Hymns and Poems, Original and Translated.* Second Edition. London: Burns, Oates & Co.

Colish, Marcia L. 1994. *Peter Lombard.* Leiden: E.J. Brill.

Connolly, William F. 1991. "A Letter to Augustine." Pp. 123-57 in *Identity/Difference: Democratic Negotiations of Political Paradox.* Ithaca and London: Cornell University Press.

Cranfield, C.E.B. 1975. *A Critical and Exegetical Commentary on the Epistle to the Romans.* Edinburgh: T.&T. Clark.

Dahl, Nils Alstrup. 1978. "The Origin of the Earliest Prologues to the Pauline Letters." Pp. 233-77 in *The Poetics of Faith: Essays Offered to Amos Niven Wilder,* edited by W. A. Beardslee. *Semeia* 12. Missoula: Society of Biblical Literature. Reprinted with revisions, 2000, pp. 179-209 in *Studies in Ephesians: Introductory Questions, Text- & Edition-Critical Issues, Interpretation of Texts and Themes,* edited by David Hellholm, Vemund Blomkvist, and Tord Forberg. Wissenschaftliche Untersuchungen zum Neuen Testament 131. Tübingen: Mohr Siebeck.

Dawson, David. 1998. "Allegorical Reading and the Embodiment of the Soul in Origen." Pp. 26-43 in *Christian Origins: Theology, Rhetoric and Community,* edited by Lewis Ayres and Gareth Jones. London and New York: Routledge.

———. 1999. "Figure, Allegory." Pp. 365-68 in *Augustine through the Ages: An Encyclopedia.* Grand Rapids: Eerdmans.

Domanyi, Thomas. 1979. *Der Römerbriefkommentar des Thomas von Aquin. Ein Beitrag zur Untersuchung seiner Auslegungsmethoden.* Bern, Frankfurt, Las Vegas: Peter Lang.

Dunn, James D.G. 1988. *Romans 1-8.* Word Biblical Commentary 38. Dallas: Word Books.

English, Edward D. (ed.). 1995. *Reading and Wisdom: The De doctrina christiana of Augustine in the Middle Ages.* Notre Dame: University of Notre Dame Press.

Farley, Edward A. 1988. *The Fragility of Knowledge: Theological Education in the Church and the University.* Philadelphia: Fortress Press.

Fowl, Stephen E. (ed.). 1998. *The Theological Interpretation of Scripture: Classic and Contemporary Readings.* Blackwell Readings in Modern Theology. Oxford: Basil Blackwell.

Fredriksen, Paula. 1999. "*Secundum Carnem*: History and Israel in the Theology of St. Augustine." Pp. 26-41 in *The Limits of Ancient Christianity: Essays on Late Antique Thought and Culture in Honor of R.A. Markus,* edited by William E. Klingshirn and Mark Vessey. Ann Arbor: University of Michigan Press.

Frei, Hans W. 1974. *The Eclipse of Biblical Narrative.* New Haven: Yale University Press.

———. 1986. "The 'Literal Reading' of Biblical Narrative in the Christian Tradition: Does It Stretch or Will It Break?" Pp. 36-77 in *The Bible and the Narrative Tradition,* edited by Frank McConnell. New York: Oxford University Press.

Gadamer, Hans-Georg. 1989. *Truth and Method.* Second, Revised Edition. New York: Crossroad.

Gerrish, B.A. 1984. *A Prince of the Church: Schleiermacher and the Beginnings of Modern Theology.* Philadelphia: Fortress Press.

Grant, Robert M. 1952. *Miracle and Natural Law in Graeco-Roman and Early Christian Thought.* Amsterdam: North Holland Publishing Co.

———. 1957. *The Letter and the Spirit.* London: SPCK Press.

Hadot, Pierre. 1995. *Philosophy as a Way of Life: Spiritual Exercises from Socrates to Foucault.* Edited with an Introduction by Arnold I. Davidson. Translated by Michael Chase. Oxford: Blackwell.

Huff, Mary Cyria. 1948. *The Sonnet "No Me Mueve, Mi Dios" — Its Theme in Spanish Tradition.* Washington: Catholic University of America.

Hurst, David (tr.). 1999. Bede the Venerable, *Excerpts from the Works of Saint Augustine on the Letters of the Blessed Apostle Paul.* Kalamazoo: Cistercian Publications.

Käsemann, Ernst. 1980. *Commentary on Romans.* Grand Rapids: Eerdmans.

Kelly, J.N.D. 1964. *The Athanasian Creed.* New York: Harper & Row.

La Bonnardière, Anne Marie. 1960-. *Biblia Augustiniana.* Paris: Études Augustiniennes.

———. 1965. *Recherches de chronologie augustinienne.* Paris: Études Augustiniennes.

———. 1986. "La Chananéenne, préfiguration de l'Église." Pp. 117-43 in *Saint Augustin et la Bible.* Paris: Beauchesne.

Lancel, Serge. 1999. *Saint Augustin.* Paris: Fayard, 1999.

Lasch, Christopher. 1991. *The True and Only Heaven: Progress and Its Critics.* New York: W.W. Norton & Company.

Lewalski, Barbara Kiefer. 1979. *Protestant Poetics and the Seventeenth-Century Religious Lyric.* Princeton: Princeton University Press.

Lubac, Henri de. 1948 [1984]. "On an Old Distich: The Doctrine of the 'Fourfold Sense' of Scripture." Pp. 109-27 in *Theological Fragments,* Translated by Rebecca Howell Balinski. San Francisco: Ignatius Press. First published in 1948 under the title "Le 'quadruple sense' de l'Écriture." Pp. 348-65 in *Mélanges offerts au R.P. Ferdinand Cavallera.* Toulouse: Bibliothèque de l'Institut Catholique.

———. 1959. *Exégèse médiévale. Les quatre sens de l'Écriture.* Vol. I. Théologie 41. Paris: Aubier.

Lüdemann, Gerd. 1996. *Heretics: The Other Side of Early Christianity.* Translated by John Bowden. London: SCM Press.

Luther, Martin. 1955- . *Luther's Works.* Saint Louis: Concordia Publishing House.

Mannheim, Karl. 1936. *Ideology and Utopia: An Introduction to the Sociology of Knowledge.* Translated from the German by Louis Wirth and Edward Shils. New York: Harcourt, Brace and Company.

Matter, E. Ann. 1997. "The Church Fathers and the *Glossa ordinaria.*" Pp. 83-111 in *The Reception of the Church Fathers in the West: From the Carolingians to the Maurists.* Edited by Irena Backus. Leiden: E.J. Brill.

Maurice, F.D. 1957. *Theological Essays.* New York: Harper & Brothers.

McNally, Robert E. S.J. 1959. *The Bible in the Early Middle Ages.* Westminster, Md.: Newman Press.

Meyer, Paul W. 1990. "The Worm at the Core of the Apple: Exegetical Reflections on Romans 7." Pp. 62-84 in *The Conversation Continues: Studies in Paul and John in Honor of J. Louis Martyn.* Nashville: Abingdon Press.

Nanos, Mark D. 1996. *The Mystery of Romans: The Jewish Context of Paul's Letter.* Minneapolis: Fortress Press.

———. 2000. "Challenging the Limits That Continue to Define Paul's Perspective on Jews and Judaism." Pp. 212-24 in *Reading Israel In Romans: Legitimacy and*

Plausibility of Divergent Interpretations, ed. Cristina Grenholm and Daniel Patte. Harrisburg: Trinity Press International.

O'Connell, Robert J., S.J. 1983. "Isaiah's Mothering God in St. Augustine's *Confessions.*" *Thought* 58:188-203.

Pépin, Jean. 1955. "À propos de l'histoire de l'exégèse allégorique. L'absurdité signe de l'allégorie." *Studia Patristica = Texte und Untersuchungen* 63: 395-413.

———. 1966. "Porphyre, exégète d'Homère." Pp. 235-58 in *Porphyre. Huit exposés suivis de discussions.* Entretiens sur l'antiquité classique, 12. Geneva: Fondation Hardt.

Pollmann, Karla. 1996. *Doctrina Christiana. Untersuchungen zu den Anfängen der christlichen Hermeneutik unter besonderer Berücksichtigung von Augustinus, De doctrina christiana.* Paradosis 41. Freiburg Schweiz: Universitätsverlag.

———. 1999. "Doctrina christiana (de)." *Augustinus-Lexikon* II:551-75.

Räisänen, Heikki. 1983. *Paul and the Law.* Wissenschaftliche Untersuchungen zum Neuen Testament, 29. Tübingen: J. C. B. Mohr (Paul Siebeck).

———. 1991. *Jesus, Paul and Torah: Collected Essays.* Translations from the German by David E. Orton. Journals for the Study of the New Testament Supplement Series 43. Sheffield: Sheffield Academic Press.

Reicke, Bo. 1973. *Die zehn Worte in Geschichte und Gegenwart.* Beiträge zur Geschichte der biblischen Exegese 15. Tübingen: J.C.B. Mohr.

Rilke, Rainer Maria. 1987. *New Poems: The Other Part.* Translated by Edward Snow. San Francisco: North Point Press.

Sanday, William, and Arthur C. Headlam. 1885. *Critical and Exegetical Commentary on the Epistle to the Romans.* Edinburgh: T.&T. Clark.

Schaberg, Jane. 1990. *The Illegitimacy of Jesus: A Feminist Theological Interpretation of the Infancy Narratives.* New York: Crossroad.

Schindler, Alfred. 1996. "Decalogus." *Augustinus-Lexikon* II: 246-55.

Schüssler Fiorenza, Elisabeth. 1984. *Bread Not Stone: The Challenge of Feminist Biblical Interpretation.* Boston: Beacon Press.

Sievers, Joseph. 2000. "'God's Gifts and Call Are Irrevocable': The Reception of Romans 11:29 through the Centuries and Christian-Jewish Relations." Pp. 127-73 in *Reading Israel In Romans: Legitimacy and Plausibility of Divergent Interpretations*, ed. Cristina Grenholm and Daniel Patte. Harrisburg: Trinity Press International.

Smalley, Beryl. 1983. *The Study of the Bible in the Middle Ages.* Third Edition. Oxford: Basil Blackwell.

Stendahl, Krister. 1962. "Biblical Theology, Contemporary." Pp. I:418-32 in *The Interpreter's Dictionary of the Bible.* Edited by George Buttrick. Nashville: Abingdon Press.

Stowers, Stanley. 1995. "Romans 7.7-25 as a Speech-in-Character (prosopopiia)." Pp. 180-202 in *Paul in His Hellenistic Context.* Edited by Troels Engberg-Pedersen. Minneapolis: Fortress Press.

Strauss, David Friedrich. 1973. *The Life of Jesus, Critically Examined.* Edited and with an Introduction by Peter C. Hodgson. Translation from the Fourth German Edition by George Eliot. Philadelphia: Fortress Press.

Swartley, Willard M. 1983. *Slavery, Sabbath, War, and Women: Case Issues in Biblical Interpretation.* Scottsdale, PA: Herald Press.

TeSelle, Eugene. 1970. *Augustine the Theologian.* New York: Herder & Herder.

————. 1999. "Holy Spirit." Pp. 434–37 in *Augustine through the Ages: An Encyclopedia.* Grand Rapids: Eerdmans.

Theissen, Gerd. 1987. *Psychological Aspects of Pauline Theology.* Translated by John P. Galvin. Philadelphia: Fortress Press.

Tillich, Paul. 1951. *Systematic Theology.* Volume I. Chicago: University of Chicago Press.

Torjesen, Karen Jo. 1986. *Hermeneutical Procedure and Theological Method in Origen's Exegesis.* Berlin: Walter de Gruyter.

Vaughan, C.J. 1886. *St. Paul's Epistle to the Romans.* Sixth Edition. London: Macmillan.

Wiles, Maurice. 1967. *The Making of Christian Doctrine: A Study in the Principles of Early Doctrinal Development.* London: Cambridge University Press.

————. 1974. *The Remaking of Christian Doctrine.* London: SCM Press.

————. 1976. *Working Papers in Doctrine.* London: SCM Press.

Young, Frances. 1994. "Typology." Pp. 29–48 in *Crossing the Boundaries: Essays in Biblical Interpretation in Honour of Michael M. Gouldner.* Edited by Stanley E. Porter, Paul Joyce and David E. Orton. Leiden: E.J. Brill, 1994.

– O N E –

Modus Inveniendi Paulum

Augustine, Hermeneutics, and his Reading of Romans

Thomas F. Martin, O.S.A.

———— ◆ ————

C For centuries, much attention has been directed to Augustine's reading of Paul's Letter to the Romans, seeking to uncover and analyze the complexities, motivations, and impact of this reading. This concern continues today, with estimations and conclusions regarding Augustine's Romans history that clearly reflect the approaches and insights of much modern scholarship. Space does not permit an exploration of these evaluations except to note that **H** little attention has been paid to the explicitly hermeneutical question in Augustine's Romans endeavors.

This is, perhaps, both surprising and not. On the one hand, given the intense concern regarding matters hermeneutical in contemporary biblical and theological studies, one would expect more attention to be devoted to this issue in Augustine. On the other hand, given the chasm that separates modern hermeneutical approaches from ancient, it is perhaps all too easy to lose sight of even the presence of hermeneutical issues, especially given the perceived difference between ancient and modern hermeneutics. Yet Augustine himself was well aware of the formal question of hermeneutics and broke new ground by being one of the very first early Christian thinkers to set out and explain an explicit hermeneutical method to guide interpretation and study of the Bible. All of this is to be found in his *On Christian Instruction (De doctrina christiana)*. In this work he defines the starting point for all who would interpret the scriptures, calling it a "way of discovering what must be understood there" — *modus inveniendi quae intelligenda sunt (De doct.chr.* I,i,1). **I** If *inventio* was a key aspect of the dialectical-rhetorical tradition that shaped

---

C Too frequently attention is devoted almost exclusively to Augustine's motivations in interpreting Romans.

H More attention should be devoted to his hermeneutics.

I *Inventio*, a rhetorical procedure, is de-centered by Augustine, who focuses attention on the biblical text, apprehended in faith, and diminishes the more subjective factors.

Augustine (Pizzolato 1994, 47ff.), now it is entirely subordinated to scriptural text and its underlying *veritas*. The notion of "what *must be* understood there [*intelligenda*]" states unambiguously that it is the obligation and responsibility of the student of the scriptures to surrender to biblical text — meaning does not come from "the investigator" but from "the investigated," the *quae intelligenda sunt*. Augustine further clarifies by calling this a *modus inveniendi*. *Modus* clearly suggests method, a "how to," and Augustine argues in his preface to the *De doctrina christiana* that there must be "objective," "standardized," "established" rules and procedures for interpreting the scriptures. He thus decries arbitrary, anti-intellectual, or purely subjective approaches to scriptural text. In so affirming the notion of a *modus inveniendi quae intelligenda sunt* Augustine provides a capsule description of the task of the ancient biblical scholar. **H** And if formally in the *De doctrina christiana* Augustine explores his understanding of this *modus inveniendi* — the theory and practice of scriptural hermeneutics — throughout all his writings but especially in his "biblical commentaries" (on John, Psalms, and Genesis in particular) there are many spontaneous hermeneutical asides and digressions where he pauses and explains his *modus inveniendi*. These tend to be concise and precise, summary capsules of how he is interpreting the scriptures, certainly a reminder or caution to his "audience" to aid them in their understanding, but also an opportunity for Augustine to clarify out loud his own method of proceeding.

It is Augustine's own frequent and spontaneous explanation of his approach to "hermeneutics" that will guide the first part of this analysis. Given the enormous attention paid to *De doctrina christiana* as indicative of Augustine's hermeneutical approach, I propose to explore a less-analyzed source, the "hermeneutical asides" that occur in the course of the above-mentioned scriptural works of Augustine (on John, Psalms, and Genesis). Paul is very present in all of these scriptural works as well, and so, I will argue, these "rules" apply equally to Augustine's reading of Paul. They will be turned practical in the second part of this paper by looking at the bishop in practice. **C** Does he, in fact, follow and apply his own rules? How, and in what way? For this I will concentrate on some final works of Augustine where Romans figures prominently (but not exclusively): *Grace and Free Choice, Admonition and Grace, The Predestination of the Saints,* and *The Gift of Perseverance.* Given the space limitations here, I must insist that these observations will be *suggestive* rather than *exhaustive* — and could certainly be more deeply analyzed and documented.

H Where are we to find Augustine's hermeneutical rules?

C Does Augustine follow his own rules?

Precepts for Treating the Scriptures

There are certain precepts for treating the scriptures (*praecepta quaedam tractandarum Scripturarum*) which I think may not inconveniently be handed on to students, so that they may make progress not only from reading the work of expositors but also in their own explanations of the sacred writings to others. I have undertaken to explain these to those able and willing to learn, provided God will not deny my putting in writing those things which He usually suggests to me in thought (*De doct. chr.*, prol. 1).

H   These opening words of *De doctrina christiana*, most likely to be dated to the winter of 396-97,[1] set the tone for what Augustine will be about in the course of the work. They suggest that even as a novice bishop Augustine was operating out of an all-encompassing theological framework that certainly placed all the *praecepta* he will be handing on into an explicit faith setting: "si Dominus ac Deus noster ea quae de hac re cogitanti solet suggerere, etiam scribenti mihi non deneget." This is confirmed in noting Augustine's most frequent "hermeneutical aside," namely the overriding "spiritual framework" within which he views the reading and understanding of the *divinae litterae*. In the *praecepta* that follow, I will cite examples of each rule, beginning with the spiritual-theological approach just mentioned, not claiming that these citations are exhaustive but nonetheless insisting that they are typical.

1. Guided by the *Regula Fidei* [2]

H   Augustine repeatedly notes a series of "theological" *a priori*'s that guided his study of scripture, all of which he will insist come from the very scriptures themselves. The leading principle is clearly Christological, as he asserts repeatedly that Christ is *the* reading key, and ultimately the final hermeneutical principle not just for the New Testament but equally for the Old Testament.[3]

The entire Old Testament is embraced [by the New] (*omnem veterem textum Scripturarum circumplexus est*). No matter what it speaks of, Christ resonates (*Christum sonat*); but only if [Christ]

H   Augustine's hermeneutic is developed out of a theological framework.
H   The "rule of faith" offers the doctrinal criteria for interpretation.

finds ears [to hear]. "And he opened its meaning to them, so that they would understand the scriptures." And so we too must pray, so that he open our understanding (*sensum nostrum*) (*In ep. Io.* 2,1).

Though commenting upon 1 John in this particular text, Augustine turns to Luke's account of Christ explaining the scriptures on the road to Emmaus (Lk 14:13ff.) for guidance and confirmation of the Christological unity of the scriptures. "*Ad illum [Christum] omnia quae divinitus scripta sunt, referentur*" (*En.Ps.* 71,18; 47,1). This will be expanded, in the light of his developing sense of the notion of *Christus Totus*, to encompass the church as well, the Body of Christ: " . . . *et totum omnium Scripturarum mysterium Christum et ecclesiam [confitetur]*" (*En.Ps.* 79,2; cf. *En.Ps.* 103,iv,10). It is here that the rich complexity of the scriptures finds both unity and univocal truth.

> One thing only (*una eademque res*) is said in many different ways, so that in this way the variety of expression catches our attention, while for the sake of harmony one [truth] is held to (*En.Ps.* 46,1).

This is supported by Augustine's placing all reading of scripture in an explicit faith context, described variously as guided by the *fides catholica* (*De Gen.adv.Man.* I,1), or *apostolica sententia* (*De Gen.ad litt.* VI,ix,15), or the *dominica et apostolica disciplina* (*En.Ps.* 8,13). Thus the scriptures are always and everywhere taken up with *pietas* — *pie quaerere* (*De Gen.adv.Man.* I,v,9), *scripturae pie credere* (*De Gen. ad litt.* V,iv,7). Given this Christological predisposition, Augustine consistently turns the act of interpretation in this direction: ". . . *erigere intentionem ad quaerendam in litteris sacris . . . christianam et evangelicam fidem*" (*De Gen. ad litt.* II,ii,5).

2. Ancient Reading

C A As much as Augustine's hermeneutic was shaped by the *a priori* of faith at the very moment he took up the sacred text, there can be no doubt that this *spiritually* driven reading of the scriptures was conditioned by the *modus legendi* given to Augustine by the world and culture of Late Antiquity (Gamble, 1995; Stock, 1996). While this certainly included the *décadence* explored by Marrou and enshrined by Augustine himself in the Book III of the *Confessions*, where he is appalled by the barbarity of Bible text (Marrou, 1938/1949), it also meant that Augustine applied to the *Litterae Sacrae* many of the same analytical tools he learned to apply to any

---

C Augustine shared a number of attitudes from the world and culture of Late Antiquity.
A Augustine used a number of ancient reading methods.

and all *litterae*. In this sense the study of the "liberal arts" or the *"disciplinae"* — grammar, dialectics, rhetoric, arithmetic, music, geometry, and philosophy *(Retr.* I,6) — conditioned him to approach any reading with the standard set of hermeneutical "givens" of his culture: its tools, questions, and methods for ascertaining meaning. Thus when Augustine speaks of *locutiones* (e.g., *En.Ps.* 104,11), *genera locutionis* (e.g. *De Gen.ad litt.* III,i,2), annotated *codices* (". . . *stella fuerat praenotata,*" *En.Ps.* 105,7), comparing *codices* (". . . *sicut alii codices habent*" becomes a veritable antiphon running throughout his commentary on the Psalms, e.g. *En.Ps* 82,4; cf. *De Gen.ad litt.* I,2), *voluntas scriptoris* (*De Gen.ad litt.* IV,i,1), *verborum ordo* (e.g. *En.Ps.* 71,4), *pronuntiatio* (e.g., *De Gen.ad litt.* V,xiv,31), *temporis verbum* (e.g. *En.Ps.* 3,5), *mutatio personae* (e.g. *En.Ps.* 4,2) — the instances could be multiplied endlessly — he is simply utilizing the standardized "reading rules" of his day, which apply to Vergil and Cicero and equally to reading scripture. Thus while affirming the divine nature of the scriptures — *"et de illa civitate unde pregrinamur, litterae nobis venerunt: ipsae sunt Scripturae . . . "* (*En.Ps.* 90,ii,1) — he will insist that one must not lose sight of the fact that these are still "human letters" with all their limitations and implied interpretative tasks:

> The human condition would be lowered if God appeared unwilling to administer his Word through humans to humans (*De doct.chr.* prol. 6).[4]

Augustine is thus well aware that "reading scripture" includes and takes for granted all the practices and approaches implied in any sort of "reading."

3. *Intellectus Fidei*

H Augustine was well trained in the art of *disputatio,* dialectics, and it is evident that this training had hermeneutical implications as well (Pépin 1976).[5] Often a text of scripture will be the center of a formal debate between Augustine and an opponent, but just as often the debate seems to be taking place within Augustine's own mind as he weighs possibilities, applies the laws of logic and dialectic, and places himself firmly *"in progressu disputationis"* in order to understand a text (see *Gen.ad litt.* IV,i,1; see also his insistence on "intelligent Christian reading of the Bible" in I,ix,38). Even the most difficult scriptural question is simply a solemn call

---

H The text of Scripture is assumed to be intelligible, but only after inquiry based upon faith.

to make even greater effort *ad intellectum,* never an obstacle before which one abandons the course:

> Because the grasping of these things is difficult for those less capable, this must not become an excuse to note or say something which we ourselves do not hold (*De Gen.ad litt.* VI,vi,9).

This requires a serious effort to integrate *discernere, credere,* and *intellegere* (ibid.), lest scripture be approached "*mente pueri*" (*De Gen.ad litt.* I,xviii,36). This dialectical and disputational approach so permeates Augustine's engagement with the biblical text as to often render the final exegetical results *polemical* in both content and "texture."[6] Augustine seems fully at home with the tensions of this approach, and will rarely make apologies for the *exercitatio* implied in all of this.

4. *Obscuritas et Mysterium*

H Augustine is clearly fascinated, attracted, and drawn to the seemingly "irreconcilable" and "incompatible" within the scriptures, and finds it a preferred field for exploration.

> There are profound mysteries (*profunda mysteria*) in the Sacred Scriptures which are made obscure to prevent us from not respecting them (*ne vilescant*). The seeking of their meaning exercises us, the finding of their meaning nourishes us (*ad hoc quaerentur, ut exerceant; ad hoc aperiuntur, ut pascant*) (*En.Ps.* 140,1).[7]

The *profunda mysteria* of scripture have, according to this perspective, a very specific function. The labor involved is a coefficient of the sacredness and dignity of the sacred text: *ne vilescant.* By means of its very difficulties, scripture proclaims its depth, dignity, and sacredness. The effort to engage the mystery is, in itself, nourishing and rewarding. It is even an encouragement to continue the pursuit: *ut pascant.* The task of the *tractator* is not to deny the apparent obstacles but to hear in them a call to enter more deeply into their hidden mystery:

> . . . lest it be thought that scripture contains foolish or repugnant things (*aliqua absurdia vel repugnantia*) to offend one who reads them, leading him to think that what the scripture tells cannot be true, or preventing him from growing in faith, or even holding him back from faith (*De Gen.ad litt.* V,viii,23).

H The profundity of Scripture stimulates further seeking.

The "resolution" of apparent contradictions even has its own rules, and are most often solvable by other clearer passages (*Ep.* 143,1; *De doct.chr.* III,xxvi,37). They can likewise serve as reminder that scripture is *polysemiotic,* offering occasion for "humility" by opportune de-construction of the hegemony of particular understandings (e.g., *En.Ps.* 74,12). Sometimes it will simply be an opportunity to relish the "pleasurable incongruity" (Cameron 1997, 46-47) of scripture's truth, inviting not only deeper understanding but, in fact, taking one even more deeply into the mystery. Exegetically speaking, this attraction to and affirmation of the seemingly contradictory as a way of more fully engaging scripture's meaning plays a persistently prominent role in all of Augustine's scriptural activity. *Factum audivimus, mysterium requiramus* (*In Io.ev.* 50,6).

5. Fallen Words

H Indeed before the fall (*ante peccatum*), God having made the green of the field and food, by which terms we indicate that an invisible creation (*inuisibilem creaturam*) is to be understood, he watered it with an interior font (*fonte interiore*), speaking into its intellect (*loquens in intellectum eius*): **so that it did not receive words from without** (*ut non extrinsecus uerba*), like rain from the already-mentioned clouds; but it was supplied by its own font (*sed fonte suo*), that is to say, by truth flowing from within (*de intimis suis manante ueritate, satiaretur*) . . . I have thus brought to your attention that we are to understand people working the earth to mean people established in the aridity of sin (*in peccatorum ariditate constituto*), and so it is necessary, like the clouds that give rain, **that divine doctrine be expressed in human words** (*necessariam esse de humanis uerbis diuinam doctrinam*) (*De Gen.adv.Man.* II,iv,5-v,6).

If the garden saw unfold the drama of fallen humanity, Augustine has no doubt that human words and human communication now bear the scars of that originating sin (*De Gen.ad litt.* VIII,xxv,46; *En.Ps.* 93,6). Despite Augustine's delight with words and fascination with the intricacies and wonders of originating human communication, this perspective is ever conditioned by a profound awareness that words are often fragile, sometimes dangerous, and ever limiting. Augustine thereby proclaims the provisional nature of all words—even the words of scripture.

There in that homeland Jerusalem [*patria illa Ierusalem*] all the just and holy who are delighted by the word of God will do so without reading and without letters (*qui fruuntur Verbo Dei sine lectione, sine*

H The necessity of speech — and its spiritual hazards.

litteris); what is written for us on pages, they will come to by seeing the face of God (*quod enim nobis per paginas scriptum est, per faciem Dei illi cernunt*). What a homeland! What a wonderful homeland! Miserable are the sojourners away from that homeland (*et miseri sunt peregrini ab illa patria*) (*En Ps.* 119,6).

"There will be no need for scripture in heaven" is a repeated affirmation of Augustine: *sine lectione, sine litteris.* All human words, even those used to compose the scriptures, partake of *miseria.* This creates tension. On the one hand, scripture is saving word, yet in its very humanness, it falls far short of its goal: *nihil enim de Deo digne dici potest* (*De Gen.adv.Man.* I,xviii,14). If on the one hand men and women can luxuriate in the verdant gardens and meadows of scripture (*Ep.* 84,1), on the other hand the serpent is always present: *susurrare serpens non desinit* (*En.Ps.* 93,20), even in the very act of exegeting (*En.Ps.* 103,iv,8). There is no doubt that Augustine loved to offer his own words to others; the nature and volume of the works he left behind is its confirmation. However, Augustine will nonetheless consistently "problematize" the very fact and necessity of words.[8] They are always *soni mortali* and can never rise to the heights of the *Verbum immortale* (*En.Ps.* 103,8). They are fraught with peril yet without them we would be sorely lacking necessary *adiutorium* and *admonitiones* (*In ep.Io.* 3,1).

6. *Mores Scripturarum*

H Commentators have consistently noted that beginning with Augustine's ordination and his "scriptural sabbatical," fervently sought after from Valerius his bishop in *Letter 21* of the Augustinian corpus, Augustine's very vocabulary becomes thoroughly imbued with the words, phrases, concepts, and even rhythms of scripture. One manifestation of this, with specific hermeneutical repercussions, is to be found in Augustine's repeated assertion that the scriptures often have a peculiar, distinct, and customary way of speaking. Augustine refers to this as "*mos scripturae*" (*En.Ps.* 71,2) or "*usitato more Scripturarum*" (*De Gen.ad litt.* V,ii,4), sometimes noting that scripture is just taking up a standard "*loquendi consuetudo*" that applies to all manner of speaking (*De Gen.ad litt.* III,iii,5), other times suggesting that it has its own idiosyncratic mode of speaking: "*more suo scriptura tanquam infirmis infirmiter loquitur*" (*De Gen.ad litt.* V,vi,19).[9] It is almost as if it is speaking in a particular dialect, if not its very own language. This is not just a question of Old Testament interpretation, for even Paul employed the "*mos scripturarum*" (*C.Faust.* XI,3), proceeded "*more apostolico*" (*De op.mon.* ii,3), and speaks "*suo more*" (C

H Scripture speaks in its own "dialect."

Faust. XI,7). Augustine intriguingly explores Paul's unique way of speaking in Book XII of *De Genesi ad litteram,* analyzing II Cor. 12:2-4 where he speaks about the "third heaven" and "paradise." To recognize and interpret correctly the *mos scripturarum* demands a close and constant encounter with the words of scripture, leading to the recognition of and submission to the scriptures' ways:

> . . . There are those who are fighting for their own opinions rather than those of the scriptures; we want the scriptures to agree with us rather than wanting to make our own what is the scriptures' own (*De Gen.ad litt.* I,xviii,37).[10]

Augustine insists on the necessity of learning, understanding, and appreciating the *consuetudines* and *mores* of scripture as a necessary step towards correct and true comprehension: "*audite scripturae sanctae consuetudinem*" (*In Io.ev.* 42,10).[11]

The Hermeneutics of Conversion

I I have been suggesting in the exploration of the previous six points that Augustine reveals important dimensions of his own *modus inveniendi* by means of the hermeneutical and exegetical *asides* that occur in the course of his explaining the text of scripture.[12] While much attention has been directed toward his formal exegetical comments in *De doctrina christiana* and other similar writings, I am suggesting that these reveal much about his own "rules" and the interpretative strategies and concerns Augustine brought to the text of scripture. I am likewise suggesting that, though these asides are often *not*, specifically Pauline in content or focus, they nonetheless reveal Augustine's "approach" to all scripture and so apply not just to John or Genesis or the Psalms or Paul, but to all. **C** In this light, I wish to propose one final "*modus inveniendi*" which permeates and conditions *all* of Augustine's scriptural activity and places that activity squarely within a framework of conversion, holiness, humility, and spiritual growth.[13] It makes abundantly clear that for Augustine the question of biblical interpretation could never be simply an academic, speculative, or scholastic exercise but was always placed within an expressly religious context and intention. This is affirmed in a variety of ways.

I Augustine's hermeneutical rules are expressed chiefly in "asides" in the course of explaining specific passages of Scripture.

C For Augustine, interpretation is set in the context of searching, growth, and conversion.

H Scripture, for example, is a *speculum* in which one ought to see oneself: *"posuit tibi speculum Scripturam suam"* (*En.Ps.* 103,4; also 30, II, s.3,1; 54,4). Hermeneutically speaking, this will predispose Augustine to locate present audience in sacred text and give this presence an objective value.[14] Thus "pastoral intention" seems to be inseparable from author's intention because this is certainly the Divine Author's intention (*En.Ps.* 38,1), such that God writes the very scriptures upon the hearts of all the faithful (*En.Ps.* 85,24). The consistent attitude and response of the *lector/auditor/tractator* before this divine condescension to human words is thus *humility*, where progress and growth in humility becomes every bit as important as progress and growth in the languages of the Bible, vocabulary, encyclopedic knowledge — all the things Augustine suggests as helpful and important in *De doctrina christiana*. Humility provides the surest guarantee of a fruitful and worthwhile encounter with scripture:

> That one attends in a holy way to the law of God and the word of God's mouth whose ears are led by humility (*En.Ps.* 77,3).

For Augustine this is clearly not a once-and-for-all event but a question of ongoing progress, conversion, growth, familiarization. This is likewise why Mt. 7:7 permeates all of Augustine's scriptural activity from beginning (*De Gen.adv.Man.* I,2) to end (*De don.pers.* xxiii,64):

> . . . so that it is given to those seeking, it is found by those searching, it is opened to those knocking (*ut detur petentibus, inveniatur a quaerentibus, intretur a pulsantibus*) (*En.Ps.* 103,ii,1).

This conversion lens or hermeneutic can perhaps be linked to Augustine's long training as a *rhetor* where he learned the importance of persuasion. This present truth of scripture operates *"ad persuasionem"* and places even greater responsibility upon the *lector/auditor* to respond to its present call.

These seven "precepts," drawn by me from Augustine's own spontaneous comments about his *"modus inveniendi,"* suggest what drove and shaped Augustine's encounter with the scriptures. How do they manifest themselves in his reading of Paul and Romans? It is to this question that we will now turn.

I The choice of attempting an interface between the seven "principles" culled from Augustine's own "exegetical asides" and four of his final works is not without risk for the investigator, and perhaps for Augustine himself. It has become virtually commonplace to see the "final" Augustine as

---

H The reader or the audience is acknowledged, on the principle that they are envisaged by the text and interpreted by it.

I How well does Augustine follow his own hermeneutical rules?

theologically self-imprisoned within a rigorist, predestinarian framework. The "love grown cold" bishop of Hippo, as many would see it,[15] could hardly be expected to have maintained any serious hermeneutical principles in the "winner-take-all" polemics that marked the final phase of the Pelagian controversy, especially with Julian of Eclanum. But such commonplaces perhaps provide the necessary and appropriate occasion for a closer look at the later "biblical Augustine," more particularly the Pauline-Romans Augustine. How does the Letter to the Romans appear in *Grace and Free Will (De gratia et libero arbitrio)* (426),[16] *Admonition and Grace (De correptione et gratia)* (426/427), *The Predestination of Saints (De praedestinatione sanctorum)* (429/430), and *The Gift of Perseverance (De dono perserverantiae)* (429/430)? The unique perspective of these works is that they lack the sharp polemical atmosphere of Augustine's writings addressed to or against Julian of Eclanum, with the particular hermeneutical challenges created and posed by polemical debate. The agonistic and antagonistic framework for polemical discourse leaves little room for nuance or irenic explanation. All four of these works, on the other hand, are addressed to monastic audiences, perplexed, perhaps, but not hostile to Augustine. Thus the aged bishop of Hippo's exposition, passionate though it may be, is restrained in its language while firm in its conviction — and the Letter to the Romans is virtually omnipresent.

Grace and Free Will
(*De Gratia et Libero Abritrio*)

C As the title makes clear, Augustine is compelled to set the monks of Hadrumetum straight regarding both grace and free choice. He wrote the work

> . . . on account of those who, when defending the grace of God, think they deny free choice, and those who so defend free choice as to deny the grace of God, insisting that [grace] is given according to our merits . . . (*Retr.* II,66).

A What strikes anyone looking at the scriptural content of the work is that the entire treatise is an elaborate tapestry of scriptural citations and allusions from the Old and New Testaments. No one biblical author bears the weight of the argument; each is subordinated to an overall scriptural strategy that suggests the overriding principle of the *regula fidei*, both the product of the *veritas scripturarum* as a whole and yet supported at each

---

C The occasion for the work.
A Passages from Scripture illuminate each other.

turn of the Bible page. Paul and his Letter to the Romans are subsumed
into this overriding framework (citations of the letter occur 42 times over
the course of its 46 paragraphs, making it the most cited biblical book in
the work). The opening chapter highlights "the abstruse nature of the
question at hand, *quaestionis obscuritas*" (i,1),[17] a certainly familiar
hermeneutical emphasis and opportunity for Augustine. **H** In the same
introduction he affirms the need to link understanding and prayer: *"ut
intelligatis orate,"* once again a familiar theme. While ever insisting that
the content of the exposition is simply biblical doctrine — *"revelavit autem
nobis per Scripturas suas sanctas"* (ii,2) — there is the equal conviction that
intellectus fidei (ut intelligatis) is the goal.

A What form does this *intellectus* take? In ii,5 he cites Romans 2:12:

> For those who have sinned without the law, will perish without the
> law; and those who have sinned under the law, will be judged by the
> law.

Augustine comments accordingly (ii-iii,5):

> I do not think that the Apostle meant to say that those who sin in
> ignorance will suffer worse punishment than those who know the
> law. It would seem that it is worse to perish than to be judged. But
> as the Apostle was speaking here of the Gentiles and of the Jews,
> since the former are without the law while the latter have received
> it, how can anyone dare say that those Jews who sin under the law
> will not perish? For they have not believed in Christ, and it has
> been said of them that "they shall be judged by the law." For
> without faith in Christ no one can be set free, and consequently they
> will perish by judgment.

C Augustine is paying close attention to the *context* of Paul's affirmation, noting that it is addressed to both Jew and Gentile. At the same
time, he affirms his overriding Christological hermeneutic: "without faith
in Christ no one can be set free." In the same section he cites Rom. 12:21,
"Be not overcome by evil, but overcome evil with good." Here dialectics
enter in, as he draws the *logical* conclusion from such a statement: Paul
would not so command our wills unless he understood those same wills to
be free: *"velle enim et nolle propriae voluntatis est."* Here he pays careful

---

H Pray in order to understand.
A Tracing Paul's argument. Rom. 2:12.
C Paul's context included both Jews and Gentiles. Rom. 2:12, read in terms of 12:21.

"logical" attention to the words of Paul, and draws their "reasonable" implications.

In vi,13 he notes to his monastic audience what "method" he is pursuing in the work:

> It is proven (*probatur*) by these and similar testimonies of Sacred Scripture (*talibus testimoniis divinis*) that God's grace is not given according to our merits. We see, in fact, that it is given, and continues to be given daily (*quotidie*).

While specific scriptural texts are constantly being brought forward for this *probatio*, there is, in fact, a "cumulative argument" (the *regula fidei* ?) operational as the real driving force behind his exposition. Augustine makes no apology for this "combining of texts," referred to generically as "testimonies of Sacred Scripture." **A** He does seem to be aware that Paul did the same:

> And in another passage, right after he had quoted the words of the Psalm: "Because for your sake we are put to death all the day long and we are counted as sheep for the slaughter" (Ps 43:22), he went on to say: "Because in all these things we overcome because of him who has loved us" (Rom. 8:36-37). We overcome, therefore, not by ourselves, but through Him who has loved us (vii,16).

On this occasion he does not pursue the *fact* of Paul's own citational method, but he does elsewhere, and it can be presumed that, if challenged, Augustine would simply point to Paul's own citational practice, certainly subsumed under the one truth of scripture.[18]

A In viii,19 Augustine ties together four separate passages from Romans: 2:6; 4:4; 11:5-6; and 6:23. The question at hand is whether "eternal life" is grace or merit. All four citations refer to grace, and he concludes:

> He has said this so plainly that it is absolutely impossible to deny it. His words do not require acute understanding, but that one merely pay attention.

A Like Augustine, Paul quotes widely from Scripture. Rom. 2:12 and 8:36-37.
A Augustine finds harmony among various passages in Romans. Rom. 2:6; 4:4; 11:5-6; and 6:23.

Here Augustine insists that careful hearing/reading of the text makes
evident Paul's intention and meaning. Certainly at this point it is the
personal authority of Augustine and the sheer weight of such an affirmation that is the basis for the assertion, though **A** in the same passage Rom.
2:6 is paired with Mt. 16:27 to further implicitly demonstrate that even
Paul's reading is part of the much larger scriptural truth.

A Augustine's most careful reading of Paul in the course of the entire
treatise occurs in x,22. Here it is a close reading of Rom. 3:20 along with
4:15a-b, 7:6, and 7:7-13.

> Accordingly, brothers and sisters, you should not do evil with your
> free will, but good; for this is what the law of God prescribes in the
> Sacred Scriptures, both in the Old and New Testaments. Yes, let us
> read and try with the Lord's help to understand what the Apostle
> means when he says: "For by the works of the law no human being
> shall be justified before him, for through law comes the recognition
> of sin" (Rom. 3:20).[19] He did not say the "destruction" of sin, but its
> "recognition." Now when someone comes to a knowledge of sin, the
> law undoubtedly works wrath unless one be aided by grace to avoid
> what is known to be sinful. This is what the Apostle says in another
> place, and these are his own words: "The law works wrath" (Rom.
> 4:15a). He said this because God's wrath is more severe towards a
> transgressor who knows sin by the law, and yet commits it. Such
> a one is indeed a transgressor of the law, as the Apostle also
> remarks in the same passage where he says: "For where there is no
> law, neither is there transgression" (Rom. 4:15b). This is why he
> also says in another place: "That we may serve in newness of spirit
> and not in oldness of letter" (Rom. 7:6). By "oldness of letter" he
> would have us to understand the law, whereas by "newness of
> spirit," nothing else but grace. Furthermore, so that no one might
> think he was blaming the law, or finding fault with it, he immedi-
> ately faced the problem by asking: "What shall we say then? Is the
> law sin? By no means!"(he follows with a full citation of the
> remainder of Rom. 7: 7-13).

Here once again there is a "close reading" of Paul with various passages
from Romans made to stand side by side, one to clarify the other. On
Augustine's part, there appears a careful attention to Paul's vocabulary

---

A Paul reads Rom. 2:6 in harmony with Matthew.

A Augustine carefully examines some leading themes in Romans. Rom. 3:20; 4:15; 7:6;
    and 7:7-13.

and method of argument: e.g., "he immediately faced the problem by asking . . ." In these instances it appears clear that Augustine is not citing from memory (perhaps his most common practice) but has his own codex of Romans open and is carefully coordinating and contrasting Paul's own words with Paul's own words!

C It is perhaps worthwhile to note two more passages that reveal the kind of reading of Romans Augustine is about. In xii,24 there is a strong polemic against the Jews. Having cited Rom. 10:3, regarding those "led by their own spirit . . .," he comments that Paul is speaking "about the Jews," who "because of their self-confidence, rejected grace and as a result did not believe in Christ." This clearly reflects the bitterness and distance that in Augustine's day had become a commonplace in Christian discourse. Finally as the treatise draws to a close, it explodes (xxii,44) with citations from Romans, prompted by a discussion of children who do not receive baptism: "these things take place by the hidden providence of God — *per occultam Dei providentiam* — whose judgments are incomprehensible and whose ways are unsearchable" (Rom. 11:33). The string of texts that follow are all Pauline exclamations of wonder before this hidden providence (Rom. 11:30-32; 11:33 [now in full]; 5:20). The treatise then ends with a repetition of the initial call to "pray for understanding — *orate ut intelligatis*," put in the light of progression in wisdom. Once again the familiar conversion hermeneutic brings a work to conclusion.

Admonition and Grace
(*De Correptione et Gratia*)

This work is an attempt to further clarify questions and concerns raised by the previous work, and it is not intended for the occasional reader:

> If you would derive the most fruit from it, determine to become entirely familiar with it by repeated reading, so that you may know very clearly the important questions that are answered therein, not by a human, but by a heavenly authority, from which we must not depart if we wish to reach the goal of our striving (i,1).

A There are some 40 references to the Letter to the Romans in the work, the most of any biblical book, yet these form part of a larger

---

C Other Augustinian emphases: anti-Jewish polemic and the mysteries of predestination. Rom. 10:3; 11:30-32; 11:33; 5:20.

A In this work, Augustine similarly makes much use of Romans, relating it to other passages of Scripture. Rom. 9:21.

scriptural repertoire that permeates the work. Thus neither Paul nor the Letter to the Romans is read without the omnipresence of an abundant array of scriptural citations from the Psalms, the Prophets, the Gospels, and the Letter of James. Along with a kind of argument by cumulative effect, there are a number of key moments in the work where the hermeneutical lens that drives Augustine is stated boldly and unequivocally. **H** One of these is found in vii,11, where his Christological reading is made explicit:

> . . . as truth itself speaks, no one is freed from the damnation accomplished by Adam except through faith in Christ.

Augustine follows this assertion with a *"massa perditionis"* conclusion, his application of the Latin *massa* of Rom. 9:21 to

> those who have not heard the Gospel, and those who, having heard it, do not persevere, and those who, having heard the Gospel call to come to Christ, are unwilling to believe in him . . . (vii,12).

This Christological key is aided by a Romans allusion:

> . . . we ought to understand that no one can be singled out of that lost mass (see Rom. 9:21) for which Adam was responsible, except one who has this gift; and anyone who has it, has it by the grace of the Savior.

A This reading and application of Romans terminology is, at this point, simply declaration, rather than exposition or explanation of scriptural text. However, in the aural-oral culture of Augustine and his world, where texts were remembered and memorized and easily called to mind, it seems evident that there is a kind of "exegesis by association": Augustine does not feel the need to justify these citations since they are held together by similar vocabulary drawn from a variety of biblical contexts.

A This is not to say, however, that in the course of the treatise there is no attempt to do a more careful reading of Romans. Augustine does this in vii,14. Here it is *propositum* that carries the reading (kept in the original to appreciate its holding force):

H The Christological basis of Augustine's interpretation.

A Use of biblical texts is sometimes more a mosaic than a close analysis.

A Augustine also engages in close textual analysis. Rom. 8:23-30; 9: 11-13.

De talibus dicit Apostolus: "Scimus quoniam diligentibus Deum omnia
*cooperatur in bonum, his qui secundum **propositum** vocati sunt: quoniam*
quos ante praescivit, et praedestinavit conformes imaginis Filii sui, ut sit
ipse primogenitus in multis fratribus: quos autem praedestinavit, illos et
vocavit; quos autem vocavit, ipsos et iustificavit; quos autem iustificavit,
ipsos et glorificavit" (Rom. 8:23-30). Ex istis nullus perit, quia omnes
*electi sunt. Electi sunt autem, quia secundum **propositum** vocati sunt:*
***propositum** autem, non suum, sed Dei; de quo alibi dicit: "Ut secundum*
*electionem **propositum** Dei maneret, non ex operibus, sed ex vocante*
dictus est ei: "quia maior serviet minori" (Rom. 9:11-13); et alibi: "Non
*secundum opera nostra," inquit, "sed secundum suum **propositum** et*
gratiam" (2 Tim. 1:9). Cum ergo audimus: "quos autem praedestinavit,
*illos et vocavit," secundum **propositum** vocatus debemus agnoscere:*
quoniam inde coepit, dicens: "omnia cooperatur in bonum, his qui secundum
***propositum** vocati sunt"; ac deinde subiunxit: "Quoniam quos ante*
praescivit, et praedestinavit conformes imaginis Filii sui, ut sit ipse
primogenitus in multis fratribus" (Rom. 8:28-30); atque his praemissis
subdidit: "Quos autem praedestinavit, illos et vocavit"; ne putentur in eis
esse aliqui vocati et non electi, propter illam dominicam sententiam: "Multi
vocati, pauci electi" (Mt. 20:16). Quicumque enim electi, sine dubio etiam
vocati: non autem quicumque vocati, consequenter electi. Illi ergo electi, ut
*saepe dictum est, qui secundum **propositum** vocati, qui etiam*
praedestinati atque praesciti.

This close reading of aspects of Romans 8 and 9, combined with other
scriptural texts carefully interwoven, is demanding upon both Augustine
and audience. The codex would need to be opened, vocabulary clearly
noted, the interconnections and movement plainly seen. **H** Yet Augustine
quickly turns to two favorite texts from Romans (9:20 and 11:33) to
highlight the *mysterium* and *obscuritas* of these demanding explorations:

At this point, if I am asked why God does not give perseverance to
those to whom He once gave the love whereby they lived a Christian life, I answer that I do not know. Not with arrogance, but in
the recognition of my condition, I heed the Apostle's words (*sed
agnoscens modulum meum, audio dicentem Apostolum*): "O human, who
are you to reply to God?" "O the depth of the riches of the wisdom
and of the knowledge of God! How incomprehensible are his

H The mystery of predestination. Rom. 9:20 and 11:33.

judgments, and how unsearchable his ways!" Insofar as He has deigned to manifest his judgments to us, let us give thanks; insofar as He has hidden them, let us not murmur against His will, but let us believe that this, too, is most salutary for us (viii,17).

Here Augustine has turned again to his "conversion" principle, and this theme of humble stupor before divine mystery will recur again (viii,18,19; ix,24,25; x,28; xii,37; xiii,40-42). It likewise returns as he concludes the treatise. We, he insists, do not know nor understand, yet it is necessary to believe whatever scripture affirms: "*nec gratia prohibet correptionem, nec correptio negat gratiam*" (xvi,49).

While there has been some effort at careful reading of Paul and while there is no doubt that Romans figures prominently in the treatise, the preferred approach is "apostolic declaration": "*Audio dicentem Apostolum*" (viii,17), Augustine affirms, and there is no doubt that this "hearing" is simply "*secundum apostolicam veramque sententiam*" (ix,21).

The Predestination of Saints
(*De Praedestinatione Sanctorum*)

C This work and the following are in many ways a single work — or at the very least are intended to be read together. They represent the last two completed works of Augustine, and while they do not contain the bitter polemics of the unfinished work against Julian, they nonetheless reflect resistance to Augustine's positions on grace, free will, and predestination, signaling a Gallic controversy that will continue well after Augustine's death. This is not the occasion to enter into these questions, since the concern here is how Augustine reads Romans in the course of these works. Yet the more controversial atmosphere will be immediately apparent throughout the work. Scripture will frequently be used starkly as proof-text, often without any introduction, explanation, or examination as such.

The very title of the work, *De praedestinatione sanctorum*, is thoroughly Pauline, since the four times the word appears in scripture are all Pauline: Rom. 8:29, 8:30, Eph. 1:5, Eph. 1:11 (Pauline authorship of Ephesians was not in question for Augustine and his theological circles). **C** The importance of Romans in prompting the work appears clear from *Letter*

C The situation of the last two works. Rom. 8:29, 8:30.
  C The work was called forth by controversy over Romans and predestination. Rom. 9:14-21.

225 from Prosper to Augustine, setting out the nature of the problem that work will address:

> . . . Quoting what the Apostle Paul wrote in his Epistle to the Romans (9:14-21) as proof of divine grace antecedent to the merits of the elect, they declare that these words have never been understood by an ecclesiastical writer as they are now understood [by you] (*Ep.* 225,3).

It is obvious that what is being challenged is his reading of Romans.

H Both the introductory and concluding paragraphs provide, it may be argued, Augustine's own suggestions for the nature of the controversy that prompts the treatise as well as the approach that ought to be taken to his comments. Four points are made at the outset regarding the attitude of mind guiding Augustine — and he invites his audience to take this same approach. The first is that the fundamental issue is grace, suggesting that predestination is a corollary to the whole question of grace; the second is that *humility* is needed to appreciate what is at stake (he cites Jer 17:5: "*Maledictus omnis qui spem habet in homine* "); the third is that even the understanding of the question is grace: "*et si quid aliter sapitis, hoc quoque vobis Deus revelabit* "; finally, it is clear that all this is guided by the *regula fidei:* "*ut credant cum Ecclesia Christi* " (i,1-2). These are the principles that will guide his arguments and expositions (and they will be echoed as he concludes the work).

A Augustine cites Romans some 51 times, once again the most-cited book of the Bible in the work. **C** There are also two lengthy citations from his *Retractationes,* the first in reference to his *Propositions on Romans* and the second to his *Ad Simplicianum.* Both are designed to demonstrate that Augustine himself has been anything but static in these questions, gentle but firm reminders that he has grown — and so ought his audience:

> The care they took to read my books, they did not apply to progressing with me in them also (iv,8).

And such progress itself has been a grace:

> This is why I said above that it was especially this testimony of the Apostle by which I myself was convinced, when I thought otherwise

---

H Augustine indictates his mode of approach.
A Romans is once again cited frequently.
C Augustine acknowledges the changes in his thinking.

about this matter; *God revealed this to me*, as I have said, when I was writing to Bishop Simplicianus, trying to resolve this question (*quam **mihi Deus** in hac quaestione solvenda, cum ad episcopum Simplicianum, sicut dixi scriberem, **revelavit***) (iv,8).

H Not only do Augustine's intended readers need to grow in the understanding of the faith, they must also reckon with the fact that Augustine himself has received this by "revelation" — an unambiguous call to accept the authority this implies. Augustine turns this into a "human fallibility" versus "divine infallibility" question:

Truly, when the Apostle says, "Therefore it is of faith that, according to grace, the promise might be firm to all the seed" (Rom. 4:16), I am amazed that people would rather trust in their own weakness than in the strength of God's promise. "But I am uncertain," someone might say, "of God's will toward me." What then? Are you certain of your own will toward yourself, and do you not fear, "Wherefore, he that thinks himself to stand, let him take heed lest he fall" (1 Cor. 10:12)? Therefore, since both wills are uncertain, why not commit one's faith, hope, and love to the stronger rather than to the weaker (xi,21)?

Here it is Augustine the *disputator* at work, showing the "logic" of trusting in God versus the "illogic" of trusting in self.

Neither has Augustine lost sight of his Christological hermeneutic in defending "the grace of God through Jesus Christ our Lord."[20] In xii,23, he highlights, in conjunction with the need for infant baptism, the case of the "man Christ Jesus":

... nor was Christ, being himself also human, made the liberator of humans by virtue of any preceding human merits.

This is a reminder that the Christological foundations and implications of all these questions remain critical for Augustine. It all gets forcefully stated in xv,31 as he vigorously affirms grace from beginning to end of the salvation event, ever placed within the framework of God's foreknowledge and predestination. **A** Paul's opening words in Romans provides the testimony:

H Human fallibility is surpassed by divine infallibility. Rom. 4:16.
  A Confirmation of predestination from Romans. Rom. 1:1-4 as confirmation of Rom. 8: 28-29; 9:12; 11:25-29.

This is what the teacher of the Gentiles proclaims in the beginning of his epistles: "Paul a servant of Jesus Christ, called to be an apostle, set apart for the gospel of God, which he had promised before, by his prophets, in the Holy Scriptures, concerning his Son, who was made from the seed of David for him, according to the flesh, who was predestined as the Son of God in power, according to the Spirit of Sanctification, by the resurrection from the dead." Therefore (*ergo*) Jesus was predestined . . .

The mere repetition of Paul's own opening words from Romans confirms the grace of predestination. This receives more detailed analysis in xvi,32, as the predestination affirmation of Rom. 8: 28-29 is linked with Rom. 9:12 (citing Gen. 25:23), 11:29, 25-27, and 28.

And the Apostle shows that this came about by God's design (*ex Dei dispositione*), who knows how to use even evil things for good; not that the vessels of wrath might be of benefit to him, but rather that by his own good use of them they might be of benefit to the vessels of mercy. For what could be said more clearly (*apertius*) than these words: "As concerning the gospel, indeed they are enemies for your sake" (Rom. 11:28)?

It is thus clear what Paul intends in Romans — grace:

It would take too long to argue these points one by one. But certainly you must see with what evidence of apostolic testimony (*quanta manifestatione apostolici eloquii*) this grace is defended, against which human merits are exalted, as if someone should first give something to God in order to receive compensation for it (xviii,37).

Yet this affirmation extends beyond Romans as Paul *himself* seems to be held up as the strongest argument for Augustine's insistence on the centrality of grace:

Behold why this most intrepid soldier, this most invincible defender of grace, gives thanks. Behold why he gives thanks that the apostles are the good odor of Christ unto God, both in those who are saved by his grace and in those who perish in virtue of his judgment . . . (xx,41).

H Augustine's focused reading of Romans is inserted into the wider interpretative framework Paul himself provides and models: *miles acerrimus et defensor invictissimus gratiae.*

The Gift of Perseverance
(*De Dono Perserverantiae*)

C The work *On the Gift of Perseverance* is Augustine's final *complete* work. It is complex, digressive, permeated with scripture, a combination handbook, apologia, tract, and spiritual exhortation. It contains a commentary on the *Our Father,* numerous citations from the likes of Ambrose, Cyprian, and Gregory Nanzianzus, reproaches directed against Pelagian and Manichaean adversaries, advice and counsel, reflections on his own *Confessions,* and even **H** a final *caveat lector:*

> I would not wish anyone to accept my opinions to the point of
> following me except in those points where they see that I have not
> erred. For that very reason I am now undertaking a review of my
> works, so that I may show that I do not even agree with my own
> views in every matter now.   However, since I did not begin
> perfectly, I do think that, through God's mercy, I have made
> progress in my writing.   Indeed I would be speaking with more
> pride than truth, if I say even now that I have reached perfection,
> without any error in my writing even in this period of my life. But
> what is of importance is to what extent and in what matters
> someone has erred and how readily he corrects, or how stubbornly
> he tries to defend his error. Certainly there is great hope for
> someone if, even on his last day of this life, he is found to be
> progressing, so that what he lacked while progressing be given him,
> and he be judged worthy to be perfected rather than punished
> (xxi,55).

Once again Augustine is providing reading key for this work, or perhaps even better for Augustine himself.

A It is clear, then, that there is much more to this work than Romans. However, it is equally important to note the place of Romans in the work

---

H Augustine's reading of Romans finds its hermeneutical frame in his reading of Paul concerning grace.

C The work as a combination handbook, apologia, tract, and spiritual exhortation.

H Augustine's approach to interpretation.

A Use of the text of Romans in this work.

itself, and to make some observations regarding this presence. Once again
it is the preeminent text throughout the work. It is cited some 41 times,
compared to 33 references from Matthew, the next most cited biblical
book in the work. His gospel figures prominently because of the
explanation of the *Our Father*. Also, there is much more than Romans that
represents Paul: 1 Corinthians is cited some 16 times, with frequent
references to Galatians and Ephesians. Further, Augustine is well into the
work (paragraph 17) before he makes explicit reference to Romans,
though this first citation suggests the approach he will take. **H** He is
exploring the mystery of why some are graced and others are not
(*numquam esse apud Deum iniquitas invenitur*, viii,17):

> "O human, who are you to respond to God — *O homo, tu quis es, qui
> respondeas Deo*" (Rom. 9:20)? You indeed see him to be a most kind
> benefactor in the case of one of your number, a most just exactor in
> your own case, yet not unjust to anyone. For since he would be
> just, even if he punished both, the one who is freed has reason to be
> grateful, the one who is condemned has no grounds for complaint.

This has by now become a familiar theme:

> So let us believe without doubt in his mercy in the case of those who
> are liberated, and in his truth in regard to those who are punished; but
> let us attempt neither to scrutinize the inscrutable, nor to search out
> the unsearchable (xi,25).

Yet despite the affirmation of the *inscrutabilia* and *investigabilia*, he in fact
pursues *intellectus fidei*, not content with simple declaration.

A C In xviii,47 he shows this by a lengthy exploration of Romans 11.
He pays close attention to Paul's terminology:

> For this reason predestination is sometimes also called foreknow-
> ledge (*nomine praescientiae*), as the Apostle says: "God has not cast
> off his people whom he foreknew" (Rom. 11:2).

He goes on to place this within context:

H The mystery of predestination. Rom. 9:20.
A Romans 11 in relation to Romans 7.
C Predestination, Election, Grace. Rom. 11:2, 4; 7:5-7.

The expression "he foreknew" (*praescivit*) is correctly understood to mean nothing else than "he predestined" (*praedestinavit*), as the context of this passage (*circumstantia ipsius lectionis*) shows.

He then explains this *circumstantia*:

For he was speaking about the remnant of the Jews who had been saved while the others were perishing.

He proceeds to explore this election and moves to its implications.

Then he added the part concerning which we are now discussing: "God has not cast off his people whom he foreknew" (Rom. 11:2). And to show that it was by the grace of God, and not by the merits of their own works that the remnant of the Jews had been preserved, he immediately added . . . (he cites Rom. 11:4, which cites 3 Kg 19:18).

He continues paying close attention to the text, what was said and what was *not* said, and how it was said:

Now he does not say (*non enim ait*), "They have been left for me," or "They have left themselves for me," but "I have left for myself" . . . and joining that which I have just introduced he asks: "*What then?*" And to this question he answers . . .

He has taken a series of texts from Rom. 7: 5-7 and considered them in sequence. This leads him to conclude:

Therefore (*ergo*), by this election, and by the remnant left "elected out of grace" he meant the people whom God did not cast off because he foreknew them (*praescivit*). This is the election by which those whom He wills He chose in Christ before the foundation of the world . . . predestinating (*praedestinans*) them to be adopted sons and daughters.

C Augustine has returned to his starting point where he affirmed identity of meaning between *praedestinatio* and *praescientia*. This careful reading of text, noting vocabulary, sequence, connections, etc. has all the hallmarks of the "reading habits" he would have learned in his own grammatical, literary, and rhetorical training. Its dialectical component

---

C Augustine's use of classical learning to deal with the text.

is evident, beginning with the assertion of identity in the terms *praedestinatio* and *praescientia.* Once this premise is agreed to, he can then proceed with logical precision: therefore — *ergo.*

A In the chapter that follows, Augustine continues to operate with this logical method:

> When we find in the works of certain exegetes of the Word of God [the expression] "the foreknowledge of God," used in reference to the calling of the elect, what is there to prevent our understanding this foreknowledge as predestination? . . . This fact I know, that only someone in error could argue against this doctrine of predestination which we are defending in accordance with Sacred Scripture (*secundum Scripturas sanctas defendimus*) (xix,48).

"*Secundum Scripturas sanctas defendere*" — Augustine restates once again his strategy. He proceeds to offer further support for his own careful analysis of Paul by the same close reading of statements of Cyprian and Ambrose. These "*tractatores excellentissimi divinorum eloquiorum*" (xix,49) provide clear testimony and evidence that Augustine's reading of *Romans* is within the *regula fidei.*

Thus, while *De dono perseverantiae* is about much more than reading Paul or Romans, nevertheless it is clear that Augustine's reading of Paul and Romans plays a critical role in the argument at hand. **H** As Augustine concludes he insists that this argument about "the predestination of divine grace" (xxii,59), though absolutely true, must nonetheless be heard and taught in a way that is *ad salutem.*

> . . . certainly this is absolutely true, yet by all means it is most outrageous, most inopportune, most inappropriate, not because what is said is false, but because it is not applied in a salutary way (*salubriter*) with respect to human weakness (xxii,61).

The communication of the *veritas scripturarum* must itself serve the conversion hermeneutic by avoiding what is outrageous and unsalutary. This exploration of how to preach/teach predestination draws upon an array of biblical texts eventually leading to a call to *pray* for perseverance. Here Rom. 8:26-27 and 8:15 provide part of the guidance necessary for this prayer. This explanation eventually and not surprisingly builds to an exhortation developed from Mt 7:7:

A Confirmation from Scripture — and from earlier ecclesiastical writers.
H All affirmations must be related to salvation. Rom. 8:15, 26-27.

Therefore, let our adversaries consider how mistaken they are to think that it is from us, and not granted to us that we ask, seek, knock; and when they say that this is [from us], that preceded by our merits, grace follows: when seeking, we receive it, and asking, we find it, and it is opened to us, when we knock. Are not these unwilling to understand that it is also a divine gift that we pray — that is, that we seek, that we ask, and that we knock: "For we have received a spirit of adoption as sons, by virtue of which we cry, Abba! Father!" (Rom. 8:15) (xxiii,64).

Even the prayer for grace, Romans teaches us, is itself a grace.

Conclusion

H The intention of this exploration was to try to enter into Augustine's own exegetical-interpretative world, first by bringing to the fore his own, as I have called them, "hermeneutical asides," and then by looking at Augustine "in operation" with the Letter to the Romans. I deliberately chose late-in-life works, precisely because it is here that it is most often suggested that Augustine abandoned any systematic approach to the Scriptures, resorting to uncritical proof-texting, driven by the heat and passions of polemics.

C In the light of the seven "precepts" outlined above, drawn from Augustine's own occasional observations about how to read Scripture, I would like to suggest that he *does* remain quite faithful to much that he himself expressed regarding his *modus inveniendi*. **I** One notes in particular the prominent role played by the *regula fidei*, the omnipresent dialectical-logical analysis, his continued fascination with mystery, and a consistent insistence on a "conversional" reading. In his own carefully digressive way, he does, in fact, return again and again to the implicit principles that drove him in all of his scriptural activities, finding in the Letter to the Romans both affirmation and expression of them. There is no doubt that Augustine shows little evidence of "technical exegesis" in these works, and debates will continue regarding whether he truly *found* Paul or simply found his own "precepts" confirmed. But the "final" Augustine and his reading of Romans certainly appears at least internally consistent with his own "exegetical asides."

H The purpose has been to identify Augustine's own hermeneutical rules.

C Augustine does follow his own rules, even in the late, polemical period.

C The complex relationship among the text, the reader, and hermeneutical principles.

Notes

1. See explanation and bibliography in *La doctrine chrétienne, De doctrina christiana,* BA11/2, 429-33.

2. Throughout this study I will use the term *"regula fidei"* to refer to the emerging sense of orthodoxy that guided early Christian thinkers like Augustine. Space does not permit a study of Augustine's particular use of this notion.

3. For patristic writers such as Augustine the Hebrew scriptures were simply the "Old Testament."

4. Many of these "hermeneutical asides" do find echoes in *De doct.chr.*

5. Solignac has suggested that it was precisely in this realm that Augustine overstepped hermeneutical boundaries (Solignac 1988).

6. Gérard Remy speaks (Remy 1991, 582) of an *"aspect conflictuel"* within the very *"texture"* of Augustine's Christological thought. I am suggesting that it be extended to his hermeneutical method.

7. Space does not permit an exploration of Augustine's preference for "antithesis," with its methodological and conceptual implications.

8. This is affirmed in his classic distinction between *res* and *signa,* as well as in his emphasis on "interiority" (e.g. *En.Ps.* 139,15) and "illumination."

9. This *"more suo"* of scripture is clearly distinguished from the *"more nostro"* of general linguistic convention; see, e.g., *En.Ps.* 12,1; 78,17; *In Io.ev.* 10,2.

10. Cf. *In Io.ev.* 28,3: *"extra usum nostrum, non quo more nos loquimur."*

11. In *De Gen.ad litt.* XII,viii,19 Augustine carefully tracks Paul's specific use of vocabulary.

12. Space does not allow an exploration of possible sources for these "rules."

13. See the perceptive comments about all ancient "study" in Hadot, 1995.

14. Augustine argued this early on in his theological career. In *Conf.* XII,xviii,27 and xxv,35 he proposes that Moses' intention does not exclude the "truth" God presently inspires in the reader. All particular "truths" are subsumed into Truth.

15. This is the famous and oft-repeated estimation of Burnaby 1938, 231.

16. For this and the following works, I refer the reader to the Latin-French volume 24 (1962) of the Bibliothèque Augustinienne, *Aux Moines d'Adrumète et de Provence.*

17. In all the translations that follow I have consulted and modified the translations of the Fathers of the Church (FOC) series.

18. See *En.Ps.* 31,ii,2 where he notes Paul's citation of this Psalm in Rom 4. This is reiterated in *En.Ps.* 118,iii,3.

19. While Augustine's text reads *"ex lege,"* the Vulgate, new in his time, reads *"ex operibus legis."* Pelagius' text likewise has *"ex operibus legis"* (de Bruyn 1993, 172).

20. Augustine is citing the Latin of Rom 7:25a which translates a Greek χάρις τοῦ θεοῦ in place of the received text's χάρις τῷ θεῷ.

Bibliography

C.Faust.	*NBA*, 14.
En.Ps.	*ACW* 29-30; *BAC* XIX-XXII; *NBA* XXV-XXVII.
Ep.	*FOC*, 12, 18, 20,30,32.
Io.ep.	*BAC* 18; *FOC* 92; *NBA* XXIV/2.
Gen.adv.Man.	*FOC* 84.
Gen.litt.	*ACW* 41-42; *BA* 48-49.
Io.ev.	*BA* LV-LXXIX; *FOC* 78, 79, 88, 90, 92; *NBA* XXIV/1 &2.
Retr.	*BA* XII; *FOC* 60; *NBA* II.

Burnaby, John. 1938. *Amor Dei: A Study of the Religion of St. Augustine.* London: Hodder & Stoughton.

Cameron, Michael. 1997. "Transfiguration Christology and the Roots of Figurative Exegesis in St. Augustine," *Studia Patristica* 33:40-47.

De Bruyn, Theodore. 1993. *Pelagius' Commentary on St. Paul's Epistles to the Romans.* Oxford Early Christian Studies. Oxford: Clarendon Press.

Gamble, Harry Y. 1995. *Books and Readers in the Early Church: A History of Early Christian Texts.* New Haven: Yale University Press.

Hadot, Pierre. 1995. *Philosophy as a Way of Life: Spiritual Exercises from Socrates to Foucault.* Edited with an Introduction by Arnold I. Davidson, Translated by Michael Chase. Oxford: Blackwell.

Marrou, Henri-Irénée. 1938/1949. *Saint Augustin et La Fin de la Culture Antique.* Paris: Boccard.

Pépin, Jean. 1972. *Saint Augustine et la Dialectique.* Saint Augustine Lecture, 1972. Villanova: Villanova University Press.

Pizzolato, Luigi. 1994. *Capitoli di retorica agostiniana.* Rome: Istituto Patristico Augustinianum, 1994.

Remy, Gérard. 1991. "La théologie de la *mediation* selon saint Augustin, son actualité." *Revue Thomiste* 91:580-623.

Solignac, Aimé, S.J. 1988. "Les excès de l'*intellectus fidei* dans la doctrine d'Augustin sur la grâce." *Nouvelle Revue Théologique* 110: 825-49.

Stock, Brian. 1996. *Augustine the Reader: Meditation, Self-Knowledge, and the Ethics of Interpretation.* Cambridge: Belknap Press of Harvard University Press.

– T W O –

Augustine and Israel

Interpretatio ad Litteram, Jews, and Judaism

in Augustine's Theology of History

*Paula Fredriksen**

———— ◆ ————

H Of all of Augustine's contributions to late Latin theology, three in particular stand out as irreducibly idiosyncratic yet enduringly important: his views on the nature of the human will; his teaching on the place of Jews and Judaism within both the history of salvation and quotidian Christian society; and his thoroughgoing secularization of post-biblical history. These three theological themes shape the final third of *The City of God,* but they originate in the fruitful confusion of Augustine's thought in the decade immediately following his conversion — most specifically, I shall argue, in his new understanding of Paul, and especially Romans, that comes into focus in the 390s, in the course of his struggle against the Manichees.[1]

 C This is the formative context within which I want to situate Augustine's novel teachings on the theological status of Jews and Judaism.[2] I will start with a brief review of the exegetical steps by which he came to the startling conclusion of the *Replies to Simplicanus (Ad Simplicianum),* and show how this in turn affected his understanding of historical time, biblical revelation, and interpretation *ad litteram.* His correspondence with Jerome, begun in the mid-390s over issues in Galatians 2, will further fill in Augustine's position on the nature of biblical narrative, historical interpretation, and thus also the religious status of Jewish observance. I will then quarry the *Against Faustus (Contra Faustum)* for Augustine's teachings on biblical Israel as a prophetic type

---

*This essay is reprinted from *Studia Patristica* 38 by permission of Peeters Publishers.

H Three defining themes in Augustine's theology.
C The context for Augustine's original teachings on Judaism.

of the Church, and current Jewish communities as its positive witness. Finally, and briefly, I shall consider his mature reprise of these themes as he presents them in *The City of God.*

The Work on Paul

H Augustine's liberating encounter with philosophy and allegory in Milan had freed him from Manichaeism's negative critique of the Old Testament and its powerful dualist reading of Paul by teaching him how to read the Bible *secundum spiritum.* He applied these techniques of spiritual understanding in his earliest exegetical attack against his old sect, the *On Genesis Against the Manichaeans (De Genesi contra Manichaeos).* His interpretation there is almost unrelievedly allegorical; and he seems to lament, at the beginning of Book II, that he could not attempt as well to read "*secundum litteram.*"[3] Four years later, in 393, he again undertook a commentary on Genesis, this time *ad litteram* — that is, "secundum historicam proprietatem" (*Retr.* I,18), "according to its historical character." This project, however, like so many undertaken during his priesthood, ran aground and remained unfinished.[4]

C Meanwhile, in part stimulated by his public confrontation with Fortunatus, in part aided by his encounter with the exegetical works of Tyconius, Augustine in this same period composed a stream of Pauline commentaries: the *Propositiones* or notes on Romans; the *Inchoata expositio,* another unfinished commentary, also on Romans; a commentary on Galatians, which would lead to an extended correspondence with Jerome; three substantial comments on questions arising from Romans, chapters 7 through 9 (*De div.quaest.* qq. 66-68); and finally, capping this period, again reviewing Romans 7-9, the answers to questions posed by his old mentor in Milan. Augustine reads Paul with the Manichees, so to speak, looking over his shoulder: against their determinist and dualist hermeneutic, he seeks to show that the Apostle "neither condemns the law nor takes away man's free will" (*Exp.prop.Rom.* 13-18,1).

C From his reading of Tyconius's *Liber regularum,* which I date to 394/95, Augustine takes over four important points: (1) that salvation history is continuous between the Testaments and (2) within the life of the individual believer – that is, salvation history is both linear and interior: the broad historical sweep from Abraham through Sinai to the coming of Christ to final redemption at the end (the argument for continuity) is recapitulated in the individual experience of each saved person to either side of the Incarnation (the argument for interiority); (3) that the person is saved not by works but by faith, which God foreknows; and (4)

H How allegory enabled Augustine's move beyond Manichaeism.
C Augustine's fresh interest in Paul during the 390s.
C The influence of Tyconius.

prophecies that seem apocalyptic are actually highly symbolic typological descriptions of current reality: the present, in consequence, is eschatologically opaque.

H Augustine systematizes both Paul's letter and Tyconius's first two exegetical points when he formulates the characteristic teaching of his notes on Romans, the four stages of salvation history: before the law, under the law, under grace, and the final eschatological stage, in peace. These stages are objective, communal and historical: they describe the linear experience of humanity. But they are also subjective, individual and transhistorical: every saved person, in whatever period of history, has passed or will pass through these grades. This rubric permitted Augustine to see the law positively, both as an historical epoch and as a stage of continuing relevance for the individual believer, thus defining as one continuous redemptive movement the divine dispensation to Israel and to the Church — a strong refutation of the Manichaean rejection of the Old Testament. On the micro-level, the interior workings of the individual, it placed at dead center the crucial moment of conversion from *sub lege* to *sub gratia.*

A How is such a transfer effected? The key, said Augustine, is the will. Insufficient to prevent man *sub lege* from sinning, man's will can at least prompt him to turn in faith to Christ and implore his aid (*Exp.prop.Rom.* 44,3). Receiving grace through faith, man will then move *sub gratia* and be able to fulfill the law through love, which could not be done through fear. But here Romans 9 complicates Augustine's picture: the prenatal choice of Jacob over Esau, the divine hardening of Pharaoh, are difficult to reconcile with a strong construction of free will. With Tyconius, Augustine responds that God elects or rejects on the basis of unerring foreknowledge whether the individual will have faith. Election must be based on some merit, and it is: the merit of faith. "Non opera sed fides inchoat meritum" (62,9).

H Within two years, in the *Ad Simplicianum*, again considering this moment of transition from "under the law" to "under grace," Augustine repudiates precisely this Tyconian understanding of the relation of divine foreknowledge, faith, and election. Man, he will now say, does absolutely nothing to merit salvation; even the first impulse to believe, to have the faith to call out to God for help, is itself God's gift, entirely undeserved (*Ad Simpl.* I, q.2,12). "Restat ergo voluntates eliguntur," that is, by God (I, q.2,22:).[5] Returning to Romans 9, Augustine takes Paul's metaphor of the the lump of clay from which God the potter forms various vessels (Rom. 9:20-23) and historicizes the image: the *conspersio* or *massa luti* now

---

H The place of the law in salvation history.

A God's foreknowledge of faith as basis for election: a way of reconciling Romans 9 with a strong construction of free will.

H A new understanding of election. Rom. 9:20-23.

reifies into a description of a universal, objective state, the condition of humanity after the fall, the *massa peccati.* Human will is compromised, broken, absolutely ineffective, because everyone is born in Adam, *una quaedam massa peccati* (1.2,16).[6]

Humanity is thus justly, universally condemned. The mystery is that God chooses to exercise mercy and save anybody. How does he make his choice, if there is absolutely no distinction between persons? We cannot know, says Augustine. God judges justly, but his justice is nothing that humans can understand or appreciate: "aequitate occultissima et ab humanis sensibus remotissima iudicat" (1.2,16). Jews, Gentiles, Pharaoh, Paul — all are from this same mass. If God mysteriously gives grace to some, the only appropriate response is praise of his inscrutable decisions.

C How had Augustine come to this new understanding? Scholars have proposed a number of causes, literary and environmental. Ambrosiaster's commentary on Romans might have suggested the new interpretation of the *massa* (I don't think so; see Fredriksen 1988, 99 and nn. 51-54). Tyconius, through the *Liber,* may have made prominent Paul's line in 1 Cor. 4:7 with reference to man's dependence on God's grace, "What do you have that you did not first receive?" (*Lib.reg.* 3, Babcock 35). This is possible, but at this point in the *Ad Simplicianum* Augustine is throwing away a key piece of Tyconius's argument, the divine foreknowledge of faith. It would be odd for such a relatively minor point as a particular citation (which he interprets differently from Tyconius in any case) to affect him so profoundly (that is, to cause the new interpretation). Then there are Paul's letters themselves. In the way that this observation is true, it is also unimportant. Many other careful and sensitive readers had studied and would study these epistles, without coming to the conclusions that Augustine came to, and even he only in 396 (Fredriksen 1988, 102 and nn. 65-66). Others invoke more atmospheric factors: cultural environment (the supposed harshness of African Christianity with its stern biblical culture), difficult working conditions (the depressing wear and tear of his job facing down a surly laity unhappy about Augustine's reform of the *laetitiae,* loath to give up swearing and recourse to astrologers). And the blush is off the rose of the life he'd thought he'd won back in Milan: "Very possibly, it could not bear the terrific weight of his own expectations of it" (see Brown 1967, 150, and the entire chapter for the effects of these intangible environmental factors).

C However we may regard the list of plausible causes for Augustine's exegetical volte-face in 396, we should certainly consider as a factor something we *know* Augustine to be doing in this period: He was reading Galatians. And we know both from that letter itself and from his

---

C Whence this new understanding?
C The effect of Galatians.

commentary and correspondence on it that he thereby encountered not
only the Paul of Pauline theology, the champion of grace, but also the Paul
of history, the Paul who speaks of his past as a persecutor (Gal. 1:13), of
his call to preach to the Gentiles (which Augustine would see as Paul's
conversion to Christianity, Gal. 1:16),[7] and most especially of his
confrontation with Peter over issues with Gentiles and Jewish law in
Antioch (2:11ff.). We know from his response to Jerome's commentary
that Augustine was worried about the nature of the historical narrative in
Galatians, because the veracity of the account affected its authority as
Scripture (*Ep.* 28; over his shoulder, again, are the Manichees).[8] The
letter's theological content, which he interprets, begins to share space
with its narrative description, which he is concerned to reconstruct
historically. In other words, and specifically with reference to Paul, by
394/95 Augustine has begun to think of the narrative content of the
Pauline letters *secundum historicam proprietatem.*

C It is this refocusing of Augustine's exegetical attention that explains
the sudden shift we see in the course of the finale of the *Ad Simplicianum,*
when he moves abruptly from the text of Paul's letter as an exercise in
exegesis to the historical Paul — Paul *ad litteram* — in order to illustrate
his new convictions about God's grace, divine justice, and human freedom.
Conversion as progress from stage two to stage three, a movement from
sub lege to *sub gratia* that depended on man's *bona voluntas*, could not
accommodate the historical description of the premier convert of biblical
history, Saul of Tarsus. The Paul of the first chapter of Galatians
(*Exp.ep.Gal.* 7-9, on Gal. 1:13f.), the "persecutor and blasphemer" of I Tim.
1:13 and the foolish, impious and hateful man enslaved to various
pleasures of Titus 3:3 (both invoked in *Inchoata expositio* on Romans,
written just after the *Propositiones*), the Paul of Acts 9,[9] did not, could not
fit Augustine's earlier formulation. No preceding good will had prefaced
this conversion. Saul was no good, and unconflicted about it:

> What did Saul will but to attack, seize, bind and slay Christians?
> What a fierce, savage, blind will was that! Yet he was thrown
> prostrate by one word from on high, and a vision came to him
> whereby his mind and will were turned from their fierceness and set
> on the right way toward faith so that, suddenly, from a marvelous
> persecutor of the Gospel a more marvelous preacher was made.
> What then shall we say? . . . "Is there unrighteousness with God?
> God forbid!" (*Ad Simpl.* I, q.2,22).

Paul *ad litteram* embodies Augustine's awareness of God's inscrutability
when choosing whom to call.

C Augustine's interest in the "historical Paul."

C 397. Augustine is still fretting over Jerome's construal of Galatians 2, and sends him another letter (*Ep.* 40). Paul's text must be read as a straightforward account of a real dispute, he insists, "otherwise, the Holy Scripture, which has been given to preserve the faith of generations to come, would be wholly undermined and thrown into doubt, if the validity of lying were once admitted" (*Ep.* 40,5).[10] He sends Aurelius of Carthage a letter nudging him to get back with his opinion of Tyconius's *Liber.* (He may have dropped Tyconius's argument about foreknowledge of faith, but obviously he's still enthused.)[11] And finally he attempts a uniquely creative and original consideration of the theological themes that have begun seriously to preoccupy him: How do we know what we (think we) know, be it ourselves, each other, the world, a text, or God? How does creation bespeak revelation? How does the mind apprehend anything — outside itself, "inside" itself, and its self? In what ways does humanity's mode of existence, after Adam, separate it from God? What sort of bridge over this chasm does God offer through creation, through his Son, through the Church, and through the Scriptures?

H I am speaking, of course, of the *Confessions.* I simply note in passing that Augustine spends his first nine books constructing an Augustine *ad litteram,* writing an historical narrative of his own past to articulate his new theological convictions. The theme of divine inscrutability shapes much of the story, despite the fact that the whole is itself addressed to God. I also note, briefly, that as he dwells on epistemology and memory in Book X, and on the elusiveness of the infinitesimally divisible moment of consciousness that we call "the present" in Book XI (past and future do not exist; the present is an interval of no duration), he articulates a defining aspect of the absolute difference between God's mode of being and ours. God is eternal; we are divided up, distended in time: "You are my eternal Father, but I am scattered in times whose order I do not understand. The storms of incoherent events tear to pieces my thoughts, the inmost entrails of my soul. . . " (*Conf.* XI,xxix,39, trans. Chadwick). Coherence comes only through memory, the seat of the self, which integrates perception and experience. Knowledge and understanding *require* retrospect, since the Present — a knife edge of reality poised between two different kinds of nonbeing, the Past and the Future — slips by too fast. Since humanity is time-bound, it can encounter God only *in* time; but God is outside time. What stable bridge can traverse this chasm between eternity and temporality, God and man? Scripture alone.

> You [God] reply to me . . . " "O man, what my scriptures say, I say.
> Yet scripture speaks in time-conditioned language, and time does

---

C A period of rethinking.
H Time and eternity.

not touch my Word, existing with me in an equal eternity. So I see those things which through my Spirit you see, just as I also say the things which through my Spirit you say. Accordingly, while your vision of them is temporally determined, my seeing is not temporal, just as you speak of these things in temporal terms, but I do not speak in the successiveness of time " (*Conf.* XIII,xxix,44).[12]

Thus God alone is eternal and unchanging. Creation reveals him as Creator; but Scripture (as both Testaments), despite its intrinsic multivocality and the difficulties of interpretation, reveals the human encounter with the divine in history. Man after Adam — both his physical, mortal self, his body; and his nonmaterial self, his soul or mind or love — is now, constitutionally, time-bound, changing. And finally, human understanding itself, dependent on memory, is intrinsically narrative, historical.[13]

With all this as background, we come to the *Contra Faustum* (398) and our topic.

On Judaism, Against the Manichees

A The *massa peccati*, the universal consequence of the sin of Adam, is the negative obverse of the law. Once the exclusive privilege of Israel, the law in the age after the incarnation is of universal benefit, available to all the nations, thanks to the coming of Christ. Here, against the anti-Judaism both of his dualist opponents and of Catholic tradition itself, Augustine picks up on the positive things Paul has to say about the law. He maintains with Paul that the law, because God-given, is and always has been the means to salvation whose *finis* is Christ (Rom. 10:4). In essential ways (Tyconius helps him with this), the law *is* the gospel, revealed as such through Christ. We can see how Augustine makes his case through typological interpretation[14] on the one hand, and *interpretatio ad litteram* on the other.

Typological exegesis had long been a staple of the Christian interpretation of the Jewish scriptures. It was a technique of Christianization, a way to stake a claim for the church in the texts of the synagogue; and it was also a tool of polemic, since the Old Testament *typos* was often regarded as inferior to the Christological datum it prefigured.[15]

H Augustine's typology was similarly motivated: it too was polemical. But his target was different. He argued — but against Manichees, not Jews as such — that the entirety of the New Testament which they

---

A The law and salvation. Rom. 10:4.
H Theological conjoining of the Old and New Testament: the Law reveals the Gospel.

claimed to revere was prefigured in the Old Testament which they reviled and repudiated. Unlike the typologies of many of his predecessors, Augustine forbears derogatory comparisons when aligning Old Testament images with New. His view of the law as constant, God-given and good both before and after the coming of Christ, affects his tone: if the Old Testament is a concealed form of the New and vice versa, then they are alike in dignity and positive religious value. And this equal valence of his typologies (both sides of the equation are positive) in turn reinforces his reading *ad litteram.*

In his massive work against Latin Manichaeism, the *Contra Faustum,* Augustine explores in exhaustive detail the myriad figurations of Christ and his church to be found (if one knows how to read aright) in Jewish scripture. He begins by quoting the Manichees' favorite Apostle against them, citing Paul's enumeration of the privileges and prerogatives of Israel in Romans 9:4, among which is the law (XII,3-4). Then his review of the "most minute details" begins: as Eve was made from Adam's side while he slept, so the church was made by the blood of Christ which flowed from his side after his death (XII,8). Abel, the younger brother, was killed by Cain, the older brother; Christ, the head of the younger people (i.e., the Gentiles), was killed by the elder people, the Jews (XII,9). Noah and his family were saved by water and wood; the family of Christ, by baptism into his crucifixion (XII,14). All kinds of animals enter the ark, all nations the Church; the unclean animals enter in twos, just as the wicked within the church are in twos, meaning easily divided because of their tendency to schism (XII,15). The ark's entrance was on its side, and one enters the church by the sacrament of the remission of sins which flowed from Christ's opened side (XII,16). Scripture mentions the twenty-seventh day of the month; 27 is the cube of 3, hence typifying the Trinity (XII,19). Entering the ark at the beginning of travail, Noah and his sons were separated from their wives; exiting, the couples were together. This prefigures the resurrection of the flesh at the end of the world, when soul and body will be reunited after death in perfect harmony, a marriage undisturbed by the passions of mortality (XII,21). "The scriptures teem with such predictions" (XII,25). Whom then, concludes Augustine, should one believe: Faustus with his accusations, or Paul and his commendation (XII,24)?

The Old Testament thus prefigures the New. But it also has its own historical reality and integrity, and the symbolic complexity of spiritual interpretation should not obscure a straightforward reading of biblical narrative: this was Augustine's principle in interpreting *ad litteram.* We see this most clearly in his understanding of the Jewish people and their observance of the law in the biblical past. **H** Earlier fathers (again, Justin

---

H Earlier fathers condemned the Jews for keeping the law *secundum carnem.*

and Tertullian spring to mind), defending the Catholic appropriation of Jewish scriptures against the dualists of their day, had lauded the text while denigrating the people. Jewish praxis in particular had stood in patristic estimate as the behavioral index of their wrong-headed carnal scriptural interpretation. If the Jews, they said, had really understood what God intended by the law (in this view, either a veiled Christological meaning, or a punishment for their proverbial carnality and stony hearts), the last thing they would have done was embrace it as a privilege, or interpret it literally. Understood spiritually (so went the argument), the command to circumcise had nothing to do with body parts; food laws were not about eating or not eating certain things, and so on.

H Wrong, says Augustine. "The Jews were right to practice all these things" — blood sacrifices, purity rituals, food disciplines, Sabbath. Their only fault lay in not recognizing, once Christ came, that a new era — not a "new" law — had begun (XII,9). The law perdured, the same from Moses to Christ (XXII,6). By keeping it, the entire Jewish people "was like a great prophet" foretelling Christ not only in word but also in deed (XXII,24). God, in other words, despite the plenitude of meanings available in Scripture, was no allegorist when giving his mandates to Israel. Whatever else his Torah signified, in the time before Christ, it also prescribed behavior.

Especially that most distinctive and most reviled observance, fleshly circumcision, Augustine urged, embodied as an *actio prophetica* the central mystery of Christianity itself. What Paul had designated the "seal of the righteousness of faith" (Rom. 4:11) marked in the organ of generation the regeneration of the flesh made possible by the bodily coming of Christ in both incarnation and resurrection (VI,3).[16] Had Jews understood God's command *secundum spiritum* without performing it *secundum carnem* (as Justin and others would have wished), they would have only imperfectly prefigured the Christological *mysterium*. In giving his law, in other words, God had not said one thing and meant another. Thus Scripture, accordingly, did not say one thing and mean another — the same point about Peter's argument with Paul that Augustine had made when arguing over Galatians with Jerome. God had commanded Israel to keep the law *secundum carnem*, and so this they rightly did.

Further, insists Augustine — and here I draw as well on letters 40 and 82 to Jerome — Jesus himself was circumcised, kept the food laws, offered at the Temple, and observed the Sabbath; so also Peter, James, Paul, and all the other Jews of the first generation. Why wouldn't they? These enactments had always been incumbent upon Israel, and never upon Gentiles, which was precisely what the apostles' quarrel in Antioch had

---

H Augustine praises the Jews for keeping the law *secundum carnem*, including circumcision. Rom. 4:11.

been about. Once Christ came, the law no longer had to be enacted, since
it was revealed in him and in the sacraments of his church. But the
relation of Jewish observances and Christian sacrament was always one
of continuity, not contrast, and the Jewish apostles of the church's
founding generation had been right in their traditional observance of the
law, "lest by compulsory abandonment it should seem to be condemned
rather than closed" (*C.Faust.* XIX,17). An essential identity of divine
intent unites the testaments ("The same law that was given by Moses
became grace and truth in Jesus Christ" [XXII,6]). To read the Old
Testament otherwise was to miss what it, and consequently what the New
Testament, was actually about — precisely the mistake, argued Augustine, that the Manichees notoriously made.

I So much for ancient, biblical Jews, and for those Jews of the founding
generation of the Church, Jesus included. But what about contemporary
Jews, and current Jewish practice? On this topic Augustine is no
enthusiast; and in many other passages throughout his works — not least
of all his sermons on John's Gospel — he can be as hateful, hurtful and
vicious as Chrysostom, Cyril, or any other father of the Church.[17] But here
again, too, we see the impress of his originality, his commitment to the
idea of divine constancy,[18] and the effect of his reading and thinking *ad
litteram*, historically.

H Augustine's conviction that Judaism was essentially, uniquely
compatible with Christianity was expressed in the typological transparency that he saw between the testaments. But this transparency does not
extend beyond them: history as directly revelatory closes with the canon.[19]
Yet in the thick darkness of this long night of post-Biblical history — a night,
he urges, that is of unknowable duration[20] — Augustine imputes an
abidingly revelatory function to carnal Israel, precisely because of the
dogged Jewish loyalty to the traditional observance of the law. Under all
previous foreign powers, including Rome, Jews had clung to their own
practices; and with the coming of the church they remained the same. "It
is a most notable fact that all the nations subjugated by Rome adopted the
ceremonies of Roman worship; whereas the Jewish nation, whether under
pagan or Christian monarchs, has never lost the sign of their law, by
which they are distinguished from all other nations and peoples" (*C.Faust.*
XII,13). Augustine takes this as a great mystery, a situation caused by
God's *occulto iustoque iudicio* (*De fid.rer.* 6,9).

And Jews will remain Jews, Augustine avers, until the end of the age
(*C.Faust.* XII,12). Left behind as history, with Christ's coming, surged to
a new stage, the Jews themselves remained relevant to divine revelation
precisely through their "carnal" practice as witnesses to Christian truth.

I The theological status of current Jewish law-observance.
H The Jews have a permanent role in God's purposes.

As a textual community, Jews preserved the oracles of God; as a halakhic community, they embodied them. Their traditional practice enacts the blindness prophesied, together with Christianity, in the very books of unquestioned antiquity and authenticity which their scattered community treasures and, through its own dispersion, disseminates.[21]

> The unbelief of the Jews has been made of signal benefit to us, so that those who do not receive these truths in their heart for their own good nonetheless carry in their hands, for our benefit, the writings in which these truths are contained. And the unbelief of the Jews increases rather than lessens the authority of these books, for this blindness is itself foretold. They testify to the truth by their not understanding it (*C.Faust.* XVI,21).[22]

In consequence of their blindness to Christian truth, contemporary Jews, scattered and bereft of their commonwealth, live in constant anxiety, subjected to the immensely more numerous Christians; terrified, like Cain, of bodily death. But as God marked Cain for his protection, so through the law has he marked the Jews. Indeed, God himself protects them from murder, vowing seven-fold vengeance on would-be fratricides (that is, on the Jews' Gentile "brothers" who might harm them, XII,12). Nor may any Christian monarch coerce conversion, that is, "kill" Jews by forcing them to cease living as Jews: again, like Cain, the Jews stand under the protection of God (XII,13). Thus until the end of time, "the continued preservation of the Jews will be a proof to believing Christians of the subjection merited by those who, in the pride of their kingdom, put the Lord to death" (XII,12).

A But the very clarity of the Scriptural prophecies of Jewish unbelief, and their unambiguous confirmation, raised once again the constellation of questions that had dogged Augustine during his earlier reading of Romans. If the sin of unbelief is mandated by heaven (as in the case of Esau, Pharaoh, or anyone languishing *sub lege*), how is God just in punishing the sinner? Augustine's answers to these questions, as we have seen, had shifted dramatically between the Romans commentaries of 394/95 and his answer to Simplicianus in 396. In 394, the sinner had the freedom to resist God's offer of grace: this resistance had informed Augustine's definition of despair.[23] But by 396, grace was not only entirely unmerited; it was also utterly irresistible: "voluntati eius nullus resistit" (*Ad Simpl.* I, q. 2,17). Hence his depiction of Saul "thrown prostrate," wrenched involuntarily into a new life *sub gratia*, chosen through some divine standard of justice that remained, by human measure, inscrutable.[24]

A Why does God leave some people *sub lege?*

Where in the *Contra Faustum* Augustine considers the Jews, both ways of conceiving these issues appear. In one passage (XII,11), developing the theme of Cain the fratricide as a type of the Jews who killed Christ and who continue to resist the embrace of the Church, the pre-396 language of uncompromised volition creeps in. Jews are "the people who would not (*nolentis*) be under grace, but under the law." Their lack of faith, within this discourse, seems the result of choice, and thus a visibly merited punishment. But in another passage (XIII,11), considering Jewish freedom of choice in the perspective of prophecy, the question of God's justice again arose, since someone might object "that it was not the fault of the Jews if God blinded them so that they did not know Christ." In defense of divine justice, Augustine again invokes divine inscrutability. Jewish blindness, Augustine grants, is indeed a punishment, but not for the sin of killing Christ (for which, evidently, the punishment was their endless exile [XII,12 and frequently]). Their continuing blindness was a penalty, though for some other sin.[25] But what? God knows, says Augustine. We can with security only affirm his justice. He punishes Israel "ex aliis occultis peccatis Deo cognitis," because of "occulti eorum meriti" (*C.Faust.* XIII,11); their blindness is God's "occulta vindicta" (*En.Ps.* 68,26); they are punished "occultioribus causis" (*De fid.rer.* 6,9).[26]

Continuing Jewish practice, then, for Augustine, is a mysterium. As carnal Israel, and only as carnal Israel, the Jews' eschatological status remains, and their religious significance as a witness to Christian truth is unambiguous. But as children of Adam, Jews are just people; and like the rest of the *massa damnata*, they languish *sub lege*.[27] Whether God chooses to leave them or to bring some *sub gratia*, he does so, for them as for anyone, for inscrutable reasons, but justly. The conversion of some Jews to Christianity in the time before the end thus has no eschatological significance whatever since, as a people, Israel as Israel shall endure until the end of the age (XII,12).

A Augustine's views on the continuous revelatory status of Israel throughout history is of a piece with his defense against the Manichees of the revelatory status of the Old Testament and the intrinsic intimacy of its relation to the New. It enables him to insist on historical simplicity and even a peculiar realism when interpreting the Bible *ad litteram* (for example, saying that God meant what he said when commanding Israel, or when praising Israel for its faithfulness to the law). But even his more figurative typological readings, when he matches events between Old Testament and New, take on an intensely dramatic dimension. The Old Testament might indeed prefigure the New, but this is no bloodless correspondence of things signifying with things signified: the actors in the history of Israel remain firmly rooted in their own time even as their

---

A History and typology in the Christian reading of the Old Testament.

words and actions point ahead to Christ. Consider this rendering (*De civ.Dei* XVI,37, Bettenson tr.) of the scene in Genesis 27 when Isaac realizes that he has given Esau's blessing to Jacob. First Augustine gives the language of the blessing, Gen. 27:27ff:

> Behold, says Isaac, the smell of my son is like the smell of a plentiful field which the Lord has blessed. And may God give you of the dew of heaven and of the richness of the soil, and abundance of corn and wine, and may nations serve you and princes do reverence to you. Become lord over your brother, and your father's sons will do reverence to you. Whoever curses you, let him be cursed; and whoever blesses you, let him be blessed.

Next comes the Christological decoding. Augustine continues,

> Thus the blessing of Jacob is the proclamation of Christ among all nations. This is happening; this is actively going on. Isaac is the Law and the Prophets, and Christ is blessed by the Law and the Prophets, even by the lips of the Jews, as by someone who does not know what he is doing....The world is filled like a field with the fragrance of the name of Christ....It is Christ whom the nations serve, and to whom princes do reverence. He is lord over his brother, since his people [the Gentiles] have dominion over the Jews. . . .Our Christ, I repeat, is blessed, that is, he is truly spoken of, even by the lips of the Jews who, although in error, still chant the Law and the Prophets. They suppose that another is being blessed, the Messiah whom they in their error still await.

Then, abruptly, we stand face-to-face with the historical patriarch:

> Look at Isaac! He is horror-stricken when his elder son asks for the promised blessing, and he realizes that he has blessed another in his place. He is amazed, and asks who this other can be; and yet he does not complain that he has been deceived. Quite the contrary. The great mystery [*sacramentum*] is straightway revealed to him, in the depths of his heart, and he eschews indignation and confirms his blessing. "Who then," he says, "hunted game for me and brought it in to me? And I ate all of it, before you arrived! Well, I have blessed him, so let him be blessed." One would surely expect at this point the curse of an angry man, if this happened in the ordinary course of events, instead of by inspiration from above. Historical events, these, but events with prophetic meaning! Events on earth, but directed from heaven! The actions of men, but the operation of God!

H When Augustine returns to the status of contemporary Israel in Book XVIII of *The City of God*, he again invokes his teaching on the Jews as witness, as such to be left unmolested. But this time he invokes Ps. 59:12 as a proof text: "Slay them not, lest your people forget; scatter them with your might" (*De civ. Dei* XVIII,46). Why?[28] Perhaps violence against Jewish communities in the Empire, mounting as the law codes of Christian emperors increasingly lumped them together with pagans and heretics, had inspired him to crystallize his teaching around this verse.[29] But since the doctrine itself, as I have argued here, seems a development internal to Augustine's theological battle against Manichees, as opposed to religious or social encounters with real Jews (here I part company with Blumenkranz[30]), it might be hazardous to venture connections to social causes that cannot be established from our evidence.

C I will close here by noting, rather, how *The City of God* brings together so many of the master themes of Augustine's teaching that he first articulated in the burst of self-confident creativity that followed (and followed from) his response to Simplicianus with its historical sketch of the apostle Paul: his reading of Genesis *ad litteram*, successfully undertaken just after our period; the *Contra Faustum*, with its comprehensive rereading of the role of Jews and Judaism in biblical narrative and contemporary history; the opacity of extra-biblical history and, accordingly, the non-millenarian reading of seemingly millenarian texts (like John's Apocalypse! again his debt to Tyconius emerges); the controlling historicized metaphor of the *massa* from Romans 9. **I** The relationship of all these themes is coordinate, symphonic. The fleshly body is and always was, *ab initio*, the native home of the soul: Adam and Eve were created both body and soul together; and the body of flesh, reunited with the soul, would participate in final redemption. So also with exegesis. The Bible must be read both for its inner meanings (*secundum spiritum*) and for its historical meanings (*ad litteram*). As with exegesis, so with biblical Judaism: Historical periods have their own importance and integrity, since God works in and through a history that the Scriptures preserve; and thus in the time before the incarnation, Jews did right to incarnate the law *secundum carnem*, literally and not just spiritually. Exegesis, history, anthropology: all three stand together.

Augustine's creative theology of history, together with his reading *ad litteram*, led him further to construct a sort of social semiotics of carnal Israel that he applied across biblical epochs and into quotidian history. The Jewish people throughout the ages, he insists, were the unique recipients of biblical revelation; and even with the closing of the canon and their rejection of Christianity, they still stood as a living sign locating

---

H Jews and Jewish observances stand under the protection of God.
C *The City of God* as a summation of earlier insights.
I The relationship of all the frames in a "social semiotics" of Israel after the flesh.

God's will in human time. This orientation toward Jews and Judaism expressed Augustine's conviction that the New Testament and the Old — like soul and body, like spiritual and historical understanding — were intimately, fundamentally, essentially connected. The task of the believing reader was to see how.

Notes

1. The present essay draws on a larger work in progress on Augustine's theological development in the 390s and the ways that it led to his original teaching on Jews and Judaism. My earlier preliminary studies specifically on Jews and Judaism, with extensive documentation, may be found in Fredriksen 1995 and 1999. As I will argue here, Augustine's views on Jews and Judaism arise out of his arguments against Manichaean anthropology and biblical hermeneutics, and his own evolving theology of history: hence the importance of the letters and the figure of Paul, and the exegetical principles of Tyconius. For convenience, I will refer to my own earlier essays on these topics, where readers will find fuller documentation and argument. Finally, I would like to thank Professor Jeremy Cohen, whose criticism of these earlier essays in his article (1998, 86ff.) helped me to sharpen my argument here.

2. A time line will help to visualize the close sequence of events and treatises that this essay will explore:

386	conversion in Milan
389	*De Genesi contra Manichaeos*
391	inducted into clergy at Hippo
392	debate *Contra Fortunatum*
393	*De Genesi ad litteram imperfectus liber*
394/95	reads Tyconius's *Liber regularum* (?)
	Propositiones ex epistulam ad Romanos; *Epistulae ad Romanos inchoata expositio*; *Expositio epistulae ad Galatas*; *De mendacio*
	Ep. 28 to Jerome on Galatians 2
395	consecrated co-adjutor bishop
	qq. 66–68 of *De 83 diversis quaestionibus*
	finishes *De libero arbitrio*
396	death of Valerius
	Ad Simplicianum
	begins *De doctrina christiana*
397	*Ep.* 40 to Jerome, again on Galatians
	Ep. 41 to Aurelius, prodding him for response on Tyconius' *Liber regularum*, "sicut saepe iam scripsi"
	Confessions
397/98	*Contra Faustum*
401–14	*De Genesi ad litteram*
404	receives *Ep.* 75 from Jerome accusing him of Judaizing
405	*Ep.* 82 to Jerome on Torah observance
410	Vandal invasion of Rome; apocalyptic panic (*Serm.* 16,8)
413/27	*De civitate Dei*
	outbreak of Pelagian controversy: attention focused again on Genesis and Paul
418	correspondence with Hesychius on Parousia (*Epp.* 197–99)
425 (?)	*Tractatus adversus Iudaeos*

3. *Sane quisquis voluerit omnia quae dicta sunt secundum litteram accipere, id est non aliter intellegere, quam littera sonat, et potest evitare blasphemias et omnia congruentia fidei catholicae praedicare, non solum ei non est invidendum, sed praecipuus multumque laudabilis intellector habendus est* (*De Gen.c.Man.* II,ii,3; PL 34:197).

4. On Augustine's struggle to find his feet in this period — aptly diagnosed by James J. O'Donnell as the "writers' block" years — see O'Donnell 1992, I: xlii-xliii, and Fredriksen 1999, 32-33.

5. For analysis of his argument see Fredriksen 1988, 94–98 and 103ff., and Malafioti 1981. Drecoll 1999 offers a fresh consideration, integrating Augustine's philosophical concerns into his reconstruction.

6. Augustine's comment on Romans 9 in his earlier essay, *De div.quaest.* q. 68,4, reveals the trajectory of his thought. There he states, concerning God's hardening of Pharaoh's heart, "He has mercy on whom he will, and he hardens whom he will; but there cannot be injustice with God. *Venit enim de* **occultissimis meritis**; *quia et ipsi peccatores cum propter generale peccatum* **unam massam** *fecerint, non tamen nulla est inter illos diversitas.*" This juxtaposition of the *massa*, Adam's sin, and the extreme hiddenness of God's criteria of judgment recurs frequently in the closing passages of the *Ad Simplicianum*, e.g, I, q.2,16 (*occultae aequitatis; massa peccati; aequitate occultissima*), 19 (*ex Adam massa peccatorum*), 22 (*occulta electio; inscrutabilia iudicia*). For the development of Augustine's ideas on the *massa* in this period, see Fredriksen 1988, 96. Rist (1994, 126–29) remarks astutely on the ways that Augustine's view of humanity's being "in Adam" as "an historical fact" complicates his ideas of personal identity.

7. For the modern historiographical problems caused by looking at this moment in Paul's career as a "conversion," and the ways that the authority both of Acts and of Augustine combine to complicate the matter, see my earlier essay, Fredriksen 1986.

8. For a review of this correspondence with these issues in mind, see Fredriksen, 1999, 37–39, and, particularly as these letters touch on the question of biblical authority, Cole-Turner 1980.

9. See, on the references to Paul's conversion in Acts that appear and cluster in the works of the 390s, Leroy 1986, esp. the charts, 17–21, and Ferrari 1982, esp. 156–68; cf. the remarks in Delaroche 1996, 98–102.

10. This thought echoes in his *Sermo super verbis Apostoli ad Galatas,* preached in 397. Dolbeau, who edited the sermon and relates it to Augustine's correspondence with Jerome, comments that Augustine "ne modifia nullement ses positions, de peur laisser une porte ouverte aux critiques scripturaires des Manichéens" (1992, 48).

11. Whence Augustine's continued enthusiasm? Though he has dropped Tyconius' construction of divine foreknowledge, he keeps the other points from the *Liber* that are more fundamental to his reading of the Bible: the continuity of the single dispensation of redemption across historical epochs — in other words, the fundamental unity of Old and New Testament, law and grace; and the de-eschatologizing of current history, so that the present is opaque and only the biblical past revelatory of the divine plan. The first point will effect particularly his positive typologies between the testaments in the *Contra Faustum*; the second, his presentation of his own past, understood only in retrospect, in the *Confessions.* See further below, n. 21.

12. *O homo, nempe quod mea scriptura dicit, ego dico, et tamen illa temporaliter dicit, uerbo autem meo tempus non accedit, quia aequali mecum aeternitate consistit. Sic ea, quae uos per spiritum meum uidetis, ego uideo, sicut ea quae uos per spiritum meum dicitis, ego dico. Atque ita cum uos temporaliter ea uideatis, non ego temporaliter uideo, quemadmodum, cum uos temporaliter ea dicatis, non ego temporaliter dico* (*CC* 27: 268).

13. For the relation of time, understanding, and memory, see XI,xiv,17–xxi,27; "I know myself to be conditioned by time," xxv,32; language, time and memory, xxvii,35; a beautiful conflation of the images of creation and a book, XIII,xv,16; on non-temporal (thus non-linguistic) angelic apprehension, XIII,xv,18; the literal and allegorical meanings of the text "Increase and multiply," 24,37.

14. In her assessment of allegory, typology and history, Frances Young points out that typology is first of all a hermeneutic of intertextuality, of textual correspondences, and "historicity" is not a criterion appropriate to identifying typology as a figure of speech (Young 1994, 48; cf. her analysis of Melito's *Peri Pascha*, 34–37, with that of J. Cohen, 1998, 89–91). It is specifically Tyconius's typology, adopted and adapted by Augustine through his more complex theology of history and *interpretatio ad litteram*, that makes the *Contra Faustum* the showcase of historical typology it is; and this, in turn, reinforces and even enables Augustine's positive "theology of Judaism" there.

15. For a brief review of the earlier, mainstream *contra Iudaeos* tradition as represented by Justin and Tertullian, see Fredriksen 1995, 313–15; 1999, 27–31; and the literature cited in the notes.

16. See further on this point Fredriksen 1999, 35–36. On Augustine's historical understanding of Scripture as a technique of biblical interpretation against the Manichees, Bonner 1986, 218–24; on the philosophical complexities of interpretation and epistemology more generally, Rist 1994, 23–40.

17. I would like to thank Professor David P. Efroymson for sharing with me his essay (1999), which includes a careful analysis of Augustine's rhetoric of abuse in those sermons. It is a sad comment on the strength and power of classical theology's anti-Judaism that the same man who produced the historical arguments against Faustus could and did author the vituperation that shapes these sermons on the Fourth Gospel.

18. This prime (biblical) theological idea particularly concerned not only Augustine, and of course Tyconius (esp. in Book III of the *Liber regularum*, "de promissis et lege"), but also the historical Paul himself, whose letter to the Romans seeks to answer how God's promises to and election of Israel can be affirmed in light of the new revelation in Christ; see Fredriksen 2000.

19. This theme of the eschatological opacity of the present dominates Book 20 of the *City of God*. See Fredriksen 1991a, 163-65, on the Tyconian sources of Augustine's view on subjective, interior opacity in the *Confessions*, pp. 165-67 for his application of these principles to public history in *De civ. Dei*.

20. It was Tyconius in the *Liber regularum* — and, if Augustine read it, in his now-lost commentary on Apocalypse — who showed him the way to read traditionally apocalyptic biblical texts as symbolic descriptions of quotidian Christian society, and who enunciated as a principle of biblical interpretation the impossibility of calculating the time of the End. No small benefit, considering that Augustine lived in one of the cultural hot zones of apocalyptic enthusiasm, Roman North Africa, and in one of the named chronological hot zones, which a specifically African chronographical tradition (Julius Africanus, Lactantius, Hilarianus) had named as the expected date of the year 6000, and thus of the Second Coming; see Fredriksen 1982 and 1991a. Aurelius would have been no less aware of the dangers of apocalyptic enthusiasm than Augustine; and the hermeneutic made available by Tyconius, as well as his anti-perfectionist (hence anti-Donatist) ecclesiology, would have more than accounted for Augustine's enthusiasm in *Ep*. 41.

21. Hence his image of the Jewish nation as both witness to the Church and as a *scriniaria*, a "desk for Christians," "baiulans legem et prophetas ad testimonium assertionis ecclesiae, ut nos honoremus per sacramentum quod nuntiat illa per litteram" (*C.Faust*. XII,23; *PL* 42:266).

22. *Nec inde auctoritas illis libris minuitur, quod a Iudaeis non intelligentur; imo et augetur: nam et ipsa eorum caecitas ibi praedicta est. Unde magis non intelligendo veritatem perhibent* **testimonium veritati***: quia cum eos libros non intelligunt, a quibus non intellecturi praedicti sunt, etiam hinc eos veraces ostendunt* (*PL* 42: 329).

23. On despair as the sin against the Holy Spirit which can never be forgiven, see *Inch.exp*. 22,3-4; for discussion, Fredriksen 1995, 307ff.

24. Hence Augustine's appeal to Paul's hymn to divine inscrutability in Rom. 11:33, cited *Ad Simpl*. I, q. 2,16.

25. *C.Faust*. XII,9-14 develops at length the typological comparison of Cain and the Jews, specifically with reference to their continued existence. There, too, Augustine affirms that contemporary Jews are "cursed," but distinguishes the reason for the curse (which remains unclear) from his description of its effects, i.e., continued Torah-observance: "The Church admits and avows the Jewish people to be cursed, because after killing Christ they continue to till the ground of an earthly circumcision, an earthly Sabbath, an earthly Passover. . . " XIII,11).

26. This paragraph draws on my earlier discussion, Fredriksen 1995, 318-20; cf. the comments of Cohen 1998, 88, 91, and n. 30.

27. *Una est enim ex Adam massa peccatorum et impiorum, in qua et Iudaei et Gentes remota gratia Dei ad unam pertinent conspersionem* (*Ad Simpl*. I, q. 2,19).

28. Jeremy Cohen, who identifies the anti-Pelagian period as the significant context for Augustine's "witness doctrine," has repeatedly argued that until Augustine began using Psalm 59:12, his teaching on the Jews was not "fully in place" or "fully ripe" (Cohen 1998, 91, reprised in Cohen 1999, 30-65). The elegance of Augustine's proof-text, and the regularity with which he repeats it once he has it, has misled Cohen. If anything, Augustine's teaching on the Jews and on the positive value for the church of their continued law observance appears *more* fully in the *C.Faustum*, where he speaks not only of the benefits that Jews as witnesses render currently, in the present — the focus likewise of his discussion in *De civ.Dei* — but also of the prophetic function of such observance in the distant past, the period before Christ, and the pedagogical function of such observances by both Jesus and his apostles in the first generation of the church. Cohen misses the broader historical sweep of the *C. Faustum's* witness doctrine in part because he miscontrues Augustine's invocation there of the image of Cain ("the

standard patristic Cain of the *Contra Faustum*...," Cohen 1999, 55). Standard patristic usage sees Cain as a type for the Jews, who oppose either Christ or his church: the force of the image is quintessentially negative. Utterly original is Augustine's positive view of Cain as the bearer of God's "mark," the sign by which God seals Cain's/the Jews' safekeeping: the perpetual fleshly observances of the law, which in turn define the Jews *as* Jews, that is, as witnesses to Christ (XII,13). Cohen's misconstrual of the image of Cain in the *C.Faustum* contributes to his distraction by the later Psalms proof text. To claim that the full formulation of Augustine's teaching on Jews and Judaism had to wait for his discovery of Ps. 59:12 is a mistake similar to saying that his teaching on original sin had to wait for his misinterpretation of Rom. 5:12 ("in quo omnes peccaverunt"), or that his teaching on the relation of will and grace (already articulated in the *Ad Simplicianum*) was not fully present until he began to quote Proverbs 8:35 ("praeparatur voluntas a deo"). On Augustine's proof-texting, and its relation to the way he formulates his arguments, see further Rist 1994, 124 and n. 93.

29. It is difficult to trace with any certainty the relationship of imperial legislation, whether affirming or eroding the centuries-long tradition of protection for Jewish religious practice, to actual outbursts of anti-Jewish activity, as the growing dossier of studies of this question attests. On the place of Jews within Roman society, the classic study is Juster 1914, supplemented by the authoritative discussions of specifically Christian views in Blumenkranz 1946 and Simon 1948; see too Blumenkranz 1958. Linder has gathered the relevant source materials in his excellent compendium (1987). This material is analyzed by Vogler 1979, 35-74; for a revisionist interpretation of the effect of this legislation, see Bachrach 1985, 399-421. See Fredriksen 1995, 321ff. and the material cited in nn. 60-67 for the situation specifically in Augustine's North Africa. On the campaign to convert the Jews of Minorca following the advent of St. Stephen's relics in 416, see now the edition, translation, and analysis in Bradbury 1996, with its valuable Bibliography (132-41). I see no warrant for Bori's opinion that "only the absence of actual opportunities prevented [Augustine] from acting as Ambrose of Milan in the affair of the synagogue of Callinicum" (Bori 1983, 310). Both he and Blumenkranz, whom he cites (1946, 212), infer from Augustine's positive views on the state coercion of heretics that he would also have sanctioned such against Jews. As I hope I have demonstrated here, Jews play a unique role in Augustine's theology, utterly different from that of heretics and Donatists; and he specifically disavows violence against Jews, be it popular or governmental, in *C.Faust.* XII,12. See too the property dispute that he adjudicates between a Jew and a fellow bishop, *Ep.**8, with full analysis by Castritius 1987.

30. See Fredriksen 1995, 320-24. Blumenkranz and Simon had both posited competitive missions on the part of Jewish and Christian communities as a fundamental reason for Christian anti-Judaism. Recent scholarship has questioned such a construal, arguing that, while Judaism in principle received converts, it did not mount missions to attract them. For a representative statement of the older view, see Feldman 1993; for the view that Judaism was not a missionary religion, see *inter alia* Cohen 1989; Fredriksen 1991, esp. 535-48; Goodman 1994; and Taylor 1995. The essay critiquing this last book, Carleton Paget 1997, serves also as a bibliographical survey and review of the *status quaestionis.*

Bibliography

Babcock, W.S. 1989. *Tyconius: The Book of Rules*. Atlanta: Scholars Press.

Bachrach, B.S. 1985. "The Jewish Community of the Later Roman Empire as Seen in the Codex Theodosianus." Pp. 399-421 in *"To See Ourselves as Others See Us": Christians, Jews, "Others" in Late Antiquity*. Ed. J. Neusner and E.S. Frerichs. Chico: Scholars Press, 1985.

Bettenson, Henry (tr.). 1984. Augustine, *Concerning the City of God against the Pagans*. Harmondsworth: Penguin Books.

Blumenkranz, Bernhard. 1946. *Die Judenpredigt Augustins*. Basel: Helbing & Lichtenhahn.

————. 1958. "Augustin et les juifs. Augustin et le judaisme." *Recherches augustiniennes* 1: 225-41.

Bonner, Gerald. 1986. *St. Augustine of Hippo: Life and Controversies*. Revised Edition. Norwich: Canterbury Press.

Bori, P.C. 1983. "The Church's Attitude toward the Jews: An Analysis of Augustine's 'Adversus Iudaeos'" Pp. 301-11 in *Miscellania Historiae Ecclesiasticae*. Brussels.

Bradbury, Scott. 1996. *Severus of Minorca. Letter on the Conversion of the Jews*. Oxford: Clarendon Press.

Brown, Peter. 1967. *Augustine of Hippo*. Berkeley: University of California Press.

Carleton Paget, J. 1997. "Anti-Judaism and Early Christian Identity." *Zeitschrift für Antikes Christentum* 1: 195-225.

Castritius, H. 1987. 'Seid weder den Juden noch den Heiden noch der Gemeinde Gottes ein Ärgernis' (1. Kor. 10,32): Zur sozialen und rechtlichen Stellung der Juden im spätrömischen Nordafrika." Pp. 47-67 in *Antisemitismus und jüdische Geschichte*, ed. R. Erb and M. Schmidt. Berlin: Wissenschaftlicher Autorenverlag.

Cohen, S.J.D. 1989. "Crossing the Boundary and Becoming a Jew." *Harvard Theological Review* 82: 13-33.

Cohen, Jeremy. 1998. "'Slay Them Not': Augustine and the Jews in Modern Scholarship." *Medieval Encounters* 4: 78-92.

————. 1999. *Living Letters of the Law: Ideas of the Jew in Medieval Christianity*. Berkeley: University of California Press.

Cole-Turner, R.S. 1980. "Anti-Heretical Issues and the Debate over Galatians 2:11-14 in the Letters of St. Augustine and St. Jerome." *Augustinian Studies* 11: 155-66.

Delaroche, Bruno. 1996. *S. Augustin lecteur et interprète de S. Paul*. Paris: Institut d'Études Augustiniennes.

Dolbeau, François. 1992. "Sermons inédits de saint Augustin prêchés en 397." *Revue bénédictine* 102:44-74.

Drecoll, V.H. 1999. *Die Entstehung der Gnadenlehre Augustins*. Tübingen: Mohr Siebeck.

Efroymson, David P. 1999. "Whose Jews? Augustine's *Tractatus* on John." Pp. 197-211 in *A Multiform Heritage*, ed. Benjamin G. Wright. Atlanta: Scholars Press.

Feldman, L. 1993. "Proselytism by Jews in the Third, Fourth, and Fifth Centuries." *Journal for the Study of Judaism* 24: 1-58.

Ferrari, Leo. C. 1982. "Saint Augustine on the Road to Damascus." *Augustinian Studies* 13:151-70.

Fredriksen, Paula. 1982. "Tyconius and the End of the World." *Revue des études augustiniennes* 28: 59-75.

————. 1986. "Paul and Augustine: Conversion Narratives, Orthodox Traditions, and the Retrospective Self." *Journal of Theologial Studies* 37: 3-34.

————. 1988. "Beyond the Body/Soul Dichotomy: Augustine on Paul against the Manichees and the Pelagians." *Recherches augustiniennes* 23: 87-114

————. 1991a. "Apocalypse and Redemption in Early Christianity, from John of Patmos to Augustine of Hippo." *Vigiliae Christianae* 45: 151-83.

————. 1991b. "Judaism, the Circumcision of Gentiles, and Apocalyptic Hope." *Journal of Theological Studies* 42:532-64.

————. 1995. "*Excaecati Occulta Iustitia Dei*: Augustine on Jews and Judaism." *Journal of Early Christian Studies* 3:299-324.

————. 1999. "*Secundum Carnem*: History and Israel in the Theology of St. Augustine." Pp. 24-41 in *The Limits of Ancient Christianity: Essays on Late Antique Thought and Culture in Honor of R.A. Markus.* Ed. W. Klingshirn and M. Vessey. Ann Arbor: University of Michigan Press.

————. 2000. "Allegory and Reading God's Book: Paul and Augustine on the Destiny of Israel." Pp. 125-149 in *Interpretation and Allegory.* Ed. Jon Whitman. Laiden: Brill.

Goodman, Martin. 1994. *Mission and Conversion. Proselytizing in the Religious History of the Roman Empire.* Oxford: Clarendon Press.

Juster, Jean. 1914. *Les Juifs dans l'Empire Romain.* 2 Vols. Paris: P. Geuthner.

Leroy, Guy. 1986. 'Saul, Saul, pourquoi me persécutes-tu?' Ac 9,4b dans la prédication de Saint Augustin," Institut d'études théologiques, section francophone. Mémoire de Licence, Bruxelles 1986, dactylographié.

Linder, Amnon. 1987. *The Jews in Roman Imperial Legislation.* Detroit: Wayne State University Press.

Marafioti, D. 1981. "Il problema dell' '*Initium fidei*' in sant'Agostino fino al 397." *Augustinianum* 21: 541-65.

O'Donnell, James J. 1992. *Augustine: Confessions.* 3 Vols. Oxford: Clarendon Press.

Rist, J.M. 1994. *Augustine: Ancient Thought Baptized.* Cambridge: Cambridge University Press, 1994.

Simon, Marcel. 1948. *Verus Israel: Étude sur les relations entre Chrétiens et Juifs dans l'empire Romain (135-425).* Paris: E. de Boccard.

Taylor, M. 1995. *Anti-Judaism and Early Christian Identity. A Critique of the Consensus.* Leiden: E.J. Brill.

Vogler, C. 1979. "Les juifs dans le code théodosien." Pp. 35-74 in *Les Chrétiens devant le fait Juif.* Paris: Beauchesne.

Young, Frances. "Typology." Pp. 29-48 in *Crossing the Boundaries: Essays in Biblical Interpretation in Honour of Michael D. Goulder.* Leiden: E.J. Brill. 1994.

THREE

Exploring the Inner Conflict

Augustine's Sermons on Romans 7 and 8

Eugene TeSelle*

———— ◆ ————

A Does Romans 7 refer to life under the law or to the Christian life? Is it to be understood *autobiographically*, as referring to Paul himself? Or *psychologically*, as referring to human experience more generally? Or *objectively*, as describing a real situation which does not necessarily correspond with personal experience? **C** Augustine always understood the chapter experientially. And when he applied it to the Christian life he intensified his awareness of — and expectations of — ongoing conflict and struggle within the Christian.

A The exact import of Romans 7 is not readily apparent.[1] **C** There are some classic alternatives, and Augustine changed his mind several times.[2]

In his first expositions of Romans during the years 394–396 he assumed that Paul in Romans 7 refers to life under the law. The law shows human beings that, because of sin, they are unable to achieve what is commanded. This leads them to repent and seek divine grace, which at last enables them to fulfill what the law requires.[3]

But in 397 Augustine becomes convinced that grace plays the initiating role.[4] **A** Texts from Paul — especially Romans 9:13 — were crucial in persuading him. But Paul's own conversion (as presented, not by Paul, but by Luke in Acts 9) was also an important factor. If Saul, in the midst of seizing and slaying Christians, could be humbled by a word from on

---

* This essay is reprinted, in a condensed form, from *Collectanea Augustiniana*, Volume V, *Augustine: Biblical Exegete* (New York: Peter Lang, 2000), pp. 333–65. Reprinted with permission of the Augustinian Historical Institute, Villanova.

A A plurality of possible analytical frame for the meaning of Romans 7.
C Augustine's intensified awareness of conflict.
A Conflicting textual analyses of Romans 7.
C Augustine's successive interpretations.
A The text suggests a key change in interpretation. Rom. 9:13.

high and be led to faith, it is convincing evidence of the role of grace (*De div. quaest. ad Simpl.* I, q. 2,22). **C** This new emphasis on grace does not have any immediate impact, however, on Augustine's interpretation of Romans 7; he still seems to assume that the struggle is prior to conversion, not after it. But there is an intensified interest in the inward dynamics of the human self, and it is not surprising that Augustine wrote his *Confessions* at this same time.

A Two decades later, in the sermons being considered here, Augustine comes to a different interpretation of Romans 7: in this chapter, he now thinks, Paul refers to the Christian life, in which, despite grace — or rather because of it — there is a heightened *conflict* within the self between obedience and sin. The clinching argument is that only those who feel God's grace can genuinely "delight in the law" (Rom. 7:22) and therefore struggle against sin.[5]

C There are other ways of reading Romans 7. Rudolf Bultmann, while he agreed that Paul refers in this chapter to life under the law, opposed the "psychological" interpretation. Paul knew that, far from failing, he was blameless under the law (Phil 3:6) and able to establish a righteousness of his own (Rom. 10:3). In denying that he was a sinner he demonstrated how sin can misuse the law and pervert it into a rival way of salvation. Paul in retrospect condemns his very zeal for the law, for his situation is now one of having been justified — declared righteous by the divine judge — in the last times (Bultmann 1951, 246-49; 1967, 16, 24, 33-48; Meyer 1990). **A** Augustine was not unaware of this dimension of Paul's theology; like Bultmann, he saw that when Paul speaks of "flesh" he refers to all forms of human self-reliance and self-assertion, even the highest forms of moral and religious zeal (*Serm.* 153,8).

A Another alternative to the "psychological" interpretation, but quite different from Bultmann's, comes from the "Scandinavian school" (Munck 1959; Stendahl 1976; Fredriksen 1986 and 1988). For them the framework is the "history of salvation." Life under the law, to be sure, is superseded by life in Christ. But God's purpose in all of this is not primarily to resolve a psychological or moral or religious conflict, but to include both Jews and Gentiles in God's saving purpose. **C** Even Paul's own experience, reported quite differently in Galatians 2 and Acts 9, is to be interpreted not as an individual "conversion" but as a call to apostleship directed toward all the nations.

C Lack of immediate impact on Augustine's total interpretation of Romans 7.
A Two decades later, a major change of interpretation. Rom. 7:22.
C How did Paul understand himself when writing Romans 7? Rom. 10:3.
A The meaning of Paul's language about "flesh."
A A different framework of interpretation.
C Paul's experience: conversion or call to apostleship.

H Augustine was aware of this dimension of Paul. In the sermons to be discussed here, he saw the Old Testament as an anticipation of the New, Israel as an anticipation of the Church (*Serm.* 152,7; 155,3-6); even where there is a contrast between the two, the same Spirit is at work (*Serm.* 155,6; 156,14). The narrative of the Canaanite woman is interpreted as prefiguring the Gentile mission that was still to come (*Serm.* 154/A [Morin IV],5).

Even more to the point, Augustine thought in terms of four successive "ages" in the spiritual history of the human race: "before the law," when there was ignorance of sin; "under the law," when sin is made known by the law; "under grace," when grace defeats sin, but does not entirely conquer it; and "in peace," when perfect harmony will at last be gained in eternal life.[6]

H There is, nonetheless, a fundamental difference between Augustine and the Scandinavian school. The Augustinian emphasis, we might say, sees the broader history of humanity as *the life of the self writ large*, always retaining its psychological or moral overtones. The Scandinavian school, by contrast, sees Augustine's moral and psychological interests as *the wider history of salvation writ small* — but erroneously, through misinterpretation.[7] **H** For them, even the strong language of Romans 7 is to be understood not as a psychological cry for help or an autobiographical reliving of an earlier experience, but as a rhetorical reinforcement of the larger argument of the epistle to the Romans (Stendahl 1960, reprinted 1976; Fredriksen 1986). For Stendahl, Paul is merely observing the obvious difference between what we ought to do and what we actually do. The problem, he says, is this:

> Unfortunately — or fortunately — Paul happened to express this supporting argument so well that what to him and his contemporaries was a common sense observation appeared to later interpreters to be a most penetrating insight into the nature of man and into the nature of sin (Stendahl 1976, 93).

H Paula Fredriksen, who is similarly convinced that Augustine's interpretation of Romans 7 was erroneous, suggests at least two ways in which it was a fruitful mistake. Not only did he go beyond the view, typical in the ancient world, that human being is "a soul occupying a body," by appropriating the body and internalizing its inclinations (Fredriksen 1988, 112). In addition, by reinterpreting the more cosmic dimensions of Paul's thinking (especially his mention of "creation

---

H Augustine's hermeneutical framework.
H A conflict over interpretive frameworks.
H The text's relation to experience, ancient and modern. Rom. 8:22.
H Augustine's interpretation: a fruitful mistake?

groaning in travail" in Rom. 8:22) he freed himself of "late antiquity's map
of the cosmos" and offered a concept of the human person that "could
survive Galileo's revolution and so endure, meaningfully, to our own day"
(Fredriksen 1988, 113).

Perhaps even more can be said in Augustine's behalf. He did not
isolate human subjectivity from the broader issues of human history. As
The City of God abundantly demonstrates, he was responsive to the whole
scope of human life as he knew it. His own conviction was that everything
in human history is to be understood as the expression of desires and fears
and potentialities that we also experience within ourselves.

The Sermons

C It has long been recognized that Sermons 151-156 have a unity, even
in the manuscript tradition. The sermons were preached in Carthage, in
several different basilicas whose names are noted by the stenographers.
They go through Romans 7 and 8 more or less sequentially. But
Augustine leaps ahead to Romans 8:3-4 in Sermon 152, probably because
he sees Romans 8 as the key to Romans 7, or, more precisely, sees the
three meanings of the law (the law of works or the letter, the law of sin
and death, and the law of the Spirit of life) as the key to the entire section.
Then he moves back to deal with the intervening paragraphs in Sermons
153 and 154. There is no discussion of Romans 8:18-23 and 8:26-28.

A Augustine had been accustomed to citing passages from this chapter
to show that the effects of sin continue even in the Christian life. But now
he specifically raises the question, "In whose person does Paul speak in
this chapter?" — an issue raised with special intensity during the climactic
phase of the controversy with Pelagius. It has generally been thought
that the year would be 419. But one of the letters newly discovered by
Divjak shows that Augustine was not in Carthage in October of 419, and
the most likely year would be 417 (La Bonnardière 1983, 129-30).

C Other surviving sermons were also preached during September and
October in Carthage. Among them are Sermons 163 and 26, based on
texts in Galatians, which deal with themes that are treated at greater
length in Sermons 151-156.

The three subsequent sermons, 157-159, do not discuss the same issue.
They are thematic discussions of hope, referring to Romans 8 almost as
though it illustrates a philosophical theory of hope: its object is not yet
experienced (Sermon 157), it is based upon divine promise (Sermon 158),

---

C The setting of Augustine's sermons on Romans 7–8. Role of Rom. 8:3-4.
A When did Augustine begin to ask: Who is speaking in Romans 7?
C Other Augustinian sermons on the same theme.

and it is animated by delight in the invisible value of justice (Sermon 159). These sermons come from approximately the same time, and it is likely that Augustine, having started through these chapters, continued to discuss the themes raised — if not in Carthage, then back home in Hippo. This would not be unusual, for Augustine, perhaps at the request of his fellow bishops, was beginning to complete his series of expository sermons on the Psalms and on the Gospel according to John, even dictating rather than preaching some of them.

Finally, in order to "complete the record" on Augustine's preaching on Romans 7, we should take note of two sermons (77/A [Guelferbytanus 33] and 154/A [Morin 4]) which use this text in conjunction with the pericope of the Canaanite woman (Mt 15:21-28).

H Augustine will often use the psalm which had been chanted between the "apostle" and the "gospel" to confirm his interpretation of Paul: if the Pelagians will not acknowledge the continuing power of sin and the need for reliance upon grace, the psalm resolves the issue. In this way Augustine anticipates a point made a few decades later by his follower Prosper of Aquitaine, who originated the slogan *Lex orandi lex credendi*, "The rule of prayer is the rule of faith" — and in the same context of polemic against those who diminished the role of grace (Pelikan 1971, 339; 1988, 264-65).

The Situation

C The sermons come from a moment of triumph in the Pelagian controversy. The bishop of Rome, Innocent, had sent a letter early in the year declaring his agreement with the two African councils of Carthage and Milevis in 416, which had condemned the "new heresy." At the end of one sermon, after mentioning those who are ignorant of God's justice and want to establish their own, Augustine exults:

> For already two councils on this question have written to the Apostolic See; rescripts have also come from there. The case is finished; would that error be finished sometime! Therefore we warn so that they might take heed; we teach so that they might be instructed; we pray so that they might be changed (*Serm.* 131,10).[8]

In that mood Augustine set about refuting them, and the series of sermons interpreting Romans 7 was preached.

The situation, as Augustine knew, was not one of total victory. The

---

H How Scripture interprets Scripture.
C Augustine's situation in preaching the sermons: toward the end of the Pelagian controversy.

Eastern synod of Diospolis had vindicated Pelagius in 415, and the two African councils in 416 had gone ahead with their condemnation in full knowledge of this other action. Thus it was necessary to use a combination of argument and diplomacy. And in a few months Augustine would learn that the new pope, Zosimus, had called two local councils which in succession declared first Caelestius and then Pelagius free of error; his letter reversing the actions of his predecessor was dated September 21, soon after the series of sermons was begun. After that the controversy would take on new earnestness and bitterness on both sides. The Africans would call upon the aid of the Emperor, who would condemn the Pelagians for their allegedly radical social views.[9] The pope would follow suit. But his doctrinal condemnation of the Pelagians, while declaring the necessity of baptism, would not affirm original sin as the Africans wished. Soon Julian of Eclanum, a young married bishop from southern Italy, would raise the controversy to a new level of intensity, provoking lengthy and detailed polemical treatises from Augustine. All of that was still to come.

At this time of cautious triumph, Augustine not only was able to take a firmer stand against Pelagius; he was under the necessity of doing so, not only to defend himself against a variety of attacks but to convince those who wavered, and even to strengthen — or to correct — those who agreed with him. The immediate target was a work by Pelagius (probably entitled *For Free Will*) in which he answered Jerome's attacks.[10]

C Jerome was always a problematical ally for Augustine. At least twenty years older, learned in Greek and Hebrew, enjoying a widespread reputation by the time Augustine became known to the Christian world, he treated Augustine disdainfully in their first rounds of correspondence. He was, furthermore, impulsive and inclined to overstatement, especially in the midst of controversy. During a dispute over the relative merits of marriage and celibacy during the 390s — which he essentially won, since the position of Jovinian was condemned by Pope Siricius — he so deprecated marriage as to shock his friends. They tried to keep the work out of circulation. Augustine's works on marriage and celibacy were written in 401 as a corrective to Jerome's violent polemic. The unknown Roman critic of Jerome during those years may well have been Pelagius himself, rehearsing, in effect, the later and better known controversy. Thus when Augustine takes pains to differentiate his views from those of the Manichaeans, he may be defending not only himself but Jerome — and at the same time correcting some of his more extreme utterances by offering a more adequate account of good and evil, spirit and flesh. As Schleiermacher would do later in his discussion of the two "natural heresies" of Christian anthropology (Schleiermacher 1928, 98, 329-30).

C Jerome, the problematical ally.

Augustine tried to show how the "Catholic faith" is the mean between the errors of the Manichaeans and the Pelagians (*De nupt.et conc.* II,iii,9; *C.du.ep.Pel.* III,ix,25).

A Even more important, however, may have been Jerome's contribution to the interpretation of Romans 7. Earlier and more insistently than Augustine he cited it as one among many proofs that the struggle with sin continues after baptism.[11] Pelagius responded by explicitly raising the question "in whose person" Paul was speaking in this passage.[12] Thus it was in large part to defend Jerome, his strongest ally in the East, that Augustine began to investigate Romans 7 more systematically.

Augustine's Theory of Willing

H The sermons with which we are dealing represent a new stage in Augustine's description of the affections and the process of willing. He becomes even more insistent than before upon the conflict within the self. "It is not what I will that I do, the good; but what I hate, evil, this is what I do" (Rom. 7:15). That is the key passage. **A** Augustine questions how someone under the law — which arouses fear — could say, "I delight in the law of God after the inward person" (Rom. 7:22). In this connection he emphasizes the repeated use of "now": "Now then it is no longer I who do it" (Rom. 7:17), "There is therefore now no condemnation" (Rom. 8:1).[13]

C In order to understand Augustine's interpretation of Romans 7, let us look at his analysis of willing as it developed through the years. The basic observation is that it is not in our power to control what will "occur to us," either from external events or through the inward association of ideas. (In addition, it was a common opinion among philosophers in the ancient world that angelic or demonic powers could influence the human imagination — but not the human mind — by commingling themselves with it and impressing their own imaginings upon it.) What is in our power is how we respond to these impressions that "come to mind" (*De diu.quaest.ad Simpl.* I, q. 2,10-13 and 21-22; *De spir.et litt.* xxxiv,60).

But it is not as simple as that, for these impressions can arouse strong feelings and inclinations toward action. They can even conflict with each other, so that we are drawn both this way and that. The outcome seems to be determined by what most delights us — or most terrifies us; or, if they equally attract or repel us, then we waver between them.[14] In addition, our inclinations are reinforced by "custom." When we become accustomed to certain things our affections remain tied to them. It was

---

A Jerome and Pelagius raise the issue of who is speaking in Romans 7.
H Interpreting Romans 7 in relation to the human self. Rom. 7:15.
A Clues within the text itself? Rom. 7:22, 7:17; 8:1.
C Augustine's theory of willing, based in Stoicism.

even a commonplace in the ancient world to say that custom becomes "second nature," so that what began as a free response to external stimuli becomes hardened into necessity. Thus Augustine is not surprised to find Paul talking about conflict within the will, and even about the bondage of the will to its own disordered affections, for phenomena like these, with varying intensity, are familiar in human experience.

Augustine typically isolates three factors in willing (*De Gen.adu.Man.* II,xiv,20-21 and xiv,28; *De serm.dom.in mon.* I,xii,34).[15] First, he says, comes the *suggestion*, which occurs to us either through the senses or through our own free association of ideas. This in turn arouses *delight* in what is presented to us. (In other connections, Augustine can also talk about fear as the other feeling which strongly motivates us.) But delight is only a movement of the affections; it does not issue in action, either inward or outward, until *consent* is freely given in the center of the self. In consent we "cede to," give in to, ratify some inclination that has already been aroused. Or perhaps we "resist" the inclination, do not cede to it, but consent to another inclination.

In this triple analysis Augustine sometimes emphasizes *suggestion* through external events or association of ideas; sometimes *consent*, for which we ourselves are responsible. But increasingly the middle factor of *delight* or *inclination* or *desire* seems to be the crucial one. And even after consent has been given, there can remain a conflict of inclinations, resisting each other and resisting what has been consented to.

The Problem of Desire

A "Do not desire." That was the example Paul chose to illustrate the commands of the law (Rom. 7:7). The word used in the ancient world (ἐπιθυμεῖν, *concupiscere*) must be translated "desire," not "covet." It is the same word used in the Platonist tradition to describe one of the basic human impulses (the other was anger, θυμός, *ira*). While the ninth and tenth commandments speaks of coveting specific things, Paul, by abbreviating the commandment and removing the specific objects, gives it a kind of generality, focusing attention upon the subjective tendency itself.[16] This serves to remind us that desire, while it may be aroused by the specific things that we encounter, reaches out more broadly. It is always there to be aroused; it may spring forth even without being presented an object; one object of desire may suggest another that is not directly encountered. **H** If Augustine, in asking for the elimination of desire, seems to demand something that is impossible and even inhuman,

---

A The meaning of desire in Paul—and in the Bible more generally. Rom. 7:7.
H An impossible demand? or a subtle analysis of the human quest for fulfillment?

the point he is making is essentially a "theological transformation" of what he had learned much earlier from Cicero: all people desire happiness, but this does not mean that people should seek whatever delights them, or that happiness consists in having whatever one desires, for one cannot be happy in possessing something inappropriate to human fulfillment (*De mor.* I,iii,4; *Ep.* 130,10; *De Trin.* XIII,v,8, quoting from Cicero's *Hortensius*).

A Romans 7 was not the only Biblical text concerned with desire. "Do not go after your desires," said Sirach 18:30. "Each is tempted by one's own desire; . . . then desire, when it has conceived, brings forth sin," said James 1:13-15. Paul had said, "You shall not fulfill the desires of the flesh" (Gal. 5:6), and, "Do not deliver your members to sin as weapons of iniquity" (Rom. 6:13).[17] Augustine is much criticized for his concern about desire (it sounds especially awful when it goes under the name of "concupiscence"). But how is desire a problem to him? Several different answers can be seen in the sermons under discussion here (for a comprehensive discussion of the term, see Bonner 1962).

H First, desire often means sexual desire. Especially as the Pelagian controversy went on, there was extended discussion between Augustine and his opponents not only about original sin but about the means of its transmission, and it was easy to quote, at least as a shorthand explanation, the words of Psalm 51[50]:7, "I was conceived in inequity." The virginal conception of Christ seemed not only appropriate but indispensable if there was this close connection between sexual activity and sin. If others are conceived through desire, Christ is conceived through faith, when Mary (Lk 1:38) believes God's Word and says, "Let it be" (*De Trin.* XIII,xviii,23; *Ench.* x,34; *Serm.* 196,1: 215,4; 293,1). Furthermore, if procreation is so closely linked with sin, other questions arise. Would there have been begetting at all apart from sin? If so, would it have been accompanied by sexual arousement? Such issues are debated at eye-glazing length in the polemics between Augustine and Julian of Eclanum — and the debate is reported in all its prurient details by modern scholars.

C And yet, quite paradoxically, Augustine may come out better, despite the polemics of his ancient and modern opponents. Julian was even more concerned than Augustine with the physiology of reproduction, which in the ancient world included many now outdated notions about the biological necessity of sexual arousal. Augustine, while he shared some of these assumptions (they were a major reason for his theory that sin is transmitted through desire and his emphasis on the virginity of Mary), shifted the emphasis to psychology. By appropriating and internalizing

---

A Other biblical texts concerning desire, including Rom. 6:13.
H Interpretations of desire.
C Other ancient conceptions of desire.

erotic desire he not only brought it closer to the center of the person but traced in it, as elsewhere in human life, the limits of conscious will and the possibilities for evil. In the process he overcame the ancient assumption that the human person is simply a soul occupying a body — and with it the scapegoating of the body or sexuality as the primary cause of sin (Brown 1988, 413-22; Fredriksen 1988, 112). This is still not enough, of course, to bring Augustine fully into harmony with modern sensibilities, or to free him from the accusation of teaching shame and repression to Western culture. Precisely in "personalizing" sexual desire he also made it the central problem of the human person, the chief obstacle to spiritual freedom (the tension is brought out by Miles 1990, 61-62).

H In the second place, sexual desire can be an illustration of desire more generally, the primary example, a part which signifies the whole. The involuntary character of sexual desire, about which the congregation shouted out in recognition when he mentioned it at the end of one of his sermons (*Serm.* 151,8), was for Augustine a dramatic illustration of what desire is in general. It seemed unlikely to him that God would allow intelligent and free beings to be subjected to involuntary movements except as the result of a moral tragedy. The course of that tragedy could be traced, and he found in it a certain poetic justice. Humanity had voluntarily turned away from God, in whom it had its true life. In consequence it was subjected involuntarily to lower desires, and in the end to death as well. This does not mean that sexual desire is identical with sin; rather it is the consequence of sin, the expression or symbolization of sin, proof of a deeper reality of disobedience. Indeed, desire is the "contention of death" (I Cor. 15:55, Old Latin), just what one would expect in the "body of death" (Rom. 7:24): having deserted God, humankind dies a spiritual death and suffers disorder as a consequence.

Third, desire can be a metaphor for all the affections (see Schlabach 1992). In one of the sermons (*Serm.* 77/A [Guelf. 33],4) the point is made explicitly as Augustine warns against "the desire which is called avarice," calls it "the root of all evils" (I Tim 6:10), and gives numerous examples.[18] Even more broadly, he often cites I John 2:16, which speaks of "the desire of the flesh [the manifold desire for sensible things], the desire of the eyes [curiosity, the desire of the mind], and the ambition of this world [anger, rivalry, desire for esteem]." The affections reach out indefinitely to all possible objects, sensible or intelligible, real or imaginary. The human heart is drawn in many directions. Augustine sees that when Paul speaks of "flesh" he often refers to "the human" — in other words, to any mode of acquiescence in human inclinations or reliance upon human capabilities, even the most spiritual (*Serm.* 153,8).

H Further interpretations of desire, including in terms of Rom. 7:24.

The Inner Struggle

Augustine thinks in terms of the sequence "suggestion-inclination-consent," which we have traced above. **I** But the inward struggle dealt with in Romans 7 makes it much more complex — especially in the Christian believer, to whom Augustine is sure this passage applies — than this simple sequence would imply.

First of all, Romans 7 speaks of two conflicting *inclinations or delights.* On the one hand there is the pervasive role of desire, such that Paul says — twice, in slightly different form — that it is not what he wants, but what he does not want, that he does (Rom. 7:15, 19), so that it is no longer he who does it but sin dwelling within him (Rom. 7:20). Augustine interprets this to mean that the will is in bondage to its own misdirected affections, delighting wrongly or in the wrong things. These affections are summed up as desire, which is characterized as sin (Rom. 7:8-11, 17) or the "law of sin" (Rom. 7:23, 25b) in the flesh. On the other hand, there is the contrary factor of delighting in the law of God (Rom. 7:22) or with the mind serving the law of God (Rom. 7:25b), even while this is resisted by desire in the flesh. As we shall see in a moment, Augustine became convinced that one cannot "delight in the good" through the law, since the law arouses only fear; thus the crucial role is played by the grace of the Holy Spirit in evoking delight in the good.

Second, one can *consent* to the good and yet not be totally untroubled and free of conflict. If it is uncertain what Paul means in saying, "I delight in the law of God after the inward person" (Rom. 7:22) — is it merely delight but not yet consent? — he has already said, "I consent to the law, because it is good" (Rom. 7:16),[19] or "I find the law a good thing to me when I will to act" (Rom. 7:21).[20] The result of this consent to the good, however, is that the conflict of delights becomes even more intense.

How and why does one "consent"? This is at the center of Augustine's wrestling with Romans 7. Earlier his explanation had been in terms of the first phase, "suggestion" or "suasion": when one is called "congruously," in a way suited to one's condition, one will respond to that divine call (TeSelle 1970, 41-42, 178-79; Burns 1980, 141-58, 183-88). Now he gives the crucial role to the second phase, delight or inclination — specifically, to the "law of grace," which is identified with the Holy Spirit (*Serm.* 152,5-7).

Augustine was already accustomed to quoting Romans 5:5 — "the love of God has been poured into our hearts by the Holy Spirit which has been

---

I Text, psychology, and theology in dialogue. Rom. 7:15, 19; 7:20; 7:8-11, 17; 7:23, 25b; 7:22; 7:16; 7:21. Rom. 5:5.

given to us." Now he understands this verse to refer to God's infusing of delight in the good, overcoming the other delight in temporal things. This new delight "draws" or "leads" the will (*Serm.* 156,10-11), inviting consent and making it possible.[21] This consent consists of faith, which Paul habitually contrasts with the law. Faith is a yielding or consenting to the authority and the appeal of God's call. And because faith is a looking beyond oneself, it can do what the law could not do through fear. What the law commands (*imperat*) faith seeks and obtains (*impetrat*), as Augustine often says (*Ep.* 196,6; *C.du.ep.Pel.* IV,v,10; *Ench.* xxxi,117), through the continuing assistance of divine grace.

This consent in the center of the self intensifies the inner conflict. There arises a mutual resistance: the "law of sin" resists the law to which the mind gives consent (Rom. 7:23), while consent to the good resists the law of sin in the flesh. Both sinful desire and consent to the good can be spoken of as ways of "acting" or "doing," prior to any external action. It is to these *inward inclinations* that Paul refers when he says, "I do not know" — meaning "I do not acknowledge" (*Serm.* 154,11) — "what I do" (Rom. 7:15), and "it is no longer I who do it but that which dwells in me, sin" (Rom. 7:16).

Thus in every phase of willing there is conflict, for misdirected desire resists consent to the good and limits the accomplishment of what one wills. The struggle is understood eschatologically, as the beginning of resurrection; indeed, it is an inward resurrection which will reach fulfillment only in bodily resurrection.

The Nature of the Conflict

C We may object to the adversarial imagery Augustine uses. He speaks of combat between opposing delights within oneself, of taking sides among delights, vanquishing or being vanquished, dominating or being dominated, even killing. Paul himself, of course, had already spoken of mortifying, putting to death, the actions of the flesh (Rom. 8:13), whose members might otherwise be yielded to sin as weapons of iniquity (Rom. 6:13).

We must be more precise, however, about this imagery of conflict.[22] In the Roman world, military references suggested loyalty and discipline and closed ranks, not the valor of single combat. Augustine's dominant metaphor, already suggested by Paul (especially I Cor. 9:24-27) is the *agon*, an athletic competition in the stadium or theater. It was not

---

C Cultural metaphors of the conflict within the self. Rom. 8:13; 6:13.

gladiatorial combat; this was no longer found in Africa, and in any case gladiators were socially degraded persons with whom Christians would not readily identify themselves. Augustine chooses the *pancratium*, the most popular entertainment in his culture; while it was fought without weapons, it was still brutal, because all blows were permitted. The Martyrdom of Perpetua, read every year on her "birth day" of March 7, authorized the use of this image. Condemned to fight the beasts in the arena, Perpetua dreamed that she was transformed into a male and defeated an Egyptian in a contest of exactly this sort. And while the violent Circumcellions in the countryside called themselves *agonistici* who "fought the good fight" (II Tim. 4:7), Augustine emphasized that the Christian *agon* is in the stadium of the heart. (Poque 1984, 83-84 and nn. 107-111). The *pancratium*, furthermore, was unlike the field of battle in that a judge was present — not to limit the blows but to declare the victor. Augustine gives the custom a new twist by making Christ a judge who not only watches but comes to the aid of the Christian lying on the ground (*Serm.* 154/A [Morin IV],3).[23]

Augustine also uses the imagery of household conflict and assumes that, when it occurs, the husband should subdue the wife (this is the one inequality which Augustine thinks to be natural rather than the result of sin). To some it may look like a comical *Taming of the Shrew*, to others like spouse abuse. The imagery, while it may have been reinforced by social custom, was actually supplied by Ephesians 5:28, where husbands are told to love their wives as they love their own bodies (*Serm.* 154,15); in other words, male and female are related like mind and body, or Christ and the Church, and it is necessary to maintain, in a spirit of love, the proper subordination. Augustine does not remain bound, however, to the cultural values of his society. Just as easily he can use the examples of Susanna's chastity and Joseph's deference toward Mary as illustrations of what happens in "the theater of our hearts" (*Serm.* 363,5-6).

And finally there is medical imagery. Augustine speaks of letting the disease grow worse so that it will fully manifest itself and treatment can begin. The treatment is surgical, without anesthesia; it hurts, but it is for one's eventual good.[24] In one way or another, then, he evokes the need for making tough choices, sacrificing one thing for the sake of something else.

And yet he does not want to be misunderstood. He denies that he is speaking of two different substances constantly at war with each other, as the Manichaeans suppose. He quotes with approval the statement of Ephesians 5:29 that "no one hates one's own flesh."

Augustine's metaphors are often those of combat between hostile parties. But he is referring, of course, to the conflict within an individual drawn in different directions. For this reason he prefers the image of a space that is already shared, but unhappily. Most often it is the stadium with its contestants, but sometimes it is the household, where we find not a friendly family discussion but disorder. Resolution of the conflict through compromise or moderation may be impossible. Decision will become inevitable. Even then — especially then — frustration, resistance, opposition will continue from one side or the other.

The conflict of "flesh and spirit" is finally resolved not by reconciling irreconcilable impulses but by framing the conflict in a new way. Augustine is able to *acknowledge* (rather than deny or exclude from awareness) the reality of inclinations against which he struggled, precisely because a *higher loyalty* has relativized them and set them in a different perspective. Mention has already been made of the philosophical point that he had learned from Cicero: when we say that all people desire happiness, this does not mean that they should seek whatever delights them, or that happiness consists in having whatever one desires, for one cannot be happy in possessing what is inappropriate. In this way it becomes acceptable to make short-term sacrifices for the sake of fulfillment in the long run, frustrating the "desires of the flesh" for the sake of eventual harmony between flesh and spirit, negating the negation brought about by evil so that more positive features can be freed.

Fate or Freedom?

H If later readers have had difficulty with Augustine's statements about desire and the ongoing conflict it causes, they have had even greater difficulty with his solution — that grace gives a delight in the good which, being stronger than desire, makes consent possible and indeed inevitable. If human willing is in bondage to its own misdirected affections, to such an extent that it cannot delight in or consent to or will the good, then it must be freed from that bondage. But is it really freed if it merely crosses from one sphere of influence to another, from the inevitability of wrong delight to the inevitability of correct delight? For that matter, once we begin thinking about inevitabilities it is not a foregone conclusion where our sympathies will lie. Popular culture more easily identifies with the overpowering but tragic love between Tristan and Isolde, Francesca da Rimini and Paolo, than with the delight in the good which claims to free the human spirit. This was already a tendency in ancient culture;

H Theological reflections on freedom and predestination.

Augustine mentions that people will often say, "Venus made me do it" or "Mars made me do it" (*En.Ps.* 40,6; 61,23). In his own youth, he recalls, he mourned the death of Dido, who killed herself from love, but not his own spiritual death (*Conf.* I,xiii,21).

Augustine believed in predestination — that is, God's election of some persons out of the lump of sinful humanity, all of whom deserved condemnation, to be offered an undeserved salvation. He came to that conviction in 396, while considering the problems raised by Romans 9. The only question was how God's purpose to save certain persons takes effect. His first theory was that it occurs through "congruous calling," ensuring that the elect are called in a way that is suited to their condition and will lead infallibly to a favorable response. In the sermons on Romans 7 and 8 we begin to see a rethinking. Because of the conflict of delights, he insists, one cannot will what is good unless one already takes delight in it. By the year 418 he came to the view that something more is needed, and he began to speak about the role of a victorious delight in the good.[25]

C   Serious inquiry along these lines was resumed in the late sixteenth century by both Catholics and Protestants as they wrestled with the relation of grace and free will. During those years a metaphorical distinction was made between two ways of thinking about the action of grace. Does it act "physically," in the way one thing acts on another? The Dominicans and many of the Calvinists chose this model. Or does it act "morally," making an appeal through meanings and affects? The Jesuits, the Arminians, and the Amyraldians, moderate Calvinists who still held firmly to predestination, chose this model.[26]   Obviously Augustine understands grace as operating in the second way, and this can mean that, even when we are "physically" capable of willing the good, we can still be "morally" unable to do so, bound by our own affections and desires until we are freed by delight in the good.

H   Under such circumstances, are we really free? Let us consider Augustine's answers to this challenge. First, he urges us to examine what our free choice really amounts to. There is a sort of underlying potentiality for affection, choice, loyalty, but it is situated "between" basic options for higher and lower values. Once it has chosen the lower values it cannot liberate itself; to be freed it must be drawn by a factor which is not its own and is not under its control. In other words, we are never in a position to make a neutral and totally autonomous choice; or, if we were once in that position in the freshness of creation (either as preexistent souls or "in Adam"), we are in it no longer. In any event, Augustine would add, we

---

C Catholic and Protestant interpretations of Augustine.
H Further reflections on freedom and grace.

can insist too strongly upon freedom of choice among alternatives, for true freedom, responsiveness to the good, is even more to be valued. We must avoid the mistake, then, of supposing that there is complete symmetry between lesser and greater values, or between delight in lesser values (which Augustine thinks will fragment our attention, distract our affections, and lead to bondage rather than freedom) and delight in higher values (which he thinks will unify the affections and give true freedom to the self and full consistency in its willing).[27]

But this is not the end of the matter. Even predestination and grace, as Augustine understands them, take into account the role of human consent. He often thinks of God's adapting the call to the individual so that it will be "congruous" with the person's needs; at times he even imagines God looking ahead to what a person "would do" under this or that set of inducements, and applying those that will tilt the affections without fail.[28] Despite the indispensable role of "delight" in human willing, however, it is "consent" that makes it one's own. And yet consent, despite its decisive role, remains fragile. Congruous calling and victorious delight may lead "infallibly" to consent, but they are not "irresistible," for there is resistance both before and after consent.[29]

Therefore Augustine not only uses the "synchronic" conceptuality of suggestion-inclination-consent in analyzing the process of willing; he is also aware of a "diachronic" drama within the self, for past judgments, past affections, past choices, retain their power in the present.[30] Even the elect do not generally experience assurance or inevitability. They are aware of struggle and anxiety, and victory is achieved only because grace persists through time and supplies perseverance. Human beings still live "under grace"; they are not yet "in peace." The difference is that, while freedom in the latter state is the "happy necessity" of responding to the good (*De perf. iust. hom.* iv,9; *C. Iul. op. imp.* I, 103), in the former there remains a conflict between impulses, such that in consenting to the better impulses one must continue to resist the worse ones.

We may object that Augustine leaves us only "technically free." In a sense that is true, for the outcome not only is certain to God but is planned by God, who calls the person "congruously" or infuses a victorious delight. And yet Augustine would say that even "technical freedom" is not to be scorned, for consent has the irreducible role of ratifying, validating, appropriating. Even if there should be no difference in *content* between an attractive "suggestion," an overwhelming "inclination," and the "consent" that is given, there is a difference in *meaning.* Consent is our own personal resolution of all the factors impinging upon us, our own way of coming to terms with them and ranking their importance or relevance to us. One suggestion, one inclination, may be so dominant that consent seems inevitable. Yet there will be other suggestions, other inclinations, as a passage like Romans 7 indicates. They not only struggle for consent *before* the decision is made; they also resist the consent *after* it is given.

C The meaning of freedom is a classic problem among modern philosophers. Ever since Locke's careful scrutiny of the meaning of free will, emphasizing the constant flow of "preferences" — but also insisting in his second edition that freedom, in the sense of a kind of "uneasiness," intervenes between desiring and willing[31] — there have been some who emphasize the aspect of inevitability. Jonathan Edwards, seeing that Locke's psychology could be used to buttress his own predestinarianism of the "moral influence" type, argued that freedom consists in following the greatest apparent good or the strongest inclination. Unlike Augustine, however, he did not differentiate between inclination and consent, and thus he did not leave room even for "technical" freedom of choice (Edwards 1957, 16-17, 156-62, 236-38, 328-33).[32]

H There are those, of course, who insist that talk about freedom has meaning because we in fact experience it, if not in every aspect of our lives, at least in some aspects. When pressed they may even acknowledge the overwhelming presence of preconditions of all sorts — our bodies, our circumstances, our experiences and character, pressures and appeals from family or friends, government or the media — yet they will still insist that the experience of freedom is not without meaning.[33] At a minimum they will adopt the position called "compatibilism," the position, in other words, that there is not a forced choice between the theories called (perhaps too starkly) determinism and libertarianism, because both of them give helpful descriptions of our experience, dealing with distinct aspects of it and from contrasting points of view.[34]

On these terms, Augustine is a compatibilist, at least with respect to grace and free will (the theological term is "congruist"). But this makes it all the more important to keep in mind his distinction between suggestion, inclination, and consent — overlooked, I think, in most of the contemporary discussion — for he identifies several distinct "layers" of considerations that must be described and related to each other in any discussion of freedom. When one adds his awareness of continued resistance from other impulses, and thus an ongoing struggle within the self, it becomes evident that he does not imagine either sin or grace to operate in a simple and uncomplicated way.[35]

C Philosophical issues concerning freedom.
H Can freedom be compatible with determination by other factors?

C "I am the field upon which I labor," Augustine once said, "with difficulty and much sweat" (*Conf.* X,xvi,25). He found this to be the case over and over, as he dealt with many different problems, and in different tones of voice. It may help us, as we seek our own way, to learn how he set his questions concerning himself in the larger framework of relationships with other beings, with other persons — and finally with the Other who, he was sure, is most intensely present.

,

C Augustine's posture of self-reflection.

–APPENDIX–

Romans 7-8 in the Old Latin Version

Eugene TeSelle

This is an informal and eclectic reconstruction of Augustine's Old Latin text of Romans 7-8. It is based on Sermons 151-159 in the Benedictine edition (reprinted in *PL*), and on other works — especially the early commentaries and questions on Paul, and the anti-Pelagian writings — as printed in the *PL* and in more recent editions in the *CSEL* (vols. 42, 60, 84) and the *CC* (vols. 44 and 44A).

The difficulties in establishing the "text" of the Old Latin version are numerous. The critical edition of the *Vetus Latina* (Fischer 1949-) does not yet include Romans. Variant readings are numerous, not only because of the hazards of manuscript copying, but because of different manuscript traditions in North Africa, Rome, and Northern Italy, and constant "contamination" by — or conscious emendation from — other textual traditions. Augustine also consulted the Greek text for himself, at least on some occasions. And as time went on the Vulgate — that is, Jerome's translation of the Old Testament from the Hebrew, his revision of the gospels, and the completion of the New Testament by others — had to be taken into account. Augustine for the most part resisted the Vulgate and clung persistently to the Old Latin translation.[36] In Sermons 151-159, for example, we find him quoting I Cor. 15:55 in the form, "Where, death, is your contention?" He knew that Jerome translated Isa. 7:9, "Unless you believe you will not endure," but he continued to cite it in the old version, "Unless you believe you will not understand." And yet, late in his career, he used Jerome's translation of a passage in Amos as the model for an examination of biblical rhetoric (*De doct.chr.* IV,vii,15-21; cf. Moreau 1986).

In the text below, I have attempted to recover Augustine's earliest text; alternative readings which appear in his later writings are in square brackets; variants which are not found in some readings are in angular brackets.[37] It will be apparent that most of the variants are minor ones, having to do with word order or conjunctions, and that others represent alternative possibilities of translation. As Augustine construes the text, he routinely ends what we call chapter 7 with the first half of verse 25 — in the wording which also occurs in Codex Bezae — and begins what we call chapter 8 with the second half of that verse, without the addition to verse 8:1 ("who do not walk according to the flesh") which is found in Codex Alexandrinus and the Vulgate. Such details indicate that ancient editors — and readers — had varying conceptions of the way Paul's argument moved from chapter 7 to chapter 8.[38]

Unusual *readings* are noted with bold type in the Latin text; unusual *interpretations* with bold type in the English translation.

Latin

7 [1]An ignoratis fratres — scientibus enim legem loquor — quia lex dominatur homini in quantum tempus uiuit? [2]Mulier enim sub uiro uiuo marito uincta [iuncta] est legi; si autem mortuus fuerit uir eius, euacuata est a lege uiri. [3]Igitur uiuente uiro uocabitur adultera si fuerit cum alio uiro [iuncta fuerit alteri uiro]; si autem [quodsi] mortuus fuerit uir eius, liberata est a lege, ut non sit adultera, si fuerit cum alio uiro.

[4]Itaque, fratres mei, et uos mortui estis legi per corpus Christi, ut sitis alterius, qui ex mortuis resurrexit, ut fructificemus Deo. [5]Cum enim essemus in carne, passiones peccatorum quae per legem sunt, operabantur in membris nostris, ut fructum ferrent morti. [6]Nunc uero euacuati sumus a lege, mortui [a lege mortis] in qua detinebamur, ita ut seruiamus in

English

7 [1]Do you not know, brothers and sisters — for I speak to those who know the law — that the law rules a person as long as one lives? [2]For a woman is bound by the law to be under her husband while he lives; but if her husband should die she is relieved from the law concerning her husband. [3]Therefore as long as her husband lives she will be called an adulteress if she is joined to another man; but if her husband should die she is freed from the law, so that she is not an adulteress if she should be with another man.

[4]Similarly, my brothers and sisters, you also are dead to the law through the body of Christ, so that you might belong to another who rose from the dead so that we might bear fruit to God. [5]For when we were in the flesh the passions of sins which are through the law were active in our members to bring forth fruit to death. [6]But now we have been relieved of the law, dead to

nouitate spiritus et non in uetustate litterae.

that which held us [the law of death in which we were held], so that we might serve in newness of spirit and not in the oldness of the letter.

⁷Quid ergo dicemus? Lex peccatum est? Absit. Sed <ego> peccatum non cognoui nisi per legem. Nam concupiscentiam nesciebam, nisi lex diceret, "Non concupisces." ⁸Occasione autem accepta, peccatum per mandatum operatum est in me omnem concupiscentiam. Sine lege enim peccatum mortuum est. ⁹Ego autem uiuebam aliquando sine lege. Adueniente autem mandato, peccatum reuixit. ¹⁰Ego autem mortuus sum, et inuentum est mihi mandatum, quod erat in uitam, hoc esse ad mortem. ¹¹Peccatum enim, occasione accepta per mandatum, fefellit me et per illud occidit.

⁷What then shall we say? Is the law sin? By no means. But I have not known sin except through the law. For I would not have know desire unless the law had said, "You shall not desire." ⁸But sin, finding occasion through the commandment, effected in me every desire. For without the law sin is dead. ⁹Once I was alive, without the law. But when the commandment came, sin revived. ¹⁰I have died, and the commandment, which was for life, has been found to be for death to me. ¹¹For sin, taking occasion through the commandment, deceived me and through it killed me.

¹²Itaque lex quidem sancta, et mandatum sanctum et iustum et bonum. ¹³Quod ergo bonum est, mihi factum est mors? Absit. Sed peccatum, ut appareat peccatum, per bonum mihi operatum est mortem, ut fiat super modum **peccator aut**³⁹ **peccatum** <delinquens> per mandatum.

¹²Thus the law is indeed holy, and the commandment is holy and just and good. ¹³Did what is good become death to me? By no means. But sin, so that it might be manifested as sin, effected death to me through that which is good, so that **the sinner or sin** might be beyond measure, [offending] through the commandment.

¹⁴Scimus autem quia lex spiritalis est; ego autem carnalis

¹⁴We know, moreover, that the law is spiritual; but I am carnal,

sum, uenundatus sub peccato. [15]Quod enim operor, ignoro. Non enim quod uolo, hoc ago; sed quod odi, illud facio. [16]Si autem quod nolo, hoc ago [facio], consentio legi quoniam bona <est>. [17]Nunc autem iam non ego operor illud, sed id quod in me habitat, peccatum. [18]Scio enim quia non habitat in me, hoc est in carne mea, bonum. Velle enim adiacet mihi, perficere autem bonum non <adiacet/ inuenio>.

[19]Non enim quod uolo facio, bonum; sed quod nolo, malum, hoc ago. [20]Si autem quod nolo <ego> hoc facio, iam non ego operor illud, sed <id> quod in me habitat [habitat in me], peccatum. [21]Inuenio igitur legem, mihi uolenti facere, bonum, quoniam mihi malum adiacet. [22]Condelector enim legi Dei secundum interiorem hominem, [23]uideo autem aliam legem in membris meis, repugnantem legi mentis meae et captiuantem me [captiuum me ducentem] sub [in] lege peccati, quae est in membris meis. [24]Miser ego homo, quis me liberabit de corpore mortis huius?[40] [25]Gratia Dei per Iesum Christum Dominum nostrum.

Igitur ipse ego [ego ipse] mente seruio legi Dei, carne autem legi peccati. 8 [1]Nulla ergo condemnatio est nunc his qui

sold under sin. [15]**I do not acknowledge what I do.**[41] For it is not what I will that I do; rather what I hate, that is what I do. [16]But if that which I do not will is what I do, **I consent to the law because it is good,**[42] [17]and yet it is no longer I who do it, but that which dwells in me, sin. [18]For I know that good does not dwell in me, that is, in my flesh. For to will is near to me, but not to accomplish the good.

[19]For it is not what I will that I do, the good; but what I do not will, evil, this is what I do. [20]But if what I do not will is what I do, it is no longer I who do it, but that which dwells in me, sin. [21]**I find, then, that the law, when I will to act, is a good thing,**[43] because evil lies near to me. [22]For I delight in the law of God after the inward person.[44] [23]But I see another law in my members, resisting the law of my mind and taking me captive under [in] the law of sin which is in my members. [24]Wretched one that I am, who will free me from the body of this death? [25]The grace of God through Jesus Christ our Lord.

Therefore I myself with the mind serve the law of God, but with the flesh the law of sin. 8 [1]Thus there is no condemnation

sunt in Christo Iesu. ²Lex enim spiritus uitae in Christo Iesu liberauit me a lege peccati et mortis. ³Quod enim impossibile erat legi, in quo infirmabatur per carnem. Deus Filium suum misit in similitudine<m> carnis peccati, et de peccato damnauit peccatum in carne, ⁴ut iustitia legis impleretur in nobis, qui non secundum carnem ambulamus sed secundum spiritum. ⁵Qui enim secundum carnem sunt, quae carnis sunt sapiunt. Qui autem secundum spiritum, quae sunt spiritus <sentiunt>. ⁶Prudentia enim carnis [sapere secundum carnem] mors est; prudentia autem spiritus [sapere autem secundum spiritum] uita et pax. ⁷Quia prudentia [sapientia] carnis inimica est in Deum. Legi enim Dei non est subiecta, nec [neque] enim potest. ⁸Qui autem in carne sunt, Deo placere non possunt.

⁹Vos autem non estis in carne, sed in spiritu, si tamen Spiritus Dei habitat in uobis. Si quis autem Spiritum Christi non habet, hic non est eius. ¹⁰Si autem Christus in uobis, corpus quidem mortuum est propter peccatum, spiritus autem uita est propter iustitiam. ¹¹Si autem Spiritus eius qui suscitauit Christum a mortuis habitat in uobis, qui suscitauit Christum [Christum Iesum] a mortuis uiuificabit et mortalia corpora

now to those who are in Christ Jesus. ²For the law of the Spirit of life in Christ Jesus has freed me from the law of sin and death. ³This was impossible to the law, in that it was weakened through the flesh. God sent his Son in the likeness of flesh of sin, and by sin condemned sin in the flesh, ⁴so that the justice of the law might be fulfilled in us, who walk not after the flesh but after the spirit.⁴⁵ ⁵For those who are after the flesh mind the things of the flesh. But those who are after the spirit mind the things of the s/Spirit. ⁶For the prudence of the flesh is death; but the prudence of the spirit is life and peace. ⁷For the prudence of the flesh is hostile toward God; it is not subject to the law of God, indeed it cannot be. ⁸But those who are in the flesh cannot please God.

⁹But you are not in the flesh but in the spirit, if the Spirit of God dwells in you. If there is anyone who does not have the Spirit of Christ, that one is not his. ¹⁰But if Christ is in you, the body indeed is dead because of sin, but the spirit is life because of justice. ¹¹But if the Spirit of the one who raised Christ from the dead dwells in you, the one who raised Christ Jesus from the dead will also give life to your mortal bodies through his Spirit

uestra, per [propter] inhabitantem Spiritum eius in uobis.

[12]Ergo, fratres, debitores sumus non carni, ut secundum carnem uiuamus. [13]Si enim secundum carnem uixeritis, moriemini; si autem Spiritu actiones [facta] carnis mortificaueritis, uiuetis. [14]Quotquot enim Spiritu Dei aguntur, hi filii sunt Dei. [15]Non enim accepistis spiritum seruitutis iterum in timore, sed accepistis Spiritum adoptionis filiorum, in quo clamamus, Abba, Pater. [16]Ipse Spiritus testimonium reddit [dat] spiritui nostro quia sumus filii Dei. [17]Si autem filii, et haeredes, haeredes quidem Dei, cohaeredes autem Christi, si tamen conpatimur, ut et conglorificemur.

[18]Existimo enim quod indignae sint passiones huius temporis ad futuram gloriam quae reuelabitur in nobis. [19]Nam expectatio creaturae reuelationem filiorum Dei expectat. [20]Vanitati enim creatura subiecta est, non sponte, sed propter eum qui subiecit eam in spe, [21]quia et ipsa creatura liberabitur a seruitute interitus in libertatem gloriae filiorum Dei. [22]Scimus enim quia omnis creatura congemiscit et dolet usque adhuc. [23]Non solum

dwelling in you.

[12]Therefore, brothers and sisters, we are debtors not to the flesh, to live according to the flesh. [13]For if you live after the flesh you will die, but if by the spirit you put to death the actions of the flesh you will live. [14]For as many as are led by the Spirit of God are children of God. [15]For you have not received the spirit of slavery again in fear, but you have received the Spirit of adoption as children, in whom we cry, "Abba," "Father." [16]The Spirit himself bears witness with our spirit that we are children of God. [17]But if children, also heirs, heirs indeed of God, joint heirs then with Christ, provided we suffer with him so that we may also be glorified with him.

[18]For I think that the sufferings of this time are unworthy of the coming glory which will be revealed in us. [19]For the longing of the creation is awaiting the revelation of the children of God. [20]For the creation has been subjected to vanity, not by its own choice but because of the one who subjected it in hope, [21]for this same creation will be freed from slavery to destruction for the glorious freedom of the children of God. [22]For we know that **all creation [i.e., each hu-**

autem sed etiam nos ipsi primitias habentes spiritus [spiritus habentes], et ipsi in nobismetipsis ingemiscimus <adhuc>, adoptionem expectantes, redemptionem corporis nostri. [24]Spe enim salui facti sumus. Spes autem quae uidetur non est spes; quod enim uidet quis, quid et sperat? [25]Si autem quod non uidemus speramus, per patientiam expectamus. [26]Similiter autem et Spiritus adiuuat infirmitatem nostram; quid enim oremus sicut oportet, nescimus, sed ipse Spiritus interpellat gemitibus inenarrabilibus. [27]Qui autem scrutatur corda, scit quid Spiritus sapiat, quia secundum Deum interpellat pro sanctis.

man being][46] groans and grieves until now. [23]Not only it, however, but also we ourselves, **who maintain the first fruits of the spirit [=faith],**[47] we ourselves also groan within ourselves until now, awaiting adoption, the redemption of our body. [24]For by hope we have been saved. But hope that is seen is not hope; what one sees, does one also hope for it? [25]But if we hope for what we do not see, we await it with patience. [26]Likewise also the Spirit helps our weakness; for we do not know what we should pray as is fitting, but the Spirit himself intercedes with unexpressible sighs.[48] [27]But the one who searches hearts knows what the Spirit understands, because he intercedes for the saints in accordance with God.

[28]Scimus quia diligentibus Deum omnia cooperantur in bonum, his qui secundum propositum uocati sunt. [29]Quoniam quos ante praesciuit, et praedestinauit conformes imaginis Filii eius, ut sit primogenitus in multis fratribus. [30]Quos autem praedestinauit, illos et uocauit; quos autem uocauit, illos et iustificauit; quos autem iustificauit, illos et glorificauit.

[28]We know that all things work together for good to those who love God, to those who are called according to purpose. [29]For those whom God foreknew he also predestined to be conformed to the image of his Son, so that he might be the firstborn among many brothers and sisters. [30]Those, further, whom he predestined he also called; and those whom he called he also justified; and those whom he justified he also glorified.

[31]Quid ergo dicemus ad haec? Si Deus pro nobis, quis contra nos?

[31]What then shall we say to these things? If God is for us,

[32]Qui etiam proprio Filio suo non pepercit, sed pro nobis omnibus tradidit illum, quomodo non etiam cum illo omnia nobis donauit? [33]Quis accusabit aduersus electos Dei? Deus qui iustificat, [34]quis est qui condemnet? Christus Iesus, qui mortuus est, immo qui et resurrexit, qui est ad dexteram Dei, qui etiam interpellat pro nobis. [35]Quis nos separabit a caritate Christi? Tribulatio an angustia an persecutio an fames an nuditas an periculum an gladius?

[36]Quoniam [quia] propter te mortificamur tota die;
Deputati sumus ut oues occisionis.

[37]Sed in his omnibus superuincimus per eum qui dilexit nos. [38]Certus enim sum quia neque mors, neque uita, neque angelus, neque principatus, neque praesentia, neque futura, neque uirtus, [39]neque altitudo, neque profundum, neque creatura alia poterit nos separare a caritate Dei quae est in Christo Iesu Domino nostro.

who is against us? [32]He who did not spare even his own Son but gave him over for us all, how will he not also give us all things with him? [33]Who shall bring a charge against God's chosen? It is God who justifies; [34]who is to condemn? Christ Jesus, who has died, yes, who has also risen, who is at the right hand of God, is the one who even now intercedes for us. [35]Who shall separate us from the love of Christ? Tribulation, or distress, or persecution, or famine, or nakedness, or peril, or sword?

[36]It is for your sake that we are being killed all the day;
We are regarded as sheep for slaughter.

[37]But in all these things we more than conquer through him who loved us. [38]For I am certain that neither death, nor life, nor angel, nor dominion, nor present things, nor future things, nor power, nor height, nor depth, **nor any other created thing** can separate us from the love of God which is in Christ Jesus our Lord.[49]

Notes

1. For the "interpretation history" of Romans 7 see Kümmel 1929; Schelkle 1956, 236-48; Wilckens 1978-82, II:101-117; Gorday 1983. Theissen 1987, 177-265, champions the psychological interpretation on the basis of parallels with Greek philosophy and literary criticism. A challenge to the psychological approach, which sees Augustine's misreading of the chapter as a crucial factor in the history of interpretation, has been issued by Fredriksen 1986 and 1988.

2. For general discussions see TeSelle 1970, 156-65, 176-82, 258-66; Gorday 1983, 137-87. The major shifts in Augustine's thinking about Paul are traced in a subtle way in Fredriksen 1986 and 1988.

3. This period in Augustine's thought is discussed in Fredriksen 1979 and Babcock 1979.

4. The transition can be seen in *De diuersis quaestionibus ad Simplicianum.* In answering the first question — which deals with Romans 7! — Augustine still assumes that the sinner seeks divine assistance. In answering the second, he becomes persuaded that grace has the initiating role.

5. This change in Augustine's thinking has been documented and traced with care by Burns 1980.

6. These four stages are developed in *Exp.prop.Rom.* 13-18 and *De diu. quaest.* q. 61,7 and q. 66,3. Augustine reaffirms them many years later in *Ench.* xxxi,118-119. This fourfold classification is related to philosophical theories of moral development by Wetzel 1987.

7. It can even be said that, for Augustine, human life is the cosmos writ small. Paul had said (Rom. 8:18-20) that all creation "groans in travail," having been subjected to vanity. Augustine understands this verse to refer to the entire human being, which includes body, soul, and mind and in this sense is "all creation," on the grounds that the text says "*omnis creatura*," not "*tota creatura*" (*De diu.quaest.* 67,5). The former adjective is understood distributively, as applying to all created things which have body *and* soul *and* mind, and only human beings meet this definition; the latter adjective is understood collectively, as applying to all created things without restriction. According to this interpretation, human being in its entirety is subjected to vanity, i.e., to earthly change and vulnerability, but in hope of resurrection (*Exp.prop.Rom.* 53; *De diu.quaest.* 67).

8. Roman Catholics have customarily seen in this papal endorsement of the African councils an early proof of the authority of the Pope. But even Catholic scholars caution that the African appeal has a large element of coalition-building through subtle flattery, and that the papal endorsement of the African councils may indicate not so much agreement with their doctrine in all details as an an attempt to maintain the dignity of the Roman see and its right to intervene in the affairs of other churches, especially in the West.

9. The more widespread, and more cynical, view is that they appealed to the imperial court in order to go over the head of the pope. The more benign view, argued by Burns 1979, is that the appeal to the court was made between September 23, when they learned of Innocent's action, and November 2, when they learned of Zosimus's suspension of that action. In the latter case, their appeal would be a "normal" request for imperial *coercitio* to back up a judgment by the church.

10. Augustine always cites the work as *Pro libero arbitrio*, perhaps to characterize its bias, perhaps because that was the title Pelagius gave it. The latter would not be unlikely, for Pelagius knew how to be assertive. He had earlier written a work *De natura* in response to Augustine's emphasis on the human need for grace; the work defending free will was issued in an even more polemical context. The expression "pro libero arbitrio" gained negative connotations as Augustine looked back over his own intellectual development, recalling, for example, how he had labored for free will but the grace of God prevailed (*Retr.* II,1).

11. Rétif 1946, 368-71, pointed out that Pelagius could not have been responding to Augustine, who had not taken a stand on the interpretation of Romans 7.

12. In *Serm.* 154,4 Augustine comments that this question had been raised by Pelagius, and his work *Pro libero arbitrio* did indeed raise it, as we learn from other passages in Augustine.

13. The emphasis on "now" — later mentioned in *C.du.ep.Pel.* I,x,22, written in 419 — is first encountered in *Serm.* 154,11 and 155,2. See La Bonnardière 1983, 133-34.

14. This is the position Augustine had already stated about the year 394 in his *Exp.ep.ad Gal.* 4 and 54. The struggle between inclinations is evoked with special power in *Conf.* VIII,ix,21, where Augustine asks how it can happen that the human spirit resists its own commands to itself; he answers that its willing is "half-hearted," inclined toward contrary things.

15. For a more thorough analysis of this theory of willing (which Augustine saw allegorized in the three figures of the Eden narrative) see TeSelle 1994.

16. Paul has a similarly brief summary of the Decalogue in Rom. 13:8-9, including "Do not desire." In Rom. 7 he seems to makes desire the basic or general sin (as also in I Cor. 10:6). It may be not only a summary of the Decalogue but a recollection of the Eden narrative (Gen. 3:6). Backgrounds in Palestinian and Hellenistic Judaism are examined in Lyonnet 1962, and more briefly in Schmithals 1980, 26, and Theissen 1987, 204-5. Many centuries later, Calvin followed Augustine (explicitly acknowledging him) and interpreted the last commandment to prohibit not only the specific kinds of "coveting" which are listed — for most of these have already been prohibited in earlier commandments — but any motivation other than love grounded in God. In this respect, he felt, the final commandment made a transition to the twin commandment of love enunciated by Christ.

17. Augustine uses these other passages to explicate the command "Do not desire" (*In eu.Io.* 41,12).

18. In *De continentia* Augustine shows that in many biblical texts "living according to the flesh" means "living according to the human" (iv,10-11) and makes the point that "the flesh desires nothing except through the soul" (viii,19).

19. Augustine's paraphrase of this verse in *Serm.* 154,10 indicates that he understands it to mean "consenting to the law," "willing what the law wills."

20. In *De diu.quaest.ad Simpl.* I, q. 1,12 this verse is paraphrased, "Therefore the law, when I will, is a good thing to me." Later, in *Serm.* 154,13 and *C. du.ep.Pel.* I,x,19, it is similarly paraphrased, "The law is a good thing to one who wills to act, but evil lies near through desire, to which one does not consent," and in *De nupt.et conc.* I,xxx,33, where it is applied to willing what the law wills, against one's own desires.

21. The *locus classicus* for this theme is *In Io.eu.* 26,4-5, where Augustine quotes Vergil's *Eclogue* II,65 to the effect that "each is drawn by one's own pleasure" and compares it with being "drawn" by the Father (Jn. 6:44). The same psychology is found in Augustine's early *Exp.prop.Rom.* 13-18, where, perhaps recalling this passage from Vergil, he speaks of being "drawn" by the desire of the flesh, without struggle prior to the law and struggling against it after the law.

22. This imagery of combat and victory is explored in Poque 1984, 53-60.

23. Poque 1984, 96 and n. 169, notes the parallel with *pius Aeneas*, who ends a combat between Entellus and Dares when the latter is endangered (*Aeneid* V:491-496).

24. For a discussion of the medical imagery see Poque 1984, 180-88, and especially Arbesmann 1954 and Eijkenboom 1960.

25. This notion of *delectatio victrix* or *vincens* is found in *De pecc.mer.* II,xix,32; *C.du.ep.Pel.* I,xii,27; *Ench.* xxii,81 and xxxi,118; *De cont.* 20; and *C.Iul.op.imp.* I,107, II,217, and II,226.

26. There is a need for an "ecumenical" survey of the disputes of this period, for Catholics and Protestants learned much from each other — positively and not merely by way of provocation or bad examples to be spoken against. For general surveys one must still consult the classic histories of doctrine or theological encyclopedias. Beyond these, there are studies of particular figures, often quite narrow in scope.

27. For a contemporary statement along the same lines see Wolf 1980, and the more extended discussion (more technical, but not adding basically new points) in Wolf 1990. As she states it, we are free when we have good reasons for acting as we do, and our action can even be said to be "determined" by those considerations. What we ordinarily call free choice is a situation of psychological uncertainty about the definitive reasons to act. And actions that go against what we consider to be true or good are not free except in a perverse sense. The theological tradition is aware of the additional complications introduced by sin and "carnal custom," so that one does not inevitably will what one knows to be right or good. This became an explicit issue at the University of Paris in 1270, when the bishop condemned the thesis that the will necessarily follows what the intellect sees to be good. Thomas Aquinas adjusted his

own position about this time, and this increased the tension in his thought between rational deliberation, which judges whether an act is "right or wrong," and motivation, which is "good or bad" because of *caritas* or the lack of it. The issues are discussed in Keenan 1992 and Westberg 1994.

28. This is what the Jesuit theologians called God's "middle knowledge" of "futuribles" or "future possibles," a knowledge, in other words, that stands "between" the knowledge of pure possibles and the knowledge of actual events. The hypothesis is that God knows what persons "would do" if offered grace under this or that set of circumstances and plans accordingly. Augustine clearly considered this, suggesting that the incarnation did not occur until the time when God knew they "would respond" to it (*Ep.* 102, q. 2,14-15). He also was aware (as Origen was earlier) of the passage in the gospels which speaks of what the people of Tyre and Sidon "would have done" (Mt. 11:20-24, Lk. 10:13-15).

29. Wetzel 1992, 198-200, insists too strongly that grace cannot be "resisted." While that would become one of the essential doctrines of the strict Calvinists, Augustine used the word differently, speaking of wrong desires "resisting" consent to the good, and vice versa (see, for example, *C. Iul.* VI,55, from the year 424). It is true that Augustine says on occasion that human beings cannot "resist God's will" (*De corr.et gr.* xiv,45), but this is because God infuses a good inclination which is both consented to in the center of the self and resisted by wrong desires.

30. This theme is traced, thoroughly and subtly, throughout Wetzel 1992.

31. Locke 1975, 249-65 (Book II, Chapter xxi, §§29-48). The very different discussion in the first edition is printed in the footnotes.

32. While Edwards did speak of "consent," he meant by it not the act of consenting but the state of being in agreement or union of heart with God, or with God's providential ordering of the world. See especially Edwards 1960, 31, 37, 61-63, 68. The subsequent discussion among the "Edwardsians" is traced by Guelzo 1989. He shows that, just as Locke felt compelled to move from a "one-stage" to a "two-stage" theory of willing, similarly many of the Edwardsians moved from a one-stage to a two-stage theory (55-59, 109-10) and some even to a three-stage theory (211, 100-05). In many ways it is a repetition of the ancient discussion, especially among the Stoics, which I have tried to trace in TeSelle 1994, 343-47.

33. The same issues appear in public policy debates. Is it true (as the National Rifle Association argues) that "Guns do not kill people, people kill people"? or (as opponents of censorship or self-regulation argue) that "Television does not cause violence, people cause violence"? When the debate is framed in this way, the sole alternative is *suggestion* versus *consent.* Sociologists and psychologists are likely to emphasize the middle factor of *inclination* and ask about the many factors that intervene between the "suggestions" that come from society (ready access to guns, images of violence on television) and the final "consent" to acting in this or that way.

34. The analyses of contemporary philosophers are strong on logical complexity and often weaker on exploration of the range of human experience. For convenient summaries see Pojman 1987, and the still-classic essay by Taylor 1967, II:359-73. The most Augustinian position is that of Susan Wolf, cited above — if one adds the complexities that come from inward struggle and resistance.

35. I have already criticized Edwards for too simplistic a conception of freedom, that it consists in following the greatest apparent good or the strongest inclination. Among Catholics, Jansenism has been similarly criticized for making the *delectatio uictrix* a sort of "concupiscence in reverse." The alternative is to emphasize a constant interaction, such that only those who consent to the good can take delight in it, and delight in turn stimulates the next act of consent. Cf. my comments TeSelle 1994, 354, and the literature cited there.

36. It was the Pelagians who first made habitual use of the Vulgate; probably the unknown scholar who completed Jerome's revision of the New Testament was Rufinus the Syrian, a member of Jerome's monastery in Bethlehem who journeyed to the West in 399 and became one of the "founders" of the Pelagian movement. See Frede 1974, I:253-55.

37. Augustine says (*De doct.chr.* II,xv,22) that the *Itala* is to be preferred. This comment has given rise to endless controversy over the nature and even the existence of regional versions. The older discussion of "African," "Italian," and "European" manuscript traditions has been replaced, among the editors of the *Vetus Latina*, by the more cautious language of "text types" called, respectively, **K**, **I**, and **D**. In any event, Augustine indicates an awareness of differences and a preference for the Italian manuscript tradition. Whether he began his career using manuscripts copied in North Africa, or brought some back to North Africa from Rome, is unclear; in any case he took an interest in checking different readings and "emending" his text. The readings I have placed in brackets come from later in his career, during the Pelagian controversy, and suggest either emendation or acquaintance with new manuscripts. What is clear is that his version of the Old Latin was quite different from the North Italian or "European" tradition reflected in Ambrose, whose citations are compiled and discussed in Muncey 1959.

38. Gorday (1983) has developed an approach to the history of interpretation that looks even more broadly at the way the interpreter construes the text as a whole.

39. This is a misreading of the Greek ἡ as ἤ .

40. For Augustine, a major reason one would want to be delivered from the "body of death" is that desire is called the "contention of death" in the Old Latin version of I Cor. 15:55.

41. This is clearly the way Augustine construes this verse in *Serm.* 154,11. In the earlier *Exp.prop.Rom.* 43 he paraphrases it "I do not approve."

42. See note 19 above.

43. See note 20 above.

44. The later Augustine insists that only those who have received grace can "delight with" the law. Even the earlier Augustine, however, notes these overtones and speaks of being not "under" but "with" or "within" the law (*Exp.prop.Rom.* 41, 44).

45. It remains a dilemma when to capitalize "spirit" in vss. 4, 5, 6, 9, 10, and 13; indeed, Augustine exploits the ambiguities to the full in Sermons 155,11-13 and 156,9-10. He opposes any flesh/spirit dualism, since both belong to human nature and both can be healed; in this connection he quotes Eph. 5:8, "You were once darkness but now are light in the Lord" (*Serm.* 155,11). If one is "not in the flesh" it is through one's own act of not consenting to the desires of the flesh. And yet, to presume upon one's own spirit means that one is still "in the flesh"; if one is not "in the flesh" it happens only because of the Spirit of God (*Serm.* 155,13). To be sure, it is "with the mind" that one serves the law of God (Rom. 7:25b); if God is spirit, the soul too is spirit, the mind is spirit, and "the [human] spirit desires against the flesh" (Gal. 5:17). But it is only "by the Spirit" (Rom. 8:13), not by the human spirit, that the actions of the flesh can be put to death. It is presumption to think that Paul means "by the spirit," i.e., by one's own will, one's own free choice; only those who are "led by the Spirit of God" (Rom. 8:14) are children of God, not those who think that they can be led by their own spirit (*Serm.* 156,10). And yet to be led by the Spirit is to be active, and to be active in the only way that is good without qualification (*Serm.* 156,11-13) namely, "active in love" (Gal. 5:6).

46. See note 7 above.

47. The "first fruits" are always understood to be of the *human* spirit, and what is meant is *faith*; the identification is explicit in Augustine's earlier writings. Augustine knew and often utilized Paul's statement that the Holy Spirit is given as a "down payment" or "earnest" (II Cor. 1:22, 5:5); he linked it, however, with Rom. 8:15-16, not with 8:23. In the anti-Pelagian writings this interpretation continues to be implicitly assumed (see esp. *De pecc. mer.* I,vi,6). The theme is paralleled by, but is never explicitly linked with, the other theme of the justice that "lives by faith" (Hab. 2:4 = Rom. 1:17; cf. Rom. 8:10), which becomes increasingly important in Augustine's later writings.

48. The Spirit's interceding with inexpressible sighs is equated in at least one passage (*Ep.* 194,16-20) with the grace of the Holy Spirit "impetrating" further gifts of grace by which to be "active in love" (Gal. 5:6) and merit eternal life (Rom. 6:23).

49. While this passage seems to be quite straightforward, Augustine could not help approaching it analytically, intertextually, and theologically, finding implications that would be missed by the casual reader, with the result that the emphasis shifts from external threat to internal temptation. In his early writings he reflected that the human mind is a *creature* and should not be separated from God by love of *other created things*, especially sensible things (*De mor.* I,xi,18; xii,21). Even more specifically, the words "nor any other created thing" ("*neque creatura alia*") led him to reflect first on *otherness*, especially on the danger that the human mind might love things other than and lower than itself; then on Paul's *total negation* in this passage, which reminds him

of Plotinus's assertion (*Enneads* V,i,3 and 6) that there ought properly to be "nothing between" God and the soul (*Exp.prop.Rom.* 58,8-9). In this relation of immediacy he emphasized the theme of love in contrast to concupiscence (*De gr.et lib.arb.* xvii,34; *De doct.chr.* IV,xx,43). By "love of God" he understood, of course, not only God's love for human beings but their love for God, inspired by the Holy Spirit (*Ep.* 145,6, citing Rom. 5:5); anticipating Karl Barth, he enunciates the theological principle that one cannot apprehend God and love God without God (*De pat.* 15). In his last writings he seems to have returned to an emphasis on the plain meaning of this passage, being comforted by the hope that all things will indeed work together for good to those who are predestined and thus are given the gift of perseverance (*De doct.chr.* IV,xx,43; *De corr.et gr.* vii,15).

Bibliography

Arbesmann, Rudolph. 1954. "Christ the *Medicus Humilis* in St. Augustine." Pp. II:623-29 in *Augustinus Magister. Actes du Congrès international augustinien.* Paris: Études Augustiniennes, 1954.

Babcock, William S. 1979. "Augustine's Interpretation of Romans (A.D. 394-396)." *Augustinian Studies* 10: 55-74.

Bonner, Gerald. 1962. "*Libido* and *concupiscentia* in St Augustine." Pp. 202-14 in *Studia Patristica* 6 = *Texte und Untersuchungen* 81. Berlin: Akademie-Verlag.

Brown, Peter. 1988. *The Body and Society: Men, Women and Sexual Renunciation in Early Christianity.* New York: Columbia University Press.

Bultmann, Rudolf. 1951. *Theology of the New Testament,* Volume I. Translated by Kendrick Grobel. New York: Charles Scribner's Sons.

———. 1967. *The Old and New Man in the Letters of Paul.* Translated by Keith R. Crim. Richmond: John Knox Press.

Burns, J. Patout. 1979. "Augustine's Role in the Imperial Action against Pelagius." *Journal of Theological Studies,* NS 30: 67-83

———. 1980. *The Development of Augustine's Doctrine of Operative Grace.* Paris: Études Augustiniennes.

Edwards, Jonathan. 1957. *Freedom of the Will.* Edited by Paul Ramsey. New Haven: Yale University Press.

———. 1960. *The Nature of True Virtue.* With a Foreword by William K. Frankena. Ann Arbor: University of Michigan Press.

Eijkenboom, Petrus Cornelis Josephus. 1960. *Het Christus-Medicusmotief in de preken van Sint Augustinus.* Assen: Van Gorcum.

Fischer, Bonifatius. 1949- . *Vetus Latina. Die Reste der altlateinischen Bibel nach Petrus Sabatier neu gesammelt und herausgegeben von der Erzabtei Beuron.* Freiburg: Herder.

Frede, Hermann Josef. 1974. *Ein neuer Paulustext und Kommentar.* Vetus Latina, Aus der Geschichte der lateinischen Bibel 8. Freiburg: Herder.

Fredriksen, Paula. 1986. "Paul and Augustine: Conversion Narratives, Orthodox Traditions, and the Retrospective Self." *Journal of Theological Studies* NS 37: 3-34

———. 1988. "Beyond the Body/Soul Dichotomy: Augustine on Paul Against the Manichees and the Pelagians." *Recherches Augustiniennes* 23: 87-114.

Gorday, Peter. 1983. *Principles of Patristic Exegesis: Romans 9-11 in Origen, John Chrysostom, and Augustine.* Studies in the Bible and Early Christianity 4. New York and Toronto: Edwin Mellen Press.

Guelzo, Allen C. 1989. *Edwards on the Will: A Century of American Theological Debate.* Middletown: Wesleyan University Press.

Keenan, James F., S.J. 1992. *Goodness and Rightness in Thomas Aquinas's Summa Theologiae*. Washington: Georgetown University Press.

Kümmel, W.G. 1929. *Römer 7 und die Bekehrung des Paulus*. Leipzig: J.C. Hinrichs.

La Bonnardière, Anne-Marie. 1983. "La date des sermons 151 a 156 de saint Augustin." *Revue des études augustiniennes* 29: 129-36.

Locke, John. 1975. *An Essay Concerning Human Understanding*. Edited with a Foreword by Peter H. Nidditch. Oxford: Clarendon Press.

Lyonnet, Stanislaus. 1962. "'Tu ne convoiteras pas' (Rom. vii 7)." Pp. 157-62 in *Neotestamentica et Patristica. Eine Freundesgabe Herrn Professor Dr. Oscar Cullmann zu seinem 60. Geburtstag überreicht*. Leiden: E.J. Brill.

Meyer, Paul W. 1990. "The Worm at the Core of the Apple: Exegetical Reflections on Romans 7." Pp. 62-84 in *The Conversation Continues: Studies in Paul and John in Honor of J. Louis Martyn*. Nashville: Abingdon Press.

Miles, Margaret R. 1990. "The Body and Human Values in Augustine of Hippo." Pp. 55-67 in *Grace, Politics and Desire: Essays on Augustine*, Edited by H.A. Meynell. Calgary: University of Calgary Press.

Moreau, Madeleine. 1986. "Sur un commentaire d'Amos 6, 1-6." Pp. 313-22 in *Saint Augustin et la Bible*, sous la direction de Anne-Marie la Bonnardière. Paris: Beauchesne.

Muncey, R.W. 1959. *The New Testament Text of Saint Ambrose*. Texts and Studies 4. Cambridge: Cambridge University Press.

Munck, Johannes. 1959. *Paul and the Salvation of Mankind*. Translated by Frank Clarke. Atlanta: John Knox Press.

Pelikan, Jaroslav. 1971. *The Christian Tradition: A History of the Development of Doctrine, I. The Emergence of the Catholic Tradition (100-600)*. Chicago: University of Chicago Press.

———. 1988. *The Melody of Theology: A Philosophical Dictionary*. Cambridge: Harvard University Press.

Pojman, Louis P. 1987. "Freedom and Determinism: A Contemporary Discussion." *Zygon* 22: 397-417.

Poque, Suzanne. 1984. *Le langage symbolique dans la prédication d'Augustin d'Hippone. Images héroïques*. Paris: Études Augustiniennes.

Rétif, André. 1946. "A propos de l'interprétation du chapitre VII des Romains par saint Augustin." *Recherches de science religieuse* 33: 368-71.

Schelkle, K.H. Schelkle. 1956. *Paulus: Lehrer der Väter*. Düsseldorf: Patmos Verlag.

Schlabach, Gerald W. 1992. "Friendship and Adultery: Social Reality and Sexual Metaphor in Augustine's Doctrine of Original Sin." *Augustinian Studies* 23: 125-47.

Schleiermacher, Friedrich. 1928. *The Christian Faith*. Translated by H.R. Mackintosh and J.S. Stewart. Edinburgh: T. & T. Clark.

Schmithals, Walter. 1980. *Die Theologische Anthropologie des Paulus. Auslegung von Röm 7,17-8,39.* Kohlhammer Taschenbücher 1021. Stuttgart: Verlag W. Kohlhammer.

Stendahl, Krister. 1960. "The Apostle Paul and the Introspective Conscience of the West." *Harvard Theological Review* 56: 199-215, reprinted in Stendahl, 1976, 78-96.

————. 1976. *Paul among Jews and Gentiles and Other Essays.* Philadelphia: Fortress Press.

Taylor, Richard. 1967. "Determinism." Pp. II:359-73 in *Encyclopedia of Philosophy.* New York: Macmillan Company and The Free Press.

TeSelle, Eugene. 1970. *Augustine the Theologian.* New York: Herder and Herder.

————. 1994. "Serpent, Eve, and Adam: Augustine and the Exegetical Tradition." *Augustine: Presbyter Factus Sum.* Edited by Joseph T. Lienhard, S.J., Earl C. Muller, S.J., Roland J. Teske, S.J. *Collectanea Augustiniana.* New York: Peter Lang.

Theissen, Gerd. 1987. *Psychological Aspects of Pauline Theology.* Translated by John P. Galvin. Philadelphia: Fortress Press.

Westberg, Daniel. 1994. "Did Aquinas Change His Mind About the Will?" *The Thomist,* 58: 41-60.

Wetzel, James. 1987. "The Recovery of Free Agency in the Theology of St. Augustine." *Harvard Theological Review* 80: 112-18.

————. 1992. *Augustine and the Limits of Virtue.* Cambridge: Cambridge University Press.

Wolf, Susan. 1980. "Asymmetrical Freedom." *Journal of Philosophy* 77: 151-66.

————. 1990. *Freedom Within Reason.* New York: Oxford University Press.

–FOUR–

A Conversion of Augustine

From Natural Law to Restored Nature in Romans 2:13-16

Simon J. Gathercole

"I write as I progress, and progress as I write" (*Ep.* 143,2).

C   Modern academia is not swamped by scholars admitting to changes of opinion, and the theological disciplines are sadly no exception. Augustine's *Retractations* come as a breath of fresh air, as do his changes of opinion in other works. One of the most interesting, and most neglected, confessions of repentance concerns Romans 2, where Augustine changes his position on the identity of the Gentiles who have the law written on their hearts. One intention of this present study is to integrate discussions of natural law with research into Augustine's soteriology, such as feature heavily in work on Augustine's reading of Romans.

A number of works deal with Augustine's interpretation of Romans, but they are concerned with a very narrow range of texts. This is understandable, and I have no desire to criticize works for not covering ground which they never intended to cover. But by and large, scholarship has concentrated on a few key texts in Romans: Romans 5:14 with its impact on the nature of original sin; Romans 7:14ff and Augustine's discussions of concupiscence; and Romans 9 and the question of predestination and grace (e.g., Babcock 1979; Burns 1979; Frederiksen Landes 1980; Mara 1984; Delaroche 1996).[1] These chapters are much discussed, because they were crucial in Augustine's articulation of his soteriology, in particular in the transition from his early to his mature thought. But none of this secondary literature really discusses Romans 2:13-16 and its relation to the doctrines of natural law, sin and salvation.

A   This essay is also intended to do a service to NT scholars, who, in their Romans commentaries and articles on this passage, do not have the

---

A Augustine's acknowledged changes of opinion. Rom. 2:13-16; 5:14; 7:14ff.
A Relevance to textual analysis of Romans. Rom. 2:13-16.

opportunity to plow through Augustine. As a result, what come up in exegetical discussions are simply citations to Augustine's works in translation. Sometimes, as we shall see, this leads to misquotation when these are taken out of the context of the works in which they appear. Further, it leads to a very incomplete view of Augustine's use of the passage, because of his wider use of the concepts — and the language as well — of Rom. 2:13-16, both of which will also be examined here. **A** This paper will, I hope, contribute to the ongoing exegetical debate among NT scholars on this passage — a debate which has come to something of a standstill.[2] Since Augustine's work is one of the most important episodes in the interpretive history of this passage, it is important to have access to something more than proof-texts.

C Augustine's change in his interpretation of Rom. 2:13-16 is a topic which has occupied NT scholars much more than Augustinians. While Augustine's use of Scripture did not require that he decide on a fixed meaning for a text, then use it with that meaning in whatever argument he was constructing,[3] his citation and allusion was not haphazard proof-texting either. I aim to show that Augustine's interpretation did evolve and change, and that the change occurred in a consistent direction. This paper will focus in particular on the "law written on the heart" in Rom. 2:15a, as well as dealing with the conscience and conflicting thoughts in 2:15b.

A One textual note before we begin. It is interesting that in verse 15, Augustine's (and Pelagius's) text differs from the Vulgate at one particular point. The Greek, some commentators note, probably supplies three distinct witnesses[4]: the work of the Law written on the heart, the conscience as a further confirmatory witness, and finally the thoughts either accusing or defending. Some, however, do take the third to be explanatory of the second (e.g. Calvin), or even all three as descriptive of the same process (e.g. Barrett). In any case, the second and third are in the genitive and are almost certainly genitive absolutes. Augustine's Latin text, however, has the work of the conscience as an ablative absolute (*contestante* [Pel. & B: *testimonium reddente*] *conscientia illorum* [*Exp.prop. Rom.* 10; *De serm.dom.mon.* II,32]) and the accusing and defending thoughts in the *genitive*, as in the Greek. Of course, this changes the meaning slightly: the genitive in Latin cannot bear the same sense as a genitive absolute in Greek. So, the verse for Augustine and Pelagius must be translated, "They show the work of the Law written on their hearts; bearing additional witness is the consciousness also of their accusing and even defending thoughts (on the day when... v.16)."

A The current impasse in textual interpretation of the passage.
C Augustine's readings of the passage were consistent — and changing. Rom. 2:15a, 15b.
A Augustine's Old Latin text differed from the Septuagint and the Vulgate. Rom. 2:16.

Augustine's Early Interpretation

C One passage that is cited as evidence for Augustine's view of this passage is in *Contra Faustum* (XIX,2). In this text, which dates from 397-98, Faustus tries to problematize Jesus' statement that he came not to abolish the Law and the prophets but rather to fulfil them. He does this by putting forward three different laws and three different kinds of prophets. The law aspect is relevant to us here: "And there are three kinds of law (*legum genera tria*): one of the Hebrews, which Paul calls the Law of sin and death; and another of the Gentiles, which he calls the 'natural' law [he quotes Rom. 2:14-15a]; and the third kind of law is the truth, which the Apostle indicates when he says 'The Law of the Spirit of life in Christ Jesus . . .'" Far from endorsing the position which Faustus expounds here, Augustine's response is more likely to be critical of it. He replies: "And do not go on straining, trying to seek (but not finding!) a way out through the three kinds of law and three kinds of prophets" (*C.Faust.* XIX,7). It is not certain that Augustine is criticizing Faustus' taxonomy of laws here,[5] but it seems to be another example where Augustine, having waited for so long for the Manichaean oracle to answer his difficulties, was disappointed with the reply.[6]

Kuss makes the mistake in his Rom.ans commentary of assuming that the text from *Contra Faustum* constitutes Augustine's own view of natural law and of this half-verse from Romans (Kuss 1963, 70-71). But it seems that this evidence, while it might function as part of the backdrop to Augustine's reading of the passage, does not actually count as direct evidence *for* Augustine's reading. In fact, as we examine our next passage, we see that Augustine uses Rom. 2:13-16 with a decisively anti-Manichaean slant.

H Augustine's *Exposition of the Sermon on the Mount* is our first text. Here the universality of natural law, of God speaking in the conscience to all persons however sinful, is the guarantee that God could speak to Satan in the story of Job. This had evidently been mocked by the Manichees and used as an argument against the authority of the OT: "Those heretical enemies of the Old Testament, when they wish to mock at it with sacrilegious mouth, brandish this above other weapons, that Satan begged that he should be tempted. For they put the question to unskillful men by no means able to understand such things, how Satan could speak with

---

C Augustine's adaptation of the Manichaeans' threefold classification of the law. Rom. 2:14–15a.

H Can God speak to Satan and to sinful human beings?

God." Augustine's reply further on is: "For when will they be able to understand that there is no soul, however wicked, which can yet reason in any way, in whose conscience God does not speak? For who but God has written the law of nature in the hearts of men? This is the law concerning which the apostle says: 'For when the Gentiles, who do not have the Law, do by nature the things contained in the Law, they, though not having the Law, are a Law for themselves. They show the work of the Law written in their hearts, their conscience also bearing witness to them, and their thoughts the meanwhile accusing or else excusing one another, on the day when the Lord shall judge the secrets of men.' And therefore, as in the case of every rational soul which thinks and reasons, even though blinded by passion, we attribute whatever in its reason is true, not to itself, but to the very light of truth by which, however faintly, it is according to its capacity illuminated, so as to perceive some measure of truth by its reasoning..." (*De serm.dom.mon.* II,32). Because of this, Augustine argues, even the faint perception of truth that Satan had discerned about Job must have come from God. Thus it makes sense that there are none so sinful that God cannot speak to them. And reason is the faculty which makes this possible. Chroust refers to this passage and comments: "Man's moral conscience, which can never be silenced, is the *lex naturalis* of these heathens" (Chroust 1973, 69).

H Book II of the *Confessions* provides another example of exactly the same function of the Law written in the heart. Here Augustine confesses to theft in the famous 'pear-stealing' incident. "Theft receives certain punishment by your law (*lex tua*), Lord, and by the Law written in the hearts of men (*et lex scripta in cordibus hominum*) which not even iniquity itself destroys" (*Conf.* II,iv,9). Chadwick and Pine-Coffin (Pine-Coffin 1961; Chadwick 1991) take this sentence slightly differently in their translations: the former distinguishes the two laws, and the latter sees them as one (the *et* being explanatory). There is probably a slight distinction, *lex tua* being the Divine Intellect, or *lex aeterna*, while the *lex scripta in cordibus hominum* is the *lex naturae*. This *lex aeterna* is crucial to the way Augustine thinks that society should function. "Briefly to express in words, as best I can, the idea of eternal law as it is stamped in our minds, I should say this: it is that all things should be in perfect order" (*De lib.arb.* I,vi,15). This means that everything should be given its proper place and treated in its right proportions. Chroust gives two examples: "This is not the proper order, nay, cannot be at all called order, when that which is superior should be sub-ordinate to that which is inferior"; and elsewhere, reason functions in a moral way when "in all its distinctions, choices and evaluations it subordinates the lesser to the greater, the corporeal to the spiritual, etc." (*De lib.arb.* I,viii,18; *Ep.* 140,ii,4, quoted in

---

H How "eternal law" becomes "natural law." Rom. 2:14–15.

Chroust 1973, 60). The *lex aeterna*, then, is the Divine Intellect by which the whole cosmos is ordered, of which the *lex naturalis*, the norm by which rational souls act morally, is a subset. Thus "the *lex naturalis*, according to St. Augustine, is the conscious participation of rational man in the *lex aeterna*" (Chroust 1973, 68). This *lex naturalis* is that which is written on the heart of every human.

A concrete example of this *lex naturae* can be seen in Sermon 1, possibly Augustine's strangest use of Rom. 2:14-15. It comes in his defense of the practice of adoption against those who, it seemed, claimed it was unbiblical. Augustine responds that it was the common practice of the wives of the patriarchs to insist on their husbands having children through maid-servants, which they could then themselves adopt. Moses was adopted; and in those times, what happened was that "the choice of the will" [Augustine's term for adoption, as opposed to "the natural way of birth"] was taken for the rule of law, as the Apostle saith also in another place, "The Gentiles who do not have the Law, do by nature the things contained in the Law" (*Serm.* 1,28). It is very difficult to determine precisely what Augustine had in mind here, except that he is giving an example of the use of the natural law.

C *Conf.* II,iv,9 does not quote all of Rom. 2:14-15, but it is a clear allusion to Rom. 2:14. Augustine asserts that evil contravenes not just Torah, but also a law in all humans which — to quote Pine-Coffin's translation — "cannot be erased however sinful they are" (*Conf.* II,iv,9). This very much echoes what we saw about the truth that "there is no soul, however wicked, which can yet reason in any way, in whose conscience God does not speak" (*De serm.dom.mon.* II,32; see further Chroust 1973, 67-70). This law of nature is evident, Augustine argues, from the fact that even a thief cannot bear being stolen from, even if the stealer *needs* what he is stealing. C Perhaps it is the "rationality" of the Law in the heart that leads Augustine to present the pear-stealing incident in such *irrational* terms. Augustine wants to make clear that he stole purely for the thrill of the communal sin: "I took pleasure in the same vices (*sc.* as my companions) not only for the enjoyment of what I did, but also for the applause I won" (*Conf.* II,iii,7). The sin itself had no rational basis. On the contrary, "of what I stole I already had plenty, and much better at that, and I had no wish to enjoy the things I coveted by stealing, but only to enjoy the theft itself and the sin. There was a pear tree near our vineyard, loaded with fruit that was attractive neither to look at nor to taste... We took away an enormous quantity of pears, not to eat them ourselves, but simply to throw them to the pigs. Perhaps we ate some of them, but our

---

C Augustine's interpretation of his own sin. Rom. 2:14.
C The rationality of the natural law heightens the irrationality of sin.

real pleasure consisted in doing something that was forbidden" (*Conf.* II,iv,9).

H The *Exposition of Psalm 58* contains something very similar. In this extended discussion of natural law he again employs Romans 2. Here, "the hand of our Maker in our very hearts has written this truth, 'That which to thyself thou wouldest not have done, do thou not to another' (Tob 4.15)." This Law is universal, given before Torah, although it was not read or heeded. The abandoning of this Law in the heart gave rise to an alienation within the human person — a fragmentation of nature — and the restoration of the person involved a return to oneself. "What does the written law cry to those who have deserted 'the law written in their hearts' (Rom. 2.15)? 'Return to the heart, you transgressors!' (Is 46.8)."[7] As we saw in the pear-stealing incident, the universal human instinct of not wishing to be cuckolded, stolen from, or murdered gives validity to the positive prohibition of these things, which is the *content* of the universal law in the heart expressed in Tob 4:15.

H In Letter 107 (written in 414) Augustine's use of the law on the heart is triggered by a reference to Rom. 4:15: "For where there is no law, there is no transgression." He goes on to argue that the law which is the precondition of transgression in the verse is not confined to Israel, *quoniam lex est etiam in ratione hominis qui iam utitur arbitrio libertatis naturaliter in corde conscripta, qua suggeritur ne aliquid faciat quisque alteri quod pati ipse non uult:* "since there is also a law, in the reason of a person who uses free will, written naturally in the heart, by which it is suggested that no person should do anything to another which he would not be willing to suffer" (*Ep.* 107,15). According to this law, then, all are transgressors according to the law, whether that law was "given in paradise, naturally embedded, or legislated on tablets" (*En.Ps.* 118,5).

The *Exposition of Psalm 118* (c. 420), also shows that Augustine's use of this passage arose not merely out of polemic but out of his own wrestling with the text in the context of the unity and harmony of Scripture. Here the motivation is to reconcile two parts of Scripture: Ps. 118:119 ("praevaricantes aestimavi omnes peccatores terrae") and Rom. 4:15 ("ubi enim lex non est, nec praevaricatio"). How can Gentiles be transgressors if "where there is no law there is no transgression"? The answer is the same: they have a *lex naturae* which they should not ignore, because what they do to others they would not put up with themselves (*En.Ps.* 118, serm. 25).[8] There was a Law before Sinai, but it was *instaurata, aucta, firmata* by the Mosaic Law (Girardet 1995, 286 n. 100).

H Natural law is universal and prior to Scripture. Rom. 2:15.
H Natural law makes *all* sinners responsible. Rom. 4:15.

Summary

H It is evident from these texts that Augustine does not merely use Rom. 2:14-15 polemically, as a proof-text. He has reflected on the passage deeply, and it is thoroughly integrated into his system. Its systemic relations and functions can be discerned from the consistent features which appear again and again in his reference to these verses. The first feature is that this law is universal, ineradicable even in the most terrible sinner, because even the most sinful person retains rationality (Chroust also mentions *De spir.et litt.* xxviii,48 and *Ep.* 157,iii,15ff. in this connection). It means that all nations are guilty of transgression, not just Adam, who received the commandment in the garden, and the recipients of the Law of Moses, though their transgressions are more serious.[9] Secondly, however, this law, though ineradicable, is ineffectual because it is not heeded. And thirdly, the content of this *lex naturalis* is consistently the negative version of the golden rule. "Man darf daher die Goldene Regel, die *lex in cordibus hominum* oder *naturaliter insita*, als Augustins *lex naturalis/naturae, 'non scripta'* bezeichnen" (Girardet 1995, 286). On an individual level, this can be seen from the fact that any (rational) person hates having certain things done to them. But it is also tied up with Augustine's political theory and theology of jurisprudence, which are based on these two foundational principles: everything in its proper place and proportion, and the Golden Rule.

The Late Works: the New Covenant Law Written on the Heart

H The *Exposition of Psalm 118* is particularly interesting because it includes both this reference to the law of nature which we have just seen, and also reference to the new covenant law on the heart, where we see that Augustine has, by this time, begun to understand this concept of "law written on the heart" in a rather different way: "You, more inward that my inmost self, have laid down a law within my heart by your Spirit, as it were, by your fingers, so that I might not fear it as a slave without love, but might love it with a chaste fear as a son, and fear it with chaste love" (*En.Ps.* 118, serm. xxii,6).

H The early Augustine's interpretation is consistent: the natural law, while universal, is not heeded, and it is equivalent with the "negative Golden Rule." Rom. 2:14-15.

H The later Augustine more clearly differentiates between natural law and the law of the Spirit.

C The most important text for Augustine's treatment of Rom. 2:14-15 is undoubtedly *De spiritu et littera* (written in 412), where we see the explanation of his new position. Here Augustine deals with the interpretation of this passage at far greater length that anywhere else. The discourse is prompted by an inquiry by Augustine's friend Marcellinus, who has been perturbed by Augustine mentioning the possibility of achieving perfection in this life. Augustine carefully sets out his premise that this is not possible by oneself, but is achievable by the human will *divinely aided*: nothing is impossible with God. Here the Pelagian polemic becomes evident: "They, however, must be resisted with the utmost ardour and vigour who suppose that without God's help, the mere power of the human will in itself, can either perfect righteousness, or advance steadily towards it" (*De spir.et litt.* ii,4). The Pelagians held that the commandments were sufficient, in view of the ability of the human will, to give that will proper direction. Perfect righteousness should be sought, and was a possibility, as one had sufficient knowledge of how to please God.[10] **H** But for Augustine, knowledge on its own is useless. In his interpretation of Rom. 1:19ff, as Madec argues, the knowledge of God which the philosophers have reached does not restrain idolatry and *superbia* (Madec 1962). Similarly, the knowledge which Israel had was not sufficient, for "the letter kills, but the spirit gives life." The Spirit, by the grace of Christ, is needed to bring the requisite divine assistance to the will. This grace was hidden in the Old Testament, but is revealed in the New, and so the central chapters of this work are concerned with the exposition of the difference between the old and new covenants. In *On the Spirit and the Letter*, two key verses which Augustine uses to explicate Rom. 2:14-15 are introduced. First, Jer. 31:31-34, with its prophecy of the law to be written on the heart, which Augustine sees as being fulfilled by the regenerate Gentiles here in Romans (*De spir. et litt.* xvi,28-xvii,29).[11] Secondly, Rom. 5:5, where love for God (Augustine takes the genitive objectively) is poured out into the hearts of believers through the Holy Spirit. Jer. 31:31-34 is expanded on, and Augustine actually defines this law in the heart: "What then is God's law written by God himself in the hearts of men, but the very presence of the Holy Spirit, who is the "finger of God," and by whose presence is shed abroad in our hearts the love which is the fulfilling of the law and the end of the commandment?" At this stage, Augustine concludes this stage of the argument by summing up the discontinuity between the covenants: "It is therefore apparent what difference there is between the old covenant and the new: in the former, the law is written on tablets, while in the latter, on hearts; so that what in one alarms from

---

C The Pelagians rely on the natural law to the exclusion of the law of the Spirit. Rom. 2:14-15.

H The natural law is not to be confused with the law of the Spirit.

without, in the other delights from within; and in the former, man becomes a transgressor through the letter that kills, in the other, a lover, through the life-giving Spirit (*De spir.et litt.* xxi,36).

A Here Augustine raises the question of the Gentiles in Rom. 2:14-15. He imagines an interlocutor asking how Augustine's distinction stands when there were Gentiles who had the law written on the hearts, the natural law of their consciences, before the coming of Christ. Furthermore, were not Gentiles better off with a law in their hearts than Israelites were, having one on tablets? Augustine answers these two questions by expounding Rom. 2:13ff. in the context of the argument of Rom. 1-2. Crucially, verses 14-15 are framed by the sentence "It is not the hearers of the law who are righteous before God, but the doers of the law who will be justified." Augustine comments on this: "Who they are that are treated of in these words, he goes on to tell us: 'For when the Gentiles, who do not have the Law, do by nature the things of the law' and so forth in the passage which I have quoted already" (*De spir.et litt.* xxvi,44). So Augustine equates these Gentiles here with the activity of God promised in Jer. 31:31-34: he interprets Rom. 2.25-29 in precisely the same way. He concludes: "God puts his laws into their mind, and writes them in their hearts with his own finger, the Holy Spirit, by whom is shed abroad in them the love which is the "fulfilling of the law" (*De spir.et litt.* xxvi,46).

H From the perspective of modern exegetes, the biggest obstacle to this interpretation is the "by nature," and Augustine felt he might be criticized by his contemporaries here as well. He replies: "Nor ought it to disturb us that the apostle described them as doing that which is contained in the law "*by nature*" – not by the Spirit of God, not by faith, not by grace. For it is the Spirit of grace that does it, in order to restore in us the image of God, in which we were *naturally* created. Sin, indeed, is contrary to nature, and it is grace that heals it" (*De spir.et litt.* xxvii,47). This is an important point: the law written on the heart is the restoration in humanity of the *imago Dei*, which has been tarnished (but not abolished) by sin (Bonner 1986, 370). It still exists in any person who participates in reason.

On the other hand, Augustine does allow the possibility of the "non-Christian" reading of these verses. Or, more precisely, he does not want the reader to think that his view of the difference between the covenants stands or falls by his interpretation of Rom. 2:14-15. "*Etiam sic*" - even if this other interpretation (from which Augustine distances himself here) is correct, his theology is not threatened. "But if those who do naturally what pertains to the law are not yet to be reckoned in the number of those

---

A How can the Gentiles follow the law "by nature"? Is this the law "written on the heart"? Rom. 2:14-15.

H Either nature is "restored," or a less sinful life receives a lesser punishment.

whom the grace of Christ justifies..." (*si autem hi qui naturaliter quae legis sunt faciunt, nondum sunt habendi in numero eorum quos Christi iustificat gratia...*). Augustine concedes that this "writing on the heart" exists in a faint and faded form in even the most depraved individual: the renewal by the Spirit means that the law is written more clearly, and the *imago Dei* is restored to some of its original glory (*De spir.et litt.* xxviii,48).

The objection that Augustine makes to the "non-Christian" reading of this passage is this: "how will 'their thoughts defending them on the day when God judges the secrets of men' be of any use except perhaps that they be punished more mildly?" Augustine then expands on this with his doctrine of gradations of reward in heaven and punishment in hell. But here, at the end of his discussion of this passage, he has still distanced himself from this non-Christian reading. **C** So by 412 he had changed his position, and argues that these Gentiles do these things by nature because grace has restored and healed their nature, and now they have to some extent reverted to the righteousness that was a reality pre-fall. His theology of the fall now meant that he was less inclined to admit the possibility of natural virtue.

C The argument surrounding Rom. 2:14-15 in *Against Julian* (IV,23-25) follows a similar pattern to *On the Spirit and the Letter*, though in a rather shorter form. The first similarity is that Augustine explains his view of the passage in direct response to Julian's use of the passage, by which Julian had hoped to dismantle Augustine's anthropology:[12] "By means of these Gentiles you tried to prove that even those who are strangers to the faith of Christ can have true righteousness, for the Apostle says they do by nature what the Law prescribes" (*C.Jul.* IV,23). **A** Augustine criticizes Julian for not explaining what he means: is "true righteousness" good things, which are not really good at all because they are not for God; or is it actually worship of God which will be rewarded with eternal life? The second feature in common with the discussion in *On the Spirit and the Letter* is the objection to Julian's view that it makes a nonsense of the "defending thoughts" in 2:15. That, at least, is the case if Julian takes these Gentiles to do some good, but *not* to receive the reward of eternal life for their good. If they do receive eternal life for these good deeds, then they could not possibly do them except by faith.[13] Thirdly, Augustine again introduces his doctrine of lesser punishment as the possible result of good deeds (i.e., in obedience to the the *lex naturae* of the Golden Rule) by the unregenerate. This is not to concede anything to Julian, but merely to rule out any possibility of escape for him. Augustine confines the function of the defending thoughts to the lessening of

---

C The later Augustine is less affirmative of "natural" virtue.

C Defense of this interpretation against Julian. Rom. 2:14-15.

A What does the natural law do for the Gentiles? Rom. 2:15.

punishment for the wicked who obeyed in small ways the law of nature, occasionally not doing what they themselves would not put up with. For his urbane interlocutor, Augustine gives the example of the virtuous Fabricius and the villain Catiline: "Fabricius will be punished less than Catiline, not because the former was good, but because the latter was more evil" (*C.Jul.* IV,25).

H But there is more in *Against Julian* than a rehearsal of the arguments of ten years earlier. There is a further development in this later period when Augustine faced Julian of Eclanum. In the early stage of the Pelagian controversy, Augustine is providing a systematic exposition of his thoughts about the Law, and explains 2:14-15 primarily as an example of the difference between the covenants. And Augustine accepts the plausibility of the non-Christian reading of the text, even though he does not hold it himself. He wants to say that his point still stands if one takes the other view of that text. This is in line with his exposition, mentioned above, of his hermeneutic at the end of the *Confessions*, where the key point is the orthodoxy of a reading that is crucial, not its exegetical accuracy. But by the time of *Against Julian*, Augustine is less willing to leave the door open to the possibility of a non-Christian reading which allows for true virtue: "nec per eos potes probare quod vis, etiam infideles veras posse habere virtutes: sunt quippe isti fideles" (*C.Jul.* IV,25). *He has decided that this reading is no longer orthodox.* Unbelievers cannot have true virtues because "all that is not from faith is sin" (Rom. 14:23) and "without faith it is impossible to please God" (Heb. 11:6). This reading of 2:14-15 is what makes Julian and his colleagues "enemies of the grace of God" and, further on, "greatly despised by the Chistian Church" (*C.Jul.* IV,23).

Yet Augustine is not unequivocal about condemning the non-Christian interpretation *per se*. What he criticizes is Julian trying to prove from these Gentiles that "those who are alien to the faith of Christ can have *true* righteousness." Augustine allows the (admittedly very slim) possibility, as he did in *On the Spirit and the Letter*, of an orthodox, "non-Christian" reading of the passage. He takes it to read that if they do not have faith in Christ, then they cannot be righteous, and so the only possible function of the excusing thoughts is the lessening of punishment. But Augustine's acknowledgement of the possibility of the non-Christian reading here in *Against Julian* is much more faint that it had been ten years earlier.

H Orthodox doctrine attenuates the scope of the "non-Christian" reading of the passage. Rom. 2:14-15.

Summary

C "Within the last few days, I have read some writings by Pelagius -- a holy man I hear, who has advanced considerably in the Christian life -- which contain very brief expositions of the epistles of Paul" (*De pecc.mer.* III,i,1). So wrote Augustine in the winter of 411-412 (Delaroche 1996, 15-17) shortly before he wrote *On the Spirit and the Letter.* A Pelagius had described in his Romans commentary, written somewhere betweeen 405-410 (De Bruyn 1993, 11), how there were two possibilities for the meaning of "they do by nature what pertains to the Law" in Rom. 2:14: either "those who were by nature righteous in the period before the law" or "those who even now do some good." Again, he supplies two possibilities for verse 15: either that nature produces the law in the heart through conscience, or that "the conscience testifies that it has a law . . . since the conscience is apprehensive when one sins, and rejoices when sin is overcome" (De Bruyn 1993, 73).

H But Augustine is not in debate with the exegesis of Rom. 2:14-15 in this commentary: Pelagius here is not particularly Pelagian.[14] At stake in the controversy between Augustine and the Pelagians over this text are the broader issues of the doctrine of sin and anthropology, whether that be defined in terms of human nature,[15] or the more relational categories that Brown and Bonner employ.[16] In Augustine's opinion, real virtue and pleasing God are impossible because of the sinful nature. Augustine provides a rather sarcastic example of this in *The City of God.* C In the course of his debate with Roman culture about the so-called Golden Age of morality, he quotes Sallust: "equity and virtue prevailed among the Romans not more by force of laws than of nature" (*Catilinarian Conspiracy* ix). He then comments himself: "I presume it is to this inborn equity and goodness of disposition we are to ascribe the rape of the Sabine women" (*De ciu.dei* II,17). This is the current "nature" of humanity: Augustine knew that Rom. 2:14-15 could not refer to the achievement of *veras virtutes*, but in his own mind, he could not envisage even partial obedience to the law in this text, such is the extent of human sin. H It is precisely this nature that is restored by conversion. Augustine's works against the Pelagians are full of references to the restoration of nature that is effected by God's grace. In *On Nature and Grace*, Augustine's first reply to Pelagius is that "if righteousness comes by nature, then Christ died in vain" (*De*

C Augustine responds to Pelagius.
A Pelagius's readings of Rom. 2:14-15.
H The debate is not exegetical but doctrinal.
C An illustration from the history of Rome.
H Human nature must be restored through grace and conversion.

nat.et gr. ii,2);[17] but he then opposes the possibility of justification "by the law of nature and the power of the will" (ix,10) with the doctrine that grace is concerned with "the *cure*, not the constitution" of nature (x,11). As a result, Augustine's favorite epithet for our Lord in this work is that of the Physician.[18] Similarly, there are three citations of Matt. 9:12, "It is not the healthy who need a physician, but the sick" (i,1; xix,21; xxi,23) and two of the parable of the good Samaritan, which Augustine uses as an extended illustration of conversion (lii,60 and xliii,50): humanity was created healthy, but "our present inquiry, however, is about the man whom the thieves left half dead on the road, and who, being disabled and pierced through with heavy wounds, is not so able to mount up to the heights of righteousness as he was able to descend from them; although if he is now in the inn, he is in the process of cure."[19] This "process" is the restoration of nature that begins when God writes the law on the hearts of these Gentiles. This law that had faded as a result of sin is now inscribed more boldly, the image of God which had been marred begins to be restored, and the motives which previously had not directed action towards God at all are now infused with the "love for God, poured out in our hearts by the Holy Spirit." It is this restored nature that now begins to please God by faith.

The Conscience and the Accusing and Defending Thoughts

A Augustine's typical method in his *Exposition of Certain Propositions from the Epistle to the Romans* (mid-390s) consists of using other short passages of Scripture to explain difficult verses: "Poi seguono gli 84 passi ripresi dalla *lettera ai Romani* che, secondo il metodo interpretativo che gli è proprio, trovano una loro chiarificazione in altre citazioni vetero e neotestamentarie" (Mara 1984, 98).[20] When Augustine comes to explain the conscience in Rom. 2:15, he uses 1 Jn. 3:20, the verse previous to that which Origen used. **C** Origen is discussing whether the conscience is different from the heart or the soul. "For this conscience is also spoken of elsewhere, since it accuses and is not accused, judges a man, but is not itself judged, just as John says, "If our conscience does not accuse us, we have confidence before God" (1 John 3.21) (Bammel 1997, 230). Augustine uses 1 Jn. 3:20, which has a rather different force: "Quod autem dicit: *Contestante conscientia illorum,* secundum illum locum loquitur Iohannis

---

A Interpretation of Rom. 2:15 is aided by other passages in Scripture.
C Similarity and contrast with Origen's interpretation.

apostoli, quo ait: *Dilectissimi, si cor nostrum nos reprehenderit, maior est deus conscientiae nostrae et cetera*" (*Exp.prop.rom.* 10). **A** Frederiksen mistranslates "*contestante conscientia illorum*" as "by their conflicting thoughts," whereas it is actually the previous phrase "their consciences also bearing witness" (Fredriksen Landes 1983, 5). The Latin translation of 1 Jn. 3 is also peculiar here, translating καρδία as *conscientia*, except in the first occurrence in 1 Jn. 3:20. Origen certainly understands the activity of the conscience here in a positive way, with an acquitting rather than a condemning function: he wrote previously of this taking place *testimonio sanae conscientiae*, "with the witness of an upright/healthy conscience." Augustine's interpretation has a slightly different, and a slightly peculiar force: with his use of 1 Jn. 3:20, he says that Paul is referring in Rom. 2:15 to God's acquittal of "us" *despite the testimony of the conscience.*

This is actually in slight contrast with Augustine's use of Rom. 2:15 in his contemporaneous reading of Psalm 9 during the 390s. Here the conscience and the thoughts are brought into the divine courtroom as testifying that God's judgment is just. That is to say, God will judge according to people's real internal guilt or innocence, "not as men judge who see not the heart" (*En.Ps.* 9,27).

In *The City of God*, in a section on the judgment of the wicked written between 425 and 427, Augustine says that God's judgment comes swiftly, "either because he is to come suddenly . . . or because he will convince the consciences of men directly and without any prolix harangue. 'For,' as it is written, 'in the thoughts of the wicked his examination shall be conducted' (Wis. 1:9). And the apostle says, 'The thoughts accusing or else excusing, in the day in which God shall judge the hidden things of men, according to my gospel in Jesus Christ' (Rom. 2:15-16). Thus then shall the Lord be a swift witness, when he shall suddenly bring back into the memory that which shall convince and punish the conscience" (*De civ.dei* XX,26, Dods translation). Here the text has a wholly negative reference, to the punishment of the wicked, with their depraved thoughts and consciences being the objects of judgment.

H We have seen that the reference to the accusing and defending thoughts in *On the Spirit and the Letter* and *Against Julian* give rise to explanations of Augustine's doctrine of gradations of reward (whereby "in the reign of God the saints differ in glory as one star does from another," *De spir.et litt.* xxviii,48) and punishment, as with Catiline being punished more severely than Fabricius. The problem comes when in these texts

---

A What is the "testimony of conscience"? Where is it "acquitting" and where is it "condemning"?

H Perhaps there are degrees of reward and punishment.

Augustine introduces his objection to his opponents' reading of the texts. He sees the main flaw in the "non-Christian" reading of Rom. 2:14-15 as not doing justice to the "defending" thoughts: "quid eis proderunt excusantes cogitationes?" (Ibid). Or again, "quid ergo eis prodest, quod secundum Apostolum defendent eos cogitationes suae, in die qua iudicabit Deus occulta hominum" (*C.Jul.* IV, 23).

Summary

C Because the references to Rom. 2:15b are so sparse and spread over such a long time frame, it is difficult to assess whether Augustine had a consistent view of these verses or not. A synthesis is certainly possible, however, though we must be cautious about how much of it was present to Augustine's thinking when he quoted these verses. Putting *Propositions from Romans* and *City of God* together (somewhat risky, considering the time gap), one might conclude that both believer and unbeliever experience a guilty conscience and accusing thoughts: the believer because of the internal struggle which we see in Augustine's later interpretation of Romans 7, and the unbeliever because the voice of God is not completely silenced by sin. For the unbeliever, the wicked thoughts are the object of God's judgment on the final day. This judgment is swift and direct, as our *City of God* passage makes clear, and entirely just, as is emphasized by the *Enarration on Psalm 9*. This is reasonably coherent, and one could imagine Augustine seeing it this way.

There are problems, however, when one combines Augustine's view of the law written on the heart with his view of the conscience and the thoughts. In the early period, Augustine's "non-Christian" reading of 2:15a sits very uncomfortably with his positive interpretation of the conscience, which we saw in *Propositions from Romans*. Conversely, his later interpretation of 2:15a, which sees the law on the heart as referring to God's fulfilment of the new covenant promise in the lives of Gentiles, is problematic alongside his negative view of the conscience and the thoughts as involved in the condemnation of the wicked in the *City of God* passage. One might be tempted to say that Augustine viewed the two halves of the verse as disparate units, were it not for the fact that he insists on the unity of the passage in *On the Spirit and the Letter* and *Against Julian*, to the point of demanding that his opponents take the two together, and criticizing them precisely for not integrating the two halves acceptably: "If they are strangers from this grace, then what use to them

---

C How consistent are the earlier and the later Augustine? Rom. 2:15a & b.

are *excusing thoughts on the day when God judges the secrets of men.*" (*De spir.et litt.* xxviii,48) This tension does not seem to be easily soluble.

Uses of Augustine's Interpretation

C This is not the place for any detailed history of interpretation of this passage;[21] rather, we will look at two striking examples (from the Reformation and modern periods) of the reception of Augustine's interpretation. His general theory of the *lex aeterna* and the *lex naturae* went on to be extremely influential: "It may be remarked here that St. Augustine's theistic definition of the *lex aeterna* was destined to become the basic concept and the authoritative pronouncement for the whole medieval (scholastic) jurisprudence or natural law theories" (Chroust 1973, 63). His reading of Romans 2, however, did not take hold: the Greek thinkers by and large followed Chrysostom, for whom these Gentiles were given grace, and did believe in one God (though not in Christ). Later, Thomas Aquinas and Bonaventure confined the passage to Gentiles before Christ, while many (Riedl mentions Bruno, Abelard, Robert of Melun and Nicholas of Lyra) assumed a natural knowledge of God which led to an anonymous, inclusive faith in Christ and divine assistance to fulfil the law of nature, which then led to a reward of eternal life (Riedl 1965, 171).

When it comes to the time of the Reformation, T.H.L. Parker makes two noteworthy points about the very short period of time which his book covers (Parker 1986, 125-41). First is the great number of commentaries written in this ten-year period: Parker has counted thirty-five (including different editions). Second is the fact that more commentaries specifically on Romans were written by Roman Catholic cardinals than by reformers. And when we look at what they have to say on Rom. 2:13-16 (to which Parker devotes a whole chapter) there is a dazzling array of interpretations, as one might expect. What they have in common is that almost none of them follows Augustine in seeing the reference to gentile Christians, which is surprising, considering how influential Augustine was on both sides of the divide. The Reformation was, among many other things, a battle over Augustine.

C Luther, whose commentary predates the spate of commentaries from 1532 to 1542, rejects both of the options that Augustine presents, saying that the truth lies somewhere in between. He prefers to understand Paul

---

C The influence of Augustine on later interpretation — or rather, the lack of influence of the *later* Augustine.

C Debates during the Reformation era. Rom. 2:14-15.

as talking of those Gentiles who prepare their hearts to receive God's grace, those who are almost in the process of becoming Christians. Melanchthon also disagrees: "Augustine," he says, "imports difficulties into Paul here, whereas the text itself is not obscure. Paul is discussing knowledge and judgment. It is plain that the unregenerate can do the external works of the law . . ." (Parker 1986, 139-40). In their different ways, Calvin and the Roman Catholic cardinals take an approach more negative than Augustine's, Calvin arguing here that "ignorance is offered in vain as an excuse by the Gentiles, since they declare by their own deeds that they do have some rule of righteousness" (Parker 1986, 47-48). On the other side, the Roman Catholic cardinals (e.g. Caietan and Guilliaud) refer at this point to the two stages of justification, the first by the sheer and unaided grace of God, the second by the person's cooperation with grace (Parker 1986, 131). Caietan further argues, "Note well that it is one thing to do the things which are of the Law and another to do meritoriously the things which are of the Law" (Parker 1986, 130). It is only *possibly* Heinrich Bullinger, the Swiss reformer, who takes these Gentiles to be regenerate, and even about his reading Parker is not sure. He writes in a rather confusing way on Rom. 2:14-15 about certain people, whose consciences will be clear on the day of judgment, much as Augustine does in *Propositions from Romans.* **C** But apart from this uncertain case, Augustine's early explanation had clearly won the day on both sides of the divide. And because this "non-Christian" reading was one on which Reformers and Cardinals were in agreement, it is no surprise that is has been so strongly held ever since. [22]

C One exception in the modern period is Karl Barth, who shares Augustine's incomprehension that an optimistic view of Rom. 2:14-15 is compatible with a properly Pauline doctrine of sin: "shortly afterwards, Paul says unmistakeably that both Jews and Gentiles collectively and individually live under sin, that none is righteous, no, not one (3:10), that the whole world is guilty before God (3:19), that all have sinned and have no glory with God (3:23). How, then, can he assume in Romans 2, even hypothetically, let alone in practice, that there are Gentiles who are not merely noble but who keep and fulfil God's law without knowing it in its revealed form, and who are thus justified before God as its doers? Something is wrong here" (Barth, 1936- , IV/4, 8).

Cranfield cites five places where Barth discusses this passage in the *Church Dogmatics,*[23] and there is a good deal of common ground with

---

C The influence is from the *early* Augustine. Rom. 2:14–15.
C The exception is the Barthian tradition, similar to the later Augustine. Rom. 2:14–15; 3:10, 19, 23.

Augustine's theological exegesis in *On the Spirit and the Letter*. Just as Augustine sees Rom. 2:14-15 as describing those who fulfil the promise in Jer. 31:31ff, so does Barth. Like Augustine, he sees the φύσει (*naturaliter*, "by nature") as unproblematical: the "nature" of the person who has been transformed by God's grace has changed so radically as to be, for Barth, a different person. They have "this other heart, this new spirit" -- a nature utterly different from their previous condition. Along these lines, Barth declares: "For in this way and on this basis, God will break the opposition of His people, creating and giving a new heart to the men of His people, putting His Spirit in their inward parts, making the observance of His commandments self-evident to them (Paul in Rom. 2:14 uses the word φύσει in relation to gentile Christians), and in that way completing the circle of the covenant" (Barth, 1936- , IV/1, 33). And so the radical otherness that takes place in this new creation is realized: "If God's Law is written on his heart, if his heart is circumcised, if he acquires a new and different heart, this means that he himself, in so far as this has a decisive bearing on his whole being and act, becomes another man. According to Rom. 2, Gentile Christians have become other men, and consequently true Israelites before God" (Barth 1936- , IV/4, 8). The main difference here[24] is that Barth sees a second birth, a second generation, which is of a radically different character from the natural birth, as "his natural origin . . . is absolutely superseded and transcended" (Barth 1936- , IV/4, 9) while Augustine sees this new nature as restored and remade into its original form.[25]

Barth's *Shorter Commentary on Romans* argues for this same view of the passage, but the major modern commentary to espouse it is C.E.B. Cranfield's two volume *magnum opus*. Here, Ambrosiaster and Augustine and Barth are mentioned as also bearing witness (Barth himself does not mention Augustine by name). Cranfield follows very Barthian lines, rejecting the hypothetical reading and the "good pagan" reading as "hardly compatible with Romans 3:9, 20 and 23" (Cranfield 1975, 156). **A** But with Cranfield an element which was crucial for Augustine has been abandoned: the φύσει is attached to the first half of 2:14a, not the second ("for when the Gentiles who do not have the law by birth carry out the requirements of the law"). This reading was not a serious option for Augustine because the Latin does not support this reading as the Greek does. But Cranfield maintains the close connection between 2:14 and Jer. 31:31ff., and says that the question of the what φύσει refers to cannot be decided with complete certainty (Cranfield 1975, 157).

A How is the text to be construed? And what is the relationship between Rom. 2 and Jer. 31?

A Most recently, this position has been argued forcefully by N.T. Wright, who has developed a thoroughgoing theology of the Christian fulfilment of Torah, in which our passage plays a important if introductory role. According to Wright, Paul leaves the precise nature of these Gentiles "deliberately vague for good rhetorical reasons" (Wright 1995, 41 n. 12). Fulfilment of Torah by gentile Christians in this passage is a theme which is being flagged initially, to be developed further in 2:26-29, 8:3-4 and 13:8-10. Thus there is a faithful remnant which adheres to the Augustinian position.

Critical Assessment of Augustine's Interpretation

1. Logical Flow of Rom. 2.13-14

I Two common views today which Augustine's reading challenges are the "negative view" (this is probably the standard view) and the "hypothetical view"[26] of this passage. Augustine argues that 2:14 is an explanation of Rom. 2:8-13 with its promise of reward and punishment first to the Jew then to the Gentile. In particular, it explains 2:13b: "not the hearers, but the doers of the Law shall be justified." The gentile here is "a doer of the law" and must be regenerate: "To what Gentiles, however, would he promise glory, honor and peace, in their doing good works, if living without the grace of the gospel? . . . How then could he [scil. Paul] say that any gentile person, who was a doer of the Law, was justified without the Savior's grace?" (*De spir. et litt.* xxvi,44). The "hypothetical" view of "the doers of the Law will be justified" is problematical, because, as Augustine says, Paul goes on to give a concrete example of a set of people who do the law and are justified.[27] And similarly, the "negative" view of Rom. 2:14-15, which argues that this passage shows that "Gentiles too are justly candidates for condemnation," is undermined because, again, these Gentiles as a group "will be justified."

2. Doing the Law *by Nature?*

A Karl Barth is almost Augustine's only modern supporter in taking "by nature" to refer, as we have seen, to the accomplishment of the Law by a

---

A Why is Paul unclear in this passage?

I Current conflicts of interpretation. Rom. 2:8-13, 14, 15.

A How is nature to be understood in the passage? In what sense can the law be followed "by nature"?

renewed nature.[28] Luther criticizes Augustine here: "this interpretation of 'by nature' is forced, and I cannot see why the apostle wanted to use this particular expression, unless he wanted to hide from the reader what he really intended to say."[29] More recently, Raïsänen, Dunn, and Byrne all say that Paul would not speak of humanity doing the law by nature.[30] But Augustine could think of "nature" in much more positive terms—"that human nature in which man was created faultless after his kind" (*De nat. et gr.* lxvii,81) — much as Paul does in Romans 1, perhaps.[31] Modern supporters of Augustine's view, however (e.g. Cranfield, Wright), actually take φύσει with the preceding clause. This is much more likely in Greek, where adverbials often follow verbs. In Latin, by contrast, *naturaliter* comes directly after a verb and so must really go with the next clause.

3. Coherence of Augustine's Reading

C We saw above that Augustine did not always use his reading of Rom. 2:14-15 very consistently. This is seen in two areas in particular: first, when he continues to use talk of the "law in the heart" as the universal law by which all nations are reckoned as transgressors even after he has changed his position by the year 412. We see this in Letter 107 (written in 414) and also in the Exposition of Psalm 118 (*c.* 420)—the exposition of v. 102 has the new reading, and of v. 119 the old. Again, it is difficult to see how these are compatible. It might be possible to harmonize the usages by resorting to Augustine's view of the law as still faintly written on the hearts of unbelievers, but made clear again at conversion; it seems more likely, however, that Augustine merely forgot. There might well have been a considerable time gap between the two sermons from Ps. 119. This lapse is surprising considering the amount of attention Augustine gives the verse in *On the Spirit and the Letter*, though we should remember that even what we see on Rom. 2:13-16 in this work is only a tiny part of Augustine's system.

Second, as we said above, there does not seem to be a simple solution to the inconsistent use of the conscience and the thoughts. In *Propositions from Romans* where Augustine tackles the question of the conscience, he seems to have come under the influence of Origen's commentary at this point and not attempted to harmonize the two halves of Rom. 2:15. Later on, his use of accusing thoughts to explain Wis. 1:9: "in the thoughts of the wicked his examination will be conducted" (*De civ.dei* XX,26) is very difficult to understand. Augustine was not infallible: "The interpretation of Scripture by Scripture is one of the most problematical aspects of

---

C Some inconsistencies in Augustine's readings of Rom. 2:13-16..

Augustine's Biblical interpretation, for it is often done in a way that is out of keeping with the meaning of the different texts" (TeSelle 1976, 175).

A Apart from these occasional lapses, however, Augustine is quite consistent in the way he uses Rom. 2:13-16. It fits well with the immediately preceding verses, and with the wider context of the first few chapters of Romans, as Augustine explains (*De spir. et litt.* xxvi,44). It is coherent, and there are no serious objections to it, contrary to the opinion of Platz.[32] Indeed, Augustine might well ask the vast majority of NT scholars today what use defending thoughts are to those who are strangers to the grace of Christ.

Conclusion

C In conclusion, it remains to be asked what the precise nature of the shift was in Augustine's thinking on the passage. It does not seem that there is much change in Augustine's *theology* as a result of his different exegesis. He did not cease to believe in a *lex naturae*; however, there is certainly a considerable development in his understanding of the relation between old and new covenants.[33] This is an important advance, as it is another example of Augustine's shift from a philosophical-traditional position to a more biblical-theological one.[34]

H In terms of the transition between his earlier position and *On the Spirit and the Letter*, the change undoubtedly took place in Augustine's description of *the ability granted to the will to produce obedience*. Now, with the new covenant, the will has been given the ability to be truly obedient: this is not perfection, yet these "feeble beginnings of the virtue of the saints," as he calls them (*De civ.dei* VI,19)[35] are of a very different character from the deeds of pagans, which "we could rightly praise because they are done according to the rule of righteousness," yet, "were we to discuss with what motive they are done, they would hardly deserve the praise and defense which are due to righteous conduct" (*De spir.et litt.* xxvii,48). Augustine's repeated emphasis throughout *On the Spirit and the Letter* is that this ability *(posse)* now granted to the will *(velle)* is very clearly a divine gift (esp. xxxi,53).

C As we have seen, the shift between *On the Spirit and the Letter* and *Against Julian* lies in Augustine's greater reluctance to admit the validity

---

A Compatibility of Augustine's reading with the broader context of Romans.

C Augustine's change was in theology more than in exegesis.

H The major shift in focus, shaped by the Pelagian controversy, is from nature to grace. Rom. 2:13-16.

C Augustine's later interpretation intensifies this contrast because of anti-Pelagian polemic.

of the "non-Christian" reading of 2:13-16, and his greater emphasis on the exclusion of reference to *veras virtutes*. Pelagius's and Julian's praise of pagan virtues[36] had evidently caused Augustine to tighten up his definition of the capacity of the unregenerate.[37]

I Souter in his analysis of Augustine's commentaries begins by describing him as "the greatest Christian since New Testament times" and "assuredly the greatest man that ever wrote Latin" (Souter 1927, 139). He concludes his chapter with the words, "Augustine was a robust and wonderfully independent thinker, always growing in power and grasp, and never afraid to retract an earlier opinion of his own, if further study, either of the biblical text or of other commentators, led him to change his opinion" (199). Many of us claim to be open to change our positions, but with the Bishop of Hippo we can actually see it in print. May Augustine's scholarly humility inspire similar exegetical and theological repentance.

Notes

1. Gorday 1983, however, gives a short assessment of how Augustine (as well as Origen and Chrysostom) treats each section of Romans.

2. Part of the discussion after N.T. Wright's paper at the Durham-Tübingen Symposium in 1993 reached an impasse on this question. See the conclusion to Dunn 1996.

3. For example, in his discussion of Genesis 1 in *Confessions* XII, he makes it clear that what is important is that an interpretation is orthodox: that is the ultimate criterion of truth (XII,xxv,34; xxxi,42). One need not be certain about whether it was what the human author meant, though Augustine did want to find the author's intention (XII,xxiii,32). If orthodox interpreters differ in their interpretations, they should exercise love for one another. For love and the unity of Scripture as Augustine's two fundamental hermeneutical principals, see de Margerie 1983, III, chapter 1, and also TeSelle 1976, 174-75.

4. Käsemann points out that the Torah required two or three witnesses for conviction.

5. Augustine does employ similar taxonomies himself. By combining Rom. 3:27 and Rom. 7:14ff, he comes up with a *lex triplex* of the law of faith, the law of works, and the law of sin (*Serm.* 152). TeSelle, in his chapter in the present volume, also notes the triad of the law of works, the law of sin and death, and the law of the Spirit of life in Sermons 151-156. The exposition of Ps. 118 talks further of the law given in Paradise, the law instilled by nature, and the law given at Sinai (*En.Ps.* CXVIII, 5).

6. For Augustine, the law of faith is what teaches that one is righteous not by one's own effort, but by divine grace (*De spir.et litt.* x,17). The law of works is explained as the law with its commandments which bring the knowledge of sin (*De spir.et litt.* xiii,21), and the law of sin is equated directly with concupiscence (*De nupt.et conc.* I, xxx,34).

7. Chroust 1973, 68: "The realization that these truths and norms are actually 'in' us, that is, in our soul or mind or heart, becomes for St. Augustine the basis of an important moral imperative, namely to know and understand ourselves."

I Augustine was willing to change his position on the basis of textual and theological reconsiderations.

8.*En.Ps.* 118, ad v. 119 (PL IV,1574): "Nullus enim est qui faciat alteri injuriam, nisi qui fieri nolit sibi . . . id quod facit non uult pati."

9. On the cosmic seriousness of Adam's sin, seen in its effects, see *De nupt.et conc.* II,viii,20; also Fredriksen 1980, 256-57.

10. On the perfectionism of Pelagian theology, see Brown 1967, 342.

11. Chroust 1973, 69 n. 57, mentions this passage in his discussion of natural law, but he does not note that Augustine is dealing with regenerate Gentiles here.

12. Julian's pithy objection to Augustine's doctrine of sin is cited in Brown 1967, 387: "It is improbable, it is untrue; it is unjust and impious; it makes it seem as if the devil were the maker of men" (*C.Iul.op.imp.* III, 67ff.).

13. Here Augustine uses two texts in particular, Rom. 14:23 ("Everything which is not of faith is sin"), and Heb. 11:6 ("Without faith it is impossible to please God").

14. He merely talks about doing "some good" — a position which Augustine is quite happy with (*De spir.et litt.* xxvii,48 talks of "actions we not only cannot blame, but even justly and rightly praise"), as long as they are not described as "true virtues" (*C.Jul.* IV,25) or as being done with good motives (*De spir.et litt.* ibid.).

15. For Augustine, however, nature can mean either the ideal created order or the condition into which one is now born as a result of Adam's sin: see *De nat.et gr.* lxvii,81.

16. Brown 1967, 351-52, sees the crucial difference in the tropes that Augustine and Pelagius use to describe humanity: Augustine talks in terms of the baby suckling at its mother's breast, depending on her for all its strength; Pelagius, on the other hand, talks of the fully-grown son who is independent of his father. Bonner 1986, 361, notes how "Julian of Eclanum did not hesitate to speak of man as 'emancipated from God' by the possession of free will, while Caelestius asserted that the will could not be free if it needed the help of God."

17. As Fredriksen (1980, 248) says of Augustine's defense of his views on baptism and original sin, he reasoned "not so much forward from Adam's sin in the garden, as *backwards* from the universal and absolute necessity of redemption in Christ."

18. See TeSelle's bibliography on this topic in his essay in this volume, n. 24.

19. The similar work *De perfectione iustitiae hominis* has a similar range of tropes: healing is the principal term for salvation in chapters ii (1 and 3), iii (5,6,7,8), xxi (44); again Mt. 9:12 is cited in iii,5 and iv,9. The healing metaphor is also used elsewhere (e.g. *De civ.dei* II,1).

20. This method was not merely his own; it was a very common approach, similar in particular to Origen's and Pelagius's commentaries, though Augustine's *Expositio* was of course not a commentary.

21. Riedl 1965 supplies the definitive history of interpretation.

22. Sanday and Headlam note, however, that the gentile Christian reading has remained very strong in certain circles: "Since the time of Augustine, the orthodox interpretation had applied this verse, either to the Gentile converts, or to the favoured few among the gentiles who had extraordinary divine assistance" (Sanday and Headlam 1902, 60).

23. The passages in the *Church Dogmatics* (Barth, 1936-) are II/2, 604; IV/1, 33ff., 395; IV/2, 561; IV/4, 7ff. = German ed. II/2, 672; IV/1, 33ff., 437; IV/2, 635; IV/4, 8ff.

24. Dr. Carol Harrison has pointed out to me, however, that both Barth and Augustine have baptism, to some degree, in view here, which reduces some of the apparent difference.

25. Packer 1986, 299, has used Augustinian categories in defense of a traditional position on the role of women: "This is part of the reality of creation, a given fact that nothing will change. Certainly, redemption will not change it, for grace restores

nature, not abolishes it."

26. This has been adopted in particular by Reformed exegetes, most recently Moo, 1996, *ad loc.*

27. Most striking is the lexical parallel between ποιηταὶ νόμου in 2:13b and τὰ τοῦ νόμου ποιῶσιν in 2:14. Much exaggerated too is the partial nature of τὰ τοῦ νόμου as "some parts of the law" or such like. A brief look at the way τὰ τοῦ / τὰ τῆς phrases function in the NT shows that they are general, but inclusive and comprehensive, not limited. See, e.g., Mk. 8:33/Mt. 16:23, Mk. 12:17 and parallels, Rom. 8:5, 1 Cor. 2:11 and 14, and 1 Cor. 7:32-34.

28. Flückiger 1952 attempts to give Barth's exegesis a more solid grounding.

29. Luther's Works, Vol. XXV, p. 186.

30. Dunn, 1988, and Byrne, 1996, *ad locc*; Raisanen, 1987, 104.

31. In fact, Ignatius in the second century can speak of the Ephesians' status as Christians, "which you have received through your righteous nature" (ὃ κέκτησθε φύσει δικαία).

32. As Gorday points out, Platz "suggests that the Pelagian dispute forced Augustine into an untenable position on the status of Gentiles who have only the natural law, and thus constrained him to take up a tortured exegesis (one which he did not hold at an earlier time)"; see Gorday 1983, 155 and 325 n. 90. Also see Platz 1938, 126-28.

33. This is a further advance on the shift that took place much earlier from the "six ages scheme" to the more existential four ages: see Frederiksen 1980, 126.

34. Just as the Manichaean controversy had driven Augustine back to Paul, so the Pelagian controversy again pushed him to reconsider his philosophical principles and review them in the light of biblical theology: in this case, from a theological *lex naturae* to the relation between OT prophecy and Paul's representation of its fulfilment. For the philosophical background, see Horsley, 1978, and Girardet 1995. Girardet 1995, 281, and Chroust 1973, 59, respectively describe the differences between the Stoic and the Augustinian positions as lying in the autonomy of the human will, and the identification of the *lex aeterna* with God, both of which Augustine challenged.

35. Cf.Cranfield's description of τὰ τοῦ νόμου ποιῶσιν in Rom. 2:14: "those works of obedience which, though but imperfect, and far from deserving God's favour, are the expression of their hearts' faith" (Cranfield 1975, 156).

36. See Bonner 1997, 365, who cites Pelagius' *Epistula ad Demetriaden* 3, and *C.Jul.* IV, 30-32. Augustine replies with Heb. 11:6 and Rom. 14:23 as we saw earlier, as well as Matt. 7:18: "non potest arbor mala bonos fructus facere."

37. As recently as Book V of *The City of God*, written in 415, Augustine had spoken of "good arts," of "virtues" of pagans who "seem to do some good," for which they have already received their reward in the human glory they have achieved.

Bibliography

Babcock, William S. 1979. "Augustine's Interpretation of Romans (A.D. 394-396)." *Augustinian Studies* 10: 55-74.

Barth, Karl. 1936- . *Church Dogmatics.* Edinburgh: T.& T. Clark.

Bonner, Gerald. 1963, 1986. *St. Augustine of Hippo: Life and Controversies.* Revised edition. Norwich: Canterbury Press.

Brown, Peter. 1967. *Augustine of Hippo: A Biography.* London: Faber & Faber.

Burns, J. Patout. 1979. "The Interpretation of Romans in the Pelagian Controversy." *Augustinian Studies* 10: 43-54.

Byrne, Brendan. 1996. *Romans.* Sacra Pagina 6. Collegeville, MN: Liturgical Press.

Chadwick, Henry. 1991. *Confessions.* Oxford: Oxford University Press.

Chroust, A.-H. 1973. "The Fundamental Ideas in Augustine's Philosophy of Law." *American Journal of Jurisprudence* 18: 59-79.

Cranfield, C.E.B. 1975. *A Critical and Exegetical Commentary on the Epistle to the Romans.* International Critical Commentary. Edinburgh: T.& T. Clark.

de Bruyn, Theodore. 1993. *Pelagius's Commentary on St Paul's Epistle to the Romans.* Oxford Early Christian Studies. Oxford: Clarendon Press.

Delaroche, Bruno. 1996. *Saint Augustin. Lecteur et interprète de Saint Paul dans le De peccatorum meritis et remissione.* Paris: Institute d'Études Augustiniennes.

Dunn, J.D.G. 1988. *Romans 1-8.* Dallas: Word Books.

1996. *Paul and the Mosaic Law.* Edited by James D.G. Dunn. Tübingen: J.C.B. Mohr (Paul Siebeck).

Flückiger, F. 1952. "Die Werke des Gesetzes bei den Heiden." *Theologische Literaturzeitung* 8:17-42.

Fredriksen, Paula. 1980. *Augustine's Early Interpretation of Paul.* Ann Arbor: University Microfilms.

1983. *Augustine on Romans.* Chico: Scholars Press.

Girardet, K.M. 1995. "Naturrecht und Naturgesetz: Eine gerade Linie von Cicero zu Augustinus?" *Rheinisches Museum für Philologie* 138: 266-98.

Gorday, Peter. 1983. *Principles of Patristic Exegesis.* Studies in the Bible and Early Christianity 4. New York: Edwin Mellen Press.

Horsley, R.A. 1978. "The Law of Nature in Philo and Cicero." *Harvard Theological Review* 71: 35-59.

Kuss, Otto. 1963. *Der Römerbrief.* Regensburg: F. Pustet.

Luther, Martin. 1972. *Lectures on Romans: Glosses and Scholia.* Edited by H.C. Oswald. Luther's Works 25. Philadelphia: Muhlenberg.

Madec, Goulven. 1962. "Connaissance de Dieu et action des grâces." *Recherches Augustiniennes* 2: 273-309.

Mara, M.G. 1984. "Note sul commento di Agostino alla Lettera ai Romani (Expositio Quarundam Propositionum ex Epistula ad Romanos)." *Annali di storia dell'esegesi* 1: 59-74.

Margerie, Bertrand de. 1983. *Introduction à l'histoire de l'exégèse. Vol. 3: St Augustin.* Paris: Cerf.

Moo, D.J. 1996. *The Epistle to the Romans.* Grand Rapids: Eerdmans.

Packer, J.I. 1986. "Understanding the Differences." Pp. 295-99 in *Women, Authority and the Bible,* Edited by Alvera Mickelsen. Downers Grove, IL: InterVarsity Press.

Parker, T.H.L. 1986. *Commentaries on Romans. 1532-1542.* Edinburgh: T.& T. Clark.

Pine-Coffin, R.S. 1961. *The Confessions of Augustine.* Harmondsworth: Penguin Books.

Platz, P 1938. *Der Römerbrief in der Gnadenlehre Augustins.* Cassiciacum 5.

Raïsänen, H. 1987. *Paul and the Law.* Tübingen: J.C.B. Mohr (Paul Siebeck).

Riedl, J. 1965. *Das Heil der Heiden. Nach Röm 2,14-16.26.27.* Mödling-bei-Wien: Sankt Gabriel Verlag.

Sanday, William, and Arthur C. Headlam. 1902. *The Epistle to the Romans.* Fifth Edition. Edinburgh: T.& T. Clark.

Souter, Alexander. 1927. *Earliest Latin Commentaries on the Epistles of St Paul.* Oxford: Clarendon.

TeSelle, Eugene. 1976. "Some Reflections on Augustine's Use of Scripture." *Augustinian Studies* 7: 165-78.

Wright, N.T. 1995. "Romans and the Theology of Paul." Pp. 30-67 in *Pauline Theology. Volume III, Romans.* Minneapolis: Fortress Press.

– F I V E –

Readings of Augustine on Paul

Their Impact on Critical Studies of Paul

John K. Riches

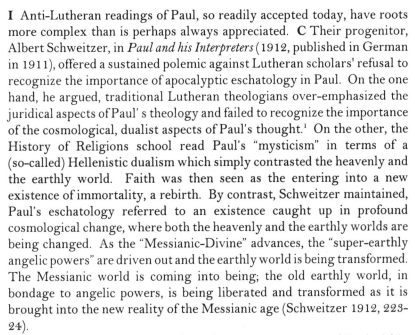

I Anti-Lutheran readings of Paul, so readily accepted today, have roots more complex than is perhaps always appreciated. **C** Their progenitor, Albert Schweitzer, in *Paul and his Interpreters* (1912, published in German in 1911), offered a sustained polemic against Lutheran scholars' refusal to recognize the importance of apocalyptic eschatology in Paul. On the one hand, he argued, traditional Lutheran theologians over-emphasized the juridical aspects of Paul's theology and failed to recognize the importance of the cosmological, dualist aspects of Paul's thought.[1] On the other, the History of Religions school read Paul's "mysticism" in terms of a (so-called) Hellenistic dualism which simply contrasted the heavenly and the earthly world. Faith was then seen as the entering into a new existence of immortality, a rebirth. By contrast, Schweitzer maintained, Paul's eschatology referred to an existence caught up in profound cosmological change, where both the heavenly and the earthly worlds are being changed. As the "Messianic-Divine" advances, the "super-earthly angelic powers" are driven out and the earthly world is being transformed. The Messianic world is coming into being; the old earthly world, in bondage to angelic powers, is being liberated and transformed as it is brought into the new reality of the Messianic age (Schweitzer 1912, 223-24).

At root Schweitzer's protest is against any attempt to read Paul within a primarily ethical/juridical framework. This can be directed both against a relatively conventional Lutheranism which sees salvation as grounded in the acquittal of the sinner before God; or against the more romantic/Idealist forms of Protestantism to be found in the History of Religions school[2] which see faith as the assumption of a new form of God- conscious-

---

I Multiple readings of Paul.
C Schweitzer's critique of Lutheran readings, and of the History of Religions school.

ness, through which the Christian spirit transcends its this-worldly limitations. Against the first, Schweitzer protests that salvation for Paul is foremost concerned with the overthrow of the angelic powers which hold men and women in thrall; against the second, that this world is overcome, not by the raising of the human spirit to a higher level of consciousness but by the invasion of the earthly sphere by the triumphant Messiah and the transformation of the earthly into "supersensual" reality.

C More recent anti-Lutheran polemic is not always directly related to Schweitzer's. Probably the most influential contribution was that of Krister Stendahl, notably in his volume *Paul among Jews and Gentiles.* This remarkable book goes back to lectures given thirty-five years ago and has its (autobiographical) setting in a New England "where there is a substantial Jewish community," in a United States which is "the first place in the modern world since Philo's Alexandria where Jews and Christians as people, as religious communities, and as learned communities, live together in a manner and in sufficient numbers to allow for open dialogue" (Stendahl 1976, 37). It is a worthy successor to Schweitzer, witty, sparkling, not overburdened with scholarly references but with a fine sense of where the nerve of those Lutheran/Protestant sensibilities lies which have so profoundly conditioned our understanding of Paul. There are, however, significant differences between Schweitzer and Stendahl which it is important to observe. Stendahl is not relegating justification by faith to the position of a "Nebenkrater" of Pauline thought whose center, "participation in Christ," lies in a wholly different mode of thinking. Rather he rereads Paul's utterances about justification by faith within the context of what he sees as Paul's fundamental concern: the question of the relation between Jews and Gentiles once the Messiah has come. Paul is not dealing in theological abstractions but is essentially attending to questions about the relation of these two peoples in the light of his own call to be apostle to the Gentiles. In making this proposal Stendahl is not, however, totally rejecting the juridical/ethical framework for interpreting Paul; he is merely attacking one particular type of juridical interpretation, one which sees Paul dealing with universal problems defined in terms of the radical failure of the human will (sin) and which therefore look more closely, "introspectively," at the nature of the will and its operations. By contrast, Stendahl argues, Paul and Pauline Jewish Christianity were both particularist and robust. The questions which exercised them vigorously were ones about the rights and duties of Gentiles now that the Messiah had come and Paul had been called to be apostle to the Gentiles. They are indeed discussed within a juridical frame of discourse; but the answers are cast in the form of a redefinition of community norms, not of exploring the springs of the human will.

C Stendahl's context — and Paul's.

C To see this is to see how different is the anti-Lutheran polemic of E.P. Sanders, so often mentioned in the same breath as Stendahl as the co-founder of a new school of Pauline studies, resisted — or better, largely ignored — only by Luther's fellow countrymen. For Sanders, the trouble with Lutheran studies of Paul is twofold: (1) that they read Lutheran polemics against a mediaeval, Pelagian "works-righteousness" back into Paul's debates with Judaizers, and thus end up misrepresenting first-century Judaism as similarly Pelagian; (2) that they construe faith and salvation in fundamentally juridical/ethical terms (faith as obedience, trust, etc.), whereas at the heart of Paul's religion lies the belief that Christians "really are one body and one Spirit with Christ" (Sanders 1977, 522). Sanders' protest is arguably the more challenging to the modern believer, because it rejects all attempts to construe Paul in juridi-cal/ethical terms. As Sanders recognizes, such terms are readily turned to in attempts to read Paul for today; Paul's actual language of participa-tion in Christ seems altogether more elusive to the modern mind.[3]

There can of course be no doubting the enormous contribution which such attacks on Lutheran readings of Paul have made to Pauline studies (however vigorously they may have been resisted in some quarters). They have forced scholars to reconsider their views of first-century Judaism and of Paul's place within it; they have encouraged a more sustained investiga-tion of Paul's engagement with Jewish apocalyptic eschatology, however alien such beliefs may appear to those within the broad cultural traditions of the West.

I Within this attempt to re-orientate Christian/Protestant readings of Paul, readings of Augustine's *Confessions* have played a small but not insignificant part. It is of course well known that Luther believed that he could find support in Augustine for his own views of faith and salvation. If one could then show that Augustine had misread Paul, or, better, that he belonged to a very different world from Paul's, this would clearly cut the support and show that Luther belonged to a different cultural world. This is what Stendahl attempts in a short passage in *Paul among Jews and Gentiles*:

> Augustine, who has perhaps rightly been called the first truly Western man, was the first person in Antiquity or Christianity to write something so self-centered as his own spiritual autobiography, his *Confessions*. It was he who applied Paul's doctrine of justification to the problem of the introspective conscience, to the question: "On what basis does a person find salvation?" (Stendahl 1976, 16).

C Sanders' critique of Augustinian and Lutheran readings.
I Is Augustine the problem, essentially misreading Paul?

It was therefore Augustine who started the whole history of Western introspection, which ran through into the struggles of late medieval piety and to which Luther sought an answer. Stendahl's views on the value of this tradition are not in doubt. "The introspective conscience is a Western development and a Western plague" (1976, 17).

Clearly if all this is true, then a major barrier has been erected between Paul and Lutheran interpretations of Paul. It is Augustine who writes the first spiritual autobiography; who develops (invents?) the introspective mode of consciousness; who asks the question about personal salvation (as opposed to questions about communal norms and salvation), and who first reads Paul in this mode. If all this is true, then such moods and achievements will no longer be able to be laid at Paul's door. But does Augustine really do all this? And what, if anything, follows for the interpretation of Paul and Romans, if some of these claims need qualification?

C Did Augustine, or in what sense did Augustine, write the first spiritual autobiography? This is clearly a question which goes beyond the scope of a paper such as this and I must restrict myself to two observations. It may very well be that this is a claim which can be upheld, more or less.

There are clearly earlier autobiographies, of which Josephus' *Vita* is one obvious example, which are self-centered enough. Was it a spiritual autobiography? Well, certainly not of the same kind of sophistication or indeed inwardness as the *Confessions*. It records Josephus' early religious search for a suitable type of religious observance from among those on offer within Judaism, but in the end it is not some inward concern that drives his choice, but concerns about public life and his standing within it (*Vita* 9-13).[4] And this it is that lies behind most of what follows, as he seeks to demonstrate his own virtue and valor and honor over against his adversary, Justus (*Vita* 340ff.). There is certainly an immense difference of tone and mood between this and the *Confessions*. The whole moves much more on the level of public esteem and standing. But what if one then tries to place Paul on a scale of "spirituality" running from Josephus to Augustine? C Certainly Paul is concerned with his standing within the churches, both his "own" and others like Rome and Jerusalem. But the deeds of valor which he puts forward are strange catalogues of weakness and trials, where the crucial factor is his own "imitation" of or participation in Christ's life, death, and resurrection. Of course Paul does not write an autobiography, but there is surely no disputing the confessional nature of Galatians and 2 Corinthians, whatever view one may take of Romans 7.

C The role of spiritual autobiography, and of personal religious quests, in antiquity.
C Autobiographical aspects of Paul. Romans 7.

C Are there other works of an indirectly "spiritual autobiographical" nature? Recently Nancy Shumate in *Crisis and Conversion in Apuleius' Metamorphoses* has argued that the *Metamorphoses* belongs to a broad genre of conversion narratives which embraces Augustine's *Confessions*, Dante's *Divine Comedy*, even the works of Sartre. It is not just that the novel ends up with a description of Lucius' conversion to the Isis cult, but that the earlier books portray the breakdown of the epistemological and moral foundations of his world, which leads up to his entering the cult.

H Thus it is Shumate's view that there are important links, for all the differences of genre, between the *Confessions* and the *Metamorphoses*:

> The basic pattern uniting the *Confessions* and the *Metamorphoses* goes deeper than any conventional act-oriented notion of sin and redemption. It hinges on the idea that the sensible world in all its aspects is characterized by *fallacia* — deception — or, in the words of a modern student of Augustine, on the growing conviction that we mortals inhabit a "bodily world of mendacious imitations of Truth" (O'Connell 1969, 15). Both narrators describe a past when they found themselves entangled in a widely accepted web of false values as an equation involving desire and pleasure: their problems began, each narrator suggests, because virtually all their activities were driven by misguided desires (Shumate, 1996, 203-4).[5]

In Augustine's case this is famously related to sexual desire, but misplaced desire is to be seen as directing a wide range of activity from his famous theft of pears to his playing truant out of a "love of playing and desire to watch frivolous performances and to imitate what transpired on the stage" (*Conf.* I,xix,30). Such desire relates not only to food and drink, *voluptaria cupiditatis fallacia* (*Conf.* X,xxxi,44) but also to intellectual pursuits, such as Augustine's study of rhetoric (he describes himself as having been "a most worthless slave of evil desires," *aequissimus malarum cupiditatum seruus*, speaking of his pursuit of these "meretricious desires," *meretriciae cupiditates* (*Conf.* IV,xvi,30). Thus Augustine can portray his contempt for his rhetorical education in terms closely resembling those which he uses to refer to his sexual desires. Speaking of his teachers he writes:

> They did not consider to what ends I might put the things that they compelled me to learn. They assumed that I would try to satisfy the insatiable desires for the poverty that they call wealth and the infamy that they call glory (*ad satiandas insatiabiles cupiditates copiosae inopiae et ignominosae gloriae*) (*Conf.* I,xii,19).

C Other examples of spiritual autobiography.
H Re-contextualizing the personal quest through a general view of the human situation.

Similar language, linking desire not only to sexual activity but also to envy, jealousy, religious divisions and theological disputes can be found in Gal. 5:16-21. Thus, if Shumate is right, Augustine is not without at least one North African precursor, who depicted the condition of those who experienced the breakdown and loss of their former world-view and the more or less sudden acquisition of a new one. Again, there are links to be made to the Paul who described his old world as σκύβαλα (Phil. 3:8) and his new mode of life as καινὴ κτίσις (2 Cor. 5:17; Gal. 6:15).

C So far we have done no more than suggest that the lines of division between Augustine and Paul may not be so sharp as some of Stendahl's formulations may suggest. Not only is the language available with which to give an account of the collapse/loss of an individual's world view and ethos, but there are texts which apply such language to individuals and not just to collectivities.

I All this still leaves undiscussed, however, the question of what is actually happening in the *Confessions.* How far is it true to say that it was Augustine "who applied Paul's doctrine of justification to the problem of the introspective conscience, to the question: 'On what basis does a person find salvation?'" (Stendahl 1976, 16). Here I must introduce a further major contribution to the debate, Paula Fredriksen's 1986 article, "Paul and Augustine: Conversion Narratives, Orthodox Traditions, and the Retrospective Self." This is based on an enviable specialist knowledge of Augustine's writing and specifically of his scriptural exegesis and is a model of the kind of work that needs to be done in this field. Nevertheless, perhaps even a non-specialist may be allowed to raise a few questions.

C Fredriksen presents the matter broadly thus: in the *Confessions,* in recounting his conversion (especially in Book VIII, chapters 7-12), Augustine "recapitulates the theological themes that contour the first seven books. . . : the weight of sin on man the child of Adam; the weakness of the divided will in the face of carnal custom; man's absolute dependence on the freely given, inexplicable grace of God." In the garden in Milan, he hears the voice commanding him to read Paul and he turns to Romans 13:13-14 and resolves to embark on a life of celibacy. By contrast (so Fredriksen), the writings of the earlier Cassiciacum period present a "different person."

This Augustine is perplexed by the problem of evil philosophically conceived. He again reports that he seized a book of Paul's letters, but they reveal to him the face, not of continence, but of Philosophy

---

C Possible links between Paul and Augustine.

I Was it Augustine, nonetheless, who began the "introspective" approach?

C The Augustine of the *Confessions* and the Augustine of the Cassiciacum writings. Rom. 13:13-14; 7:15-16.

(*C.Acad.* II,ii,5). This is a different conversion, one viewed not as
the struggle of the will, sin, and grace, but as progress in philosophy (Fredriksen, 1986, 20).[6]

Further, she argues, these fundamental differences in approach (philosophical as against introspective-theological) correspond to different readings
of Paul, notably of Romans. Paul "scarcely appears in the Cassiciacum
dialogues" and later — only, in effect, when Augustine wishes, as in *De
moribus ecclesiae,* to reclaim him from the Manichees. When he does turn
to Paul, in 395, Augustine "pursue[s] the problem of moral evil through
an analysis of the dynamics of love, memory, and human motivation as
these express the interplay of grace and free-will." Nevertheless in 395,
when he comments on Rom. 7:15-16, Augustine "argues against a
deterministic reading . . . : the sinner under the Law . . . can freely choose
to respond in faith to God's call." In *Ad Simplicianum* (397), however,

> he argues that faith is not man's work, but God's gift, and hence no
> ground for merit. . . Not man's will, but solely the absolute
> unmerited gift of God's grace, can correctly orient man's love
> toward the Divine. Augustine makes his case exegetically in the *Ad
> Simplicianum* and autobiographically in the *Confessions,* demonstrat-
> ing it through his description in Book VIII of the conversion
> (Fredriksen 1986, 22-23).

C Fredriksen's explanation for the differences between these two
accounts is twofold: on the one hand Augustine is reacting to the
pressures of his ecclesiastical situation on his return to North Africa in
389/390:

> [t] here, before the watching eyes of his own church and its
> schismatic rival, the Donatists, Augustine had to confront publicly
> a well-organized Manichaean sect that based much of its determin-
> istic and dualistic doctrine on the Pauline Epistles. To proceed
> against the Manichees, Augustine had to reclaim Paul (Fredriksen
> 1986, 22).

On the other, his reading of Paul is deeply influenced by the picture of
Paul's conversion (itself inspired by ecclesiastical orthodoxy) in Acts 9.
Thus she concludes:

C Was Augustine reclaiming Paul against the Manichees and interpreting him in the light
of Acts 9?

Augustine's account of his conversion in the *Confessions*, in other words, is a theological reinterpretation of a past event, an attempt to render his past coherent to his present self. It is, in fact, a disguised description of where he stands in the present as much as an ostensible description of what occurred in the past. And he constructs his description from his reading of Acts 9 as well as from his new theological convictions (Fredriksen 1986, 24).

C It is not difficult to see how this construction of the relationship of the *Confessions* to Augustine's "philosophical" conversion and to his understanding of Paul can serve to draw a very sharp line between "Augustinian," Western, introspective readings of Paul and Paul "as he actually was." It is powerfully argued and wonderfully earthed in Augustine's writings of the time. Nevertheless, in what follows I want to suggest that while there is indeed significant development in Augustine's beliefs about the will and its relation to God's grace throughout the 390's, such developments flow from the philosophical debates which he had conducted with Manichaeist beliefs in his Milan and Cassiciacum period. I want to question, that is to say, the view that there is a major sea-change between Augustine's engagement with philosophy which led to his initial conversion and his move to Cassiciacum, and his subsequent engagement with Paul which leads to the very different, retrospective account of his conversion in the *Confessions*.

H This can best be done, I think, by showing how the philosophical debates continue to play a central role in the argument of the *Confessions*. For if Shumate is right to portray the *Confessions* and the *Metamorphoses* as narratives which depict the breakdown of one set of epistemological and moral conventions and their replacement with another, then Augustine is particularly concerned throughout the *Confessions* with his escape on the one hand from the metaphysical errors of Manichaeism and on the other from his own misplaced desires, for fame, wealth and the satisfaction of his sexual appetites. The exchange of one set of metaphysical beliefs for another is an integral part of the story that Augustine tells in the *Confessions*, together with the story of his grappling with his misplaced desires and his struggle to overcome his divided will. Moreover the two are related, because the outcome of his metaphysical debate is to locate the source of evil precisely in the human will.

H Let me then turn to the question of the place of philosophy in the *Confessions*. Fredriksen, we have seen, makes a sharp distinction between

---

C In reclaiming Paul from the Manichees, Augustine was developing his own intellectual position?

H The interrelation of metaphysical and moral questions as key to the continuity of Augustine's development.

H Philosophical/theological issues in the *Confessions*.

Augustine's account of his conversion in *C.Acad.* II,ii,5 as a philosophical conversion and his account in Book VIII of the *Confessions*, which "recapitulates the theological themes that contour the first seven books" (Fredriksen 1986, 20): sin, the divided will, and grace. Now it is true that the conversion story in Book VIII does emphasize such themes; but is it correct to say that they "contour" the first seven books? My reading of the first seven books is that they document a many-stranded debate concerned not only with the question of the will and human sinfulness, Augustine's in particular, but with questions of the nature of God's presence in the world, the relation of the eternal, unchanging substance to the universe of existents; the question of God's supposed materiality, and of course the central challenge posed by the Manichees: whence is evil?[7] It is important, moreover, to see that the "theological" questions of the weakness of the divided will in the face of carnal custom do not "contour" these debates but flow directly from them. Once Augustine had adopted a broadly Platonist metaphysic he had of course clearly ruled out explanations of the origins of evil cast in terms of a metaphysical dualism, for that would have limited God, and therefore rendered him corruptible. But if there was no second power which was evil in itself, and if God himself was good and therefore also not the source of evil, then whence was it, *unde malum?* (*Conf.* VII,v,7).

Augustine's answer, set out in Book VII, is that it derives from the will:

> And I enquired what iniquity was, and found it to be no substance, but the perversion of the will, turned aside from Thee, O God, the Supreme substance, towards these lower things, and casting out its bowels, and puffed up outwardly (*Conf.* VII,xvi,22).

The Scriptural allusion to Sirach 10:9-10 is not to be denied; but the rest of the language, and indeed the sense of the Scriptural allusion, is deeply "philosophical."[8] Once Augustine has come to the clear conviction that all things owe their being to God, in so far as they participate in him, though he alone is pure substance, then the origin of evil has to be sought in the corruption of dependent being. Things which are dependent on God, the supreme substance, are, since they are derived from God, but also are not, because they are not what God is (*Conf.* VII,xi,17). Within such a great chain of being, there is room for the corruption of that which is yet derived from God. Augustine sees that even things which are corrupted are still in a measure good, because they still exist and so are still dependent on the good. That is to say, things are corrupted in so far (but only in so far) as they are deprived of good (*omnia quae corrumperentur, privantur bono*). To be wholly corrupt would therefore be to be wholly deprived of good and therefore to cease to exist. Hence Augustine comes to his doctrine of evil as *privatio boni*, as a lack of goodness, of reality, which is of course in turn a rejection of cosmic dualism, which affirms the reality of evil, independent of the good (*Conf.* VII,xi,18).

What Role Does Paul Play in This?

C It would be relatively simple to say that it is neo-Platonism that is responsible for Augustine's release from Manichaeism, while Paul illuminates Augustine's sense of moral dividedness and so prepares the way for his release from the bondage of his will. But this neat division of roles is too simple. There is certainly little serious doubt that much of the main force of the argumentation against Manichaeism in the *Confessions* is drawn from the neo-Platonists. Augustine's belief in the unreality of evil, as well as his belief in the transcendent, unitary nature of the Good and the distinction between the being of God and all other existents whose being is derived from God, are clearly Platonist in inspiration. But the question which the Manichaeans pressed against the Catholics, Whence is evil? was one which, if it were to be answered in terms of the *liberum arbitrium voluntatis*, required profound reflection on the nature of the human will. It was here that Augustine's reading of Paul played its part, not least because Paul was contested territory. The Manichaeans appealed to Paul, and Augustine therefore needed to extract himself from interpretations of Paul which he had himself presumably espoused in the past. That is to say: engagement with Paul was an integral part of Augustine's debate with the Manichaeans, partly because the Manichaeans could with some justice appeal to the cosmological dualist elements in Paul, partly because this was (may well have been) part of Augustine's own intellectual formation. If Augustine was to disentangle himself from Manichaean dualism, he had to discard, or better reinterpret, just those elements in Paul's thought which Schweitzer would later bring into his debates with the Lutherans.

I With the doctrine of *privatio boni* Augustine firmly turns his back on any kind of dualist explanation of evil. At the same time, such a move raises fresh questions about the nature of the *liberum arbitrium voluntatis* as the source of evil. What is it for the will to choose evil rather than good? It is here that the Pauline literature enters the debate for two related reasons. One is that it is disputed territory between Augustine and the Manichees; the other is that Augustine uses it (whether in accordance with its original sense or no) to reflect more deeply on this question.[9]

C Was Paul or neo-Platonism the key to Augustine's self-interpretation?

I Does Paul support Platonism against Manichaeism? or Manichaeism against Platonism? Rom. 7:15-16.

Let me develop this point a little further. The problem for Augustine was this: by identifying the freely acting human will as the source of evil in the world he could certainly offer an alternative view to the Manichaean one, that the source of evil lay in an evil substance independent of God, and indeed offer a view which, he could argue with some force, was consistent with belief in a good God, the source of all reality. For this, indeed, Paul might seem to give him support, and he appeals in an early exposition of Romans (*Exp.prop.Rom.* 44,3), as Fredriksen points out (1986, 22), to Rom. 7:15-16 as proof that the "sinner under the law can freely choose to respond in faith to God's call" (22). But he then had to face the Manichaean challenge that men's and women's freedom to act seemed to be remarkably constrained; and here not only common sense but also Paul seemed to be against him. The objection was urged by the Manichee, Fortunatus:

> It is plain from this that the good soul . . . is seen to sin, and not of its own accord, but following the way in which the "flesh lusteth against the spirit and that which you wish not, that you do." And, as Paul says elsewhere: "I see another law in my members" (*C.Fort.* 21; cf. Brown 1967, 149).

Augustine's answer is two-pronged. It is, on the one hand, broadly salvation-historical. Adam exercised free will, and "there was absolutely nothing could resist his will, if he had willed to keep the precepts of God. But after he voluntarily sinned, we who have descended into his stock were plunged into necessity." Augustine then backs this up with an appeal to common experience of how habits ensnare us.

> When by that liberty we have done something and the pernicious sweetness and pleasure of that deed has taken hold of the mind, by its own habit the mind is so implicated that afterwards it cannot conquer what by sinning it has fashioned for itself (*C.Fort.* 22).

What wars against the soul, as he says in the *Confessions*, is *violentia consuetudinis*, which outweighs his delight in the law.

> In vain I delighted in thy law according to the inner man, when another law in my members rebelled against the law of my mind, leading me captive in the law of sin which was in my members. That law of sin now is the violence of custom, by which the mind of man is drawn and holden even against its will; deserving to be so holden, for that it so willingly slides into that custom (*Conf.* VIII,v.12).

Clearly here large theological perspectives are opened up which will play an increasingly important role in the forthcoming controversies with the Pelagians; but in the *Confessions* it is the argument from habit that will be in the forefront.

H What is happening here? In the first place there is a conflict of interpretations. Augustine and the Manichees are contesting the meaning of passages in Paul which are easily and, as Schweitzer and Sanders would argue, most properly, read in a dualist way: Romans 7 and Galatians 5. Augustine's non-dualist interpretation paves the way for an interpretation of Paul in entirely juridical/ethical terms, and this is as much a part of his legacy to Western Christianity as is his introspection, which, I suggest, grows out of such a shift to the juridical. Augustine has taken a tradition characterized by a dialectic between juridical and cosmic-dualistic views of the world and purged it of its dualism. The effect of this is to locate sin within the human heart/will and its overcoming in the mysterious intervention of the divine in the lives of individuals as opposed to their liberation from dark powers. This is clearly marked in the earlier writings from Cassiciacum, where, alongside the strong affirmation of the freedom of the human will and its role in the embracing of salvation, we also find an equally strong assertion of the role of the Holy Spirit in separating the creature from vanity and uniting it to the truth.

But attributing to the human will that evil which the Manichees had located in an independent spiritual agency has of course profound implications for our understanding of the human will. Rather than being enslaved by "beggarly spirits," it is itself the cause of its own enslavement to habit; and if it has enslaved itself, then it cannot free itself from the consequences of its own actions but can look only to the grace of God for such liberation. The rejection of cosmic dualism leads to a much darker view of the human will, which in turn calls for different accounts of human salvation. The more Augustine ponders these matters, the more he inclines to see God as the cause of aspects of human experience which on a dualist view might have been attributed to the agency of supernatural powers. Doctrines of election and the divine hardening are brought in to explain human malice, as well as human goodness (*Exp.prop.Rom.* 61-62). The long-term effect of such a shift to the forensic away from the cosmic dualist perspective is to make central sections of Paul's letters (largely?) unintelligible to Western, Protestant readers, as indeed Sanders suggests.

H If this fails to convince, let me suggest another way of showing the continuity between the metaphysical debates and the moral struggles which Augustine portrays in the *Confessions*. By the end of Book VII, Augustine has effectively resolved his metaphysical debates with the

---

H A conflict of interpretations: "the powers" or the human will? Romans 7.

H Was an intellectual conversion followed by an affective conversion?

Manichaeans. He has attained to a new world-view of which he is confident; but he has not as yet made it his own, has not so embraced it that it shapes his own attitudes and ethos. His former doubts have gone, but he is still not firmly grounded in this new world view: "*nec certior de te, sed stabilior in te esse cupiebam*" (*Conf.* VIII,i,1). The rest of the *Confessions* represents Augustine's struggle to appropriate this world-view, to come to a real apprehension of the verities of which he has persuaded himself, and to live out their implications for his own life. Much of that struggle is with his own attachment to his old way of life, and this provides the stuff for his reflection on the bondage of the will to the force of habit and the refusal of the will to delight in the objects of true desire, even when presented with them. Part of the consequence of this struggle, that is to say, is further reflection on the nature of the will and the relation between divine and human agency. The shifting opinions about the nature of the will and its freedom which Fredriksen documents so well in her article bear witness to Augustine's continuing struggle with this question. The process of appropriating this new world view with its heavy emphasis on human choice, of developing a corresponding ethos, in turn leads to modification and further clarification of the world view and not, pace Fredriksen, an ἀνάβασις εἰς ἄλλο γένος from philosophy into theology. The more he becomes aware of the weakness of the will to move the mind to action and choice, the more he is forced to contemplate the role of divine grace in moving the human will.

H As Fredriksen and Brown both argue, the decisive break in Augustine's thought here comes in Augustine's reply to Simplicianus' question, Why was it that God said: "I have hated Esau"? As Brown observes, "It is a long journey from the contemplation of a Logos, whose existence can be 'hinted at by innumerable rational proofs,' to this acute posing of the unfathomable nature of individual destinies" (Brown 1967, 153). A long way indeed, but one which both the Platonist Simplicianus and the former Manichee Augustine undertake as part of their coming to terms through Paul with the nature of the will's role in bringing evil into the world. A purely Platonist reading of Paul as the exponent of a spiritual ascent, of the renewal of the "inner" man, the decay of the "outer," would no longer satisfy either of them as they grappled with the realities of the corruption of the human will, which had become pivotal for their defense of the sovereignty of God against Manichaean dualism.

Augustine's answer to Simplicianus is characteristically nuanced. He needs to assert the sovereignty of God's grace, the "divine overruling" of men and women's wills, over against any suggestion that the evil inclination of the human will is the result of demonic forces and influences.

H A non-dualist ontology is reconciled with the bondage of the will through predestination and grace.

Augustine later says that he "had previously tried hard to uphold the freedom of choice of the human will; but the grace of God had the upper hand" (*Retr.* II,1, referring to *Ad Simpl.* I, q. 2,10-22). There was no way out but to conclude that the Apostle must be understood to have stated the most obvious truth when he said: "Who has made you different? What have you got that you did not first receive? If you have received all this, why glory in it as if you had not been given it?" (1 Cor. 4:7). And this assertion of God's sovereignty is complemented by a profound analysis of human motivation. Central to this discussion is a consideration of the notion of "delight." What is it that attracts us to a particular object, and which then motivates our will, so that we act with regard to it? The problem is that there is no direct correlation between the beauty of a particular object and the delight that it arouses within the soul. This is as true in the religious life as elsewhere. "The fact that those things that make for successful progress towards God should cause us delight is not acquired by our good intentions, earnestness and the value of our own good will — but is dependent on the inspiration granted us by God...[For] Who can embrace wholeheartedly what gives him no delight? But who can determine for himself that what will delight him should come his way, and, when it comes, that it should, in fact, delight him?" (*Ad Simpl.* II, q.2,22).

I Augustine's search for an ethos, a model for reality which would correspond to his Platonist world-view, is a long and difficult one. He notes at one point how in the church, though it was full, "one went this way, and another that way." What sort of way of life is appropriate for those who believe that they as human beings bear the — sole — responsibility for the evil that is within the world? that the human freedom which was the cause of such universal disaster is now in bondage to habit? that salvation can lie only in the (free?) acceptance of divine grace, the empowerment by God's Holy Spirit? What sort of "long-lasting moods and motivations"[10] chime in with such a view of reality? And how will the attempt to embody such beliefs in a Christian spirituality in turn affect the understanding of the beliefs themselves?

C The answer to such questions lies of course in a long, rich and varied history of spirituality of which Lutheran piety forms only a part, though of course an immensely influential one. Augustine's contribution to this quest in the period up to and including the *Confessions* is (at least) twofold: first he develops an account of the motivation of the will which sees it as profoundly in bondage to the power of habit and able to be liberated only through the renewing force of delight-inspired-by-God.

I Augustine's search for an "ethos" of human responsibility appropriate to his world view.
C Augustine's anthropology is still shaped by its philosophical/theological framework. Rom. 5:5.

This still allows a sense in which the human will is the ultimate source of evil in the world, namely in so far as Adam's disobedience was freely willed. It even allows a sense in which the human will may regain its freedom through divine inspiration prompting it to follow that in which the heart delights. It can encourage a simple and joyful trust in God, as it can profoundly undermine confidence in the human will and inspire moods of profound melancholy, guilt and self-doubt, the kind of introspection which Krister Stendahl has rightly described as a plague. It suggests that there is an arbitrariness in the renewing action of God and so casts a shadow over God's goodness and mercy which will lengthen with the development of Augustine's predestinarian views in his controversies with the Pelagians.

It would be a mistake, however, to suppose that such reflections on the bondage and weakness of the will form the whole of the second part of the *Confessions* or that this is Augustine's sole legacy to the history of Christian spirituality. Concentration on the narrative of his conversion certainly lends support to the view that it is Augustine who single-handedly inaugurated the new age of Western introspection and left us with the plague of a guilt-ridden and oversensitive conscience. But this is to overlook elements in the latter books which point in a different direction. Crucial here is Augustine's use (*Conf.* X,iii,3 and v,7; XIII,xxxi,46) of I Cor. 2:11-12 with its affirmation of both the unknowability for human beings of the "thoughts of God" and the gift of the Spirit of God so that believers might understand the gifts of God.[11] While it is true that for Augustine the Christian life is principally to be described in terms of pilgrimage (Brown 1967, 152, 202, 210), Book XIII nevertheless celebrates the gift of the Spirit to Christians, the "pouring out of God's love into our hearts through the Holy Spirit" (Rom. 5:5). And what is most striking, for our purposes, about this final book is the way that here cosmology, world view, and ethos, the description of the new life which Augustine the convert now leads, are linked together through the device of an allegorical interpretation of the Genesis creation narrative. Augustine returns to the very issues which had occupied him all through the first seven books — of cosmology, of the relation of the supreme substance to finite existents, of the nature of God's creative act — and draws out of his exposition of the creation narrative an account of the new creation which believers undergo, of the transformation of their minds by the work of the Spirit.

What bearing might such debates about the interpretation of Augustine's *Confessions* have on our understanding of Paul? Are we to speak of conversion or call?

Paul: Conversion or Call?

I Let me start by trying to tie together the discussion of Apuleius and Augustine with respect to the question of conversion. In what sense, one might ask, are both of these texts which describe the breakdown of an individual's epistemological and moral universe and the embracing of another? In broad terms this seems to me a most persuasive way of portraying what is happening in both works, despite the entirely different genres and degrees of reflexivity. What is in detail interesting are the differences that emerge between Lucius and Augustine and shed light on Augustine and from there on his treatment of Paul. It is not the case with Augustine that his world simply collapses around him in such a way that he no longer knows what to think or what to do. He is himself actively involved in the breaking down of the world-view that he has made his own, and in this he is greatly helped by the work of the Platonists. As I have tried to show there is a fairly continuous line of development in his story, which leads him on from the engagement with Manichaean views of the nature of the two powers in the world to consideration of the origin of evil in the free judgement of the will and from there to considerations of the bondage of the will to desire and habit. The drama of his story comes precisely from this mixture of, on the one hand, self-conscious questing and critical scrutiny of his cherished beliefs and desires and, on the other, his powerlessness to embrace the goals that his good will wants. This is not purely a matter of his inability to control his sexual appetites, though ultimately that is the bond that ties him the longest. The story is of someone who has shared fully in the contemporary ethos of his society and its search for honor and wealth. His encounter with the beggar in Book VI shows the extent to which by then he has already moved to a position where his world view and ethos are no longer consonant with each other. This struggle to conform world-view and ethos continues for Augustine beyond the actual moment of his conversion; the later books give some indication of how the two are brought closer together.

All this is of course very different from Lucius' conversion, and also from Paul's. Does this mean that we should not speak of Paul's spiritual development in terms of conversion at all, but rather of call? Perhaps some of the grounds for arguing against conversion begin to look a little less clear-cut. Fredriksen argues against such a characterization on the grounds that the move from Pharisaism to a Jewish group which recognized Jesus as the Messiah would not have constituted a "movement between religions, from one articulated symbol system to another" but only "a lateral movement within Judaism" (Fredriksen 1986, 15). Stendahl makes similar points about Paul's not having changed religion but having

---

I How are we to read texts which express a change of world view or ethos?

received a particular charge which caused him to revise certain views about the Messiah and the place of the Gentiles in relation to the law. He is not a "Jew who gives up his former faith to become a Christian" (Stendahl 1976, 9).

Now it is true, I would judge, that the religious group/movement into which Paul moved did not see itself as forming a separate religious movement from other Jews, and if "conversion" is going to be restricted solely to changes of affiliation from one (or no) religion to another, then we should not use it to describe Paul's experience. Nevertheless, the question remains: how far had he moved within Judaism? Pharisees, for example, who entered the community at Qumran would, like the fictional Lucius and the autobiographer Augustine, have experienced a breakdown of past beliefs and ethos (now seen as mendacious and the prompting of the angel of darkness) as they embraced a new set of beliefs and values, even though these still related to the same central symbols. Was Paul's "conversion" like this?

A Stendahl wants to play down the extent of Paul's change of world-view. Paul, he says, did not cast "doubts as to the worth of his background but point[ed] out that his former values, great though they were, [we]re as nothing in the light of his knowledge and recognition of Christ" (Stendahl, 1976, 8-9). And he cites Phil. 3:7-9. But to refer to one's former way of life ("values") and beliefs as excrement, σκύβαλα, seems some way from saying that they "were great." It actually seems closer to saying that they were "fallacious" or "mendacious," but it clearly is also not that. That is to say, it is like but unlike (yet not wholly unlike) Augustine's and Lucius' experiences, which were of course also like but unlike each other. What all three do have in common is a sense of having moved out of one world into another. The texts that Augustine singles out to describe the new life that he has entered, whether from Romans 12:2 or the texts about leaven (I Cor. 5:7f.) and the conferring of the gift of the Spirit (I Cor. 2:11-12), talk about a new life which has involved a radical change from that which he had lived before. One great difference between Paul and Augustine in this respect might be that Paul in both his old and his new life had "served the one and the same God" who was attested by one and the same scriptures (Stendahl 1976, 7). This is true, but the differences can be exaggerated: Augustine's Manichaeism was a Christian heresy which rejected the Old Testament and selected parts of the New, but it still contested the interpretation of these scriptures with the church. Paul is clearly engaged in continuing debate both with Jews and Jewish and Gentile Christians about the meaning of Scripture, and this is for him and them a matter of life and death. Evidently his new views and behavior were sufficiently repugnant to some Jews to call on

---

A The way Paul speak about his struggle. Rom. 12:2.

more than one occasion for the most severe of synagogue punishments.

But would we not then expect clearer evidence of inner turmoil in Paul, such as we certainly find in Luther and, in a measure, in Augustine? Maybe. The problem here is that it is not all that easy to know what stress and turmoil Paul may have undergone. Is viewing your past values as σκύβαλα altogether without stress and strain? Nor should we overestimate the element of inner turmoil in Augustine. Fredriksen is right to stress the sense of continuity in Augustine's earlier account of his conversion; I have been wanting to argue that, even in the account in the *Confessions,* the sense of turmoil is qualified by a clear sense of intellectual certainty: *nec certior de te, sed stabilior in te esse cupiebam (Conf.* VIII,i,1). We must guard against reading Augustine too much through Luther's eyes and recognize the different psychological manifestations of conversion.

Differences Between Paul and Augustine about Individualistic and Collective Matters?

I In what sense do we see the differences and continuities between Paul and Augustine as being more or less about individualistic and collective matters? Paul, it is said, again by Stendahl, was concerned not with questions about "on what basis does a *person* find salvation,"[12] but with ones about the possibility of Gentiles being included in the Messianic *community.* The contrast here seems to be between two different types of religion, one which is personal (and universal) and which relates to a common human predicament which any person can share; and one which is about the way a particular group articulates its values and behavior: how it regulates membership of the community: who's in, how you might get in, how you stay in, etc. The one is personal, existential, inward-looking; the other is something you just get on with without much soul-searching, where changes of allegiance might at best be effected by reports of miracles,[13] not by the kinds of processes of self-examination and self-criticism which Augustine has blessed us all with.

Such a view of the matter seems to assume that there were very stable ethnic religious communities in the ancient world where world-view and ethos were closely coordinated and where changes to the symbolic system (or to its construal by the group) were relatively rare and accomplished without much soul-searching. Maybe this was indeed so, but it is not the case with Judaism, where there was great variety in the ways in which people construed the central Jewish symbols and evidence of considerable change of allegiance between different groups and of enmity and rivalry between them. This does not mean, of course, that first-century Judaism

---

I Weighing the aspects of personal struggle and of community definition.

in its various manifestations sat light to questions of ethnicity or of shared values and practices, which defined them over against other groups. But it does mean that there was a great deal more scope for personal choice and decision for at least some: there were different ways of upholding group norms, of defining the group, of resolving questions about the fate and future of those outside the group.[14]

For Augustine ethnicity played very little part in his religion. This does not mean, however, that he was not interested in group values of any kind. The questions he asked about group allegiance were spelled out not in terms of physical descent but in terms of the value of wealth and rhetoric and of the kind of life-style and goals which he himself pursued in the course of a successful career. In trying to make up his mind about the right course to follow in such matters, he turns to the Bible, the sacred text of a particular community, as a source of truth and guidance. His search is not just for some personal way, but rather for the right way for the church to which he feels called through the teaching of the Platonists. In all this there are perhaps more lines of similarity between Augustine and Paul than Stendahl suggests.

What is of course striking is the emphasis in the *Confessions* on the dynamics of Augustine's decision, on the mobilization of his will. Was he wholly wrong to find in Paul someone who could help him address such questions? Was Paul wholly concerned with questions about the adjustment of the boundaries of the Jewish people in the light of the coming of the Messiah? Did he not also have a burning concern with human action, motivation and choice? How could the Galatians go back on their earlier course of action? How could they abandon his Gospel? What was the nature of the freedom for which Christ had set them free? And what the nature of the bondage from which they had been delivered? Augustine was surely right to see in Paul someone who grappled with such questions about the nature of the human response to the word of God, about human freedom and bondage. For in redefining humanity in terms which transcended former ethnic definitions (Gal. 3:28) — in terms, that is, not of Jews and Gentiles but of sonship of God and participation in Christ — Paul was putting an enormous weight on human choice and motivation.

The Nature of Evil and its Overcoming
for Paul and Augustine

I But did Augustine read Paul's answers to these questions aright? Martin de Boer (1989) has argued that first-century Jewish eschatology

---

I The relative importance of "the powers" and of personal responsibility. Romans 1–3. Rom. 2:1; 5:12. Romans 7.

was of two kinds: one cosmic dualist, which saw the root of evil as lying in the invasion of the world by demonic forces, which held men and women in bondage and which could be overcome only by a final battle between God and the demonic forces (I Enoch 1-36); another forensic, which saw the source of evil as lying in the human will, of which the resolution lies in some final assize (2 Baruch). These two views may be found in isolation but more often they are found in some kind of dialogue within the same work. It is not too difficult, I think, to see how Paul himself engages with, indeed, in some sense embraces, both these views. Rom. 1-3 asserts the accountability of all (ἀναπολόγητος 2.1) for the sin which is nevertheless seen to be omnipresent in the world; Rom. 5:12 asserts the universality of sin as a power which has engulfed the world, while still wanting to attribute responsibility for sin to all, ἐφ᾽ ᾧ πάντες ἥμαρτον). Romans 7 similarly speaks of the struggle of the will with the power of sin which, as Schweitzer was keen to argue, is portrayed in personal terms. It is the interplay between these two opposed mythologies that in many ways accounts for the richness and elusiveness of Paul's thought. Without an appeal to some kind of supra-human source of evil, it is hard to make sense of the universality of human sin: explanations in terms of the failure of individual wills break down at this point. On the other hand, without an assertion of the moral accountability of each and every human being, human dignity is undermined.

H Augustine, I have been wanting to argue, is engaged in the same debates about the nature of evil and its overcoming, as were those who wrote in the traditions stemming from Jewish apocalyptic eschatology. He is battling against dualist accounts of the origin and reality of evil in the world; he struggles in the light of the pervasiveness of corruption and moral infirmity to hold on to some view of the freedom of the will as the moral agent responsible for evil in the world. It seems to me that we might do better in trying to understand both Paul and Augustine if we were to see them, for all their differences, as addressing certain fundamental questions which were of wide influence and interest in the ancient world, rather than taking their differences of temperament and affective style as definitive. Of course there is a great deal more reflexivity in Augustine's account of his entry to the Christian community than in Paul's of his entry into the Jesus movement. But it is not the case that Augustine is only interested in questions of personal salvation, of how he can find release from sin and guilt, whereas Paul is interested only in questions about the nature and boundaries of the people of God in the light of the coming of the Messiah (existential theology as against some kind of salvation history). Augustine is engrossed in questions about the nature of being; about creation and the relation of finite existents to the

---

H Continuity of questions about evil and how evil can be overcome.

ultimate source(s) of reality; about universal history as well as about questions of the freedom of the will, the divided nature of the will and the operation of desire. He is engaged with the Judaeo-Christian tradition, with its dualist interpretation by the Manichees and with the tradition of Greek and Latin philosophy, with which, of course, Jews like Paul and Philo had also engaged in varying measure. **I** That is to say, Augustine's conversation partners are not the same but not so far different from Paul's; both Paul and Augustine, furthermore, are attempting to deal with some of the same fundamental issues. Maybe we could begin to see both the Pauline texts which Augustine picks up to illuminate his own enquiries about the dividedness of the will, and those which he adopts to describe the new life in Christ, as belonging to the same world of discourse, and not as having been wrenched from their context and distorted out of recognition.

H But having said that, then we also need to recognize that Augustine has read Paul in a way which eliminates precisely the dualist elements in his thought. How indeed, after his struggle with Manichaeism, could he do otherwise? Thus what we have in his reading of Romans 7 and Galatians 5 is an exclusively forensic reading of Paul. Paul speaks to him of the weakness and bondage of the will not to some angelic agency but to the force of habit which has enslaved all wills since the time of Adam's fall. And where that fails to satisfy, he speaks of the divine hardening. What in Paul is explained partly in terms of bondage to spiritual forces outside human control, partly in terms of human weakness and failure, partly too in terms of the divine hardening and punishment, is in Augustine presented exclusively in terms of the psychology of the human will and the divine action upon it. This indeed opens the way to the "introspective conscience of the West." It also lays the whole responsibility for the world's ills at the door of the will.

Conclusion

In conclusion, let me return to my opening remarks about the different strands of contemporary anti-Lutheran polemic in Pauline studies. Does

---

I Similarity of context, relevance of Paul's texts to Augustine.
H Augustine's diminution of "dualistic" elements in Paul. Romans 7.

the view of Augustine's *Confessions* I have been arguing for reinforce or modify such polemic?

I Stendahl's work forcibly drew scholars' attention to the enormous emphasis which Augustine places upon the human will and its predicament in his theology. As I have indicated, I think that this is not purely the result of a change in mood and temperament; that such a focus grows out of the central theological issues which Augustine addresses; and that here there is common ground with Paul. Nevertheless, it is important to realize the extent to which in Augustine and his Lutheran successors the focus has shifted away from the issues of ethnicity which occupy Paul in Romans and which reflect indeed concerns of great importance to Paul and his fellow Jews. But here I think some caution is required. If we contrast Augustine's conversion and Paul's calling as apostle to the Gentiles too sharply, if we underplay the sense in which Paul has parted company with his inherited Jewish world-view, we may miss the sense in which the writers of the New Testament are also engaged in recasting religious and ethnic identity. Certainly issues of ethnicity were important for Paul and others in a way that they were not for Augustine. But they were profoundly problematical issues, which led to deep changes in world-view and ethos. Whether these are properly described as conversion may be a matter of linguistic convention. I hope to have shown that there are at the least instructive points of comparison with Augustine.

I What I have been trying to show about the way Augustine suppresses the dualist elements in Paul suggests, I think, that Schweitzer was essentially right to argue that the apocalyptic aspects of Paul's thought had not merely been overlooked in the Lutheran tradition, but that they were in some profound sense inimical to it.[15] The concentration on the forensic aspects of Paul's thought, which is given such powerful impetus in Augustine's writings, creates a cultural, theological tradition which, as Sanders asserts, simply does not have the conceptual tools to make sense of Paul's belief in the believers' participation in Christ.

I Schweitzer himself attempted to break out of his cultural bondage by invoking the category of mysticism. He placed Paul's Christ-mysticism on a line between primitive magical mysticism and intellectual mysticism, which latter he found in "Platonism, Stoicism, Spinoza, Schopenhauer and Hegel" (Schweitzer 1931, 2). Although this move has been widely dismissed by Protestant scholars,[16] it interestingly attempts to read Paul in terms of the wider intellectual tradition to which Augustine belonged. Schweitzer of course recognizes the sense in which Pauline mysticism

---

I Similarities and differences between Paul and Augustine.

I Augustine's suppression of the apocalyptic aspect of Paul.

I Schweitzer's attention to mysticism, suppressing other aspects of Paul.

does not conform to the higher forms of "intellectual mysticism," as he recognizes the clearly dualistic elements in Paul's thought which had been emphasized by his heroes, Everling and Kabisch. Nevertheless, the categories which he employs to make sense of Paul's doctrine of participation in Christ are monist, non-dualist categories and so are in principle inimical to the beliefs he is trying to interpret. Moreover, he does not recognize the sense in which Paul's thought is dialectical, dependent on the interplay between dualistic and forensic modes of thought: for him the forensic modes of thought are no more than a side-show. So what he offers is a monist interpretation of the dualist elements in Paul's thought, to the exclusion (largely) of the forensic. It is not an interpretation which has found many followers, though his work enjoyed some popularity in England in the 1930s.

H We are left, then, with the dilemma that the most fruitful interpretations of Paul in the West are those which, stemming from Augustine and Luther, emphasize the language of obedience, trust, and righteousness/ justification; but that precisely the success of such interpretations has made it increasingly difficult for us to offer effective contemporary interpretations of Paul's beliefs in liberation from bondage to the powers and participation in Christ. Such Lutheran interpretations, I want to insist, are indeed interpretations of Paul: they draw on and provide powerful readings of Pauline texts from the context of their own metaphysical and theological debates. But they also suppress, reinterpret, demythologize other elements of his thought and their subsequent readings and so destroy what some at least would see as the inner dynamic of Paul's thought, the interplay of the dualistic and the forensic. Does this mean that Paul is lost to us for ever? Maybe it does. If to find Paul would be to recover the sense of real participation in Christ of which he speaks, then maybe we have to say that from the mainstream of our culture we can discern only the outer shell of such doctrines, nothing of the life inside. But maybe then we need to recover those readings which have been more marginal to the dominant culture of the West: the readings of the "radical Reformation," of millenarian Christianity, of the Pietists and of liberationist theology, as well as of the mystical groups to which Schweitzer referred. Perhaps then a conversation can develop which will, in its own time, recapture something of the inner dynamic of Paul's texts.

H The complexity — and perhaps strangeness — of Paul's theology.

Notes

1. Writing of Otto Everling's 1888 work on Paul's angelology and demonology, he says: "From the moment when Paul's statements regarding God, the devil, the angels, and the world are apprehended in their organic connexion, it becomes abundantly evident that for him redemption, in its primary and fundamental sense, consists in a deliverance from the powers which have their abode between heaven and earth. It is therefore essentially a future good, dependent on a cosmic event of universal scope" (Schweitzer 1912, 57).

2. Chapman 1993, 43-44, comments that "most of the members of the History of Religions School sought refuge in a primordial mystical experience expressive of non-rational feelings, of emotions, moods and fantasies."

3. Sanders comments, "We seem to lack a category of 'reality' — real participation in Christ, real possession of the Spirit — which lies between naive cosmological speculation and belief in magical transference on the one hand and a revised self-understanding on the other. I must confess that I do not have a new category of perception to propose here" (Sanders 1977, 522-23).

4. See Mason 1989, on the question whether Josephus was a Pharisee, and the comment of Baumgarten (1997, 52) that "there is no doubt that the pattern which Josephus claimed to have followed, *of having tried out several groups before making a final choice*, was typical."

5. Public spectacle is another matter which is the object of false desire, as in the description (*Conf.* VI,viii,13) of Alypius' attraction to the public games in Carthage: "The cesspool of Carthaginian morals had absorbed him with its passion for frivolous shows and had drawn him into a mad obsession with the games in the circus . . . but I myself neglected to try to persuade him not to destroy his good character by his blind and headlong desire for empty spectacles (*vanorum ludorum caeco et praecipiti studio*)."

6. Throughout her article she appeals to Brown for support, here to his view that the account which Augustine offers of his conversion in the Cassiciacum period is one which stresses continuity and appears as "an astonishingly tranquil process" (Brown 1967, 113). But Fredriksen ignores Brown's rather more nuanced account of the differences in presentation of the two accounts. Brown suggests that the tranquility of the Cassiciacum writings "may have had deep, personal roots" which were "only revealed ten years later" and that the difference in presentation had a good deal to do with the different audiences for whom Augustine was writing: the Cassiciacum writings are formal works, which he "wrote as one public figure to other public men." The "classic scene in the garden is passed over in silence. Yet it is only in this scene that we can glimpse the depth of the reorientation which was taking place in Augustine. . . . When Augustine retired to Cassiciacum, a change had already taken place in him at that deep level" (Brown 1967, 114). Thus Brown emphasizes the fundamental agreement between the two accounts: continuity was in fact a feature of Augustine's "conversion"; the later account brings out aspects which the earlier more formal account glosses over. His later emphasis on the deep "reorientation" which was occurring in him was not occasioned by subsequent pressures of ecclesiastical orthodoxy and the influence of the account of Paul's conversion in Acts 9, as Fredriksen asserts, but was a matter of "deep psychological authenticity" (Brown 1967, 114).

7. Even in the conversion narrative, it is not insignificant that Augustine refers to his reading of Cicero's *Hortensius* (*Conf.* VIII,vii,17), thus keying the ensuing narrative back into the discussions which have largely dominated the work to this point.

8. Augustine also discussed Sir. 10.9-10 in *De musica* VI,xiii,40, written about 391; here he interpreted it as referring to "placing oneself far from God, not by distance of place, but by the affection of the mind" (*longe a se facere deum, non locorum spatio, sed mentis affectu*). See O'Donnell 1992, II:453.

9. Fredriksen agrees that "[a]t several points in the preceding decade [sc. 380-90], both as a Manichean 'hearer' and later, in Italy, as a Catholic catechumen and budding Neoplatonist, [Augustine] had occasion to read Paul attentively" and that he "turns to Paul continually in this decade [sc. 390-400] to construct a non-dualistic anthropology and a response to the problem of evil" (Fredriksen 1982, ix and n. 4).

10. The phrase is taken from Geertz 1973, 90. Note also the distinction Geertz makes between "models of" and "models for" reality, between world-view and ethos.

11. As O'Donnell points out (1992, III: 165; cf. 410), the first part with its assertion of the "unknowability of humanity and divinity" brackets the meditative books X-XIII and is completed only at its final citation. Nevertheless the fact that the citation is completed at the culmination of the work (*Conf.* XIII,xxxi,46) is of no small significance.

12. "His statements are now to be read as answers to the quest for assurance about man's salvation out of a common human predicament" (Stendahl 1976, 86).

13. Such views about Paul's lack of inwardness and introspection are also broadly supported by A.D. Nock, who argues, on the basis of his survey of paganism, that there is "little reason to expect that the adhesion of any individual to a cult would involve any marked spiritual reorientation, any recoil from his moral and religious past, any idea of starting a new life..." (Nock 1933, 138). Macmullen (1981, 1983, 1984) argues that views of conversion in this period have been based too much on the literary accounts of the elite, not enough on brief third-person and anecdotal accounts. What these suggest overwhelmingly is that it was miracles which were the catalyst for mass conversions: "*That* was what produced converts. Nothing else is attested" (Macmullen, 1981, 95-96).

14. For a brief sketch of such diversity, see Riches 1990.

15. Cf. Schweitzer's account of the treatment of Richard Kabisch: "But for all that theology held to the old way and was determined to cast out anyone who set foot upon the new. That is the explanation of the fate which befell [sic] Richard Kabisch's 'Eschatology of Paul'" (Schweitzer 1912, 58).

16. Bornkamm 1971, 155, speaks of mysticism as "a blurring of the boundary between God and man."

Bibliography

Baumgarten, A.L. 1997. *The Flourishing of Jewish Sects in the Maccabean Era: An Interpretation.* Leiden: E.J. Brill.

Bornkamm, Gunther. 1971. *Paul.* Translated by D.M.G. Stalker. New York: Harper & Row.

Brown, Peter. 1967. *Augustine of Hippo: A Biography.* Berkeley: University of California Press.

Chapman, Mark D. 1993. "Religion, Ethics and the History of Religion School." *Scottish Journal of Theology* 46: 43-78.

De Boer, Martin. 1989. "Paul and Jewish Apocalyptic Eschatology." Pp. 169 -90 in *Apocalyptic and the New Testament: Essays in Honor of J. Louis Martin,* ed. Joel Marcus and Marion L. Soards. Sheffield: JSOT Press.

Fredriksen, Paula. 1982. *Augustine on Romans: Propositions from the Epistle to the Romans and Unfinished Commentary on the Epistle to the Romans.* Chico: Scholars.

————. 1986. "Paul and Augustine: Conversion Narratives, Orthodox Traditions, and the Retrospective Self." *Journal of Theological Studies* 37: 3-34.

Geertz, Clifford. 1973. "Religion as a Cultural System." Pp. 87-125 in *The Interpretation of Cultures: Selected Essays.* New York: Basic Books.

Macmullen, Ramsay. 1981. *Paganism in the Roman Empire.* New Haven: Yale University Press.

————. 1983. "Two Types of Conversion to Early Christianity." *Vigiliae Christianae* 37: 174-92.

————. 1984. *Christianizing the Roman Empire (A.D. 100-400).* New Haven: Yale University Press.

Mason, S.N. 1989. "Was Josephus a Pharisee? A Re-examination of *Life* 10-12." *Journal of Jewish Studies* 40: 31-45.

Nock, A.D. 1933. *Conversion: The Old and the New in Religion from Alexander to Augustine of Hippo.* Oxford: Oxford University Press.

O'Connel, R. 1969. *St. Augustine's* Confessions: *The Odysee of Soul.* Cambridge, Mass.

O'Donnell, James J. 1992. *Confessions /Augustine.* Oxford: Clarendon Press.

Riches, John K. 1990. *The World of Jesus.* Cambridge University Press: New York.

Sanders, E.P. 1977. *Paul and Palestinian Judaism: A Comparison of Patterns.* Philadelphia: Fortress.

Schweitzer, Albert. 1912.*Paul and His Interpreters: A Critical History.* Translated by William Montgomery. London: A.& C. Black.

————. 1931. *The Mysticism of Paul the Apostle.* Translated by William Montgomery. London: A.& C. Black.

Shumate, Nancy. 1996. *Crisis and Conversion in Apuleius' Metamorphoses.* Ann Arbor: University of Michigan Press.

Stendahl, Krister. 1976. *Paul among Jews and Gentiles, and Other Essays.* Philadelphia: Fortress.

– S I X –

Jews and Gentiles, Galatians 2:11-14, and Reading Israel in Romans

The Patristic Debate

Peter J. Gorday

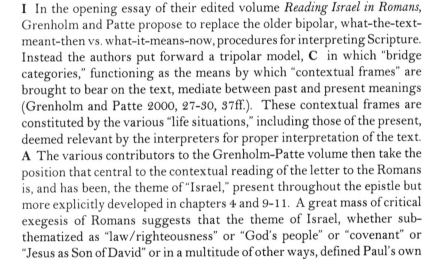

I In the opening essay of their edited volume *Reading Israel in Romans,* Grenholm and Patte propose to replace the older bipolar, what-the-text-meant-then vs. what-it-means-now, procedures for interpreting Scripture. Instead the authors put forward a tripolar model, **C** in which "bridge categories," functioning as the means by which "contextual frames" are brought to bear on the text, mediate between past and present meanings (Grenholm and Patte 2000, 27-30, 37ff.). These contextual frames are constituted by the various "life situations," including those of the present, deemed relevant by the interpreters for proper interpretation of the text. **A** The various contributors to the Grenholm-Patte volume then take the position that central to the contextual reading of the letter to the Romans is, and has been, the theme of "Israel," present throughout the epistle but more explicitly developed in chapters 4 and 9-11. A great mass of critical exegesis of Romans suggests that the theme of Israel, whether sub-thematized as "law/righteousness" or "God's people" or "covenant" or "Jesus as Son of David" or in a multitude of other ways, defined Paul's own work of interpreting the gospel. At the same time, different aspects of the problematic of "Israel" inform our contemporary efforts to make sense of Paul's theologizing in Romans. From Paul's time to our own, "Israel" names a problem, a challenge, a major *crux interpretationis* in reading Romans accurately and powerfully.

I Bipolar or tripolar approach to interpretation?
C The importance of contextual frames.
A Perhaps the central "theme" of Romans is a contextual one, the relation to Israel. Romans 4 and 9–11.

Peter J. Gorday

- I -

C For much exegesis, pre-modern as well as modern, the life situations relevant to the contextual understanding of Paul have encompassed what interpreters perceived to be the original setting, or historical location, of his epistles. In this essay, my concern is precisely with this dimension of *historical* context as it has been differently construed and interpreted by particular students of the letters of Paul, Romans included. It is true, of course, that modern critical readings of Paul have attempted, until recently at least, to make the determination of his historical setting the primary, if not sole, means of clarifying his thought; but serious concern with historical context did not begin with critics of the recent past. In fact, efforts to discern Paul's setting arose quite early in the church's life among the patristic exegetes, and these were debated vigorously. As I try to illustrate here, the patristic interpreters developed elaborate, diverse scenarios in their explanations of Paul's context and then used these constructions to defend their own contemporary theologizing about Paul's meaning. Certainly one element in these construals, and thus in patristic reading(s) of Romans in particular, was the problem of Israel as they imagined such a difficulty to have existed in Paul's ministry and as the apostle then wove it into his thought. "Israel" as a problematic in Pauline interpretation, then, is not new; it is only newly defined for us by a history and circumstances that did not exist quite yet for the patristic writers.[1]

H To move closer, moreover, to the specific ways in which the patristic exegetes unfolded their understanding of Paul, and the import of Israel for his theology, I want to make a connection with one notable way in which Paul formulated the theme of Israel. It is an approach that applies especially to the interpretation of Romans but extends to all of Paul's letters. It is a theme that has found particular resonance among modern interpreters of Paul and has allowed, therefore, the kind of empathic reading of the apostle that Krister Stendahl has called for in his classic study of biblical hermeneutics (Stendahl 1962, 418).[2] It is, moreover, a theme that allows for that special dynamic between believers and sacred scripture in which, as Grenholm and Patte say, "Believers read the biblical text with the expectation that this scriptural text in turn will 'read them'" (Grenholm and Patte 2000, 37). This way of reading Paul, and of reading Israel in Paul, including Romans, is the now immensely popular one of "Jews and Gentiles."

C Interest in Paul's context is found among ancient as well as modern commentators.
H "Jews and Gentiles" as the defining theme of Romans.

C When I say that this theme is now popular, I mean that it has become newly salient as a result of current events. For one must admit that at first glance the theme is entirely unremarkable, let alone controversial. That is, "Jews and Gentiles" is a staple of all historically minded interpretation of Paul, since everyone recognizes that evangelizing the Gentiles was the central and characteristic action of Paul's ministry, and that this evangelization involved a complex appropriation of the heritage of Israel. However, "Jews and Gentiles" as the center of the interpretation of Paul has in recent years taken on a cutting edge and indeed has become a polemical center. The reasons are multiple: our context is shaped by the shadow of the Holocaust, by the dynamics of renewed dialogue between Christianity and Judaism, and by post-modern and pluralistic versions of the human situation, to name only a few. For exegetes of Paul, these have come to roost very notably in the work of Krister Stendahl. He has made the idea of "Jew and Gentile" a call to arms for a reading of Romans, and of Paul generally, that is at once more *historical* and at the same time, he has claimed, more pertinent to the present. Such a reading, argues Stendahl, is less clouded by dogmatic issues that emerged in the post-Pauline history of the church. **C** Stendahl's specific target is the theology of personal redemption that emerged from the Protestant Reformation and that has undeniably and profoundly shaped modern interpretation of Paul, all to the detriment of authentic Christianity. The reference is to the teaching of justification by faith alone, or, in its more recent theocentric, less anthropocentric, formulation, "the righteousness of God." Stendahl's opponents have been quick and sharp in response. Led by Ernst Käsemann, they have argued that *their* justification-based reading of Paul is more true to the character of Paul's historical setting and speaks to our own world with perennially compelling force.[3]

H I would like to argue here, on the premise of Grenholm and Patte that exegesis operates multi-contextually, that both Stendahl and his critics are right. Both are making good-faith efforts to read Paul, especially Romans, historically. The problem is that there is more than one way to read a text "historically," that is, to extract meaning from the text's original historical setting and then insert this meaning into the setting of the contemporary interpreter. Since we are not generally in a position to say that one approach to reading a text "historically" is more valid than another, the evidence being ambiguous, we can at least clarify what these differing approaches are, assess their impact, and then bring them more explicitly into conversation with one another. What the

---

C The contemporary importance of the relationship between Jews and Gentiles.

C The "theme" of personal redemption, an influence from Augustine and the Reformation?

H *Both* themes are relevant to Romans and mutually correcting–Gorday's thesis.

history of exegesis sometimes helps us to do is to recognize that we are struggling with new forms of old dilemmas, and that the "solution" has to be sought at some sort of meta-level that yet eludes us. For the present, however, and as I suggest below in the conclusions, the differing approaches to reading history, and specifically Israel in Romans, can exercise a mutually corrective influence. In what follows I formulate the opposing positions on reading Israel in Paul in terms of either a privileging of what seem to be the theological/universal components or, alternatively, the apparently situational/personal components in the historical context.

C Now a major part of the modern debate about how to read Paul's historical context with regard to the problem of Israel has centered primarily on texts from the letter to the Romans, especially, as mentioned, on chapters 4 and 9-11. The texts in these two chapters constitute Paul's primary arguments from Scripture for the status of believing Gentiles within the new people of God. The figure of Abraham as the exemplar of faith in chapter 4, and the examples of God's extraordinary mercy in chapters 9-11, function so as to make it clear that Gentiles have been fully included in the scope of the redemptive activity begun by God with the people of Israel. In the course of detailed reflection, however, other questions arise, including that of "Jews and Gentiles." How are Gentile Christians to see themselves in relation to Jews, both Christian and non-Christian? How are Gentile Christians to make sense of their own status in light of the fact that some Jews have chosen to follow Jesus and most others have not? And, so on. Issues of continuity and discontinuity bristle on all sides. It is clear that Paul, precisely as apostle to the Gentiles, deals directly here with *Israel* as a foundational category for his thinking. These passages from Romans have thus functioned as magnets for Stendahl and his critics, who assess them along the lines of the split I have mentioned with regard to how meaning is to be extracted from an understanding of Paul's historical context.

H I have argued elsewhere (Gorday 1983) for a certain parallel between aspects of Stendahl's position and the patristic understanding of chapters 9-11. I have contended that Stendahl and the "Scandinavian School" of interpreters of Paul are the heirs of those patristic exegetes who, different though their philosophical presuppositions may have been in some ways from those of modern exegetes, gave a central and structurally pre-eminent place to chapters 9-11 in the elaboration of Paul's thought in Romans. The hallmark of their approach was, and is, that it

---

C Paul, precisely as apostle to the Gentiles, was repeatedly confronted with the presence of Israel. Romans 4 and 9–11.

H The problem of Israel as linchpin for Paul's theology of redemption. Romans 9–11.

takes the problem of Israel very seriously, indeed, makes this problem a linchpin in trying to discern the meaning of Paul's theology of redemption. What is particularly noteworthy, I have suggested in the earlier work, is that Israel exists for these exegetes not just as an abstract category or way of thinking about the identity of God's people and, more generally, of the human situation, but also concretely and empirically as a living presence in Judaism and its faith. By the end of the patristic age, and until modern times, this awareness gradually diminished, almost to extinction, for exegetes of Paul, given the gradual dominance over culture and society by the church. Our modern situation, however, in its pluralism, revives some of the conditions existing in the patristic age.

C What I offer in this essay, therefore, is an effort somewhat parallel to my earlier work by incorporating a different, indirect piece of patristic debate about the meaning of Israel in Romans for Paul. The ancient exegetical contest that is my concern here focuses not on the letter to the Romans as such, but on a passage from the letter to the Galatians. But consideration of Galatians has implications for reading Romans as well, since these two are often closely yoked in the history of exegesis.[4] I make use of this debate because its ancient documentation is particularly rich and instructive, and because it took place in an unusual way, in the form of actual, sustained, and detailed exchanges between two preeminent exegetes. In a way that the pre-modern history of exegesis rarely provides (no journals existed yet!), we thus have the privilege of "listening in" while the disputants engage one another's arguments directly.

C In the last years of the fourth and early years of the fifth century of the common era, Jerome at Bethlehem and Augustine at Hippo wrangled over how to understand a vital incident in the history of Paul's ministry. This was the meeting of Peter and Paul in Antioch, as related by Paul at Galatians 2:11-14. The views on this passage put forth by these two exegetes, and by their predecessors, were intended to apply to the whole of Paul's work, including by implication the message in Romans and the other epistles. My effort here is to examine yet again this ancient debate about the Antioch incident in order to highlight the contrasting readings of Jerome and Augustine, and their forebears and contemporaries, with regard to the historical context of Paul's life and teaching. I then use that contrast somewhat as I did in my study of Romans 9-11 to shed more light on what is at stake in the modern disagreement between Stendahl and Käsemann. These debaters about Paul are respectively, *mutatis mutandis*, the heirs of Jerome and Augustine.

C The "incident at Antioch" as a key context for Paul's approach to the relation of Jews and Gentiles. Galatians 2:11-14 and Romans 4 and 9-11.

C The debate between Jerome and Augustine, and its similarities with the debate between Stendahl and Käsemann. Galatians 2:11-14 and Romans 4 and 9-11.

Indeed, Käsemann, in a way reminiscent of the old Reformation-era Protestant-Catholic debates, has claimed to be Augustine's true exegetical successor where an emphasis on justification by faith in interpreting Paul is concerned (1971c, 67).[5] This lineage would go back through the Protestant Reformers to aspects of medieval penitential theology, and even Rhineland mysticism, to the struggles of Augustine with Pelagius and Julian of Eclanum.[6] What is much less clear, however, despite the fact that he has hinted at it (Stendahl 1976, 17 and 85), is that Stendahl's emphasis on Jew and Gentile in understanding Paul has patristic roots in Augustine as well. This is so since, as I suggest below, Augustine very much cared about Paul's historical context; but Stendahl's roots are even more in the Greek tradition that comes to a head with Jerome and John Chrysostom.[7]

C In the interpretation of the Pauline epistles, one of the common factors in their work lies in the fact that Augustine and Jerome both, as well as their forebears, attempted to make sense of Paul's historical context in terms of Jews and Gentiles. **H** What separated them, as in the modern debate, was a divergence about what it is in Paul's historical context of Jews and Gentiles – the theological/universal or the situational/personal elements – that translates into present meaning for the Christian and speaks to the perennial issues of faith. There was no clear winner in the ancient debate[8] nor is there one in the modern, probably because elements of truth were (are) present in both positions, and a satisfactorily comprehensive formulation still eludes us. I suspect that neither position in the modern debate has been adequately subjected to Grenholm and Patte's tripolar critique.[9]

- II -

C In their correspondence between 394 and 405 Augustine and Jerome stood on two sides of a divide as they tried to capture the special qualities of Paul's message.[10] The difference was manifested in their alternative scenarios for the relations of Jews and Gentiles in the apostolic age. Central to the disagreement was the interpretation of Galatians 2:11-14, where Paul narrates his encounter with Peter at Antioch. In that passage the apostle Paul had continued the process, begun at the very outset of the letter, of defending his apostolic authority and work, as well as his version of the gospel, to the Galatian Christians. Following his account of the

---

C Divergent interpretations agree on the importance of Paul's context.

H The theological/universal or the situational/personal elements as hermeneutical frames.

C Jerome and Augustine try to understand the "incident at Antioch." Gal. 2:11-14.

meeting with the "pillar" apostles in Jerusalem (Gal. 2:1-10), where, as he
told it, he had been fully legitimated in his mission to the Gentiles, he
recounted the story of his meeting with Peter at Antioch.[11] In that incident
Paul claimed to have confronted Peter "face to face" in public about
behavior for which he, Peter, stood condemned (2:11). The specific
indictment was that Peter, who had formerly been observing a fraternal
table fellowship with Gentile believers, had been influenced by representa-
tives from the apostle James in Jerusalem: they had frightened him,
claimed Paul, into separating himself from fellowship with Gentile
believers (2:12). Noting that even Barnabas, as well as the other Jewish
Christians, joined in Peter's "hypocrisy" (2:13), some Gentile believers had
started to follow Peter's example (2:14). Paul proceeded to castigate Peter
for not living in accordance with the truth of the gospel (2:14,
ὀρθοποδοῦσιν), and through his living first as a Gentile (ἐθνικῶς), and then
as a Jew ('Ιουδαϊκῶς), of setting up a pressure for Gentile Christians to
"Judaize" ('Ιουδαΐζειν) (2:14). Paul then used the occasion to make a
strong, fresh statement of his central claim that justification for all comes
only from Christ, not from their observance of the law (2:15-21). As his
way of correcting the abuses existing in the Galatian churches, Paul went
on for the rest of the letter to develop his theology of the status and
purpose of the law of Moses for those who have faith in the Lordship of
Christ.

C To be sure, on one level Paul's narratives posed no problem for
Augustine and Jerome. They were quite clear in their agreement about
the final implications for faith and practice of the encounter between the
two apostles at Antioch. Christians may on no account feel bound to
observe Jewish ritual law as a required, inherent part of their discipleship.
In Christ, the law has been dethroned as the means of salvation. C On
another level, however, questions remained about what had really been
going on in the encounter between the two apostles. H Was it a
straightforward matter of the clash of two opposed points of view, in
which one man was right and the other wrong? Was the outcome a
simple submission of one to the other? Further, was Peter not only
theologically wrong but also morally flawed in his behavior? Was Paul
arrogant, or worse, inconsistent, in administering rebuke? Was there a
triumph here of the Gentiles' understanding and practice of the gospel
over that of their Jewish fellow believers? Or were there deeper, hidden
dimensions of the meeting of Peter and Paul, in which a more fundamental
unity, even concord, was more significant than their opposition?

C Jerome and Augustine agree on implications for faith and practice.
C The conflict was over the nature of the confrontation.
H Theological and moral issues raised by this confrontation.

Furthermore, and more basically, was the abrogation of the law as the means of salvation a simple, straightforward matter? Why then did not only Peter but Paul as well continue on occasion to observe its requirements? The answers arrived at by Jerome and Augustine to these questions, based in part on their historical reconstructions of the special circumstances affecting Paul's theology, then enabled them to arrive at **H** somewhat different understandings of the continuing significance of the law of Moses in the history of salvation. **I** Different theological assumptions and frameworks [hermeneutical frames] came into play as part of their differing historical construals [contextual frames], but so too did different ways of gathering what is significant in a historical construction [analytical frames].

C Actually, both Jerome and Augustine voiced a number of concerns in their exchanges about the passage. In his commentary on Galatians of 388, in a way clearly reminiscent of Origen, Jerome took the view that Paul was writing to the Galatians as one attempting to straddle two worlds (*"ita caute inter utrumque et medius incedit, ut nec Evangelii prodat gratiam, pressus pondere et auctoritate majorum, nec precessoribus faciat injuriam"* (*Comm.in Gal.* ad loc. [PL 26:334B]). He wanted on the one hand to reaffirm for Gentile converts that the observance of the law is superseded in Christ, but also, for the sake of Jewish converts, that the law is still to be valued and respected. **C** Jerome also made it clear here, and later (*Ep.* 112.6), that his, Jerome's, purpose was to rebut Porphyry's claim, based on part on Gal. 2:11-14, that the primitive apostles had, through their disagreement, revealed the fact that the "gospel" was each person's personal and mendacious construction in the first place, *"communem ficti dogmatis . . . mendacium"* (*Comm.in Gal.* ad loc. [PL 26:335A]).

C Jerome took the position that Paul and the Jerusalem apostles had carefully worked out a division of labor in the mission to non-believers. Paul would preach the law-free gospel to the Gentiles, and Peter would preach the gospel to Jews in a way that continued to allow for observance of the law. In Jerome's view, this last concession was granted lest there be too sudden a disruption of ancient and venerable customs to the scandal of many.[12] The letter to the Galatians, Jerome argued, was written to Gentile believers in order to make it clear that they as Gentiles must not fall into ritual observance of the law of Moses, however much such

---

H Differences over the continuing significance of the law of Moses in the history of salvation as different hermeneutical frames.

I Hermeneutical, Contextual, and Analytical Factors in the disagreement.

C Peter and Paul's concern with the ways Jews and to Gentiles are affected. Gal. 2:11-14.

C Jerome's apologetic concern with Porphyry's attacks on Christianity. Gal. 2:11-14.

C The apostles' division of their labors.

practice might still be allowed for Jews. Given their different missions and the different strategies involved, no substantive disagreement existed, therefore, between Peter and Paul about the nature of the gospel and the work they were authorized to do.

C Jerome then took the view that when Peter first came to Antioch he, along with Barnabas, had shared table fellowship with Gentile believers on the premise that in Christ nothing is unclean. Here, of course, Jerome was using the perspective of Acts 10 and 11 to imagine what Peter might have believed.[13] Peter, however, observing that Jewish believers had withdrawn from table fellowship with Gentile believers and being mindful of his own particular mission, then chose to withdraw from a fellowship that had become objectionable to some Jewish believers. What followed was a misunderstanding on the part of these same Gentile believers, who began to think that observance of the law represented a superior form of Christian discipleship. Jerome suggested that these Gentiles were unaware of the agreed-upon division of labor between the apostles and then began to practice the law as something necessary once again (*"non intellegentes dispensationem Petri, qua Judaeos salvari cuperet, sed putantes ita se Evangelii habere rationem"* [ibid., 363D]). Peter in fact had intended not to set a bad example but only to honor the original agreement. C Paul on his side, "like a shrewd old warrior" (*nova bellator vetus usus est arte pugnandi* [ibid., 363D]), saw an opportunity to rebut publicly a position that, were Gentile believers to accept it, would compromise their salvation. He and Peter then cooperated to stage, that is to "simulate," a debate. This staging was much as biblical figures in the past had done for the benefit of others, or as lawyers sometimes do in court in order to cut through procedural verbiage to the matter at hand (*"utilem vero simulationem...simulare pro tempore...ob suam et aliorum salutem...fictis litibus"* [ibid., 364C-365A]). In the process Paul was able to make a point valid for both Jews and Gentiles, but differently weighted for both, that salvation is from Christ alone. The truth had been spoken in a way that saved all believers, Jew and Gentile, while not humiliating the Jewish believers, whose salvation was Peter's business and not his own. All of this was so that "the peace of believers might prevail, and that there might be real agreement in the faith through a holy contention between the two men (*"nisi ut eorum simulata contentio, pax credentium fieret, et ecclesiae fides sancto inter eos jurgio concordaret"* [ibid., 365B]). Jerome emphasized that there was no effort on Paul's part here truly to contradict Peter, but only to act "so that those for whose sake Peter had engaged in a simulation might be corrected, that the Jews might be relieved of their pride, and the

---

C Peter honored the original agreement, but was misunderstood by Gentile Christians.
C Jerome: A simulated debate.

Gentiles of their despair (*Unde et Paulus eadem arte qua ille simulabat, ei restiti in faciem, et loquitur coram omnibus; non tam ut Petrum arguat, quam ut hi, quorum causa Petrus simulaverat, corigantur, vel ut etiam Judaeis superbia, gentibus desperatio tolleretur)"* [ibid., 365A]).[14]

C In his commentary on Galatians of 394–395, written in tandem with his first expositions of Romans, Augustine took a different tack (*Exp.ep.Gal.* 15). Rejecting the notion of simulation out of hand, he argued that Paul's work was from first to last one of presenting the gospel in such a way that new believers might retain their existing customs and manner of life. Such an allowance on Paul's part was accompanied, however, by the warning that believers not place their hope of salvation in these non-essential customs, even if there were a risk of offending those weak in faith (*"tantum admonens, ne quis in superfluis poneret spem salutis, etiam si consuetudinem in eis propter offensionem infirmorum custodire vellet"*) [*Exp.ep.Gal.* 15,2).[15] Paul thus stated his principle that neither circumcision nor uncircumcision matters for salvation (Gal. 5:4).[16] The situation, then, was that Peter was rebuked by Paul not because he continued to keep his ancestral custom as a Jew in observing the law, but because he wished to impose this requirement on Gentile believers after being intimidated by those who came from Jerusalem.[17] These persons represented the position that salvation does depend on observance of the law, and Peter by yielding to their error worked a gross deceit on Gentile believers. It is thus clear in Augustine's interpretation that Peter's fault lay not in his loyalty to Jewish customs as such, but in creating a situation where Gentiles felt forced to live as Jews. Paul thus rebukes Peter openly for his error, for the instruction of all, on the principle *"Non enim utile erat errorem, qui palam noceret, in secreto emendare"* (ibid. 15,9), and Peter, mindful of the Lord's great charge to him, submits as charity and strong faith require. He becomes a sterling example of the humility intrinsic to authentic discipleship (ibid., 15,11).

C About the same time (i.e., 394–395) Augustine made it clear that he had become aware of Jerome's interpretation, and he wrote a first response to him, followed by a second about three years later when it seemed that the first one had been lost (*Ep.* 28 and *Ep.* 40). In the first of these letters he expressed shock at Jerome's contention that Peter and Paul had staged a debate, when, in fact, the apostle Peter had committed a "dangerous deceit." To say that any kind of falsification took place, believed Augustine, was tantamount to saying that lying was acceptable to a biblical writer. Jerome's interpretation implied that Paul was being insincere

---

C Augustine: Simulation is out of the question; dispute about Paul's concern that new believers might retain their existing customs and manner of life. Gal. 5:4.

C Correspondence between Jerome and Augustine over the dispute in Antioch.

when he rebuked Peter for forcing the Gentiles to live like Jews, as if he, Paul, had really approved of Peter's actions and wanted also to avoid offending those who might rebel. **H** But the real brunt of Augustine's communication at this point was reflected in his position that a "useful lie" is a contradiction in terms for a Christian. The only usefulness of such fabrications would be to open the doors to heretics who liked to argue that some passages in Paul's letters, such as those in support of marriage, are misrepresentations that do not reflect the Apostle's true views (*Ep.* 28,3-4).

Augustine's work *On Lying*, written about the same time, expanded the argument. While contending that anyone who tells a lie in order to accomplish some good is still a liar and still morally culpable, he had to face the difficulty that on some occasions biblical figures did in fact lie. **H** In the case of the meeting of Peter and Paul in Antioch, the only simulation or lie that existed was the hypocrisy of Peter and Barnabas in rejecting table fellowship with the Gentile believers. This hypocrisy was truly confronted and corrected by Paul. It is indeed the case that Paul observed the Jewish ritual requirements as well, but he was not thereby engaging in practices for which he hypocritically condemned Peter later. Paul's observance of the law, as in circumcising Timothy, was done as an act of freedom, since Timothy's salvation was neither helped nor hindered by the practice. Gentiles need not submit to the law, and Jews need not jettison their ancient customs. Jewish believers are permitted, says Augustine, to leave off their ancestral practices, particularly if there will be no offense to their fellow Jewish believers in doing so. If, however, a Jewish believer chose to maintain the old ways, it was vital to understand that these do not confer salvation. What matters in deciding to retain the old rituals is that we recognize that they are not to be despised or feared as harmful, for they are a "sign" (*signaculum*) whose own time has passed.[18] Paul's decision to observe the law on occasion was a matter of respect, but Peter's observance at Antioch was done in slavery and as a hypocrisy.

H It is clear, however, that Augustine saw a difficulty in the fact that Paul had indeed observed the law of Moses and had defended this observance. Consequently, he picked up the matter again in 397 in his second letter to Jerome. Paul's statement in I Cor. 9:20 that he became a Jew and became subject to the law in order to win Jews is taken to mean that he was compassionate and merciful toward Jewish practice, not deceitful and acting in pretence. "Paul was without doubt a Jew, and when he became a Christian he did not give up the practices of the Jews which

---

H Deception as inappropriate hermeneutical frame.

H Hypocrisy of Peter and Barnabas.

H Observing the law, not a matter of salvation, but of appropriate respect for the Jewish heritage. I Cor. 9:20.

that people had accepted as lawful and suitable for the times" (*Ep.* 40,v,4 [tr. White, 77]). He wanted to show that these observances are not hurtful, if Jewish believers wish to honor the heritage passed to them from earlier generations. Again, however, it is a matter of understanding that these observances do not form the basis of salvation, Peter's fault at Antioch consisting of the fact that he imposed these on Gentiles as if they were necessary. Such is the fundamental Jewish error, and such is the fundamental error of Christians like Peter who would mandate the law for Gentiles. Paul, therefore, may not be accused of hypocrisy when he criticized Peter, since the Apostle's only wish was to preach the gospel while exercising *appropriate* respect for the Jewish heritage as well.

H What is striking at this point in the unfolding of the debate between Jerome and Augustine is that both of them recognized that some continued observance of the law by some Christians, including Peter and Paul, constituted a historical and theological dilemma. Both, furthermore, posited with regard to this observance the existence of some kind of special conditions in the apostolic age. The accurate discernment of these conditions would be the key to understanding what was at stake in the incident at Antioch. By implication at least, they both saw that a case would have to be made for Paul's particular stance toward continued observance of the law of Moses for Jewish believers, if his rebuke of Peter at Antioch was to make sense. They both saw that indeed Paul had countenanced such continued observance, and each man then introduced to the exegesis a favorite concept to resolve the difficulty (*Ep.* 40,iv,6).[19]

H We have seen that Augustine had begun to use the distinction between things necessary and things unnecessary, things essential to salvation and things non-essential, but permissible.[20] The distinction was especially useful in his ongoing struggle with the Manichaean teachers, as in the work *Contra Faustum.*[21] In response to the Manichaean dismissal of the Old Testament, Augustine had to make the point that Paul indeed venerated in a certain way the traditions of the Jews and the Old Testament. One way he did this was to make particular allowance for their temporary observance as non-essential for, yet preparatory to, salvation by the Jewish converts of the time. The same distinction was used by Augustine with particular force when he preached at Carthage in Lent of 397 and contended that the institutions of the law of Moses – circumcision, the keeping of the Sabbath, the dietary regulations – were "*sacramenta*" and "*a deo praecepta sunt in futura temporum futurorum*" (*Serm.* 162C = Dolbeau 27 [Dolbeau 1996, 55]). By comparison with the rituals

---

H Theological dilemma constituted by obervance of the law by Peter and Paul, and by other Christians.

H Augustine: distinction between things necessary and essential to salvation and things non-necessary and non-essential, but permissible.

of Gentile paganism these Jewish institutions were necessary things in their own time, but they ceased to be so with the arrival of the gospel. **H** Jerome, on the other hand, was to lean heavily on the concept of "economy," the "dispensation" in the course of salvation history by which God "accommodates" to human needs and limitations in conferring the gift of salvation. We have seen that he called the division of labor between Paul and Peter in their separate missions to Jews and Gentiles such an economy, and, following a tradition going back at least to Origen, he was to lean heavily on the concept. The notion of "economy," perhaps originating with the Valentinian Gnostics as an exegetical theme, found its first orthodox use in interpreting Scripture in the work of Irenaeus. It describes a structured and dynamic unfolding within a lower order of plans and intentions that emanate from a higher order. Thus salvation history itself can be understood as such an economy, originating with God and developing graciously and in sovereign fashion according to a pre-set plan. Applied to the whole divine work of creation and redemption, as with, say, Gregory of Nyssa, "economy" is sweeping in its coverage, but when applied, as with Jerome, to missionary strategy, the term provided a useful way of thinking about why inspired persons might have acted as they did. That is, their actions are the playing out, on a mundane level, of a higher drama.

C In late 404 Jerome dispatched a response to Augustine. He chose to sharpen even further the issue of Paul's own observance of the law by arguing that "he could not accuse someone else of pretence when he himself was guilty of it" (*nec [potuisse] in alio arguere simulationem, cuius ipse tenebatur reus*) [*Ep.* 112,4 (p.370)]. Here Jerome appealed to the Greek tradition of exegesis that he claimed to be following. The task, he suggested, is to show that Peter did not actually sin and that Paul was not insolent in rebuking him, as well as to show how Paul could criticize Peter for doing something that he himself had done. Jerome recalled that he was framing his exegesis with one eye on Porphyry's charge that Paul was a hypocrite. He further claimed that John Chrysostom had endorsed such a perspective through his own approach to the passage (*Ep.* 112,6 [p.373]). Chrysostom had indeed taken such a position, though in a substantially more subtle way than had Jerome. Chrysostom made careful and measured use of the idea of accommodation to explain the understanding about mission between Peter and Paul, and to clarify what had gone

---

H Jerome: "economy," the "dispensation" in salvation history by which God "accommodates" to human needs and limitations; Paul's and Peter's actions play out, on a mundane level, a higher drama.

C "Economy" as a useful H Frame to describe the disagreement between Peter and Paul in view of Porphyry's charge.

wrong in their agreement and thus led to confusion. This is a good point, therefore, at which to review that exegete's constructions.

C Both in a sermon of 388 (*"Homilia in illud: In faciem ei restiti,"* *PG* 51, 371-88) and in his commentary on Galatians of 393 (*PG* 61:640-45) Chrysostom argued that Peter, in the division of the mission agreed to at Jerusalem, would follow a policy of allowing Jewish converts to continue with ritual observances based on the law of Moses. This permission, Chrysostom contended, was based on Peter's fear of overturning the law too quickly, lest he cause these converts to abandon the gospel as well. Chrysostom compared this practice to that of a shrewd farmer who has the sense to see that a new tree growing alongside an old one can have its roots preserved only if he is careful not to uproot the old one too soon (*"In faciem ei restiti"* 12 [PG 51:381-82]). Paul, on the other hand, had to observe no such precautions: his task was to usher his Gentile converts into the freedom of the gospel by helping them make a complete break with any other means of salvation. With Jews, however, he could, and did, function, in the οἰκονομία, much like Peter. Both men would thus tolerate the observance of the law as a συγκατάβασις, that is, an agreed-upon plan for a certain period of time. This is the condescension or "accommodation" (in Latin, *dispensatio*) (ibid., 13 [PG 51:382]).

What then was the basis of Paul's confrontation with Peter at Antioch? Chrysostom's views here were nuanced and appear to have evolved between the sermon and the commentary. In both places he contended that Peter, in being anxious to comfort the Jerusalem brethren by backing away from table fellowship with Gentile believers, had created a dilemma that he recognized and that needed some resolution. In the sermon, Peter makes the mistake of overstepping περὰ τοῦ μέτρου the accommodation to Jewish sensitivity, and Paul rightly (καλῶς) rebukes him (ibid., 16 [PG 60:381]). **C** In the commentary, on the other hand, Chrysostom suggested that Peter had intentionally generated a "reasonable pretext" for Paul to rebuke him(εὔλογον τῆς ἐπιτιμήσεως πρόφασιν) (*Comm.ad Gal.*, 2,4 [PG 61:640-641]). In any case, an offense to the gospel had been created, the need for fresh teaching had arisen, and Paul was the one to correct matters. Peter and Paul then worked out an understanding, a διάνοια, so that the plan, the οἰκονομία, could be fulfilled (*"In faciem ei restiti"* 16 [PG 51:385]; *Comm.ad Gal.* 2,4 [PG 61:641]). Both apostles, Chrysostom argued, wanted to remind their followers that life in Christ does not require submission to the law, but both also recognized that Peter himself could not state this view openly because of his peculiar mission to the

---

C Chrysostom's concern for Peter's and Paul's responsibility to Jewish and Gentile Christians.

C Peter letting Paul send a message "indirectly."

Jews. Peter then consented to be publicly, and, by implication at least, deservedly (Chrysostom's term is καλῶς) rebuked for the confusion that he himself had triggered.

This arrangement of, as it were, orchestrated blame, then enabled Peter to send a message to his fellow Jewish believers that he himself could not directly teach (καὶ ἐπιτιμᾶται μὲν ὁ Πέτρος διορθοῦνται δὲ οἱ μαθηταί) ("*In faciem ei restiti*" 16 [PG 51:385]). Peter could not be the bearer of this message for two possible reasons: that he would have been offending the very Jewish converts who were his special charge (the view in the commentary), or that he would have been perceived as submitting to that same apostle whom "the Jews could not bear" (the view in the sermon, based on Acts 22:17ff.) (*Comm.ad Gal.* 2,4 [PG 61:641]; "*In faciem ei restiti*" 10 [PG 51:380]). His silence under rebuke was then an assent to the position voiced by Paul to his face, but intended through him for all fellow Jewish converts. Chrysostom summed up this interpretation with the idea that Peter with Paul's help made himself an ἀπολογία for his Jewish kinsmen by, we might say, "taking the heat" for doing the very thing that he wishes them to be able to stop doing, i.e., observing the law (ibid. 20 [PG 51:388]).[22] **C** Chrysostom's ways of formulating the simulation are thus much more finely shaded than that of Jerome, and thereby allow for a measure of real offense on Peter's part and thus for a substantive confrontation between the apostles, however diluted this may be by their collusion.[23] The commentary of Theodoret of Cyr, composed sometime before 450, despite its fragmentary state with regard to this passage, appears to have taken much the same line (*Comm.in ep.ad Gal.* ad loc. [PG 82:472B]).

C Jerome appealed, in addition, to Origen as the fountainhead of Greek exegesis of the Antioch incident (*Ep.* 112,6). Jerome is not well known, however, for correctly understanding Origen, and later on Origen became a convenient whipping boy for him. Here also he was probably being a bit ham-fisted. The use of the concept of simulation for interpreting Galatians 2:11-14 is usually laid at Origen's door-step because of Jerome's statement, but no sure evidence exists. The most significant direct reference in Origen's extant work is in the *Commentary on John*, where Origen had been discussing the apostle Peter's ignorance in remonstrating with Jesus, when the latter attempted to wash his feet (Jn. 13:6ff.). Origen's observation was that Peter failed on that occasion to understand what was "expedient" (σύμφερον) and that he often made such mistakes (*Comm.in Ioh.* XXXII,56 and 61). Notice the use of the term "fitting," which again refers back to the ethical categories of the Stoa. The striking

---

C For Chrysostom, Peter really committed an offense against the gospel of justification.
C Origen's interpretation: an error, corrected to the benefit of all.

thing, however, was that God used such mistakes on Peter's part to advance the divine purposes, and Peter, having recognized this, had learned to be strong and patient. Thus Origen indicated that Peter remained both silent and penitent under Paul's rebuke at Antioch (XXXII,63), the deeper meaning of all this being left, said Origen, to his exposition elsewhere on Galatians (XXXII,63). What those good things might have been, that God worked through Peter's suffering of (just) rebuke, is perhaps indicated in his *Contra Celsum* (II,1). In that place Origen was engaged in a rebuttal of Celsus' charge that Christians stupidly abandon all ancient tradition and wisdom in their rush to embrace the new savior Jesus. Not so, said Origen, for we see from Peter's actions at Antioch, and from Paul's activity elsewhere, that both greatly respected the law of the Jews, and that Peter above all, with his special mission, should not jettison that law. There is at least the suggestion, therefore, that the good being worked through Paul's rebuke of Peter was some kind of salutary reminder of the correct understanding of Jewish tradition from the perspective of the gospel. We can only imagine that in Origen's view such an understanding would have centered on a properly "spiritual" reading of the law, such that in this point he would not have been so very different ultimately from Augustine.

C In the case of Origen, moreover, we also have evidence from his *Commentary on Romans* that he saw Paul's role and calling as an apostle in a very particular way. This role, argued Origen, can be summed up in the notion of the *iustus arbiter*, the fair judge who can balance the implications of the gospel *pro gentibus* and *pro Israel* (Gorday, 1989). In Romans Paul defended the ancient status of God's covenant people at the same time that he defended the claims of the Gentiles to have become in Christ part of that people. Origen saw Paul as engaged in a constant effort to establish the right relationship between these claims, so that truth would be served not through victory of one group over another but in the purposeful unfolding of a drama in which each party has its role to play and that ultimately benefits all. In the introduction to his commentary, Origen suggested that the Apostle had to enlighten the Roman Christians about the real nature of the law of Moses, so that they might avoid the Marcionite error of a thoughtless rejection of the Old Covenant. In this apostolic work, Origen told us, Paul would be working out his own striving for perfection in the special calling of an apostle (*Comm.in epist.ad Rom.* I,1 praef.).

Again, we can only imagine how Origen might have seen the situation at Antioch from this perspective: Paul being faithful to his explanatory work, and Peter erring one more time, but in both cases the advance of the

---

C Origen: Paul was finding the proper balance between Israel and the Gentiles.

gospel being facilitated. Consequently, and somewhat contrary to Jerome's assertion, Origen may be the originator of the use of simulation not so much as a contrived performance, but rather as a collaboration. This last would have its element of rebuke, but the emphasis would fall on a kind of fundamental faithfulness in both men, even where one was more "correct" than the other.

C In returning, then, to his response of 404 to Augustine, Jerome was at some pains to argue that both Paul and Peter had observed the ritual requirements of the law on various occasions, and that they had a clear agreement at the conference in Jerusalem about division of the mission. He then took the tack of interpreting the "fear" felt by Peter "of those from the circumcision" mentioned by Paul (Gal. 2:14) as a reference not to cravenness on Peter's part but to a fear that he would lose his Jewish converts if he acted unwisely in this crisis (*Ep.* 112,8). He thus enters not into a lie, contended Jerome, but into "honest diplomacy" (*honestam dispensationem*) intended to display the wisdom of the apostles and to put a stop to Porphyry's blasphemy and impudence. For Porphyry alleged that Paul and Peter had fought like children, or rather that Paul, in his envy of Peter's virtues, flared up and wrote an account of things which Peter had not done or, if he did, it was wrong of Paul to rebuke Peter for something of which Paul himself was guilty (*Paulum et Petrum puerili dicit inter se pugnasse certamine*) (*Ep.* 112,11 [tr. White]). H His final objection, then, to Augustine's reasoning involved a rejection of the distinction between the essential and the non-essential-but-good in the case of the law of Moses, for it seemed to Jerome to imply that there was something inherently important about continued observance of the law by Jewish converts. To Jerome, such a view compromised the belief that salvation is only, and totally, through faith in Christ, and that this salvation has come about in one fell swoop through Christ's death and resurrection. Augustine seemed to be making room for a kind of neo-Ebionism on the part of Jewish converts, for there can be no such thing as a qualified submission to the law's observances. How can one be "compassionate" toward the Jewish law at this point, said Jerome, when it must be rejected *in toto* and without qualification?[24]

C Augustine's rejoinder in a letter of 405 was his final public statement (*Ep.* 82). He attempted to draw the sting from the Porphyry/Jerome position that Paul appeared to be rebuking Peter for something that he himself had done. He argued that, if there had been any such inconsistency on Paul's part, then he had clearly repented of his own prior actions.

C Interpreting Peter's fear "the men from Jerusalem."

H Observance of the law by Christians, at least during the first generation.

C Augustine: If there was a genuine dispute between Peter and Paul, Paul was inconsistent with his own practice.

Nothing, Augustine believed as he glanced at the Manichees, must be allowed to compromise the literal truthfulness of Paul's report. Augustine reiterates his earlier positions by describing the law and its institutions as venerable sacraments and prefigurations of the gospel, by rejecting the whole notion of a well-intentioned lie as ethically acceptable for Christians, and by insisting that the idea of "things indifferent" for Christian practice makes perfectly good sense. Jerome's charge of Ebionism is dismissed as foolish, since he, Augustine, has wanted to argue only that the law was permitted for Jewish converts as a special arrangement for the apostolic age. Therefore the salvation given through Christ's work required a kind of temporal unfolding in stages for converts from Judaism. Here Augustine admitted that he had been a bit unclear, and now he wanted to set matters straight. The reason for the allowance was not an accommodation in the Greek sense, i.e., an evangelistic strategy, but **H** a temporally bounded acknowledgement of the permanent sign-value of the law, after which all actual observance was to be abandoned. Thus it is that Peter "received with a devout, holy and good-natured humility the rebuke which Paul gave him for his benefit with the frankness of love." Peter not only "took the heat," he "took his medicine," we might say. Finally, Augustine appealed to *his* tradition as support for his views, this being the tradition of Cyprian and Ambrose (*Ep.* 82,ii,21).[25] As Augustine closes out his side of the debate, therefore, we can look briefly at his sources as well.

    C While neither side made reference to Tertullian, this writer's view is significant. He seems to have seen the encounter between Peter and Paul at Antioch as an altercation reflecting the fact that in the apostolic period the ritual aspects of the law had not yet been definitively abrogated. Thus some practices were *"pro temporibus et personis et causis"* (*Adv.Marc.* I,xx,2 and IV,ii,3; *De praescr.haer.* 24,1-4). Consequently both Peter and Paul observed the law and denied it, for this was not a time of settled faith and practice. Perhaps in his final notion of the provisionality of arrangements in the apostolic age Augustine echoed this idea; but his conviction that Paul was of a definite mind, had formulated his views once and for all, is quite different in spirit. Cyprian (*Ep.* 71,2-3) introduced the idea that at Antioch Peter submitted to a thoroughgoing rebuke in order that the peace of the Church be maintained.[26] Certainly Augustine, locked in struggle with the Donatists, would have found Cyprian's exegesis immensely appealing. We catch an echo of it in Augustine's idea of Peter's humility and charity as he submits to Paul's orthodoxy. **H** Perhaps it was the anti-Jewish tradition of the Marcionite prologues and Marius

---

    H Augustine: Permanent value of the law as a sign.

    C Augustine's debt to the African tradition of Tertullian and Cyprian.

    H Rejection of Jewish adulteration of the way to salvation, resulting from anti-Jewish Marcionite influences.

Victorinus and Ambrosiaster that fed his inclination to see Paul's stance as a principled, uncompromising, straightforward rejection of Jewish adulteration of the way to salvation.

In the Marcionite prologues (introductory notes to the epistles in the Latin version), we encounter the idea that in all of his epistles Paul contended with false apostles who had led believers "in the name of our Lord Jesus Christ into submission to the law and the prophets" (these prologues are reproduced in Harnack 1921, 136*-38*). Victorinus in his commentary during the latter part of the fourth century argued that Peter had genuinely betrayed the faith by his behavior and stood condemned by the whole congregation; Paul simply confronted Peter with this standing judgment. Peter's sin was that he yielded to pressure from James and the men from Jerusalem and decided to resume observance of the law. This observance, thus, was hypocritical, for it was undertaken not as a matter of principle as a missionary strategy but out of craven fear. Peter's courage had failed him. Thus, when Paul rebuked him, Peter returned to the faith that he had held all along but in a moment of weakness compromised (*Comm.in ep.Pauli ad Galatas* I, ad.loc.).

Ambrosiaster in his commentary did acknowledge the harmony and authority relations that emerged for Peter and Paul from the Jerusalem conference (*concordiam societatis et honorificentiam primatus*), but felt that somehow (*causa neglegentiae vel erroris*) things had broken down in Antioch (*Comm.in ep.ad Galatas*, ad loc. [26-28]). The problem was that the Jewish converts in Antioch had been intimidated, along with Peter and Barnabas, by the men from Jerusalem. These latter were truly followers of the law and as such put Christ and the law on an equal footing. Out of fear that these Jerusalem men would be scandalized, Peter began practicing the ritual requirements again. Had the matter ended here, averred Ambrosiaster, no harm might have been done. The problem was that Peter withdrew from fellowship with the Gentile believers and then put pressure on them to conform to Jewish practice. For Gentile believers Peter's inconsistency would have generated total confusion, thought Ambrosiaster, about how they ought to conduct themselves with regard to the law. It was Paul's service to cut through the confusion and uproar and restore order by clarifying again how Gentiles are to relate to the commandments of the law, that it might be fulfilled in Christ who justifies us. Perhaps Augustine appropriated from Ambrosiaster's type of reasoning about the passage a view that after all Peter had fallen into error through his human weakness and as a result the truth was obscured. The "furor" of the Jews hides the true nature of the law, and only the light of the gospel can illuminate the truth contained beneath the Judaizing obfuscations.

C Both Jerome and Augustine, therefore, presented themselves in the debate as synthesizers of the traditions that preceded them in East and West respectively. Augustine carried out this intention, I believe, somewhat more honestly than did Jerome, but he was not saddled with a problematical past, as was Jerome with Origen. In both streams of exegesis, however, the preoccupation with clarifying the historical context of Paul's thought in terms of "Jew and Gentile" is massively evident, though H the Greek tradition presses more in the direction of situational/personal, and the Latin more toward theological/universal constructions. What remains is to clarify the parallels and connections with reading Israel in Romans and, then, to make the link with the modern debate already mentioned between Stendahl and his critics.

- III -

H What then might be the implications of this examination of Galatians 2:11-14 for reading Israel in Romans? Until the nineteenth century the question would have had an obvious answer: the theology taught by Paul in Galatians is so similar to that in Romans that any perceived differences are purely minor and contingent. The implied comparison here was always between Romans 1-8 and Galatians 2:15ff., that is, between the "doctrinal" portions of both letters. Increasing attention to Romans 9-11, however, on the part of exegetes since the time of F.C. Baur has changed the picture.[27] Baur recognized that Paul in those chapters turned to the history of Israel and Israel's status in the light of the gospel in a way seemingly not paralleled in Galatians. What is notable about Romans 9-11, and then in Romans 4 as well, is that Paul actually defends the status and prerogatives of Israel (Rom. 9:1-5, 11:17ff., 11:25ff.) and makes Abraham the father of *all* nations in Romans 4 (see especially Neubrand 1997).

As recognition of the import of these passages and themes dawns on the exegete, other themes and references throughout the epistle begin to click into focus. The gospel is for the Jew "first" (1:16) and then for the Greek. The contrast of the true and false Jews in chapter 2 sets Jew and Gentile on a plane of equality and calls both to a higher righteousness. At 3:29ff. we are informed that God is the God of both Jews and Gentiles. At 7:13 we learn that the law is holy, just, and good. The amount of exegesis

---

C Jerome and Augustine continue, respectively, the Greek and Latin traditions of interpretation.

H The Greek tradition is more situational/personal, the Latin more theological/universal.

H Paul's position(s) on the issue of "Jews and Gentiles" in Galatians and Romans. Romans 1-8 and 9–11; Romans 4; Romans 2; Rom. 9:1-5, 11:17ff., 11:25ff.; Rom. 1:16, 3:29ff, 7:13.

of Hebrew Scripture in Romans and its import for Paul's thinking are striking. The possibilities multiply. Gradually, and then with massive impact, the Jewishness of Romans begins to register in a way that seems quite different from the assault on the law in Galatians. Modern exegesis of Romans is now heavily preoccupied with the strikingly pro-Jewish qualities of Paul's presentation in Romans and their contrast with the passages that seem to make faith in Christ the one way of salvation. Exegetes are widely in agreement that Paul seems to have a different agenda in Romans from that in Galatians, and proposals for explaining the difference fill the horizon.[28]

C At the end of the twentieth century, therefore, we find ourselves in a radically different situation from that of earlier exegetes who assimilated Romans and Galatians. The usual explanation of the divergence is now in terms of historical setting: Paul must defend Gentile Christians against Jewish Christians in Galatians, and must do the opposite in Romans.[29] In dealing with the Roman congregation there is for some reason the need to come to the defense of Jewish Christians who are not receiving proper respect from Gentiles for the heritage and understanding which they bring to the gospel; therefore Israel must be vindicated, and the "weak" of 14:1ff. must be treated with compassion. In the case of the Galatian congregations there is the need to make it clear to Gentile Christians that they must not Judaize, that ritual adherence to the law is not for them necessary, and thus Israelite claims must be relativized and compromise forbidden. The differentiation of the two epistles thus serves to clarify their individuality.

C A good case can be made, however, that the contrast between Romans and Galatians may be overdrawn, without having to harken back to an uncritical assimilation of the two. An example is the very contemporary work of Mark Nanos (1996), who embraces, as a Jewish interpreter, the view that Paul teaches in Romans that Jews and Gentiles must be considered as equals under the care of the one God (Nanos 1996, 179ff.; a somewhat related argument from the "Scandinavian school" is Halvor Moxnes 1980). The great sin against which Paul inveighs in Romans, according to Nanos, and which draws down the wrath of God, is the self-righteousness of Jews and Gentiles toward one another. Gentiles tend to despise Jews and Jewish Christians for their Jewishness, which includes keeping the law, and Jews feel superior to Gentiles for their lack of the marks of covenant status. Both groups forget thereby the supreme truth, that God through the Messiah Jesus has made them one. Both groups act out their sin when they imagine that they can gain status by giving up

---

C Galatians and Romans written in different contexts. Rom. 14:1ff.

C Was Paul always "pro-Jewish"? Romans 7.

either Jewish or Gentile membership and transferring to the other group. Nanos further argues that in Romans 7 Paul anguished with his conscience over this very issue, that he, Paul, is constantly tempted to seek special status with God by clinging to the righteousness of the law, thus falling into the sin that is the special weakness of Jews and leads to exclusiveness. Nanos makes a connection with the Antioch incident in Galatians by arguing that Paul rebukes Peter for having fallen into the very temptation described in Romans 7. By separating himself from his Gentile Christian brethren, Peter made group membership the means of salvation, made it seem as if belonging to one group was better than belonging to the other. Nanos suggests, therefore, that Paul never accused Peter of apostasy, only of hypocrisy, of not living out what he believed. The point of the argument both in Galatians and in Romans is that in Christ we have become equals, that our righteousness is from a gracious God who has made us both different and the same, different as Jews and Gentiles, the same as human beings under a single sovereignty. Romans and Galatians contain an argument essentially the same, but cut, so to speak, for two different audiences (Nanos 1996, 337-71).

H Whatever the merits of Nanos's proposals, which are considerable, I hold him up in this context as an example of how things come full circle in exegesis. We are listening here to one version of what Jerome and Augustine struggled to clarify. The issue of Israel, highlighted in one way in the Antioch incident of Galatians, *ripples outward to the entirety of the total human situation* and appears to be closely related to, if not identical with, the issue of Israel in Romans. Nanos' approach, like that of many today who read Israel in Romans, is one of painstakingly reconstructing the human drama within Paul both as Jew and as apostle to the Gentiles and unfolded in his particular controversies with Peter and others. This was the approach of the Greek exegetes, described above — an effort to see into the virtue of the human actors — but it was also the approach of Augustine in his determination to draw more than a narrowly ecclesiastical significance from the text. Augustine sought universal truth about the human situation, and so does Nanos, though they occupy different anthropological systems. But it is the wrestling with Israel in the texts of Romans and Galatians, under the rubric of "Jews and Gentiles," that constitutes the common core of their exegetical endeavors.

A return to the contours of the Stendahl/Käsemann debate can now round out our reflections and bring them to a sharp formulation.

H General views of the human situation emerging from both the Greek and the Latin wrestling with the problem of "Jews and Gentiles."

- IV -

H In the contemporary controversy about the use of the theme of "Jews and Gentiles" in interpreting the theology of Paul, the "flash-point" presentation was Stendahl's 1963 essay "The Apostle Paul and the Introspective Conscience of the West" (Stendahl 1963, reprinted in Stendahl 1976, 78-96). The author made a number of claims. He argued that in the interpretation of Paul since the time of Augustine, the apostle has been made the keeper of a conscience-focused, morbidly sin-centered form of spirituality, which is grounded in a general theological anthropology. In this doctrine of universal human nature, a "deep and sensitive introspective conscience," whose awareness of its bondage to sin (Romans 7) sets the stage for authentic conversion to Christ, also provides the setting for the psychological process of individuation and the formation of the mature self. Contending that this reading of Paul has its roots in Augustine, Stendahl went on to suggest that such a view could have arisen only when Paul's original struggle to find a place for the gospel of Gentile Christianity within the heritage of Israel had been forgotten. Paul, in fact the possessor of a "robust conscience," had actually focused his energies on "the problem about the nature and intention of God's Law" once the Messiah had arrived in Jesus.[30]

Paul's true concern, according to Stendahl, was an accurate understanding of the unfolding of "sacred history" or of "the plan of God" (Romans 9-11) for Jews and Gentiles. "Paul's references to the impossibility of fulfilling the Law is part of a theological and theoretical scriptural argument about the relation between Jews and Gentiles." Indeed, "Paul had not arrived at his view of the Law by testing and pondering its effect upon his conscience," but rather "it was his grappling with the question about the place of the Gentiles in the Church and in the plan of God, with the problem Jews/Gentiles or Jewish Christians/Gentile Christians," that tormented him. It was this problematic "which had driven him to that interpretation of the Law which was to become his in a unique way." That interpretation, averred Stendahl, was based on a kind of family argument between Paul and his fellow Jews about whether specific customs such as circumcision would be required in the messianic age. **I** The tendency of subsequent Christian theology to turn such a local dispute into a matter of principle has arisen from a grandiose, triumphalistic over-generalization that represents the political power of the church since the fourth century. The result has been the theology of justification characteristic of

---

H The Stendahl thesis. Romans 7.

I Was the "introspective" interpretation possible only after the original issue of the Gentiles' relation to Israel had been forgotten?

Peter J. Gorday

the church in the West but distinctly not present in the Eastern churches or the patristic church before Augustine.[31]

What Stendahl has proposed as a more authentically historical reading of Paul is, as he has testified, a product of his own background in the work of Anton Fridrichsen and Johannes Munck. These exegetes, mindful of the work of Albert Schweitzer and deeply committed to an interpretation of Paul that would honor the eschatological-apocalyptic context of his life and work, focused above all on the nature of Paul's apostleship. **H** Paul's apostolic identity functioned, they believed, as a union of his person and work and therefore as the key to his message (Fridrichsen 1947). Everything in his writing was subordinated to the central importance of his divine calling and appointment. Paul was to preach the messiahship of the crucified and risen Christ, to bring the Gentiles under the sway of Christ's lordship, and to do these things within the setting of the last days and the approaching ingathering of all of the elect people of God. Fridrichsen particularly emphasized the kerygmatic, ecclesial dimensions of Paul's apostleship, whereby a high level of cooperation existed with the apostle Peter and others in the universal mission.

Munck was more concerned with the eschatological significance of the taking up of the collection for Jerusalem, with Paul's concern for the redemption of his fellow Jews as part of universal salvation, and with the timetable and mechanics of the approaching end (Munck 1959). Stendahl has then refined the views of Fridrichsen and Munck to characterize Paul's thought as a theology of *missions*. The apostle struggled to understand "his own humble yet important role" within God's grand plan for "Israel and the Gentile Church, two minorities whose witnesses were somehow necessary to God's mysterious dealings with the world" (Stendahl 1993, 41).

H Ernst Käsemann has responded to Stendahl's invitation to a more historical, i.e., more eschatological-apocalyptic, reading of Paul's context in several essays and in his commentary on Romans, particularly on Romans 9-11. There is first of all Käsemann's fundamental view that the "righteousness of God," as the central theme of Paul's theology, be understood as "God's 'salvation-creating power' by which he conquers evil and establishes his rule over the whole cosmos" (Käsemann 1961, reprinted in Funk 1965; cf. Wright 1982, 10). This righteousness of God is the "gift given to the believer that he might be recaptured for obedience to God," and is thus a modern derivative from Augustine's emphasis on the grace and consequent charity engendered in the faithful Christian by

---

H Paul's apostolic calling, the key to his theology of mission.

H Käsemann's emphasis on the "righteousness of God" in Paul.

God's work in Christ. **H** Consequently, in Käsemann's view, Paul does offer a universal anthropology, based on the two-aeon structure of his thought and thus thoroughly eschatological in nature (Käsemann 1971a). Paul's theology of the cross is a universal proclamation of the nature of God and the nature of the human situation before God (Käsemann 1971b). There is a real danger, contended Käsemann, that in the enthusiasm for the notion of redemptive history and the importance of historical events in salvation we will lose sight of the one thing necessary, "faith in one thing and one thing alone: Christ is Lord." **I** In direct rebuttal to Stendahl, he agreed that a universalizing anthropology is not the main thrust of Paul's thought. The central place in Paul's thought *does* belong to a salvation history, whose true significance is initially unclear (Käsemann 1971c). "It cannot be denied," he says, "that even the Pauline texts do not have an anthropology in view, and it is highly questionable whether anthropology even represents their central concern" (1971c, 65). Closer examination reveals, however, that this salvation history is essentially that of Augustine, that of the two cities set in dialectical relation and correlative with the grounding of Paul's theology in the apocalyptic idea of the two ages. **I** He further grants to Stendahl that there has been historically a psychologizing of Paul's thought that has led to the abuses which the latter characterizes as the "introspective conscience." There has also been an illegitimate individualizing of salvation in the usual understandings of justification (1971c, 74) so that Käsemann proposes, and actually carries out in the commentary, a reinterpretation of justification along "cosmic" lines (Käsemann 1980). Absolutely everything in the commentary is framed in terms of the cosmic-eschatological nature of God's work, presupposed by Paul's roots in the apocalyptic world-view of early Christianity. This task is carried out, he has claimed, with the help of a properly eschatological understanding of the notion of "salvation history." As he says, "salvation history is not the consummation of, let alone the substitute for, justification, but its historical depth, i.e., one of its aspects" (Käsemann 1971c, pp. 73-74).

H One example may serve to illustrate how Käsemann handles the theme of "Jews and Gentiles." In discussing portions of Romans 9, Käsemann argues that "Paul is no longer concerned with two peoples and their destiny, but timelessly with the election and rejection of two persons who are elevated as types" (Käsemann 1980, 264). That is, Paul concerns himself with the elect who possess true faith and inherit the promises and

---

H Paul's "universal" perspective based in apocalyptic eschatology. Romans 9–11.

I Paul's universalizing anthropology in the context of salvation history, also for Käsemann.

I An excessively psychologizing or "introspective" approach is a misinterpretation of Augustine.

H Käsemann's interpretation of Romans 9.

the non-elect who do not have faith and come under consequent judgement. This way of construing the Jew and Gentile theme, i.e., abstracting and universalizing it, is carried out from beginning to end.

I The debate between Stendahl and Käsemann is thus the old debate in modern form. The struggle is that between a situational/personal approach and a theological/universal approach to the understanding of Paul's historical context. I The former, represented by the Greek exegetes and Jerome in antiquity and Stendahl in the present, is focused on the particularities of the place, the time, the character of the players, and all of the contingent and cultural circumstances. Significance for the present arises from the ways in which God is perceived to have acted through concrete human interactions to effect a larger purpose. The hermeneutical leap is accomplished by a kind of empathic bridge from one thought-world (that of the past) into another (that of the present), from one set of particularities to a different set. Thus Jerome and the Greeks were much preoccupied, often with considerable psychological realism, with the virtues of Peter and Paul and their import for us; Stendahl similarly is much concerned with Paul's humility and human weakness as an apostle and its import for us. Historical particularity is one kind of window into the reality of God and, so to speak, feels after transcendence in its own way.

I Augustine and Käsemann represent on their side the theological/universal approach, in which the tendency is to search for essences in a historical situation in order to grasp the point of it all. What matters is that the truth be distilled, stated propositionally, and then passed on as a sacred deposit in more or less systematic form. History and historical context are profoundly important here as well, though their particularities tend to recede quickly in the face of an overarching principle once that is clarified. I In the case of Augustine, this tendency is clear in his need to formulate the encounter of Peter and Paul at Antioch as a clash of distinctly opposite points of view. In this way the characteristic truth of Christianity, its *proprium*, would prevail, and no mere dimension of human contriving such as a simulation be allowed to cloud, or compromise, the outcome. For the Greeks and Jerome, the human contingencies with all of their nuances are everything, even if the exegete here becomes subject to fancifulness, since the gospel itself is precisely about the concrete transformations of human beings in their place and time.

We are finally left, in assessing the ancient and modern quarrels about

---

I Situational/personal approach or theological/universal approach?

I The situational/personal approach of the Greek tradition, Jerome, and Stendahl.

I The theological/universal approach of Augustine and Käsemann.

I Are specific episodes to be interpreted as manifestations of basic principles, or are their contingencies and nuances to be explored in detail?

Paul's historical context in terms of "Jews and Gentiles," with three issues.

H 1. There is the matter of the use of the concept of "salvation history." What is its import? In his treatment of the differing views held by Augustine and Jerome about the authority of the law for Christians, Henning has emphasized, through their contrasting views of the law, the radically divergent notions of the two men about salvation history as well (Hennings 1994, 265-91).[32] **H** Jerome formulated a kind of two-stage position according to which before Christ the law is valid and predicts the coming of the Messiah, and after Christ the law is extinct as a practice and meaningful only as prophecy. The economy of salvation history for Jerome was rather like the modern theory of evolution: it posits an irreversible process of change. What is past is past, though it pointed to what was to come. For Jerome, therefore, the Jews become an atavism, a holdover from a bygone era, instructive in their own way but superseded.

H Augustine took a three-stage position, seeing a before-Christ period, where the law is valid and salvific, and an after-Christ period which is subdivided. The first stage after Christ is that of the apostolic age, where "special" arrangements prevailed for a qualified observance of the law by Jewish converts, and then a second stage of complete abrogation of the law. **H** The law after Christ has become a sign, a sacrament, a pointer to the purposes of God perfectly represented in Christ as these unfold both within the lives of the elect (those who have faith) and the non-elect (including unbelieving Jews), but still incomplete within the conditions of earthly temporality. Such was Augustine's reading of Israel in the encounter at Antioch, as well as in the letter to the Romans.

Prescinding from all the metaphysical questions about the nature of history and the nature of divine "action" in history, the practical implications of the Jerome-Augustine and Stendahl-Käsemann debates remain unclear. A good example is the stance of Christian exegetes towards the Jewish people considered as "the people of the law" or "Judaism" or "Israel" or "the synagogue," and the implications of such a stance for understanding Christian faith itself. The question as such is an open one, but the way we construe salvation history, and its implicit horizons of providence and theodicy, will make a significant difference.[33] This is a central issue for reading Israel in Romans.

I 2. The second issue concerns the presence or absence of a theological

---

H Differing conceptions of "salvation history."
H Jerome's "two-stage" interpretation.
H Augustine's "three-stage" interpretation.
H The law after Christ continuing to have a sign-character.
I Is interpretation focused upon the situation, or does it seek universally applicable insights?

doctrine of human nature, or the human situation, in Paul's thought. In the modern debate Käsemann has suggested that Stendahl makes the idea of salvation history so comprehensively explanatory of Paul's theology that any specified understanding on the apostle's part of the human plight is excluded. In the ancient debate, as we saw, the Greek exegetes appealed to the concept of "accommodation" to explain why Jewish converts were allowed to continue observance of the law for a time. Accommodation was both a missionary strategy and a reflection of the nature of God's saving action in history on behalf of humankind. Augustine, on the other hand, followed a different strategy when he described the law as good and its observance allowable so long as it was treated as an indifferent thing, that is, as helpful but not necessary for salvation. Here he was appropriating, and extending, an anthropological doctrine. The Stoics had classed objects of desire as good, bad, or indifferent in their impact on the person seeking to live a virtuous life. The modern contrast of salvation history with anthropology as different ways of construing Paul thus existed in the past as well.[34] ❡ The question that arises, then, is a challenge from the theological/universal perspective to the situation/personal one: just what are the implications for human self-understanding of Paul's preaching of the law-free gospel for the Gentiles? What are the human implications for Jews who remain Jews? What perspective on human need or human desiring is implied in saying that Paul's thought is based on his apostleship and that his thought is really a theology of mission?

❡ 3. The third question is a challenge in reverse, from the situational/personal perspective to the theological/universal, though there is a difficulty for the former perspective as well. Both the patristic and the modern debates about the meaning of "Jews and Gentiles" for understanding Paul are premised on the desire to clarify with greater precision the unique and special features of his personal identity and his peculiar work. In making sense of his context we are also trying to make sense of *him*, and not necessarily through anachronistic psychologizing interpretations. Consequently, the patristic exegetes go to great lengths to unravel what they see as the rhetorical, tactical, and interpersonal subtleties everywhere present in Paul's letters. Whether it is a matter of understanding the "I" who speaks in Romans 7, or the Paul who agonizes for his kinsmen in Romans 9:1-5, or the Paul who grandly announces that "all Israel will be saved" (Rom. 11:25), or the Paul who rebukes Peter at Antioch, his human reality is of consuming interest. They recognize that real human beings

---

❡ A challenge from the theological/universal to the situational/personal perspective.

❡ How can we pay proper attention to Paul himself without isolating him in the past? Romans 7; 9:1-5; 11:25.

with roles to play and agendas to be pursued are involved here, and as exegetes they try to fathom the actions narrated in the text in real human terms. **I** The advantage of the situational/personal approach in understanding Paul is that this interest in his person and activity in all of their particularity can be given free rein. The problem with this method, as represented by Stendahl, is that Paul is seen as an entirely unique character with a unique task in a unique time. Such a representation makes him nearly as remote from our normal categories of human understanding as does the theological/universal labeling of him as *the* Apostle to the Gentiles and arch-expositor of justification by faith.[35]

C What makes the debate between Augustine and Jerome perennially interesting and instructive is the fact that, though they anticipated the contours of the modern debate, they are not yet limited by it. They both struggled mightily to discern accurately the human motives, the human limitations, the degree of virtue or its lack, and the fashioning of each character's understanding of his faithfulness to a mission and a constituency, when they viewed Peter and Paul at Antioch. It seems to me that when we on our part wrestle with "context" in understanding Paul, we might operate with somewhat different tools and different assumptions from our patristic forebears. We cannot improve, however, on their vision of what needed to be done if Paul and his thought are to be grasped with empathy, perhaps even with saving power.

Notes

1. Does the approach which I thus describe make me guilty of the "cherry-picking" from pre-modern exegesis that Michael Cahill (2000, 340) deplores? The essence of such cherry-picking, as Cahill describes it, is that the modern interpreter fails to take due account of the historical context of the earlier exegetical efforts, then appropriates the older work in an uncritical way for the present. Cahill's constructive offer is an integration of older methods of exegesis with contemporary postmodern literary theory of multiple meanings, or layers of meaning, in classic texts. My solution is different. Closer examination of ancient exegesis often suggests, as I argue in this paper, that those exegetes resorted to strategies that also typify even the most "critical" of modern critical interpreters as they extract historical meaning from sacred texts. It is not necessary to make an appeal to postmodern hermeneutics to justify interest in the history of exegesis.

2. The actual statement is that the history-of-religions school of biblical scholarship made it possible for exegetes to appreciate the historical context of Scripture as something with its own character and integrity. Therefore, "What emerged was a descriptive study of biblical thought – empathetic in the sense that it was beyond sympathy or antipathy." Empathy is an act of understanding in which I know the other and am known by that other simultaneously; it is the intersubjective act *par*

I A challenge from the theological/universal to the situational/personal perspective.
C Jerome and Augustine, preceding this contemporary debate, were not limited by it.

excellence.

3. My detailed treatment of the Stendahl-Käsemann standoff, with references, is in part IV below.

4. Since Grenholm and Patte (2000) focus on reading Israel in Romans, I might suggest a companion volume on *Reading Israel in Galatians.*

5. Stendahl certainly agrees with the idea of the Reformation as the heir of Augustine, much of his argument (Stendahl 1963, and the first chapter of Stendahl 1976) being intended to show that this dogmatic, universalizing, conscience-stricken reading of Paul originates with Augustine and is transmitted to the Protestant Reformers. The truth is that such a reading did not originate with Augustine but has ample precedent in his Latin forebears and in Origen.

6. Such is the standard account, at least. In the first chapter of my work (1983) on the patristic exegesis of Romans 9-11, I sketch out some of the development. The contention of Protestant apologists during and after the Reformation was that the doctrine of justification derives from Augustine and, through him, from Paul. Eventually the Protestant form of the argument turned into the "Hellenization thesis" that the dogmas and creeds of the early Catholic Church were a product of the Greek spirit and caused the original essence of the gospel to be obscured or lost altogether. As Augustine fought against Pelagius for the principle of radical grace, he fought against the contamination of the Gospel by pagan philosophy. At the same time he refought, so the argument went, the battle of Paul against the Judaizing false Christians, and he anticipated the struggles of the Reformers with the legal ecclesiasticism of the Roman Church in the sixteenth century. It is quite true, of course, that Catholic exegetes have also claimed the authority of Augustine. Much of the modern history of Protestant-Catholic debate about Paul might be written as the effort to discern which communion is the true heir of Augustine and his understanding of Paulinism.

7. Somewhere in the linkage of this hypothesized connection of Stendahl with the work of the Greek exegetes of Paul is his own background in the patristically informed theologies of Gustaf Aulén and Gustaf Wingren.

8. This would seem to be the case despite the fact that statements in works Jerome composed after the time of his exchanges with Augustine seem to concede some points to Augustine. In one place Jerome says (*Dialogus contra Pelagianos* I,22) that Peter did not live in accordance with the gospel, that he led Barnabas astray, and that Paul rebuked him. In another place (*Epistula Hieronymi adversus Rufinum* 2 = *Apologia contra Rufinum* 3,2) Jerome pointed to Paul's confronting Peter at Antioch with the latter's error as an example of friendship in the Gospel that transcends disagreements. These statements by Jerome are not necessarily inconsistent with the interpretation of the Antioch incident by the Greek exegetes, who allowed for a measure of blame on Peter's part. Thus I disagree with Kelly (1975, 272 n. 41, following de Bruyne), who believes that these passages show that Jerome had adopted Augustine's explanation as superior. On the contrary, they suggest that Jerome stuck to his notion of some kind of collusion between the two apostles at Antioch.

9. See my points in the conclusion to this essay.

10. The latest and most comprehensive monographic treatment of the debate is Hennings (1994), whose analysis is particularly commendable in clarifying the theological issues at stake for Augustine, but is less adequate in the analysis of the Greek writers and sources. All of the epistles between Augustine and Jerome are introduced and translated by White (1990).

11. There was no possibility among the patristic exegetes for the tactic resorted to by some modern exegetes in order to explain how Peter and Paul could come into conflict

Galatians, Reading Israel in Romans: the Patristic Debate

so soon after an accord (e.g., Lüdemann 1983, 75ff., 291), namely of dating the incident at Antioch *before* the Jerusalem Conference of Gal 2:1-10.

12. A major theme in the debate between Jerome and Augustine about the nature of what happened between Peter and Paul at Antioch is the veneration of ancient tradition. Part of the apologetic, first of Hellenistic Judaism and then of the Christian church, was the claim that the law of Moses represented wisdom passed down from ancient times and therefore of even greater worth than pagan wisdom. Both Jerome and Augustine adhered to this way of thinking about the traditions of Judaism, though they reasoned out its implications in quite different ways.

13. It is difficult to be clear about the nature of what Peter, as an observant Jewish Christian, would have been doing at Gentile meals. The evidence taken from Acts is routinely used in ancient and modern exegesis to suggest that he would have followed the premise that in Christ, and with Gentile believers at the very least, he would have been completely free to partake of whatever was served. This is the usual understanding of what Paul is saying when he refers to Peter's having lived like a Gentile (Gal. 2:14). But Murphy-O'Connor (1996, 150ff.) and Nanos (1996, 349) make it clear that the matter was not so simple. Halakhic regulations of the time made it entirely possible for Jews to eat with Gentiles as long as certain precautions were observed. Thus Peter's having lived like a Gentile cannot have been about food *per se*, for as an observant Jewish Christian among presumably accommodating Gentile Christians he would have been able easily to eat with them at the same table. Thus the separation from this table fellowship would have been about something else than the keeping of the dietary laws. The exegete, ancient or modern, is forced to speculate at this point about the reason for Peter's withdrawal; usually it is related to the nature of the pressure being put on him by the "men from James."

14. It is easy enough to find modern parallels to the psychology of Jerome's interpretation. The intent is to preserve the integrity of Peter's behavior while supporting the thrust of Paul's teaching. Murphy O'Connor's treatment (1996, 151ff.) shows one way of doing this. For him Peter joins those Jews from Jerusalem who fear the loss of Jewish nationalistic identity in a sea of Gentile converts; he therefore withdraws into a situation where Jewish Christians will have complete control of their meal preparation and not be dependent on Gentile generosity in such situations. E.P. Sanders (1991, 53) suggests a somewhat similar scenario, in which too much fellowship with Gentiles was casting suspicion on the Apostle to the Jews. The point is that Peter had to be true to himself and his mission. Hence the withdrawal.

15. There is an element of continuity here, despite the enormous differences, with the recent work of Mark Nanos (1996, 353ff.), who makes heavy use of Gal. 3:28 and I Cor. 7:17-24 to argue that it was Paul's intention to leave all converts in the state of life in which he found them, *including that of Torah-observant Jews who had become Christians.* Nanos's intention is to build a case for understanding Paul as one who taught Gentile believers to respect Jews as followers of the one God. While this modern egalitarianism is unknown to Augustine, the common element between the ancient and modern exegete here is the recognition that Paul accorded a special status to law-observant Jewish Christians.

16. Jerome cites the same passage at the end of his last communication to Augustine about their disagreement (*Ep.* 112,14), but he makes a different point. For Augustine circumcision will come to seem valuable to the Christian in the present as a "sign," while for Jerome it will have no value for the present at all.

17. Augustine (*Exp.ep.Gal.* 15,7) thus made use of the idea, perhaps appropriated from Marius Victorinus (see below), that Peter was genuinely intimidated by, and afraid of, the men from James. But why? Betz (1979, 109) suggests tentatively that Peter feared losing his political power, i.e., his position of influential leadership, by getting into trouble with the leaders in Jerusalem. Lüdemann (1989, 237) insists that the fear felt

by Peter for the circumcision party in Jerusalem, i.e., the Jewish Christians, was a "theologically grounded" fear linked to the authority of James. But such an interpretation is linked to Lüdemann's comprehensive argument for the presence of Jewish-Christian anti-Paulinism in the early church.

18. I believe that this is the first appearance in the dispute about Gal. 2:11-14 of Augustine's developing theory of signs. For masterful exposition, I refer the reader to Cameron (1999), who relates Augustine's sign theory to his project of unifying the Old and New Testaments in *Contra Faustum.*

19. Augustine says that Paul observed the law "*non ut fallaciter ... sed ut misericorditer.*" Jerome was to insist that this is a sophism; but then again Jerome could not comprehend the significance of what Augustine meant by a "sign."

20. The distinction originated in the ethics of the Stoics, but it was transmitted especially through Cicero's *De finibus.* An often quoted passage is *De finibus* III,58, where human actions are classed as good, bad, and indifferent. The last type is described as "*officium medium quiddam esse, quod neque in bonis ponatur neque in contrariis*"; that is, indifferent actions are neither inherently good or bad, but are dependent for their moral quality on the circumstances under which they are performed. For Augustine, continued observance for Jewish believers of the law of Moses would come under this heading. See Rist 1969, 97-111 (the citation from *De finibus* is on p. 97).

21. At one juncture in his discussions with Jerome (*Ep.* 82,ii,17), Augustine referred back to a point he had made in a debate with the Manichaean leader Faustus (*C.Faust.* XIX,17), that observance of the law for Jewish converts made sense for a short time. The reason was not that the law brings salvation, but that it sets the stage for salvation by creating the condition of demand that only charity can satisfy. The demand for righteousness contained in the law and incumbent on humankind is fulfilled through Christ, as God's Spirit works love in our hearts. The first generation of Jewish Christians in their continuing observance of the law become a timeless reminder of this progression. As they reverenced the law, so should we all, that we may learn definitively that it does not bring salvation. To the law's commandment must always be added Jesus' "but I say to you." Contrariwise, the plight of contemporaneous Jews for Augustine is that, in their unbelief, they testify to the inscrutable will of God in election. Though they are the carriers of God's word, they have been rejected by God so that others may be chosen. Paula Fredriksen (1995) analyzes Augustine's attitude toward Jews as "a protected witness people" (320) with great care, and concludes that it was essentially a product of his debates with the Manichaeans, not a product of actual struggles with real Jews. I agree with this argument. Actual contact with Jews on the part of Christian thinkers, such as Origen and even Jerome, seems to have been livelier, and more likely, in Egypt and Palestine.

22. In *Comm. ad Gal.* 2,5 (PG 61:641), Chrysostom says with regard to 2:14, "[Paul] does not condemn Peter, but so expresses himself for the benefit of those who were to be reformed by Peter" (NPNF, 2,19).

23. Thus Augustine's charge that the "simulation" is simply lying under another name may be a bit severe, even lacking, in its own way, in psychological sophistication. Collusion in relationships is quite different from lying, even though, of course, an "untruth" is propagated. At some level, moreover, it is clear that Augustine embraced in a way quite different from that of Jerome a particular, and complex, understanding of how divine truth is mediated through the word of Scripture. Mark Vessey (1999) expertly compares the views of the two men.

24. J.N.D. Kelly (1975, 269) believes that Jerome is here indulging in a "caricature" of Augustine's argument. But this is not true. Jerome understood very well Augustine's use of the necessary vs. unnecessary for salvation rationale, but found the special class into which Augustine put the law of Moses a sophism. It is only in his *Ep.* 82, in response to Jerome, that Augustine makes it clear that he considered the apostolic age

a special time with special provisions, so far as the status of the law went.

25. Augustine argues that all of Jerome's talk about an "economy" is a sophism for covering up the fact that a lie is a lie (*Ep.* 82,ii,24). Here Augustine begins the appeal to his own *auctoritates*. By "Ambrose" he must mean the commentator known since Erasmus' time as "Ambrosiaster," though Erasmus may not have actually originated the name.

26. He suggested that at Antioch Peter had the good sense to see that, under the conditions of the moment, Paul had the stronger case (had *ratio* on his side), and that it was more important to submit than to argue (as he might have). This sounds like an ancient form of preferring to be a "team player"!

27. The remarks of Jervell (1984, 63-67) are particularly helpful here, not so much as a resuscitation of old Tübingen School arguments about the predominance of Jewish Christians in the Roman church but as a reminder of the profound influence of F.C. Baur on the whole subsequent history of the problem.

28. The bibliographies in Fitzmyer (1993) are state-of-the-art, but I especially recommend Lübking (1986) for his massive assimilation of the history of exegesis on Paul and Israel in Romans. Zeller (1973) is also important, but much too diffuse and bogged down in detail.

29. The classic collection of essays now is Donfried (1977), especially the essay by Wiefel on the Jewish community in Rome.

30. Gratuitous though it may be to mention it in this essay, Stendahl was in his own way answering the old Freudian charge that religion is an obsessional neurosis which, by its very nature, contains at its core the guilt-and-fear-driven superego of the modern neurotic work ethic. Stendahl seems to be saying that the gospel, *rightly understood,* is no such thing. Paul had a *robust* conscience, not a morbidly conflicted one.

31. I have re-arranged the order of some of the sentences to highlight the thrust of Stendahl's argument as it pertains to this essay. It should be evident from this essay, and from others in this collection, that Stendahl greatly overstated the originality of Augustine's exegesis. It is true, though, that Augustine's Western Latin tradition, with a different set of apologetic needs, construed Pauline texts in a way significantly different from that of the Greek East.

32. Hennings suggests that in essence what divided Augustine and Jerome was that the former was able to understand the continuing practice of the Law in apostolic times as genuinely good (though not necessary for salvation!), whereas Jerome always saw its practice as essentially shameful for a Christian (286).

33. Thus Wright (1982, 15), in his review of Käsemann's work, can claim that this exegete does not really deal in the final analysis with "Israel's hope," with the particularity of Israel we might say. Stendahl, on the other hand, claims to be doing just that by arguing that Paul's theology is about a mission that admits Gentiles to Israel's promises, i.e., takes those promises seriously, first for Jews and then for Gentiles. What is noteworthy as well in Stendahl's constructions is that respect for the particularities of historical setting that results in a kind of re-anthropologizing of Paul's theology. The chapters of Stendahl 1976 are organized around themes that reflect on Paul's scarred humanity. These include his call, his weakness, his humble love and endurance, the triumph not of his faith (which was bizarre, as apocalyptic eschatology always is), but of his faithfulness (which bespeaks something central to *homo religiosus* in any age).

34. Jerome's use of the concept of "accommodation/economy" and Augustine's use of the notion of "things indifferent" as a background to the necessary/not-necessary distinction might stand, then, as examples, in the language of Grenholm and Patte, of the bridge concepts that facilitate contextual frames. Accomodation/economy would fit the Grenholm-Patte class of bridge categories that deal with lack of knowledge in

the reader, i.e., the reader who would misunderstand the real nature of the interaction between Peter and Paul. Things indifferent would fit the category of terms that deal with lack of will or wrong will in the recipient, i.e., the person who would strive to acquire salvation through works of the Law (cf. Grenholm and Patte 2000, 36-38).

35. This is the element of truth in the criticism aimed at Stendahl by Espy (1985). He claims that Stendahl misuses the autobiographical statements made by Paul as if they were "self-indulgent" and boastful, rather than "purposeful" components of a larger theological and pastoral intent on Paul's part (p.164). "Stendahl," says Espy, "sets out to challenge 'the traditional Western way of reading the Pauline letters as documents of human consciousness,' but he and many others have rather perpetuated it; the difference is that they regard the letters as documents of just *one* human consciousness" (164). So far as their opposition to the universalizing reading of Romans goes, "the only difference [for Stendahl and his followers] is that, while their predecessors believed that the letters revealed a general human nature, the moderns seek only the marks of Paul's own personality. They continue in the fault which they condemn but limit its application" (165). It is true that Stendahl draws from his exegesis of Paul the rudiments of an anthropology. The chapter headings of Stendahl (1976) — such as "call rather than conversion," "justification rather than forgiveness," and especially "weakness rather than sin" – lean toward a doctrine of universal human nature. With regard, for instance, to his chapter on Paul's weakness, Stendahl says, "And his [Paul's] insight into the role of weakness in the life of religious people remains equally indispensable for all Christians" (1976, 76). What is completely untrue in Espy's critique of Stendahl is that the latter fails to understand Paul's autobiographical statements as central to his theological and apostolic project. Quite the contrary is the case. The problem is the claim that the kind of post-modern understanding of the human situation that Stendahl believes he has found in Paul is quite different from Espy's classical anthropological paradigm.

Bibliography

Primary Sources

Ambrosiaster. *Commentarius in epistolam ad Galatas.* Ed. H.-J. Vogels. CSEL 81,3. Vienna: Tempsky, 1966.

Augustine. *Expositio epistolae ad Galatas.* Ed. J. Divjak. CSEL 84. Vienna: Hoelder-Pichler-Tempsky, 1971.

Augustine. *De mendacio.* Ed. J. Zycha. CSEL 41. Vienna: Tempsky, 1900.

Augustine. *Contra Faustum Manichaeum.* CSEL 25,1. Ed. J. Zycha. Vienna: Tempsky, 1891.

Augustine. *Vingt-Six Sermons au Peuple d'Afrique.* Ed. F. Dolbeau. Collections des Études Augustiniennes, Série Antiquité, 147. Paris: Institut 'des Études Augustiniennes, 1996.

Augustine. *Epistulae* (Pars I, epp. I-XXX; Pars II, epp. XXXI-CXXIII). Ed. J. Goldbacher. CSEL 34,1; CSEL 34,2. Vienna: Tempsky, 1895-1900.

Cyprian. *Epistulae.* Ed. G.F. Diercks. CCL 3C. Turnhout: Brepols, 1996.

Harnack, Adolf von. *Das Evangelium vom fremden Gott. Eine Monographie zur Geschichte der Grundlegung der katholischen Kirche.* Leipzig: J.C. Hinrichs, 1921.

Jerome. *Commentarius in epistolam ad Galatas libri iii.* Ed. D. Vallarsi. PL 26. Paris: Migne, 1884.

Jerome. *Dialogus contra Pelagianos libri ii.* Ed. D. Vallarsi. PL 23. Paris: Migne, 1865.

Jerome. *Apologia contra Rufinum.* Ed. P. Lardet. CCL 79. Turnhout: Brepols, 1982.

Jerome. *Epistulae: Pars II, Epistulae LXII-CXX.* Ed. I. Hilberg. CSEL 55. Vienna: Tempsky, 1912.

John Chrysostom. *Homilia in illud: In faciem ei restiti.* Ed. B. de Montfaucon. PG 51. Paris: Migne, 1862.

John Chrysostom. *Commentarius in epistolam ad Galatas.* Ed. B. de Montfaucon. PG 61. Migne: Paris, 1862. (ET, Nicene and Post-Nicene Fathers, 2, 13. Grand Rapids, MI: Eerdmans, 1994).

Marius Victorinus. *Commentarius in epistolam ad Galatas.* Ed. A. Locher. Leipzig: Teubner, 1972.

Origen. *Commentaria in evangelium Iohannis.* [*Origène, Commentaire sur Saint Jean, tome V, (livres 28 et 32).*] Ed. C. Blanc. SC 385. Paris: Cerf, 1992.

Origen. *Commentarius in Epistolam ad Romanos libri xvi. Der Römerbriefkommentar des Origenes: Kritische Ausgabe der Übersetzung Rufins, Buch 1-3.* Aus der Geschichte der Lateinischen Bibel 16. Ed. C. P. Hammond Bammel. Freiburg: Herder, 1990.

Origen. *Contra Celsum libri VIII.* Ed. C. and V. Delarue. PG 11. Paris: Migne, 1857.

Tertullian. *Adversus Marcionem, De praescriptione haereticorum.* CCL 1. Turnhout: Brepols, 1954.

Theodoret of Cyr. *Commentarius in epistolam ad Galatas.* Ed. J. Schulze. PG 82. Paris: Migne, 1864.

White, C., tr. *The Correspondence (394-419) Between Jerome and Augustine of Hippo.* Studies in the Bible and Early Christianity, 23. Lewiston, Queenston/Lampeter: Edwin Mellen, 1990.

Secondary Literature

Betz, H.D. 1979. *Galatians: A Commentary on Paul's Letter to the Galatians.* Philadelphia: Fortress.

Cahill, Michael. 2000. "The History of Exegesis and Our Theological Future." *Theological Studies* 61:332-47.

Cameron, Michael. 1999. "The Christological Substructure of Augustine's Figurative Exegesis." Pp. 74-103 in Pamela Bright, ed., *Augustine and the Bible.* Notre Dame, IN: University of Notre Dame Press.

Donfried, K.P., ed. 1977. *The Romans Debate.* Minneapolis: Augsburg.

Espy, J.M. 1985. "Paul's 'Robust Conscience' Re-examined." *New Testament Studies* 31:161-88.

Fitzmyer, J.A. 1993. *Romans: A New Translation with Introduction and Commentary.* New York: Doubleday.

Fredriksen, Paula. 1995. "Excaecati Occulta Justitia Dei: Augustine on Jews and Judaism." *Journal of Early Christian Studies* 3:299-324.

Fridrichsen, Anton. 1947/1994. "The Apostle and His Message." Pp. 233-50 in *Anton Fridrichsen, Exegetical Writings: A Selection.* Edited by Chrys C. Caragounis and Tord Fornberg. Tübingen: J.C.B. Mohr (Paul Siebeck).

Fürst, Alfons. 1999. *Augustins Briefwechsel mit Hieronymus.* Jahrbuch für Antike und Christentum, Ergänzungband 29. Münster Westfalen: Aschendorf.

Gorday, Peter. 1983. *Principles of Patristic Exegesis: Romans 9-11 in Origen, John Chrysostom, and Augustine.* Studies in the Bible and Early Christianity 4. New York and Toronto: Edwin Mellen.

————. 1989. "The *iustus arbiter:* Origen on Paul's Role in the Epistle to the Romans." *Studia Patristica* 18,3: 393-99. Kalamazoo, MI: Cistercian Publications.

————. 1990. "*Paulus Origenianus:* The Economic Interpretation of Paul in Origen and Gregory of Nyssa." Pp. 141-63 in *Paul and the Legacies of Paul.* Edited by William S. Babcock. Dallas, TX: Southern Methodist University Press.

Grenholm, Cristina, and Daniel Patte (eds.). 2000. *Reading Israel in Romans: Legitimacy and Plausibility of Divergent Interpretations.* Harrisburg, PA: Trinity Press International.

Hennings, R. 1994. *Der Briefwechsel zwischen Augustinus und Hieronymus und ihr Streit um den Kanon des Alten Testaments und die Auslegung von Gal. 2,11-14.* Supplements to *Vigiliae Christianae*, 21. Leiden: E.J. Brill.

Jervell, Jacob. 1984. *The Unknown Paul: Essays on Luke-Acts and Early Christian History*. Minneapolis: Augsburg.

Käsemann, Ernst. 1961. "God's Righeousness in Paul." Pp. 100-110 in *The Bultmann School of Biblical Interpretation: New Directions?* Edited by Robert W. Funk. Tübingen: J.C.B. Mohr (Paul Siebeck)/New York: Harper & Row, 1965.

————. 1971a. "On Paul's Anthropology." Pp. 1-31 in E. Käsemann, *Perspectives on Paul*. Translated by Margaret Kohl. Philadelphia: Fortress.

————. 1971b. "The Saving Significance of the Death of Jesus in Paul." Pp. 32-59 in E. Käsemann, *Perspectives on Paul*. Translated by Margaret Kohl. Philadelphia: Fortress.

————. 1971c. "Justification and Salvation History in the Epistle to the Romans." Pp. 60-78 in E. Käsemann, *Perspectives on Paul* (pp. 60-78). Translated by Margaret Kohl. Philadelphia: Fortress.

————. 1980. *Commentary on Romans*. Translated and Edited by Geoffrey W. Bromiley. Grand Rapids: Eerdmans.

Kelly, J. N. D. 1975. *Jerome: His Life, Writings and Controversies*. New York: Harper & Row.

Lübking, H.-M. 1986. *Paulus und Israel in Römerbrief: Eine Untersuchung zu Römer 9-11*. Frankfurt: Peter Lang.

Lüdemann, Gerd. 1984. *Paul, Apostle to the Gentiles: Studies in Chronology*. Translated by F. Stanley Jones. Philadelphia: Fortress.

————. 1989. *Opposition to Paul in Jewish Christianity*. Translated by M. Eugene Boring. Minneapolis: Fortress.

Moxnes, Halvor. 1980. *Theology in Conflict: Studies in Paul's Understanding of God in Romans*. New Testament Supplements 53. Leiden: E.J. Brill.

Munck, Johannes. 1959. *Paul and the Salvation of Mankind*. Translated by Frank Clarke. Richmond: John Knox.

Murphy-O'Connor, J. 1996. *Paul: A Critical Life*. Oxford: Clarendon.

Nanos, Mark. 1996. *The Mystery of Romans: The Jewish Context of Paul's Letter*. Minneapolis: Fortress.

Neubrand, M. 1997. *Abraham – Vater von Juden und Nichtjuden: Eine exegetische Studie zu Röm 4*. Forschung zur Bibel 85. Würzburg: Echter Verlag.

Sanders, E.P. 1991. *Paul*. Oxford/New York: Oxford University Press.

Stendahl, Krister. 1963. "The Apostle Paul and the Introspective Conscience of the West." Pp. 78-96 in Krister Stendahl, *Paul Among Jews and Gentiles*. Philadelphia: Fortress, 1976.

————. 1976. *Paul Among Jews and Gentiles*. Philadelphia: Fortress .

————. 1995. *Final Account: Paul's Letter to the Romans*. Minneapolis: Fortress.

Vessey, M. 1999. "The Great Conference: Augustine and His Fellow Readers." Pp. 52-73 in Pamela Bright, ed., *Augustine and the Bible*, pp. 52-73. Notre Dame, IN: University of Notre Dame Press.

Wiefel, W. (1977). "The Jewish Community in Ancient Rome and the Origins of Roman Christianity." Pp. 100-119 in K.P. Donfried, ed., *The Romans Debate*. Minneapolis: Augsburg.

Peter J. Gorday

Wright, N. T. 1982. "A New Tübingen School? Ernst Käsemann and His Commentary on Romans." *Themelios* 7:6-16.

Zeller, D. 1973. *Juden und Heiden in der Mission des Paulus: Studien zum Römerbrief.* Stuttgart: Verlag Katholisches Bibelwerk.

– CONCLUSION–

Augustine's Reading of Romans, a Model for the Practice of "Scriptural Criticism"

Daniel Patte

Biblical Critics Engaging Augustine's Interpretation of Romans and Being Engaged by It

C How should I approach these essays on Augustine's interpretation of Romans? Church historians (all the contributors to this volume, except John Riches, Krister Stendahl, Peter Gorday, and I) and theologians have their own goals, which range from seeking to understand Augustine in the context of the church of his time to assessing the relative value of his theological insights for the development of contemporary theology (one of Eugene TeSelle's concerns). But what stake in Augustine should I have as a biblical critic whose primary concern is responsibility and accountability in the interpretation of Romans?

The title of this volume, *Engaging Augustine on Romans*, is deliberately ambiguous. It refers to confronting Augustine's interpretation of Romans — "engaging" it by critically assessing his interpretation. Yet this title is also to be read as a reference to the "engaging" and attractive character of Augustine, which invites us to emulate his way of interpreting Romans.

A In this volume and in their published work, two of my colleagues in New Testament studies, Krister Stendahl and John Riches, engage Augustine in the first sense. On the basis of their critical studies of Romans, each in his own way assesses the legitimacy of Augustine's interpretation and seeks to correct his misinterpretations. I readily join them; in so doing, I learned much from them about Augustine, about Paul, as well as about my own interpretation of Paul. Yet, something is missing.

C Reading Augustine as theologians, church historians, or biblical critics.

A Critically assessing Augustine's interpretation of Romans.

A With Peter Gorday I believe we also need to ask: What do we biblical critics learn *from* Augustine? Addressing this question should complement Stendahl's and Riches's contributions. In other words, I believe together with Peter Gorday that it is also appropriate for us, biblical critics, to allow ourselves to be fascinated by "an engaging Augustine on Romans," and thus to be engaged by Augustine. Thus, with the help of colleagues in church history, I approach Augustine with the expectation that, as a biblical critic, I have much to learn from him, both about Romans and about the way to perform a critical study of it. Yet this is a counterintuitive attitude for us as biblical critics.

I In his essay, Peter Gorday begins to break down our resistance by showing the similarities of the debates between Jerome and Augustine and between Stendahl and Käsemann (the latter embodied in this volume by the debate between Stendahl and Riches). Since the fourth century and the twentieth debates concern similar contextual, analytical, and hermeneutical choices, is it not appropriate to take seriously the interpreters of the patristic period? To acknowledge that they have much to teach us? That both sides in this debate have plausible interpretations? And therefore that our task as biblical critics is not to pursue an elusive single true interpretation, but to practice along with Augustine and Jerome a broader, more open type of critical biblical studies?

I More specifically, I want to argue that Augustine provides a model for *practicing* "scriptural criticism." New Testament scholars might feel relieved: "Then, Patte does not suggest that we take Augustine as a model for our critical work in biblical studies!" As if scriptural criticism were an interdisciplinary endeavor subsequent to, or at least separate from, our "true" work as biblical scholars! "Is it not our vocation to offer analytical interpretations which strive to be as free as possible from the hermeneutical circle?" For sure, as Daniel Boyarin suggests, scriptural criticism does not provide an exit from the hermeneutical circle; rather, it draws such a circle around the interpreters, making its role more visible.[1] But precisely, the overall point Cristina Grenholm and I make in the "Overture" to the first volume is that a practice of critical biblical studies which implicitly or explicitly pursues the illusory goal of a preunderstanding-free interpretation is neither academically nor ethically responsible and accountable.[2] In order to be truly critical, an interpretation must acknowledge that it takes place in a hermeneutical circle, i.e., that its analytical frame is related to a hermeneutical and a contextual frame. In other words, a critical interpretation must acknowledge that a biblical text is necessarily

---

A Learning from Augustine how to interpret Romans.

I Results of Gorday's analysis of the patristic and modern debates.

I Augustine, a model for the practice of "scriptural criticism."

interpreted in terms of the readers' religious views and life-situations, and vice versa, that the biblical text interprets, challenges, and redefines the readers' religious views and their perception of their life-situations. Thus, scriptural criticism is a form of biblical studies which must also be practiced by biblical critics. Explaining the ways in which Augustine is a model for the practice of scriptural criticism that biblical critics should emulate will, hopefully, clarify why biblical critics might want to adopt this practice.

It is not by accident that I see in Augustine a model for the practice of scriptural criticism. At the time Cristina Grenholm and I formulated this approach, we were already participating in the discussion of Augustine's interpretation of Romans as presented in several of the essays found in this volume. Thus, from the outset, Augustine and these essays influenced our formulation of scriptural criticism, which deliberately seeks to reflect the kind of biblical criticism that New Testament scholars, theologians, church historians, and specialists in present-day receptions of Romans *collectively* practice in the context of the SBL seminar, "Romans Through History and Cultures."

I Perceiving the emergence of this tripolar approach to critical biblical studies in the dialogue among theologians, church historians, and biblical critics about the interpretations of Romans is one thing. Rethinking how to perform our specific tasks as theologians, church historians, and biblical critics from the integrated perspective of scriptural criticism is quite another matter. Each of us needs to learn *how to practice* scriptural criticism in our own field. First, we should not expect a uniform practice. Because of our distinct research and pedagogical goals, the practice of scriptural criticism can be expected to take different forms; and, for the sake of our collective endeavor, this distinctiveness among our fields needs to be respected. For instance, Cristina Grenholm as a constructive theologian tends to make use of the tripolar approach of scriptural criticism in order to develop her theological understanding [H] of contemporary issues [C] in light of a biblical text that she analyzes [A].[3] By contrast, as a biblical critic concerned with issues of responsibility and accountability in the interpretation of biblical texts, I tend to focus on the ways in which a biblical text is interpreted in existing interpretations, so as to identify the textual dimensions they found most significant and most helpful [A] for addressing the hermeneutical [H] and contextual [C] issues which also frame these interpretations (Patte 1999). A brief definition is à propos:

- For biblical critics, scriptural criticism is the *integrated critical practice* through which we seek to assume responsibility and accountability in biblical studies by comparing the interpretation we propose to advocate

---

I Conceiving of the practice of scriptural criticism by biblical critics.

with other existing interpretations. This comparative process involves:
(1) elucidating the different interpretive choices reflected by each of
these interpretations (in each case, choices of particular analytical,
hermeneutical, and contextual frames); (2) analyzing the ways in which
each interpretation affects those who receive it as a "word to live by"
that posits a meaning and a purpose for their life; and (3) assessing the
relative value of the types of behavior and relationship with others which
each interpretation promotes.

Even though in other fields, such as constructive theology, church history,
pastoral theology, homiletics, the practice of scriptural criticism takes other
forms and has different orientations, our collective work suggested that all
of us can learn to practice scriptural criticism by emulating the same
models, because they make explicit the integrated character of their
interpretive practice. Thus, Cristina Grenholm and I pointed to certain
exemplary preachers, from whom all of us have much to learn regarding
how to integrate the analytical study of the biblical text with the believers'
contextual lives and their religious experiences. Following them we
recognized the tripolar character of any interpretation of biblical texts.
Three things are simultaneously interpreted: not only the scriptural text, but
also the believers' life-context, and the believers' religious perception of
life.

I Augustine is one of those exemplary preachers, in addition to being a
believer who read the Bible as Scripture, a theologian, and an interpreter
who self-consciously reflects on his interpretive practice. In fact several of
Augustine's interpretations of Romans discussed in this volume are found
in sermons. Whatever the genre of his works, it is clear that Augustine
brings together in his interpretations (1) close analytical studies of the texts,
(2) the contextual needs of the church in his time, and (3) the believers'
religious experience. Augustine is, therefore, an excellent potential model
for the practice of scriptural criticism.

Biblical critics can easily imagine that Augustine might be a model for
theologians. But for biblical critics? I expect resistance to this claim. Do
I really mean that, as biblical critics, we should listen to Augustine and our
colleagues who specialize in Augustinian studies to learn from them how
to practice critical biblical study in such an integrated way?

A This receptive attitude toward Augustine may seem inappropriate on
the part of biblical critics. Is it not our role to assess critically
interpretations, including Augustine's hermeneutical and pragmatic
interpretations of Romans, in terms of the "canon" of scholarly

---

I Augustine as a potential model for the practice of scriptural criticism by biblical critics.

A The critical assessment of Augustine's interpretation from our scholarly stance.

interpretations? Of course! **A** But we should not forget that our own interpretations also need to be assessed. And how could we do so if we do not consider other interpretations as potential alternatives? If we are not open to learn something from other interpreters, including Augustine?

H This point is self-evident when we consider scholarly interpretations: of course, we should review the history of the scholarship. Yet it must be argued, it seems, as soon as we deal with religious or dogmatic interpretations. The point of contention is clear: religious interpretations preclude the possibility of appropriate analytical interpretations. Thus, is it not a nonsense to suggest that Augustine with his use of a *regula fidei* for assessing the legitimacy of an interpretation be viewed as a model by biblical critics? I do not think so. Because, to paraphrase Paul (Romans 2:1), we who frown upon the use of a *regula fidei* for assessing interpretations are doing the very same things, as becomes apparent when we consider our own interpretations from the perspective of Augustine's. Thus, by suggesting that we take Augustine as a model, I am not *advocating* the use of a *regula fidei* in biblical interpretation (be it a creed of the church or some personal convictions). Rather I simply describe what is implicitly or explicitly involved in any interpretation of a biblical text.

I still need to clarify why a receptive attitude toward Augustine needs to *complement* the critical assessment of his interpretations, as practiced for instance by Krister Stendahl and John Riches. Then, it will be clearer how Augustine can help us progress from a general understanding of "scriptural criticism" to its practice as a refined form of critical biblical studies.

Critical Biblical Studies Assessing the Legitimacy of Interpretations of Romans by Augustine and Others

A In his epoch-making essay "The Apostle Paul and the Introspective Conscience of the West" (first published in 1960) and the no less remarkable 1963 and 1964 lectures gathered together in *Paul among Jews and Gentiles* (1976), Krister Stendahl's primary goal in studying Augustine is clear. As is well-known, for him it is a matter of correcting fundamental and ongoing misinterpretations of Paul which originated with Augustine, **H** who read Paul's letters from the perspective of an "introspective

---

A   Allowing our own interpretations to be assessed in terms potential alternatives--interpretations which belong to the history of scholarship as well as Augustine's.

H   Acknowledging the role of some kind of *regula fidei* in biblical interpretation.

A   Stendahl's critical assessment of Augustine's (mis-)interpretation of Romans.

H   "Instrospective Consciousness" as hermeneutical frame of Augustine's reading of Romans.

conscience" (85). **C** This misinterpretation "reaches its climax in the penitential struggle of an Augustinian monk, Martin Luther, and in his interpretation of Paul" (85). "Where Paul was concerned about the possibility for Gentiles to be included in the messianic community, his statements are read as answers to the quest for assurance about [human] salvation out of a common human predicament" (86). Why this misinterpretation? Because of a "shift in the frame of reference" (86). "Primarily," Stendahl says, "it is our own Western introspective thinking that leads us astray" (14), away from "Paul's original intentions" (6). Our interpretation of Paul's letters in terms of conversion, troubled conscience, forgiveness of sins is a mis-representation of "what the text meant" due to a misreading of these letters in terms of hermeneutical categories which are foreign to them. Ultimately, Stendahl emphasizes, **H** this misapprehension is closely related to the fact that Christians read Paul's letters *as Scripture* for a teaching for their own lives today (15; 22; *passim*). Part of the problem is that our interpretations posit a particular view of the Bible as Word of God, according to which "one should perceive the message as coming directly to us" (22) as individuals, a view of Scripture already found in Luther (86 - 87) and even in Augustine.

Rereading these lectures, I am left with the question: What is the actual issue which Stendahl seeks to address? That Romans is read as Scripture? Or that it is read with an inappropriate view of Scripture? The tone of his lectures suggests the latter.

I For Stendahl, the perceived Augustinian misinterpretation of Paul must be confronted in the name of maintaining a clear distinction between "what the text meant" and "what it means." From the perspective of the historical paradigm of his 1962 essay on "Biblical Theology (Stendahl 1962)," Stendahl emphasizes that "what it meant" and "what it means" should not be "carelessly intermingled." Otherwise biblical critics and theologians fail to fulfill their role as theological educators: "the theology as well as the preaching of our churches becomes a mixed or even an inarticulate language" (Stendahl, 1962, 422). Augustine's interpretation of Romans must therefore be denounced and corrected for carelessly intermingling the theological and hermeneutical concerns of his days with Paul's text. **H** As a result, Paul's intention to deal with the relationship

---

C Penitential struggle of an Augustinian monk, Martin Luther, and the problem it is in the church today.

H The view of Scripture presupposed by this (mis-)interpretation of Romans.

I Inappropriate intermingling of "what the text meant" (analytical frame) and "what the text means" (hermeneutical frame).

H Relationship between Jews and Gentiles, the appropriate hermeneutical frame for an interpretation of Paul's letters according to Stendahl.

between Jews and Gentiles is totally ignored. In sum: for Krister Stendahl (in his publications of 40 years ago), in order to elucidate Paul's intention, a biblical critic's task involves correcting Augustine's misinterpretations of Romans by identifying the foreign features which he brought to the text out of his own religious experience and out of the theological preoccupations arising from his church context in his time.

The questions are: Is it truly possible for an interpretation to avoid intermingling the text with the interpreter's theological and hermeneutical concerns? And even if it were possible, is it helpful? Clearly, for Stendahl the problem arises from certain inappropriate readings of Romans as Scripture. Does this mean that all readings of the "text as Scripture" are inappropriate? Stendahl does not seem to want to say so.

Assessing our own interpretive practices from Augustine's perspective will help us address these issues.

A   For John Riches, despite his critical discussion of Stendahl's approach,[4] the task of a biblical critic remains, in practice, essentially the same. It is still a matter of correcting Augustine's misinterpretations of Romans. **H** The difference concerns what Riches perceives to be the essential features of "what the text meant" which have been obscured or repressed by the Augustinian interpretation: the apocalyptic eschatology of Paul and its cosmic dualism, rather than the relation between Jews and Gentiles.   What is problematical in the Augustinian tradition of interpretation of Romans is not so much that it has read into the text something which is not there, as Stendahl claimed regarding the introspective and forensic view of justification. **H** Rather, for Riches, Augustine ignores a significant feature of Paul's letter to the Romans, namely the "dialectical" "interplay between dualistic and forensic modes of thought" (193) which must be maintained in a legitimate interpretation. In sum, as TeSelle notes in his introduction: for Riches, a biblical critic's primary task is still to elucidate Augustine's misinterpretations or re-interpretations of Romans by confronting them with the results of critical studies which have established "what the text meant."

I Yet the form of Riches's argument is noteworthy. On the one hand, he notes the differences between the Lutheran interpretations and the anti-Lutheran ones (Schweitzer's, Stendahl's, Sanders's, Fredriksen's) that reject the emphasis on the individual forensic mode of thought and emphasize

---

A Riches's critical assessment of Stendahl's interpretation.

H "Apocalyptic eschatology and cosmic dualism" as a part of hermeneutical frame of Riches's reading of Romans.

H The dialectical interplay between dualistic and forensic modes of thought, the appropriate hermeneutical frame for an interpretation of Paul's letters according to Riches.

I The scriptural critical form of Riches's argument.

either the community dimension (Jews and Gentiles) or a cosmic, apocalyptic dualism (evil having its source beyond the individuals' free will). On the other hand, he underscores that each interpretation has in fact chosen as most significant one of the several textual dimensions of Romans. Riches further notes that this choice is in each case linked with contextual issues with which the interpreters have to contend, and arises out of the hermeneutical issues which originate with the interpreters' religious experiences and the "worldview" they share with their communities. Thus, in a discussion of the *Confessions* (176, above), Riches argues that Augustine suppressed the community and/or cosmic dimensions and exclusively retained the forensic mode of thought, because of his context and of the hermeneutical issues he needed to address.   In that particular context Augustine struggled not merely with personal issues but also with issues concerning the ethos of the church in specific times and locations. Furthermore, Augustine constantly dealt with hermeneutical and theological issues concerning the religious perception of human experience.   For instance, there are "cosmic dualistic elements in [Augustine's] thought" which Augustine had to suppress in his struggle with Manichaeism. Otherwise, how could he reject the Manichees' dualism? (193, above).

I Although Riches's overall critical discourse still aims at establishing what the text truly meant—thus, for him, Romans presents a "dialectical interplay between dualistic and forensic modes of thought"—the form of his discourse implies a recognition that any given interpretation involves choosing a certain textual dimension as most significant and subordinating to it other dimensions. Then, the critical discourse of the biblical scholar has, in effect, another goal; it needs to discern the kind of interpretive choices reflected by each given interpretation—here, Augustine's —, the hermeneutical and contextual grounds upon which these choices have been made, the textual dimensions they emphasize and those they suppress. Thus, critical biblical study seems to have two goals: *the establishment of what the text truly meant* and the *elucidation of interpretive choices* in given interpretations. Of course, one cannot pursue both of these goals without subordinating one to the other. Thus, Riches subordinates the latter to the former. Consequently, as a biblical scholar, his role includes assessing the relative legitimacy of Augustine's interpretation. With Stendahl, Riches finds Augustine's interpretation wanting, but now for different reasons: it fails to account for the dialectical interplay between Paul's two modes of thought.

I The two goals of critical biblical studies for Riches: establishing "what the text truly meant" and elucidating interpretive choices.

I I am sure John Riches would deny that he engaged in a quest for some kind of "objective" interpretation—an a-contextual, a-hermeneutical interpretation.[5] In fact, for him, historical and hermeneutical issues cannot and should not be separated, although it is difficult to find how they should be kept together.[6] Furthermore, as he volunteered during the discussion of his paper at the SBL meeting, his concern for the apocalyptic cosmic dualism of Paul's thought grew out of his confrontation with the massive character of evil which he witnessed shortly after World War II in refugees camps. And beyond this, in his interactions with African churches as well as in Glasgow, he is more than willing to underscore the hermeneutical and contextual character of any interpretation of biblical texts. Yet, when he puts on his biblical scholar's hat, he feels the pull of an approach to the biblical text *as object.* Then the establishment of "what the text truly meant" seems to be the primary task at hand, *as if* the teaching of this text for people today were to be construed as the "application" of some objective content of the text to a present-day situation—a view which is an oversimplified, and indeed, distorted view of hermeneutics, as both Stendahl and Riches would agree. Neither one nor the other would want to claim that critical biblical studies have a veto power over theological interpretations.   And yet their critical *practice* implicitly claims and exercises such a power.

The question is: How can we envision a goal for our practice of critical biblical studies which would neither contradict our theoretical understanding of the hermeneutical process nor claim a veto power over the interpretations of theologians, including Augustine and our colleagues today? How can we conceive of a critical practice which both accounts for the text and what it meant as object, and is ethically responsible by facilitating accountability in the theologians', the church historians', and the believers' interpretations? I want to suggest that the answer to both questions is: By making sure that our critical practice involves a two-way assessment of Augustine's interpretation in terms of ours, and of our interpretations in terms of Augustine's. This simply asks from us, biblical critics, to approach Augustine with the expectation that we have something to learn from him about Romans and its interpretation. Yet this shift in attitude requires us to abandon old habits.

I The tension between theoretical views of the interpretive process and one's practice of critical biblical studies.

The Scope of the Biblical Critical Task and Augustine

Our collegial experience in the SBL seminar on "Romans Through History and Cultures" led Cristina Grenholm and me to suggest that biblical critics have much to learn from readers of Romans who are not biblical critics, including Augustine.

This attitude was readily adopted by biblical critics in the context of the SBL seminar. In dialogue with church historians, theologians, and practical theologians, it was unthinkable for us biblical critics to claim that we have the legitimate interpretation of Romans which others should use as a benchmark. As is illustrated by the first volume in this series subtitled, appropriately, *Legitimacy and Plausibility of Divergent Interpretations,* biblical critics are far from agreeing. Furthermore, there would be no point to such a seminar if we were not listening to each other's interpretations with the expectation that we have something to learn from each other about Romans and its interpretation. And, as we soon discovered, our expectation is warranted. We biblical critics are learning much about Romans and its critical interpretation from church historians, from theologians, from practical theologians, and, by extension, from preachers, and from "ordinary" believers. Then, why should we not expect to learn much about Romans and its interpretation from someone who was a believer who read the Bible as Scripture, a renowned preacher, a bishop, a sophisticated theologian, as well as a remarkable semiotician and hermeneut?

But, if we biblical critics approach interpretations of Romans by theologians, preachers, believers of the past and today with the expectation that we have to learn from them, what is our role as biblical critics? Does any interpretation go? Is not our task to make sure that the text as object be respected? Is not our responsibility to denounce interpretations that betray the text and to affirm, promote, and perform "legitimate" interpretations that truly account for the teaching of the text?

Of course. This is indeed our task. But what is "the text as object" that we want to respect? What is a legitimate interpretation? What is the "teaching of the text" that we want to account for? As John Riches repeatedly underscores, "the abiding temptation of the historian is to pretend to know more than [one] knows." In this case, the temptation is for us to pretend that we already know what the text as object and its teaching are, and therefore that we do not need to learn anything about Romans from Augustine. As Thomas Martin shows, Augustine has much to say on these issues.

Understanding with Augustine the Nature of the Biblical Text as Object: Beyond the Subject/Object Dichotomy, *"modus inveniendi quae intelligenda sunt"*

Thomas Martin reminds us that "Augustine himself was well aware of the formal question of hermeneutics and broke new ground by being one of the very first Christian thinkers to set out and explain an explicit hermeneutical method to guide interpretation and study of the Bible" (64, above). Indeed, "in his *De doctrina christiana*... [Augustine] defines the starting point for all who would interpret the scriptures, calling it a 'way of discovering what must be understood there'—modus inveniendi quae intelligenda sunt" (64, above). This formula is, in and of itself, a good designation for a critical methodology: it is "a way of discovering" something about a text. Most fascinating is the way Augustine defines this object of the investigation. Martin explains:

> The notion of "what *must be* understood there [*intelligenda*]" states unambiguously that it is the obligation and responsibility of the student of the scriptures to surrender to biblical text—meaning does not come from "the investigator" but from "the investigated"—the *quae intelligenda sunt* (64, above).

A Together with traditional understandings of critical biblical studies, Augustine's view of critical interpretation underscores that meaning is not subjective. As Martin puts it: "Meaning does not come from 'the investigator.'" The teaching of the text is not "read into the text" by the interpreter; it is encountered as something new by the interpreter. The distinctive character of the text as object, and thus its otherness, must be respected by the interpreter. But (and this is a departure from the traditional understandings of critical biblical studies), the fact that the text is an object does not mean that it should be analyzed, dissected, manipulated, categorized, observed in a detached way. In fact, it should *not* be treated as something to be kept at a distance from the interpreter. Rather "it is the obligation and responsibility of the student of the scriptures to surrender to biblical text." The text is objective in the sense that it has a presence that affects the interpreter who is somehow transformed by this encounter. *A responsible reading demands that interpreters allow the text to affect them.*
I I have long been aware of the hermeneutical circle, of the impossibility to fully separate subjectivity from objectivity in biblical interpretation, as well as of the ethical problems resulting from a practice

---

A The text is an object both because it can be analyzed and because it affects the interpreter.

I Needed: a critical practice beyond the subject/object dichotomy.

of critical biblical studies which perpetuates the subject/object dichotomy. Thus, I have long been convinced that we need to move toward a practice of critical biblical studies beyond this dichotomy.[7] Yet, for me, conceiving of this practice remained elusive. Seeking to address the problems of the ethics of interpretation convinced me that the contextual and the hermeneutical frames of any given interpretation must be accounted for in our critical practices (Patte 1995). Formulating scriptural criticism with Cristina Grenholm opened the way. But old habits are difficult to abandon. The pull of an approach to the biblical text *as object* remains.

A Now, listening to Augustine opens for me the possibility of envisioning how to approach the biblical text as object without reducing this approach to an objective interpretation, and without being caught in a subject/object dichotomy. As Carol Smith argues (Smith 1997), traditional critical biblical studies of the stories of Lot's daughters (Gen. 19:30-38) and Tamar and Ammon (2 Sam. 13:1-22) call for an objective, detached reading of the text, even as one acknowledges the shocking character of the stories. "The reader is being asked to believe that the message is that it is intended that this account should shock and challenge him or her, but not if the reader happens to be a biblical scholar" (131). The question is: "Even if it is possible, is it helpful?" Without even entering the debate regarding the possibility of a detached, objective reading, with Carol Smith I want to underscore that one misses an essential feature of the text if the interpretation is not framed by the way it affects the readers.[8] Such stories as literary objects are aimed at stirring emotions in the readers. Accounting for these objects involves accounting for the readers' emotions stirred by these objects.

A More generally, accounting for biblical texts as objects involves accounting for the way in which these religious texts challenge the readers as believers and claim authority over them so much so that they surrender to them. Thus, the Augustinian "surrendering to biblical text" does not renounce approaching the text as object. Rather it involves recognizing the way in which this object challenges the reader, be it by stirring emotions or by engendering resistance.

H Conversely, "surrendering to biblical text" does not negate the place and role of the subject who interprets. This approach acknowledges and marks the distinctiveness of the subject who encounters the text as a

---

A Accounting for literary objects involves accounting for the readers' emotions stirred by these objects.

A Accounting for religious texts as objects involves accounting for their effects upon readers/believers.

H Bringing to the text one's knowledge of oneself in the present and the past and "thinking with history" this knowledge.

historical object which challenges the reader. This is the kind of critical approach the historian takes into account when studying intellectual history, as Carl Schorske does in his book, *Thinking with History*. Thus, as he comments upon his autobiographical essay, "Encountering History" (17-34), he underscores the complex relationship between a subject and history.

> Through ever-renewed encounters with the shifting elements in the stream of history one can come to know oneself in the present, and also acquire an altered understanding of what one has been in the past. In autobiography, to think with history helps to establish a certain distance from one's self by seeing it as both shaped by the structures and conflicts of society and as responding creatively to their pressures. Thus if I deflect in my life story the larger development of the society, I also reflect (as knowing subject) on that particular historical consciousness, its formation and changes, that my personal encounters with my time elicited as modes of coming to terms with it, whether by resistance or adaptation. (Schorske1998, 5-6).

Similarly, through encounters with the biblical texts as Scripture, "one can come to know oneself in the present, and also acquire an altered understanding of what one has been in the past." This is the still uncritical reading of the biblical text by believers. Then, the critical assessment of this scriptural reading by believers can be envisioned as "thinking with history," as in Schorske's intellectual autobiography. It is what allows someone "to establish a certain distance from one's self by seeing it as both shaped by the structures and conflicts of society and as responding creatively to their pressures."

H Augustine's *modus inveniendi quae intelligenda sunt*, although it affirms as object the biblical text and "what must be understood there," does not deny the place and role of the subject, because it involves "thinking with" the biblical text, as Schorske thinks with history. Then, for Augustine, reading the biblical text as Scripture, as Word of God, as revelation of mystery, as food for life, is not in tension with an analytical interpretation of it. On the contrary, scriptural reading and analytical interpretation necessarily belong together, as Thomas Martin demonstrated by listing for us the seven interpretive "principles" presented by Augustine in his "exegetical asides." Before discussing more specifically what we, biblical critics, can learn from these principles, we still need to clarify why, despite our knee-jerk reactions, we should acknowledge that scriptural

---

H "Thinking with" the biblical text as Scripture one's religious and theological views.

interpretations and analytical interpretations belong together in critical biblical studies.

Critical Biblical Studies Acknowledging the Scriptural Character of Biblical Texts

The scope of the "obligation and responsibility of the student of the scriptures" as envisioned by Augustine is further clarified by Lévinas's reflections on what constitutes a responsible reading of the Hebrew Bible. Burggraeve's comments on this point, based upon Lévinas's *Difficile Liberté* and *"La révélation dans la tradition juive,"*[9] are worth quoting at length. I intersperse his comments with observations about Augustine's view. Burggraeve begins:

> According to Lévinas, in order for the "founding" Word to truly become a Word to live by, it must first become a Word to learn from. An existential engagement with Scripture can never be achieved in the blind obedience which suspends critical judgment from reading and reflection. One can look into the mirror of God's Word only with clear and open eyes (Burggraeve 2000, 165).

C Similarly, for Augustine a biblical text is first of all Scripture, a Word to live by. This is for Augustine the necessary starting point for any reflection on "the way of discovering what must be understood there." But, should it also be so for biblical critics? Traditionally critical biblical studies have rejected this option. **I** They have taken their starting point with a non-scriptural definition of the text: for instance, the New Testament as "early Christian literature," a historical witness to the development of the early church best studied when one keeps one's distance from it. In this mode of historical studies, no "thinking with history" (Schorske) is allowed. Yet this traditional stance has been challenged over the last 20 years, not only by the development of approaches for the study of intellectual history, but also by the development of "Canon Criticism" (Childs 1979 an 1985), then by a series of studies on the phenomenon of Scripture.[10] **I** Sandra Schneiders's vigorously claims in *The Revelatory Text: Interpreting the New Testament as Sacred Scripture* (Schneiders 1991) that studies which do not account for

---

C   The biblical text as Scripture, a Word to live by.

   I   The long-recognized impossibility of isolating the analytical from the contextual and the hermeneutical in critical biblical studies.

   I   Schneiders's formulation of scriptural criticism.

the revelatory or scriptural character of biblical texts cannot claim to be truly critical are most significant. She develops her argument (1) by pointing out that we cannot and should not bracket out of critical biblical studies our convictions regarding the scriptural character of the text; she does so by reviewing Gadamer's and Ricoeur's hermeneutical theories, and by her very evocative discussion of what it means to approach the biblical text as Scripture; (2) by showing that whether one focuses on what is "behind the text," or "in the text," or again "in front of the text," one cannot but recognize that the text points to, or embodies, or again effects for its readers, revelatory moments; and finally (3) by proposing an example of a practice of feminist critical reading of a text as Scripture. These three moves approximately correspond to the three poles of "scriptural criticism"[11]: (1) the hermeneutical pole, (2) the analytical pole, (3) the pragmatic/contextual pole (following the order of Schneider's presentation).

Sandra Schneiders's important *analytical* observation that a critical study of a biblical text must account for its revelatory or scriptural character might need to be underscored, both because at first it is surprising for many biblical critics and because it is so clear as soon as one's attention is drawn to it. For this, some brief remarks about the "scriptural character" of Romans are enough.

I Reading Paul's letter as Scripture means reading it as "a Word to live by," and therefore expecting that its teaching for us is contained not in the text itself but rather in the way the text relates to our lives. Therefore, reading Romans as Scripture is reading it as "a Word to think with" about all aspects of our lives; reading Romans in terms of our lives, and conversely, "reading our lives" in terms of this letter.

A The first reaction of biblical critics is that this is not acceptable in critical biblical studies, because it is "reading into the text" rather than "reading the text." But, along the line of Schneiders's argument, I want to underscore that as long as our studies do not take into account such "scriptural readings" they fail to account for an essential aspect of Paul's letter: the fact that it is a pastoral letter offering a very rich teaching for the Romans by calling them to think with it about their life as Christians. Be it enough to say here that, besides urging them to think about their lives in community and in Roman society (see the exhortations and instructions of chapters 12-16), this teaching concerned their theological outlook on human

---

I The teaching of a scriptural text is not a content of the text but the way the text relates to our lives. Reading the text as "a Word to think with" about all aspects of our lives.

A An analytical study of Romans needs to account for the way in which this text helps its readers to rethink their lives.

existence under God. Therefore, the intended effect of Paul's letter is that it would lead the Romans to reflect upon the view of human existence under God they hold as well as to rethink and eventually change their way of life and their behavior. In brief, Paul is expecting his readers to read his letter as a "Word to think with" and "Word to live by"—indeed, as a Word addressed to them by "a servant of Jesus Christ, called to be an apostle, set apart for the gospel of God" (Rom. 1:1). *The meaning of Paul's letter to the Romans which critical biblical studies needs to account for is the way in which this text helps its readers to rethink their lives.*

H C A Since it is clear that Paul anticipates that there is in Rome a diversity of readers with quite different religious outlooks and kinds of behavior, from its inception the meaning of this pastoral letter was plural. It involved rethinking different life situations and different views of human existence under God. From this perspective, we can recognize that readings of Romans as Scripture in other periods by theologians and believers, who assume a position as receivers analogous to that of the Romans and rethink their lives and views of human existence from the perspective of this letter, account for an essential dimension of this letter which traditional critical studies unduly neglect.

I We biblical critics have difficulties conceiving of interpretation in this way, because we continue to think about biblical studies as exclusively limited to "the interpretation of given texts," as if, in each instance, only one thing was interpreted: a text. We theoretically know that this unipolar view of interpretation is unduly constricted; thus we move in the direction of conceiving of interpretation as bipolar, when we acknowledge that we interpreted the text with hermeneutical preunderstandings. Yet when we do so, we still fail to take into account the reverse movement of the interpretation process, namely, the interpretation of the *interpreters' life* by the text. Consequently, in the present case, even as we acknowledge the pastoral or rhetoric character of the letter, often we still conceive of its pastoral or rhetorical effect in its original context as a "meaning content" (what the text meant) to be appropriated in a new context. And from this perspective, this appropriation is legitimate, when, and only when, the two contexts are shown to be truly analogous.[12] But, for both Augustine and Lévinas (and also for Schorske, when one views the text as history), it is not a matter of

---

H C A Through their hermeneutical and contextual readings, theologians and believers who rethink their lives and views of human existence in terms of Romans assume a position as receivers analogous to that of the Romans according to analytical studies.

I Scriptural criticism does not suspend critical judgment; it applies it to the entire interpretive process.

critically recognizing the analogy between "the text in its context" and "today's readers and their context" in order to understand how to "apply" the teaching-content of the text to the new situation. Rather, it is a matter of participating in the interpretive process opened by the biblical text. As Martin says describing Augustine's approach, it is a matter of "surrender[ing] to the biblical text." As Schorske says, it is a matter of "thinking with history." Or, as Lévinas emphasizes, it is a matter of thinking with the Bible. Once again, Burggraeve explains that for Lévinas:

> The Bible is a Word which gives rise to thinking and in which our entire existence can live so that we come to the truth... Biblical texts call for the reflective resources of thinking readers so that the enduring insights and values contained there can continue to nourish souls. We must turn to the Scriptures not so much for plausibility as for instruction, basic and directive insights about human beings, society, and the meaning of life (Burggraeve 2000, 165).

Thus, "surrendering to the biblical text" is neither for Augustine, nor for Lévinas, "the blind obedience which suspends critical judgment from reading and reflection" (Burggraeve 2000, 165). As is clear from the essays by Martin, Gathercole, Fredriksen, TeSelle, and Gorday, far from suspending critical judgment Augustine had quite self-consciously developed hermeneutical principles and did not hesitate to reject his own earlier interpretations by using these principles. But this critical judgment does not involve mastering the text, reducing it to a "meaning-content" that one can choose to appropriate or not to appropriate, following a critical analysis. Rather, this critical judgment takes place within the to-and-fro of an encounter with the text. As a critical interpreter who seeks to account for the text *in its otherness*— that is, as other than I, as an "object" distinct from the "subject" I am—I must respectfully encounter this text as a presence which is beyond me even as I am in dialogue with it. In other words, the text should not be approached like a "thing," but as we approach a person, like another human. For Burggraeve, this is an essential aspect of Lévinas's approach to Scripture.

> Scripture can appear human only if one looks at it *as a human*, which is to say, as a thinking being. This is why an existentially engaged relation to the Bible must be mediated by reflective consideration which presupposes but also goes beyond historical-philological and literary analysis. In order to truly understand the life-giving meaning and proper bearing of Scripture, immediate sensibility and spontaneous intuition are not enough; one has need of keen attention which thinks, thinks again,

and thinks through (Burggraeve 2000, 165).

I Envisioning our relationship to a text as to a person further clarifies the scope of the interpretive process.[13] The text as a discourse by a person re-presents this person, manifests the presence of this person. Thus, as we read the text we enter in relationship with this text/person, who then participates in all the modes of our existence (and not simply in the existence of its original intended readers). Our relationship to the text can then be understood according to the model of our relationship with persons. This clarifies why, as suggested in the "Overture" (Grenholm and Patte, 2000), an interpretive discourse (the end-product of the interpretation of a scriptural text) reflects the three modes of human existence (autonomy, relationality/contextuality, heteronomy). But beyond this, we can now recognize that the interpretation of a text is always in process, as our relationship with a person is always in process. This is so because:

1. Out of our *autonomy*, we approach the text/person as having an autonomy of its/her/his own which we must respect by taking the time to listen and/or to analyze it/her/him. This is commonly done in critical *analytical* readings of the text.

2. In the *relationality* of our lives interwoven with the lives of others, we can now weave the text (which we might use for our own purpose in our relationship with others) or, conversely, we can enter into the relational world of the text (for instance, by participating in the life of a community based on this text). This is the two-way contextualization of interpretation, which is made most explicit in the believers' devotionals and the preachers' sermons, but is also necessarily involved in any critical interpretation which takes into account the socio/anthropological rhetoric of the text and/or its hortatory character.

3. Furthermore, in the same way as we surrender to God or to a beloved Other and his/her mystery in a face-to-face heteronomous encounter, so we can enter into a *heteronomous* relationship with the text/person, contemplating its mystery as we totally open ourselves to it. This is the two-way hermeneutical process which characterizes faith-interpretations of scriptural texts, but is also necessarily involved in any critical interpretation

---

I Envisioning the interpretive process as our relationship to a person in the three modes of human existence; autonomy, relationality, heteronomy.

which takes into account the religious and/or ideological character of the text.

With such a tripolar conception of critical biblical studies, we can more easily recognize that Augustine practiced a kind of scriptural criticism, and that we have much to learn from him. This is most apparent as we ponder all that surprises us in his way of interpreting Romans.

Augustine and the Overall Scope of Disciplined Biblical Interpretations

As I pondered the significance of the differences between the way in which Augustine approached Romans (as presented in the essays in this volume) and present-day practices of critical biblical studies, a shift in overall attitude toward the biblical text became apparent.

A Much of the energy of biblical critics is devoted to striving to make the biblical text accessible to believers/readers, because we commonly presuppose that a gap separates them from the text. This is what Cristina Grenholm[14] appropriately named Gabler's gap, tying it with the advent of historiography and underscoring that it is most commonly conceived of as a historical divide. For modern readers, the text is filled with difficulties, obscurities, nonsensical features, which prevent understanding when they are heeded as they should be, or lead to misinterpretations when they are ignored. Therefore, biblical critics commonly view their task as the overcoming of textual difficulties with appropriate critical tools, which vary according to the perception of the textual difficulties, which could be, for instance, historical, linguistic, religious, literary, sociological, anthropological, or cultural. In sum, in most instances we conceive of critical biblical studies as bridging the gap which separates the biblical text from its readers, including believers who misinterpret it because they overlook its difficulties.

Augustine has a very different attitude. Textual difficulties encountered when reading scriptures are not to be overlooked. The readers/believers need to struggle with them: "Even the most difficult scriptural question is simply a solemn call to make even greater effort *ad intellectum*, never an obstacle before which one abandons the course" (Martin, 67, above). Yet, for Augustine, we should seek not to overcome them but to ponder them as mysteries concerning our lives. This becomes clear in Martin's presentation of the seven "precepts" he identified in Augustine's hermeneutical asides.

A Approaching textual difficulties as mysteries rather than as gaps to be bridged.

Martin's quotation from Augustine's comments on the Psalms makes the point regarding *obscuritas and mysterium*:

There are profound mysteries (*profunda mysteria*) in the Sacred Scriptures which are made obscure to prevent us from not respecting them (*ne vilescant*). The seeking of their meaning exercises us, the finding of their meaning nourishes us (*ad hoc quaerentur, ut exerceant; ad hoc aperiuntur, ut pascant*) (*En.Ps.* 140,1):

A H C Martin notes that "the effort to engage the mystery is, in itself, nourishing and rewarding" (68, above). I believe we can go beyond this. As Augustine says, "the finding of their meaning nourishes us," because their meaning is nourishment for life. Indeed, for Augustine, "it is necessary... *that divine doctrine be expressed in human words*" (69, above; Martin's emphasis). Thus, with Martin we can say that for Augustine "words are often fragile, sometimes dangerous, and ever limiting." (69, above). This fallen, human character of words creates tension with the mystery they seek to convey. But it is precisely because of the fall that Scripture is necessary for our salvation, and therefore that Scripture needs to be expressed in human words so that it might be nourishment for life. The textual difficulties and obscurities are actual reminders that the meaning of the biblical text occurs when the text is read in terms of the reader's life—both the religious and contextual dimensions of life— and the reader's life in terms of the text.

From this perspective, textual difficulties and obscurities do not separate biblical text and readers from each other. On the contrary, they are a bridge integrating the interpretation of this text and of the readers' life experience in all its aspects. The analytical study of the text and the *intellectus fidei* go hand-in-hand, as two parts of the same interpretive process. Thus, of course, "Augustine applied to the *Litterae Sacrae* many of the same analytical tools he learned to apply to any and all *litterae*" (66, above), namely, the mode of reading of the world and culture of late antiquity. Taking Augustine as a model means that, in turn, present day biblical critics should apply to the biblical text the same analytical tools the diverse academic disciplines use for the study of similar texts, including all the range of historical, literary, anthropological, socio-scientific, rhetoric, structural, cultural, gender, postcolonial, etc., critical methods.

A H C Textual difficulties as reminders that the text is to be read in terms of the reader's religious and contextual life and the reader's life in terms of the text.

H For Augustine, the analytical reading of the text is nothing but one aspect of an overall interpretive process which also includes bringing to understanding the readers' faith, and which, in Martin's words, "requires a serious effort to integrate *discernere, credere,* and *intelligere*, lest Scripture be approached 'mente pueri' (67, above). As a result, Augustine's interpretation of the text is far from being disengaged! "Often a text of Scripture will be the center of a formal debate between Augustine and an opponent, but just as often the debate seems to be taking place within Augustine's own mind..." (67, above). And, of course, this debate concerns not only points concerning the analysis of the text, but also the relative values of different conclusions as assessed from the perspective of the *regula fidei*, as well as of what they reveal about the readers/believers, since Scripture is a mirror, "a *speculum* in which one ought to see oneself" (71, above), and places upon the readers/believers the responsibility to respond to its call (72, above); Augustine's "hermeneutics of conversion"). Furthermore, as Eugene TeSelle (in the introduction) and Paula Fredriksen show in their respective discussions of *ad litteram*, typological, allegorical, and metaphorical interpretations, for Augustine disciplined biblical interpretations account not only for the theological/religious but also for the contextual/relational mode of existence - including the relationship between Jews and Christians. Once again, Augustine's practice of disciplined biblical interpretation has a scope comparable to that of scriptural criticism.

Understanding the relation between Augustine's practice and scriptural criticism has already helped us better to understand why we need to practice biblical studies in a scriptural critical mode and gave us a clearer view of what this practice by present-day biblical critics should entail. The question is: How can we start practicing such an integrated critical study of Romans which, following Augustine, would include not only (1) performing an analytical interpretation of the text, but also assessing it (2) "from the perspective of the *regula fidei*" and of the nature of the call the biblical text addresses to the readers/believers, and (3) from the perspective of the contextual implications of this interpretation? How can we start? Simply by *reading with* Augustine.

H   The role of the *regula fidei* in interpretation and the role of hermeneutical frame.

"Reading With" Augustine Following the Essays in This Volume

A Way of Proceeding to a Scriptural Critical Study of Romans

I have noted that, for biblical critics,[15] scriptural criticism is practiced in order to help us to assume responsibility for the interpretation we propose to advocate by comparing it with other existing interpretations, so as to elucidate the different interpretive choices reflected by each of these interpretations, including our own. By making us aware of the choices of particular analytical, hermeneutical, and contextual frames involved in our interpretation and in those of others, such comparisons free us to assess the value of our proposed interpretation. We can now consider how it affects those who receive it as a "Word to live by" which posits a meaning and a purpose for their life and calls for certain types of behavior and relationship with others. How is this view of life related to our deepest convictions (that often are for us a *regula fidei*)? Does the chosen interpretation promote, in some ways, a view of life which, in a given setting, is plausible, healthy, constructive, wholesome, open to encounters with the mystery of the Other? Or one which is dubious, sick and sickening, destructive, vicious, hellish? Similarly, what kind of relationship with others in the community and in society at large does this interpretation promote? A self-centered one or an other-centered one? One that uses and belittles others or one that affirms and empowers them? An oppressive one or a liberating one? One that condones injustice or one that fights for justice? On the basis of such a scriptural critical assessment we should be in a better position to decide whether or not we should advocate our original interpretation or another one. With this goal in mind, it is clear that scriptural criticism cannot be practiced by an individual in splendid isolation, as Cristina Grenholm and I have repeatedly underscored in the "Overture" of the first volume. More pointedly, it is a collective endeavor which involves "reading with" others who come to the table with different interpretations (Patte 1995). As one respectfully acknowledges and appreciates the distinctiveness of the other readings, one becomes aware that one's own reading is characterized by analytical, hermeneutical and contextual frames different from those of other interpretations.

I   Goals for a practice of scriptural criticism by biblical critics: elucidating the choices involved in each interpretation and helping readers to assess the value of their choices.

The critical process has begun, and soon one has to assess the relative value of the choices made. Yet, as in the case of a preacher choosing a focus for her sermon, this assessment is done with the full awareness that it is itself hermeneutically and contextually/ethically framed; it is never a totalizing gesture which completely and definitively dismisses other interpreters and their interpretations. As is exemplified in our interdisciplinary SBL seminar of *Romans Through History and Cultures* where everyone acknowledges he/she speaks as an outsider to the disciplines of the others, no one can have a veto power by claiming that he/she has a special hold on the truth. Otherwise, how would we learn from each other?

It remains that the goal of scriptural criticism is to assess interpretations, including ours, in order to identify one of the interpretations as particularly worthy, and to advocate its adoption. Since three poles—the text, the readers' relational/contextual life, and the readers' heteronomous/religious experience—are interpreted, a practice of scriptural criticism can be primarily focused on the interpretation of any of the three poles. For biblical critics, the primary concern is to advocate a specific interpretation of *the text*, because it is "better" (makes more sense, is more appropriate, more helpful, etc.) in a given contextual situation and from a specific theological/hermeneutical perspective. For constructive theologians, the primary concern might be different; as suggested earlier, it might be to advocate a specific interpretation of *given life-situations* and/or *religious experiences*. Whatever might be our goal, starting the process of scriptural criticism is simply a matter of joining reading companions and beginning to read with them.

Augustine promises to be an excellent reading companion for all of us, because in addition to being an astute exegete who analyzes Romans with the tools of his time, he does not hesitate to make explicit the hermeneutical and contextual frames of his interpretation. Practicing scriptural criticism is, therefore, as simple as "reading Romans with" Augustine, by respectfully receiving his interpretation with all the attention due to another legitimate reading, and by comparing it with our own. Note: *Reading with Augustine does not mean adopting his interpretation.* It means joining him with our own interpretations, and entering in dialogue with him in order to take note of the different choices each of us has made, and in this way putting ourselves in a position to assess the relative value of our own choices.

The Marginalia as Help for Reading Romans with Augustine

By distinguishing among analytical, contextual, and analytical frames as we do in this volume, we seek to facilitate the comparison of Augustine's interpretation with ours. The marginalia in the preceding essays are designed to help in this comparative process.

Biblical critics, with a primary concern for the interpretation of *the text,* will usually begin by comparing their own interpretation with others in terms of their respective analytical frames.

(1) **A** *Comparing the Analytical Frames of Augustine's and of Our Interpretations.*

Regarding the *analytical frames* of our respective interpretations, we ask: What are the textual features and the passages of Romans which are the most significant for Augustine and for us?

By raising this question we prolong the discussion opened by Krister Stendahl and John Riches, though in a slightly different direction. As they did, we take note of the textual dimension each interpretation views as most significant: for instance, the textual dimension concerning the introspective consciousness as part of Pauline anthropology, or concerning the relation between Jews and Gentiles, or again concerning the apocalyptic eschatology of Paul and its cosmic dualism. Yet, in this practice of scriptural criticism, one does not need to exclude interpretations which are not like ours. On the contrary, we simply acknowledge that each interpretation reflects certain analytical choices and we seek to elucidate the nature of these choices. From the perspective of scriptural criticism, it is inappropriate (and strangely arrogant!) to reject as inept and irresponsible the many scholars who happen not to share our interpretation, for instance, because they followed Augustine by underscoring the anthropology of Romans and the introspective consciousness, or because they emphasized with Krister Stendahl the relationship between Jews and Gentiles, or again because they emphasized with John Riches the apocalypticism of Paul's teaching. Because certain exegetes advocate interpretations which are analytically different from mine it does not mean that they "read into the text" something which is not there, while I alone was able to discern what the text truly says! As if the words of Paul originated with me![16]

A   Analytical Frames of Augustine's and of our interpretations.

A more reasonable assumption held by scriptural criticism is that each group of scholars has chosen a particular analytical frame; that is, their interpretation reflects their view that certain textual features are particularly significant, and therefore that other features are less significant. And of course it is also assumed that each group of scholars made this choice with the conviction that it can be justified in one way or another. Then, respecting the work of our colleagues is far from formal politeness or false humility.[17] We can adopt a receptive attitude toward other interpretations, including Augustine's. But this is not so much in order to identify what we can appropriate from these so as to build up and reinforce our own interpretation. Reading with others involves appreciating and respecting the distinctiveness of their interpretations, and in the process becoming aware of the specificity of our own interpretation. In this perspective, what is different in other interpretations is the most instructive for us, because these differences allow us to become aware of the analytical choices we made, while we might have thought we simply presented "what the text originally meant."

In order to facilitate comparison of the analytical frame of Augustine's interpretation of Romans, throughout this volume we highlight the passages of Romans and the textual features with which Augustine framed his interpretation in the "A" marginalia and in the indices. In this way, when we biblical critics study a given passage of Romans, we can easily identify in the preceding essays where Augustine's interpretation of this passage is discussed, and then take note of the differences between Augustine's and our interpretive choices regarding the textual features to be viewed as most significant.

(2) **C** *Comparing the Contextual Frames of Augustine's and of Our Interpretations.*

As we continue "reading with" our companions, Augustine cannot but call our attention to the contextual frames of our respective interpretations. This is so because he did not hesitate to make explicit that his interpretation of Romans aimed at drawing a teaching which would hopefully contribute to address issues and problems of the church in his time. By contrast, in most instances we biblical critics tend to ignore this aspect of our interpretations. We fail to pay any attention to the fact that, on the basis of our exegetical interpretations, believers envision teachings of the text by which they live

---

C Contextual Frames of Augustine's and of our interpretations.

and act in particular contexts. Our analytical choices, which appeared to be innocent, have in fact concrete consequences for the lives of believers and of people around them. Our exegetical/analytical choices have ethical implications which need to be assessed, as feminist and other advocacy interpretations have pointed out to us (Schüssler Fiorenza 1988 and 1999; Patte 1995). Reading with Augustine who readily makes explicit the contextual frames of his interpretation of Romans will help us to recognize the contextual frames of our own interpretations.

In order to facilitate the comparison of the contextual frame of Augustine's interpretation of Romans with the contextual frames of our own interpretations, throughout this volume we have marked in the "C" marginalia (and in the indices) not only the context in which Augustine read Romans with the hope to find a "Word to live by," but also the kind of contextual problems and issues that this teaching sought to address in the church of his time—as is remarkably elucidated in the essays by the Augustinian scholars, TeSelle, Martin, Fredricksen, Gathercole, and Gorday. In this way, we biblical critics are prompted to identify the kind of teachings for believers our own interpretations point toward, as well as the kind of contextual problems and issues such teachings could address. Then we can begin the ethical assessment of the effects of this teaching upon believers and people around them.

(3) **H** *Comparing the Hermeneutical Frames of Augustine's and of Our Interpretations*

Finally, as we read Romans with Augustine, he cannot fail to call our attention to the hermeneutical frames of our respective interpretations. Augustine used a *regula fidei* in order to select what was for him the most appropriate interpretation. And so do we, whether we admit it or not. The main differences is that he did so deliberately and openly, while the form of our interpretations most often hides this process. As we already discussed at length, our interpretations have hermeneutical frames which presuppose certain views of religious experience; we approach the text in terms of specific theological categories and questions which directly reflect our convictions (in the proper sense of "truths we hold as self-evident"), a kind of collective or individual *regula fidei*. In our case as in Augustine's case, the hermeneutical frames of interpretations include a specific view of Scripture which relates either our convictions and theological preunderstandings, or Augustine's *regula fidei*, to the biblical text and to the

---

H Hermeneutical Frames of Augustine's and of our interpretations

readers/believers' life. This is to say that different hermeneutical frames involve different views of the text as Scripture—contrary to our common presupposition that there is a single view of Scripture. Reading with Augustine will help us to elucidate the view of Scripture our interpretation presupposed, and to assess the relative value of this choice of a particular view of Scripture.

Since this point might be somewhat unexpected, in concluding this essay I need briefly to suggest how different views of Scripture are correlated with the different kinds of *regula fidei*, as illustrated in Augustine's work.

Martin and Gathercole emphasized two roles of Scripture in their discussion of Augustine's interpretation of Romans: Scripture as either

- *Lamp to my feet*, that is, as a guideline for the believers' life; then the role of a *regula fidei* for the interpretation of Scripture is to provide guidelines for the interpretive process and rules to discern what are doctrinally and morally orthodox interpretations.

Or as

- *Canon* (in a more forensic sense); then, another and similar role of a *regula fidei* for the interpretation of Scripture is to provide rules for discerning and judging whether or not interpretations are orthodox.

Yet, there are many other possible roles of Scripture (Patte 1999, 58-59, *passim*) correlated with many other possible roles for a *regula fidei*. Augustine seems to have alluded to several of them. Scripture can be viewed as:

- *Good News,* offering to believers a loving word about God's grace and mercy. Then, the *regula fidei* is the principle though which one scrutinizes the Scriptures for their "plenitude and end," namely the mystery of God's on-going love. Is this not the role of the *regula fidei* for Augustine which de Margerie points to when he refers to Augustine's comments on "the plenitude and end" of Scripture as the mystery of God's love? (Margerie 1983, 174-75, commenting on passages from *De Doctrina Christiana*).

- *Family Album*, establishing and reinforcing the believer's identity and vocation as a member of the family of God (God's people). It gives believers a true sense of relationship to others and to God. Then, the *regula fidei* would be the principle though which one would scrutinize the Scriptures for the vision which brings human beings to love God and to love others. Could this be the role of the *regula fidei* for

Augustine, which de Margerie suggests when he points out that the double divine charity, which is the ultimate end of the Scriptures, is universal, that is, for all the people of God (Margerie 1983, 50-51, commenting on passages from *De Genesi ad litteram*).

- *Corrective Glasses*, that is, as promise, prophecy, and/or type being fulfilled, allowing believers to see their lives/experiences with the eyes of faith, discerning in the midst of evil "what is good and acceptable and perfect" (Rom 12:2) and what God is doing. Then, the *regula fidei* would be a typological principle though which one would scrutinize present-day experience in terms of the Scriptures and the Scriptures in terms of one's experience. It is not one of the roles of the *regula fidei* for Augustine suggested in TeSelle's introduction?

- *Empowering Word*, conjuring a new reality (e.g., preliminary manifestations of the kingdom and of God's justice) in the present situation characterized by overwhelming human weakness, thus empowering believers for salvation and for a life characterized by charity. Then, the *regula fidei* would be a principle through which one opens oneself to be empowered by God as promised in the Scriptures—a function of the *regula fidei* directly related to the *ad salutem* principle of interpretation (mentioned by Martin).

- *Holy Bible*, confronting believers with the holy, with the mystery of God's presence, a transforming experience. Then, the *regula fidei* would be an interpretive principle focused upon the mystery in Scriptures (as mentioned by Martin).

These examples should be enough to dissipate our misconceptions concerning the rigidity which, accordingly, would be involved in reading Romans as Scripture, in assessing an interpretation in terms of a *regula fidei,* and which would characterize its hermeneutical/theological frame. To the contrary, such frames and the attendant views of Scripture and of the *regula fidei* are constantly in flux, depending upon the passage being read and the context in which it is read. This is also true in the case of our own interpretations. In the same way that we could not pretend that our interpretation does not points to a teaching that affects believers and others in specific ways in their lives, we cannot pretend that our interpretation does not presuppose certain view of the relationship of the text as Scripture to the believers. Similarly, our interpretation cannot avoid focusing on certain theological categories which, because of some hidden *regula fidei*, we view either as despicable and to be rejected or as most valuable and to be preserved.

In order to facilitate the comparison of the hermeneutical frame of Augustine's interpretation of Romans with the hermeneutical frames of our own interpretations, throughout this volume we have marked in the "H" marginalia (and in the indices) not only the views of Scripture, but also the theological categories which Augustine used, whether or not they belonged to his explicit *regula fidei*, as our colleagues the Augustinian scholars have shown. In this way, we biblical critics are prompted to identify the kind of views of Scripture and hermeneutical categories which our own interpretations presupposed, and sometimes made explicit. Then we can begin the assessment of the choices of theological, religious, and hermeneutical categories involved in our own interpretation. Are these categories plausible, or otherwise meaningful, in the specific cultural/religious setting for which we are interpreting Romans?

In sum, for me as a biblical critic, the essays in this volume persistently ask the question: How can we, present-day biblical critics, envision a practice of scriptural criticism which would follow Augustine's practice as a model? From the perspective of our collective work, I suggested that these essays invite us to "read Romans with Augustine." As we proceed, we cannot but assume responsibility for our own interpretations. And we discover again and again that being a biblical critic has nothing to do with mastering the text. On the contrary, we become all the more critical when we encounter the text as one encounters a person in all her/his/its mystery, and then respectfully ponder this mystery, rather than perceiving it as a cesspool of textual gaps, difficulties and obscurities in which we will disappear if we do not find a way to bridge it.

Notes

1. Boyarin wrote: "I leave it to readers to decide whether the authors' answer provides a way out of the hermeneutical circle that they draw around themselves and us." Daniel Boyarin, "Israel Reading in 'Reading Israel,'" *Reading Israel in Romans*, pp.247-48.

2. See the co-authored "Overture" by Grenholm and Patte, in *Reading Israel in Romans*, 1-54, and especially our comments on the problems with "unipolar" and "bipolar" practices of biblical critics, 19-30.

3. See for instance, Cristina Grenholm, "Scriptural Criticism and the Story of Annunciation," in Gary Phillips and Nicole Wilkinson Duran, eds. *Reading Communities Reading Scripture* (Harrisburg, PA: Trinity Press International, forthcoming). The letters between parentheses, (H), (C), (A), signal to use of hermeneutical, contextual, and analytical frames.

4. John Riches comments on Krister Stendahl's proposal in his detailed analysis of the unsuccessful efforts to reconcile historical and theological New Testament studies. See,

Riches 1993, 198-232). He criticizes Stendahl for driving a wedge between the historical and theological components of Bultmann's hermeneutical model.

5. "The abiding temptation of the historian is to pretend to know more than [one] knows" (Riches 1993, 233, 240).

6. The overall thesis of Riches, 1993.

7. My effort to look for a practice of critical biblical studies beyond the subject/object dichotomy is similar to Joel Green (2000, 239) who writes in the context of his discussion of "the crisis of history" which lies in the Modernist fascination with the historical: "The dilemma we face is historical and is grounded in modernity's firm embrace of a historicism that postmodernity has just as firmly rejected. The resolution is not to be found in the false choices thus offered, voting yea or nay for a modernist historicism oriented around scientific objectivity and facts. The way forward is in learning to think (and live) with history, to borrow a phrase from historian Carl Schorske. 'Thinking *with* history implies the employment of the materials of the past and the configurations in which we organize and comprehend them to orient ourselves in the living present.'" Green refers to Carl E. Schorske, *Thinking with History: Explorations in the Passage to Modernism* (Princeton: Princeton University Press, 1998), 3-16.

8. "If the reader is not moved to some sort of emotion by the accounts in Genesis 19 and 2 Samuel 13—whether it is horror, sympathy, or anger— one can only feel that the biblical writer has failed in what he or she intended to do" (Smith 1997, 130).

9. The corresponding English translations are: Emile Lévinas, *Difficult Freedom: Essays on Judaism,* translated by Seán Hand (Baltimore: Johns Hopkins University Press, 1990) and "Revelation in the Jewish Tradition," in *The Lévinas Reader* (Oxford: Blackwell, 1989).

10. Most important has been the "functional" definition of Scripture provided by Smith 1993, *What is Scripture? A Comparative Approach*— by contrast with the "knowledge" (informational) emphasis of Biderman 1995.

11. Yet this third pole is primarily conceived as an application of the two preceding ones. As we formulated the tripolar interpretive practice of "scriptural criticism," Cristina Grenholm and I readily embraced the overall perspective of Sandra Schneiders, although taking note that she emphasized the first two poles (and therefore spirituality) while we proposed to amplify the third one, the pragmatic/contextual pole, so as to acknowledge the equal status of all three poles. Thus the pragmatic aspects of interpretation (the way in which it addresses problems arising in a given context) which is apparent in feminist interpretations and also in believers' interpretations is viewed as an integral part of the interpretive process (rather than as the application of a superior level of interpretation which, for Schneiders, combines the analytical and the hermeneutical). I emphasize this point by proposing a pedagogical and critical approach which takes its starting point with the pragmatic/contextual, "the teaching of the biblical text for believers today," in Patte 1999, 211-234.

12. These comments apply even when one envisions in a tripolar way the two interpretive contexts between which one looks for analogies. This is the case of Alain Gignac 1996 and 1997. These two essays are remarkable because of the way in which they emphasize and clarify the tripolar hermeneutical process practiced both by Paul and by present day interpreters. Yet, in these essays (in forthcoming works he abandons this perspective), Gignac remained in the traditional critical pattern by implicitly keeping the dichotomy between "what the text meant" and "what the text means," although for him the bridge between the two was through a "critical analogy."

13. As I have learned from Per Folkesson during an extraordinarily rich interdisciplinary workshop at Hagegården (Arvika, Sweden, May 2000) on "The Pleasure of Reading" with the participation of Helene Blomqvist (literature), Sören Dalevi (theology), Per Folkesson (psychology), Cristina Grenholm (theology), Maria Jansdotter (theology), Anders Palm (literature), Anders Tyrberg (literature).

14. Cristina Grenholm 1996, 265-72, 278-80. Referring to Gabler's 1787 essay, "On the Proper Discrimination Between Biblical and Dogmatic Theology and the Specific Objective of Each," Grenholm underscores the gap between "critical and creative interpretations" which reflects the gap between the text in its historical context and present day theological interpretation.

15. As distinct from scholars in other fields, such as constructive theologians, church historians, practical theologians, and homileticians.

16. Echoing Paul's words: "Did the word of God originate with you? Or are you the only ones it has reached?" (1 Cor 14:36).

17. The possibility, indeed the necessity, that each interpretation is focused on a specific textual dimension is readily understandable as soon as one considers how meaning is produced and communicated, and as soon as one takes into account the role of the readers or hearers in this process. Semiotics has been most helpful for me at this juncture. See Daniel Patte 1990. For an analysis of diverse critical exegetical studies which shows how each focuses on a specific textual dimension and brackets out others, see Daniel Patte 1996.

Bibliography

Biderman, Shlomo. 1995. *Scripture and Knowledge: An Essay on Religious Epistemology.* Leiden: E.J. Brill.

Bloechl, Jeffrey. ed. 2000. *The Face of the Other and the Trace of God : Essays on the Philosophy of Emmanuel Levinas.* Perspectives in Continental Philosophy, 10. New York: Fordham University Press.

Boyarin, Daniel. 2000. "Israel Reading in 'Reading Israel,'" in Grenholm and Patte, eds, *Reading Israel in Romans,* 247-48.

Brenner, Athalya and Carole Fontaine, edrs. 1997. *A Feminist Companion to Reading the Bible: Approaches, Methods and Strategies* (Sheffield: Sheffield Academic Press.

Burggraeve, Roger. 2000. "The Bible Gives to Thoughts: Lévinas on the Possibility and Program Nature of Biblical Thinking" in Bloechl, ed. *The Face of the Other and the Trace of God,* 165-183.

Childs, Brevard S. 1979. *Introduction to the Old Testament as Scripture.* Philadelphia: Fortress.

————. 1985. *The New Testament as Canon : An Introduction.* Philadelphia: Fortress.

Gignac, Alain. 1996, "Comment élaborer une théologie paulininienne (première partie)" *Science et esprit,* XLVIII, 307-326.

————. 1997, "Comment élaborer une théologie paulininienne (deuxième partie)" *Science et esprit,* XLIX, 25-38.

Green, Joel B. and Max Turner. 2000. *Between Two Horizons: Spanning New Testament Studies and Systematic Theology.* Grand Rapids, Michigan, Cambridge, UK: Eerdmans.

Grenholm, Cristina. 1996. *The Old Testament, Christianity and Pluralism.* Beiträge zur Geschichte der biblischen Exegese, 33. Tübingen, Mohr.

————. 2002. "Scriptural Criticism and the Story of Annunciation," in Phillips and Wilkinson Duran, eds. *Reading Communities Reading Scripture.* Harrisburg, PA: Trinity Press International.

Grenholm, Cristina and Daniel Patte, eds, 2000. *Reading Israel in Romans, Legitimacy and Plausibility of Divergent Interpretations.* Romans Through History and Cultures vol. 1. Harrisburg, Penn.: Trinity Press International.

————. 2000b. "Overture. Receptions, Critical Interpretations, and Scriptural Criticism.," in *Reading Israel in Romans,* 1-54.

Lévinas, Emmanuel. 1989. "Revelation in the Jewish Tradition," in *The Lévinas Reader.* Oxford: Blackwell,

————. 1990 *Difficult Freedom: Essays on Judaism.* translated by Seán Hand. Baltimore: Johns Hopkins University Press.

Margerie, Bertrand de. 1983. *Introduction à l'histoire de l'exégèse. Vol. III. Saint Augustin.* Paris: le Cerf.

Patte, Daniel. 1990. *The Religious Dimensions of Biblical Texts: Greimas's Structural Semiotics and Biblical Exegesis*, Semeia Studies Series. Atlanta: Scholars.

—————. 1995. *Ethics of Biblical Interpretation: A Reevaluation.* Louisville: Westminster/John Knox.

—————. 1996. *Discipleship According to the Sermon on the Mount: Four Legitimate Readings, Four Plausible Views of Discipleship, and Their Relative Values.* Harrisburg, PA: Trinity Press International.

—————. 1999. *The Challenge of Discipleship: a Critical Reading of the Sermon on the Mount as Scripture* (Harrisburg, Pa: Trinity Press International, 1999).

Phillips, Gary and Nicole Wilkinson Duran, eds. 2002. *Reading Communities Reading Scripture. Essays in Honor of Daniel Patte.* Harrisburg, PA: Trinity Press International.

Riches, John. 1993. *A Century of New Testament Study.* Valley Forge, Penn.: Trinity Press International.

Schneiders, Sandra M. 1991. *The Revelatory Text: Interpreting the New Testament as Sacred Scripture.* San Francisco: HarperSanFrancisco (Second edition, Liturgical Press, 1999).

Schorske, Carl E. 1998. *Thinking with History: Explorations in the Passage to Modernism.* Princeton: Princeton University Press.

Schüssler Fiorenza, Elisabeth. 1988. "The Ethics of Interpretation: De-Centering Biblical Scholarship." JBL 107:3-17.

—————. 1999. *Rhetoric and Ethic: The Politics of Biblical Studies.* Minneapolis: Fortress.

Smith, Carol. 1997. "Challenged by the Text: Interpreting Two Stories of Incest in the Hebrew Bible," in Athalya Brenner and Carole Fontaine, *A Feminist Companion to Reading the Bible: Approaches, Methods and Strategies* (Sheffield: Sheffield Academic Press, 114-135.

Smith, Wilfred Cantwell. 1993. *What is Scripture? A Comparative Approach.* Minneapolis: Fortress.

Stendahl, Krister. 1962. "Biblical Theology, Contemporary." in ed. George A. Buttrick. *The Interpreter's Dictionary of the Bible*, Vol. 1. Nashville: Abingdon, 418-32.

—————. 1976. *Paul among Jews and Gentiles and Other Essays.* Philadelphia: Fortress.

– A L A S T   W O R D –

Krister Stendahl

◆

C When forty some years ago I began to speak of Paul as an extrovert with a robust conscience, and that in sharp contrast to the sensitivities of Augustine and Luther as they read and expounded the Apostle, my focus was of course justification by faith as it was taught in my native land.

H I still think that for Paul that concept was the central vehicle for defending/understanding how his Gentile converts could be legitimate children of Abraham. It was not as an insight growing out of some inner struggles with his moral conscience. His "exegetical find" was in Gen. 15, where [the uncircumcised] Abraham believed and was approved and affirmed. That quotation is decisive in the only two letters that do present the Pauline understanding of justification. We have it in two keys: in Galatians re judaizing Gentiles, in Romans re Jews and Gentiles.

H Hence I made Augustine—the author of the Confessions—into the pioneer of the introspective reading of Paul. I think our two papers on Augustine basically substantiate that view. And it is intriguing to welcome Apuleius as a precursor. Riches' move, as I understand it, is to lift up confessional and moral and psychological elements in Paul that change my forbiddingly separating canyon into a walkable valley. His chief vehicle for this landscaping activity is Nancy Shumate's definition of conversion narratives: " . . . narratives of the breakdown of one set of epistemological and moral conventions and their replacement with another" (quoted by Riches; see above, p. 177). Riches applies this cool definition of conversion also to Paul, as having "parted company with his inherited Jewish world view." **H** But is not Paul's whole mission to find the place for his Gentiles *within* that "world view"? The reversal of the eschatological timetable (Rom. 11), and the whole structure of Paul's

---

C The context of Stendahl's interpretation.

H Paul's central problem was how Gentile believers could be children of Abraham (Gen. 15:5-6; Gal. 3:6-9; Rom. 4:2-5).

H While the "introspective" reading of Romans originates with Augustine, his interest in conversion may have had predecessors, as Riches' essay suggests.

H Paul did not abandon Judaism but tried to find a place for Gentiles within its framework.

argumentation about the law, presuppose and affirm that Jewish world view. To put it boldly, Paul is not really a Christian as we use that word, he is a Jew who knows himself to have been called by Christ to be Apostle to the Gentiles.

C And as to the inner struggles, I still find it striking that the only sin he admits to is that he had persecuted the church—for which he says he has more than made up by his good apostolic work. The inner struggle of which he speaks is rather with what he calls his weakness, never equated with sin, but obviously referring to his medical condition (was he epileptic?). That weakness interferes with his ministry and thus becomes the thing that teaches him that he is not indispensable—which must have been hard for him.

H Any discussion of Paul and Augustine comes sooner or later to Romans 7. It was fascinating for me to learn more about how Augustine read it in various ways. But speaking of "world views," this is really another world. TeSelle's subtitles say it all: Theory of Willing, The Problem of Desire, Fate and Freedom.

As I read both TeSelle and Riches here, I become more convinced that my old guess was basically right: The common sense observation that we do not always do what we want to do (and vice versa) is used by Paul in order to prove that—as he says—the law is holy and the commandment holy and just and good. No spirit of contrition here! The fact that we recognize our shortcomings shows that we "agree that the law is good." Our true selves serve God's law. But the tragedy is that sin has come into the system, in "this body of death" from which Christ will deliver us. H So what to Paul was an illustration (the words about the will) became the message. It could hardly go otherwise once the introspective mind found such an overtly psychological passage in the Bible. Here was now the key to the understanding of the self, and Augustine struggled valiantly with those words, "condelector enim legi dei," and they engendered deep insight. But Paul must feel like Moses when, according to the Talmud, he did not understand a word of what rabbi Akiba discussed with his students.

H TeSelle says, "It could even be said that, for Augustine, human life is the cosmos writ small." This conformity between the macro- and micro-worlds is of special importance for our discussion. Let me point to an interesting feature of Romans. Toward the end of chapter 5 Paul gets excited about how "the more sin increased, grace abounded all the more." A beautiful pattern in accordance with justification by faith. But then

---

C Paul's struggles were not those of Romans 7.

H Rival interpretations of Romans 7 operate with quite different "world views."

H The illustration came to be interpreted as the message.

H We cannot assume that the cosmic and the personal, the macro and micro levels, follow the same patterns.

Paul breaks off, recognizing that such a theological model does not work on the personal level. So he brings in a new and totally different paradigm: baptism as a dying with Christ. Such a move by Paul tells me that one cannot always take a theological macro-paradigm and use it for micro-issues. And I like to stress that for Paul justification by faith is a macro-argument. Its transfer to the individual is not unproblematic.

H Riches' concluding and mind-opening discussion of Augustine's monism and Paul's dualist elements brings us back to Schweitzer, but also forward toward roads not yet taken in Pauline interpretation. Let me add a wild suggestion: If Paul is about how to deal with communities and their relation to each other in a world that is a community of communities, does he by implication have something to say toward the construction of a Christian theology of religions?

H Paul's interest in the relations between communities may be pertinent to the construction of a Christian "theology of religions."

Contributors

———— ◆ ————

Paula Fredriksen is the Aurelio Professor of Scripture in the Department of Religion, Boston University. An historian of ancient Christianity, her books include *Augustine on Romans* (Scholars Press 1982), *From Jesus to Christ* (Yale 1988/2000), and *Jesus of Nazareth, King of the Jews* (Knopf 1999). Her latest study, *Augustine and theJews*, is forthcoming from Doubleday. For a full listing of publications, go to www.bu.edu/faculty.

Simon J. Gathercole teaches New Testament at the University of Aberdeen, Scotland. He is the author of *Where is Boasting? Early Jewish Soteriology and Paul's Response in Romans 1-5* (2002) and several articles including "The Critical and Dogmatic Agenda of Albert Schweitzer's Quest of the Historical Jesus" (2000), "A Law unto Themselves: The Gentiles in Rom 2.14-15 Revisited"(2002), and "Torah, Life and Salvation: The Use of Lev 18.5 in Early Judaism and Christianity" (forthcoming).

Peter J. Gorday is an occasional adjunct professor at the Candler School of Theology of Emory University in Atlanta. He is the author of *Principles of Patristic Exegesis: Romans 9-11 in Origen, John Chrysostom, and Augustine,* various essays on patristic thinkers in collections, and editor of *New Testament IX: Colossians, 1-2 Thessalonians, 1-2 Timothy, Titus, Philemon,* in the Ancient Christian Commentary on Scripture series. He is an Episcopal priest and licenced marriage and family therapist in private practice in Atlanta.

Thomas F. Martin teaches ancient Christianity and patristic theology at Villanova University, Villanova, PA. He is the author of "Rhetoric and Exegesis in Augustine's Interpretation of Romans 7:24-25A" (2001); "Our Restless Heart: The Augustinian Tradition" (forthcoming); published essays on Augustine and Paul in "Journal of Early Christian Studies" (2000, v.8,2) "Augustinian Studies" (2001, v.32,2) and "Vigiliae Christianae" (2001, v.55). He is an Associate Editor of "Augustinian Studies."

Daniel Patte is Professor of New Testament and Early Christianity, the Divinity School, and Professor of Religious Studies at Vanderbilt University. Among his books are *Paul's Faith and the Power of the Gospel* (1983), *Preaching Paul* (1984), *Ethics of Biblical Interpretation* (1995); with Cristina Grenholm, co-editor of *Reading Israel in Romans:* (2000), and co-author of "Overture: Receptions, Critical Interpretations, and Scriptural Criticism." He is the general editor of two forthcoming reference works: *A Global Bible Commentary* and *The Cambridge Dictionary of Christianity.*

John K. Riches is Professor of Divinity and Biblical Criticism at the University of Glasgow. He is the author of books on the New Testament and its world, including *Jesus and the Transformation of Judaism* (1980), *Conflicting Mythologies: Identity Formation in the Gospels of Mark and Matthew* (2000). His long standing interest in the history of biblical interpretation is found another series of books, including *A Century of New Testament Study* (1993), *The Bible: A Very Short Introduction* (2000), his forthcoming Blackwells Biblical Commentary on *Galatians* (from a reception historical perspective) and forthcoming contribution to the *Global Bible Commentary* as a member of the Scottish Contextual Bible Study Group.

Bishop Krister Stendahl, to whom this book is dedicated, is the Andrew W. Mellon Professor of Divinity Emeritus at the Divinity School, Harvard University. His seminal work, *Paul Among Jews and Gentiles* (1976), brought about what is appropriately called "The New Perspective on Paul." It includes the essay, "The Apostle Paul and the Introspective Conscience of the West" (Swedish original, 1960) and its critique of Augustine's interpretation of Paul – the origin and center of the discussion of the present book. Among his publications is *Final account : Paul's letter to the Romans* .

Eugene TeSelle is Oberlin Alumni/ae Professor of Church History and Theology Emeritus at the Divinity School, Vanderbilt University. His field of specialization is the history of doctrine, especially in the early and medieval periods. Among his books are *Augustine the Theologian* (1970), *Augustine's Strategy as an Apologist* (1974), and *Living in Two Cities: Augustinian Trajectories in Political Thought* (1998). He is one of the associate editors of the forthcoming *Cambridge Dictionary of Christianity.*

Index of Scriptural References

Index of Augustine References

———— ◆ ————

Index of References to Other Ancient
and Medieval Authors

——— ◆ ———

Index of Authors Cited

———— ◆ ————